CHARLES REED BISHOP

Man of Hawaii

CHARLES REED BISHOP
Man of Hawaii

By HAROLD WINFIELD KENT

A little schooner with two masts,
well manned with captain and sail-
ors, ready to sail out on the far ocean.
Such is the Hawaiian Kingdom
KAMAKAU

PACIFIC BOOKS
Publishers
Palo Alto, California
1965

To Ethel

Foreword

AN INDIVIDUAL OF innate modesty and natural reserve rarely in his lifetime receives widespread public appreciation or criticism. If the trend in his life and works is toward the common good of all he may and likely will create a reputation for integrity, but his light can fade as the memory of his contemporaries dulls and the generation of those who remember him passes on.

This would have been so very possible with Charles Reed Bishop had I not, in casting about for a suitable essay subject for the Social Science Association of Honolulu, come upon this *Man of Hawaii* as a man almost of mystery and yet one who somehow, as the story unfolded, seemed to touch at some point or other every major historical event and significant community agency during his fifty years in Hawaii. The essay was written under the same title as this book, and even the uncomplicated doing of that revealed a story of a man almost completely unknown.

The Bishop story is plain, unostentatious, singularly free of nuance and intrigue; it is chiefly a story of integrity and only a little less so of loyalty and devotion to the causes minor and major with which he was associated throughout his long, useful life.

In many respects this book is drawn from the correspondence of Mr. Bishop. He was—without more than a New England grammar school education—literally a man of letters. Other important sources are the minute books of the many organizations, agencies, and institutions with which Bishop was associated.

This book is not a biography, chronologically arranged, of Charles Reed Bishop. While there is some conformity to chronology—we start with his birth, and we end with his death—the story arises from the institutions and people entering his life story; and since these are usually grouped because of some basic affinity of purpose, the telling necessarily results in a seesawing through the years.

Another point needs stating: This is the Bishop story. Despite the slant in the material, the picture of Charles Reed Bishop emerges clearly from the shadows of the slowly yielding past and shows him for what he is—Man of Hawaii.

It is impossible to list all who have in some way or other extended a helping hand to the telling of the Charles Reed Bishop story. It would be fitting to remember several great libraries of Hawaii and their people: Archives of Hawaii and Agnes Conrad; Hawaiian Historical Society and Mrs. Willowdean Handy; Hawaiian Mission Children's Society and Sophie Cluff; and the Bishop Museum and Margaret Titcomb.

On the mainland, welcome assistance was extended by the staff of the Sutro Library, Glens Falls Public Library, Essex Museum, Newburyport Public Library, Library of Congress, and the National Archives. Special thanks go to the Bruce Inverarity family of the Adirondack Museum.

Many *kamaaina* agencies and firms in the Hawaiian Islands have opened their early minute books and correspondence files: Bernice P. Bishop Estate, Charles R. Bishop Trust, Bernice Pauahi Bishop Museum, Alexander and Baldwin, First National Bank of Hawaii, Lihue Plantation, Hackfeld and Company,* and Oahu Railway and Land Company. Willis Warner of the Bank of California in San Francisco and Edward L. Joesting of the First National Bank of Hawaii have been most helpful in this research.

The trustees of the Bernice P. Bishop Estate, Edwin P. Murray, Frank E. Midkiff, Atherton Richards, Richard Lyman, Jr., and Herbert Keppeler, have been most helpful not only in reading the manuscript but in publication of the book.

Community institutions both in Hawaii and the San Francisco Bay area willingly allowed access to old records: Central Union Church, Honolulu YMCA, Hilo Boys' Boarding School, I. O. O. F., Social Science Association of Honolulu, Leahi Hospital, Punahou School, Queen's Hospital, The Kamehameha Schools, Sailors' Home, the Unitarian Churches of San Francisco and Berkeley, Starr King Library of Berkeley, and others.

Bishop relatives and friends from around the world have assisted in one way or another: Mrs. Edna Lucile McCaffery, Mrs. Elizabeth B. Bettis, Mattie Washburn, Leland Stanford Bishop, Raymond B. Bishop, Maida Rumsey, Mrs. Charles P. Baker, Gordon Smith, Helen Wilcox Salazar, Henry Damon, Alexander F. Meyer, William H. Hill, Mr. and Mrs. Alexander W. Miller, John Nelson McElroy, and Lawrence Judd.

Then and in a sense most of all among these, I would list Annie

* American Factors, Ltd.

Smith Bishop (Mrs. E. Faxon Bishop), who regaled Mrs. Kent and me with endless yarns of people and incidents in the Bishop days.

To my secretarial staff, Sara Woodyard and Harriet Oana, I would say *Aloha nui loa a me mahalo nui kakou!*

My warmest gratitude goes to George M. Collins, Agnes Conrad, Bernice Judd, and Don Mitchell for their willingness to read this manuscript. The late, highly esteemed Meiric Dutton also read the first half of the manuscript before having to lay all work finally aside. Luryier Diamond has helped most generously with the photography, Ray Lanterman with the pen and ink drawings, and Cecil Keesling with technical advice.

HAROLD WINFIELD KENT

Honolulu, Hawaii
September, 1964

Contents

List of Illustrations

List of Illustrations

An early print which represents the bridge over the Hudson River at Glens Falls, New York, as it existed in 1822. The gatehouse, birthplace of Charles Reed Bishop, appears in the center of the print. The title "Glenns [sic] Falls" is given to the print which is No. 6 of the Hudson River Port Folio, published by Henry I. Megarey, New York, 1824. It was painted by W. G. Wall and engraved by I. Hill.

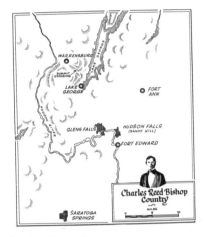

Upper left: Glens Falls Academy occupied this building from 1836 to 1841. Here, Charles Bishop attended school for about two years. The building which was erected by Sidney Berry, was torn down in 1961.

Upper right: Charles Reed Bishop country in and near Glens Falls, New York.

Below: This mural by Griffith Bailey Coale is in the Queensbury Hotel, Glens Falls, New York. The gatehouse on the bridge over the Hudson River at Glens Falls was directly above the celebrated cave. "At the farther extremity of a narrow, deep cavern in the rock . . . was seated the scout holding a blazing knot of pine," James Fenimore Cooper, *The Last of the Mohicans,* Chapter VI.

Charles Reed Bishop

MAN OF HAWAII

1

Foundation

THE HUDSON RIVER AND
GLENS FALLS, NEW YORK

MOUNT MARCY, RISING to a height of 5844 feet, is the highest point in the state of New York. Nestled close against this ancient upthrust of an Adirondack is the clear-water Lake Tear of the Clouds, more commonly known as Summit Lake. Here the Hudson River timidly begins its march to the sea. Slowly and in great meanders, it wanders its chosen course over the glaciated plateau which covers northern New York. This is a part of the Labrador Ice Cap, which had its center far to the north in Eastern Canada during an early ice age. Finally the river comes to the terminal moraine of the plateau, plunges in several beautiful rock falls one hundred fifty feet to the Hudson gorge, where it begins to earn its reputation as a mighty stream of history and commerce.

The Hudson River played a profound role in the life of Charles Reed Bishop, even cradling him at birth in the very center of its hospitable bosom at a point marked by the riotous drop of river waters at Glens Falls, New York. He spoke of this years later in a letter to an old friend, Charles Bellamy Culver. The letter was dated December 6, 1909:

. . . The roar of the waters of Glens Falls helped to lull me to sleep when I was a child, for I was born quite near there. I love the river, the rocks and caverns near them, so well known and described by Cooper. . . .

In the 1820's there was a bridge across the Hudson from Glens Falls to Moreau. The bridge consisted of two rude spans meeting on an island in the middle of the river. On this island stood a tollhouse. The collector of tolls in 1822 was Samuel Bishop, who had but recently been married, February 14, 1821, to a frail, hard-working,

3

New England woman named Maria Reed. In this tollhouse on January 25, 1822, Charles Reed Bishop was born. His mother in giving birth to another son, Henry Bostwick Bishop, May 11, 1824, had some fatal physical difficulty for her death was recorded on May 24, only two weeks later.* Because Maria Bishop was also ill following Charles' birth, he was taken by his mother's sister Lucy Jane Reed (Blood) to Fort Ann, New York. A little later he was taken to his grandfather Jesse Bishop, who in addition to running a foundry and blacksmith shop managed a 123 acre farm and acted as collector of tolls on the Lake George-Warrensburgh,† New York toll road. The farm straddled the road at a point called Summit Crossing about halfway between the two valleys. He had been baptized in the Methodist Church at Glens Falls, and while he was a member of no church again until the twilight of his long life, he was a staunch defender of the denomination of his baptism.

A generous start in Charles Bishop's education was given him at the grandfather Jesse Bishop farm. There were more than the usual farm chores. In addition to caring for sheep, cattle, and horses, he assisted in keeping the toll collector's records in good order and repairing the wagons, buggies, and even the stage coaches. These experiences in some way possessed elements of work information which became helpful in practical ways throughout his life.

After a few years Charles was sent to the Glens Falls Academy which he attended for the seventh and eighth grades. This constituted his formal schooling. As he ventured beyond this schooling, the impact of the river's combination of natural resources was important.

One other highway, this one of war and commerce, was closely associated with the Hudson River—the great valley extending in a straight north and south line from New York City to the St. Lawrence River. This was the Great War Path of the French and Indian Wars, of the struggles among the British, the French, and the Dutch. It was the land of the Mohicans, the Indians-Who-Lived-Where-The-Waters-Flow-Both-Ways. James Fenimore Cooper, in *The Last of the Mohicans,* uses much of the Great War Path as the locale of that story. The climactic hiding place of his characters, Cora, Alice,

* Samuel Bishop was remarried on February 16, 1825, to Saphronia King. One child, half brother to Charles and Henry, was born of this marriage and carried the given name, George King. The child died in infancy.

† Old spelling.

the Major, and the tuneful David, is actually centered at about the half-way point across the river in the cave that is in the midst of the falls at Glens Falls. The island housing this cave was the foundation at the mid-point of the bridge where Charles Reed Bishop was born. Traveled successively by Champlain, Marin, Montcalm, Burgoyne, Prevost, and a host of others, the Great War Path was so given to bloodshed and the pursuits of war generally that it was strongly fortified in strategic spots and, therefore, was lacking in genuine communities and settlements of people. With the conclusion of the Revolutionary War, in which Charles Bishop's maternal forebears had fought heroically, peace came to the Great War Path.

There were certain natural resources which were compulsorily unused until peace was assured. This entire country was traversable by either land or water. With a short connecting canal, commerce could move all the way by water from New York City to Quebec. The forests of hard and soft woods contained beautiful, clear lumber that could be fashioned into a thousand items of usefulness to human living. There were great prairies holding deep fertility for grains of several kinds. The marble corridor of the Hudson River in the falls section could supply lime and marble, and the rushing water could supply power. The turning of the economic wheels at Glens Falls only awaited the signing of the Declaration of Independence.

A state dam was constructed about two and a half miles below Glens Falls as a feeder for the canal connecting Fort Edward and the Hudson River with Whitehall on Lake Champlain. This enabled the engineers to piece together an all-water route for shipping from New York City to the St. Lawrence River. In a sense, the system made an island of all of New England. Just above the dam the Great Boom was constructed to impound all logs that floated down from the tributaries and main body of the upland Hudson, following the winter logging operations and the spring thaws. The logs were diverted to saw mills in the falls section of the Hudson at Glens Falls, Sandy Hill (now called Hudson Falls) or Fort Edward. This was Charles Reed Bishop country.

Leaving the eighth grade at Glens Falls Academy, young Bishop hired out to Nelson J. Warren, who presided over the largest mercantile house in Warrensburgh. This experience constituted the second phase of his education. The practical demands of clerking, barter, bookkeeping, inventory, maintenance, and janitorial duties, served to sharpen his business skills. At the age of twenty, in 1842, he moved closer to the wheels of industry and trade. He went to work as bookkeeper and head clerk for Charles Dewey in the Old Stone Store next to the Herald office in Sandy Hill, about three miles from Glens Falls. There in the store he met William Little Lee who was a brother-in-law of Mr. Dewey. Lee's sister, Eliza, had earlier been married to Charles Bishop's Uncle Linus. Lee, only a year older than Charles Bishop, was born in Sandy Hill, in February, 1821. He entered the University of Norwich with the class of 1842, graduating with the degrees of A. B. and M. C. E.

In 1839 Captain Alden Partridge, of Norwich University, founded the Virginia Literary, Scientific, and Military Institute in Portsmouth, Virginia. Lee directed this military academy as principal for the school year 1842–1843. To round out his education, he entered Harvard Law School in 1843; and with only one year of graduate work, under such famous legal lights as Judge Joseph Story and Professor Simon Greenleaf, he obtained his law degree and went to Troy to open an office.

Charles Bishop, during the last four years of this portion of the Lee story, worked on at the Sandy Hill store. Any day at the store was crowded, and every transaction added to his merchandising skill. He became an expert in barter, supervised the store's post office, and ran a lumber yard and a farm. He became familiar with saw mills and grist mills and gained a valuable knowledge of stage coaches, roads, and communications. In addition to becoming closely familiar with money and its function in exchange, he possessed an integrity which was to be absolutely unassailable throughout the rest of his long life. Developing a capability as a shrewd judge of character became one of his greatest assets, both in building his enormous fortune and in his ponderation of community and cultural institutions.

In such a position, and growing in mental stature as he did, he naturally would reflect on the changing times. He carefully read the newspapers of Sandy Hill and Glens Falls. About 1837, when he was fifteen, he noted that the old Northwest fur trade had about died out. Even while this traffic was languishing, settlers began flocking into New England. Glens Falls enjoyed this population explosion too, for it was more nearly New England than New York at this time.

The whaling industry boomed; and the newspapers bannered stories of that new industry and its substantial contributions to the New England economy in home building, ship building, and trading. From Boston in 1820, the Congregationalists through the recently organized (1810) American Board of Commissioners for Foreign Missions dispatched the First Company of Missionaries to Hawaii. Oregon was entering the news headlines. Settlers were invading the Middle West and preempting land in the fertile valleys of Illinois, Iowa, and the other great prairie states. People were stirring.

Bishop became restless. He had saved some money. He did not, however, see his future in the Glens Falls area. Undoubtedly, had he remained, he would have been a power in the business world and might have emerged with a great record of public service and have achieved many times over the status of millionaire. Glens Falls came to be known as the maker of millionaires, and most of them had their start about the time Bishop was in Sandy Hill. His restlessness, however, overruled all considerations of local affiliation after his employer sent him on a business trip to Troy, New York, in January 1846. Since Lee was practicing law in Troy, the two friends had a reunion and after an exchange of news and views, determined upon an ocean trip to the promising land of Oregon.

OREGON

In 1829, Hall J. Keeley, an enthusiastic but somewhat erratic schoolmaster of Boston, started the Oregon Colonization Society and gained the support of many distinguished citizens of Boston, among them, Edward Everett. In 1832, Nathaniel J. Wyeth with much fanfare organized a company in Boston and pioneered a notable transcontinental trip to Fort Vancouver. The Methodists and Presbyterians started their missions to Oregon in 1833–1836. This was the time (1836) when Dr. Marcus Whitman made his historic journey to the junction of the Walla Walla and Columbia rivers. Washington Irving added his skillful literary art to the publicity on the Oregon country with his narrative on the stirring achievements of Captain Benjamin L. E. Bonneville, published in 1837. To cap the climax John C. Fremont in 1843, on his second expedition, visited the valley of the Columbia River.

All of the eastern newspapers featured the Oregon country. Migration companies were organized, and settlements were established. Inevitably, the general pace of migrations and commerce sparked an argument of jurisdiction over the Oregon country between Great Britain and the United States. It was the promising romance of lush, fertile, green valleys and the mushrooming mercantile establishments and counting houses in the new untamed Oregon country that ultimately reached the willing attention of Bishop and his good friend, William Little Lee. The mounting commerce of whalers, serving as a means of communication between Oregon and New England, constituted an infectious stimulation to these pioneer-minded Americans. Bishop, long years afterward, gave an account of the eventful days of discussion and decision in a letter, April 29, 1901, to his friend Frederick B. Richards:

. . . My first acquaintance with Lee was during a [visit] home at vacation from the University. He, his brother Stephen B. his friend W. W. H. Davis and others walked back to Norwich, one hundred miles, in two days! His father, Stephen Lee, was a noted pedestrian, and lived as you know to a good old age greatly beloved by his family and highly respected by all who knew him.

In 1845 and during the presidential campaign which resulted in the election of James K. Polk there was an exciting dispute with Gt Britain about the North West boundary, which brought the then Territory of Oregon into public notice. Lee and his friend Church were practicing law as partners in Troy. The former was somewhat out of health and ready for a change to a new field. I went to Troy on business for Charles Dewey and on visiting Lee, whom I admired very much for his talents and nobility of character, we talked of our respective condition and prospects. I had determined to leave Sandy Hill to go West or South, or to some other new place. This was in January 1846. We finally agreed to go to Oregon together, he to take his Law books and I a surveyor's compass etc.

We sailed from Newburyport, Mass. Febry 23 1846 in the Brig "*Henry*," a vessel of less than 160 Tons, expecting to reach Honolulu about July 1st and after a short stay—not longer than a month—then, to go on to and up the Columbia River. We made one stop on the way, St. Catherines, Brazil, where we spent about ten days pleasurably, and after experiencing *all kinds* of weather which may be met with during many months and covering many degrees of latitude and longitude on two great oceans, we arrived at Honolulu Oct 12th 1846! . . .

As they were meeting in Troy and discussing plans for the trip the local press carried a report of federal action regarding the Oregon question. The *Glens Falls Clarion*, on February 12, 1846, printed the story:

Passage of the Oregon Resolutions

The Resolutions directing the President to give notice to the British Government of the abrogation of the treaty for the joint occupancy of the Oregon Territory were adopted by the H of R on the 9th of February by a vote of 163 to 54.

Resolved by the Senate and H of R of the U. S. A. in Congress assembled; That the President of the United States cause notice to be given that the connection between the U. S. A. and Great Britain concerning the territory on the northwest coast of America, west of the Stoney Mountains, of the 6th of August 1827, signed at London, shall be annulled and abrogated twelve months after giving such notice.

Many of the votes against the resolution were given by Southern members—men who were so vociferous in their shouts for "Texas and Oregon," until they had acquired the former, when they were seized suddenly with the sober second thought, "that the area of freedom" had already become sufficiently "extended."

A timely advertisement with an attractive description of transportation to Oregon via the Sandwich Isles appeared in late January and early February, 1846, in the Troy, New York papers. The two men moved swiftly. They checked the stage coach run to Newburyport, Massachusetts and were shortly on their way. They made the trip in three days, stopping at Manchester, New Hampshire, the first night; Keene, New Hampshire, the second; and Newburyport, Massachusetts, the third. They stayed at the Franklin House in Newburyport, Thomas Brown, proprietor. There was little time for cultural indulgence in the next few days. They did manage to attend a lyceum lecture by Ralph Waldo Emerson on the evening of February 6.

In the meantime the *Newburyport Advertiser*, January 6, 1846, recorded the arrival of the ship in question, the "brig *Henry*, Kilborn, Salem to load for the Columbia River," and on February 24, 1846, carried the further notation, "cleared, brig *Henry*, Kilborn, Saturday, February 21, Sandwich Islands, and Columbia River. (She sailed yesterday.)." Preparations for departure were watched by the local Newburyport citizenry, and their interest was well described in the *Herald's* February 20, 1846, issue:

For Oregon. A large number of people, have within a few days, visited the brig *Henry*, lying at Bartletts Wharf, nearly ready for sea, and carrying out a reenforcement in the valley of the Wallamette [*sic*]. A second cabin has been fitted on board the brig, and her accommodations are equal to those usually found in a ship of three times her tonnage. She takes out eighteen passengers, twelve males and six females; and her cargo, consisting of every conceivable Yankee notion, is valued at $13,000. Capt. Kilborn, and Mr. Swasey, the first officer of the brig, both of whom have an interest in the voyage, are skillful mariners, and if their business capacities are equal to their seamanship, and a good Providence protects them from unknown dangers, will no doubt find a prosperous career opening upon them. As we stepped on board yesterday, one of the passengers, a young shoemaker, was taking on board a huge box, filled with lasts, tools, and leathers. We thought if his judgment was as clear as his courage and enterprise were undisputed, twenty years hence might see him the associate of the mighty men of the earth, and exerting, perhaps, a powerful influence upon the destinies of the world.

The vessel will probably be ready to sail tomorrow, direct for the Columbia River; and we wish her crew and passengers favoring gales to waft them from our own coast and around the headlands of the southern continent, and into their destined haven. Success in all else will depend upon their own efforts and sound discretion.

Despite the heavy traffic in arrivals and departures of ocean brigs and barkentines, the *Henry* and its mission and interesting passenger list continued to attract much newspaper comment. The *Newburyport Advertiser,* on February 24, 1846, said:

The Oregon Expedition. The brig *Henry*, Capt. Kilborn, sailed for Columbia River, via Sandwich Islands, at 9 o'clock, A.M. yesterday. At the request of the owners and passengers, the Rev. Randolph Campbell and the Rev. Dana, addressed them and their assembled friends in a short but appropriate address and prayer.

The concourse of citizens to witness the embarkation of their friends was numerous, and a more deep feeling of regret at parting, we have never witnessed—such affectionate salutations could only come from hearts truly sincere. . . .

Three days later the *Newburyport Herald* thus described the departure:

The brig *Henry*, with the Oregon expedition, sailed yesterday, at 9 A.M. Three or four hundred spectators gathered at the wharf to witness her departure, and there were many moist eyes among those who took leave of their friends. Religious exercises were had on the occasion, prayer being offered by Rev. Mr. Campbell, and a brief address made by Rev. Dr. Dana. One of the passengers arrived from Boston, in the cars a few moments after the brig cast off, and was put on board by a pilot boat. —The vessel went down the river in good style, with a fine breeze, and as the barometer was rising, there is a good probability, that she will carry pleasant weather with her till clear of the coast. The people on the wharf gave them a parting salute of three cheers, which were responded to from the brig.

The list of officers and passengers was not long:

W. R. [K.] Kilborn	Master		Newburyport, Mass.	
Mrs. Kilborn and three children			"	"
Capt. George Swasey and two children	1st Mate		"	"
Gilbert Watson, M.D.	Ship's Doctor	Age 34	"	"
Mrs. A. Watson and one child			"	"
Hannah Peabody	[Miss]		"	"
George C. Lawton	Merchant	Age 24	Waltham, Mass.	
Col. Wm. L. Lee	Civil Engineer	Age 26	Troy, N. Y.	
James [George] Patterson	Carpenter	Age 23	Charleston, Mass.	
Charles A. [R.] Bishop	Age 23 [*sic*]		Sandy Hill, N. Y.	
John [James] McKeen [McKean]	Shoemaker	Age 23	Charleston, Mass.	
John K. [H.] Wood	Shoemaker	Age 35	Boxboro, Mass.	
Ora R. Wood	Shoemaker	Age 27	"	"

In a book, *Ship Registers of Newburyport 1789–1870,* published by the Essex Institute, Salem, Massachusetts, are details of the *Henry:*

Henry, brig 153 tons, Built Nobleboro, Maine 1837. Length 81 feet 6 inches, breadth 20 feet 8½ inches, depth 8 feet 3 inches; billet head. Registered February 13, 1846. William K. Kilborn, Charles Currier, Gilbert Watson, George A. Swasey, Atkinson Stanwood, all of Newburyport, George D. Johnson, John Gilbert, Calvin Hagar, all of Boston, owners; William K. Kilborn, master.

The ship's papers list the brig as having a "burthen" of 153 59/95 tons.

One of the owners mentioned, George A. Swasey, was also first mate and a passenger as far as Brazil. It was John H. Wood, the shoemaker from Boston, who wrote an adjective-filled, colorful journal of the trip covering the voyage as far as the Falkland Islands. Wood was the grandfather of the late Maude Jones, director of the

Archives of Hawaii. There is no journal known covering the rest of the trip. A few entries from the journal illustrate the hopes and the despairs of the little ship's company. The trip was arduous and beautiful alternately:

Diary of a voyage in the Brig Henry from Newburyport to the Columbia River by way of the Hawaiian Islands.

John H. Wood.

Monday, February 23, 1846:

Today, I have but one favor to ask, and if that could be granted I should be willing never to ask another. *Id est,* to be set on *terra firma.* Good God! What can a man be thinking of when he says he loved the sea?

Thursday, February 26th:

They say we are in the *Gulf Stream* today; but *I* say the d——l, take the gulf stream, and all the rest of the ocean, with all its treasures, its poetry, its mermaids, its dolphins, its whales, and numberless other wonders and beauties. Give me *one foot* of good solid land, and you may have the whole ocean.

Friday, February 27th 1846:

About midnight as I was watching Charles as he lay in his berth, when all of a sudden a huge wave struck the side of the house just opposite his berth and out he came, straight as he lay, clear over the table nearly into my nest, a distance of about ten feet. I thought the whole side of the house was knocked in, and after looking for the big waves, I turned to look for my companion. There he stood all dumb with terror, his mouth open, his eyes out gazing at his vacant berth as if in search of the unknown power that had unceremoniously helped him from his lodge. With fear, and saying in look and action, "come on old wave and I'll look out for #1." This was such a faithful and pleasing exhibition of human nature that despite the danger and awful solemnity of the scene around us, I laughed outright. Charles bunked in again and was soon rocking in old style.

Sunday, March 8th:

If we could have such weather as this I might endure the sea, perchance might learn to love it.

Sunday, March 15th:

Charles read in the Bible, this morning from Luke where Christ raised to life the son of the widow of Nain.

Friday, March 27th:

The sea *is* pleasant after all in good weather. Good bye happy day, and may the morrow be like this.

Thursday, April 9th:

Our evenings are so lovely that any description I might give of them were I to attempt it, would be mere mockery.

Sunday, April 26th:

Never was more lovely day enjoyed by mortal. All is joy and gladness. The whole western heavens were bathed in a flood of glory, and the sun seemed to linger in its flight as if loathe to quit the scene of its own beauty. The sky of the west smiled like a healthy hillside, and all the east catching the cheerful reflection threw back the joyous smile and the approaching stars seemed to sing with gladness. And oh the clouds! the clouds! Who shall attempt a description of *their* superlative beauty? Not I—not I—Heigh-ho; ye landsmen! I tell you it is *good* to live, —it is good to be at sea.

Friday, May 13th:

Head winds and cold, wet, dirty weather. May Heaven pardon me for looseing [*sic*] my patience.

Sunday, May 17th:

A fine breeze sprung up at 12N and Charles and myself spent most of the afternoon sitting at the masthead watching the beautiful changes of land, and on a keen-lookout for St. Catherine's [Brazil]

Monday, May 18th:

After spending a few moments with Mr. Wells (U. S. Consul) Charles George and myself went to the public square, and filled ourselves with fruit and then took a grand stroll over the whole city.

Wednesday, June 17, 1846:

Dear, thrice dear friends! Every night as Charles and myself kneel on the transom to offer up our feeble prayers, their spirits seem to hover near us and bless us—Oh, God help them! Bless them all as they may need!

Thursday, July 16th:

Capt., Charles and myself have spent the day in breaking out the hold for wood and stove pipe and the exercise of handling barrels, boxes etc. has made us warm. In our search for wood we discovered a large leak but so high up as not to endanger the safety of the brig. The tempest increases and God only knows how soon we shall be in eternity.

There was a sea chest crammed with books, and Charles Bishop read avidly—sometimes aloud, sometimes silently. The character of the ship's library is revealed by a partial list of its books: Blair, *Effect of Religion on Adversity;* Cooper, *Naval History of the United States;* Tupper, *Proverbial Philosophy;* Jefferson, *Memoirs;* Rollins, *Life of Alexander;* Gibbon, *World History.* The lack of distraction aboard ship would suggest that even a reasonable concentration upon such works would leave its mark.

The *Henry* likely suffered severely in the unduly long three months of the Falkland Islands-Honolulu leg of the voyage. An only reference in a U. S. Consulate letter is a clue: "the Brig *Henry* encountered a severe gale off Cape Horn and sustained damages to amount of $5500." This was not minor damage in terms of the currency of the day. Battered and beaten, the *Henry* hove to outside the harbor of Honolulu, October 12, 1846. Instead of the estimated four months to Oregon, the voyage had taken almost eight months; and they were still more than 2,000 miles from Oregon. A large party of Hawaiians appeared with a tow rope and pulled the brig through the channel in the reef, up to the wharf. Gorham D. Gilman, highly regarded by the chiefs, young and old, came aboard the ship to greet any newcomers. He was a clerk in a retail store at Fort and King Streets and was destined to be Bishop's friend for the next fifty years. Gilman was accompanied by Reverend Samuel Chenery Damon.*

Lee and Bishop decided not to continue on to Oregon, and Bishop discusses this in a letter to Frederick Richards: †

On examination it was found that the necessary repairs upon the vessel would consume many weeks, carrying the time for her arrival on the stormy coast into the rainy winter season. We listened to the strong advice of gentlemen who had resided in Oregon, and others, and decided to postpone going on until the following spring. We both received offers of employment, Lee quite tempting offers in his profession. We were pleased with the climate and soon came to like the friendly people, both whites and natives, and the result was as you know that we became permanent residents in Honolulu. In 1891 I passed through Oregon on my way from the East—more than forty years behind time.

The somewhat ill-fated *Henry,* after many weeks of repair, sailed for its original destination, without Bishop and Lee. It arrived off the Columbia River in seventeen days, but as a consequence of bad weather and lack of water and provisions it put in at Victoria. The passengers had to make their way across rough land to the Columbia River. The brig finally arrived at the river on March 12, 1847, having lost both anchors and chains and having narrowly averted grounding at one point. For a while the little ship plied the Pacific in the lumber trade, occasionally reappearing in the Honolulu harbor. National Archives contains a record of the "surrender" of this vessel at Salem, Massachusetts, October 15, 1849.

---

* Samuel Chenery Damon was sent to Honolulu in 1842 by the American Seamen's Friend Society to take charge of the Oahu Bethel Church. He served for forty-three years, visited each vessel while in port, and founded *The Friend,* a monthly English publication. This book makes reference to two of his four sons: Samuel Mills Damon p. 48 and Francis Williams Damon p. 237.

† See p. 38.

EARLY HONOLULU YEARS

THE SENSE OF RELIEF upon disembarkation must have been a strong incentive to prolong the stopover. This was an enforced indulgence anyway, since the *Henry* was in no condition to carry out its original mission for many weeks.

Bishop was twenty-four and of unquiet purpose. Here he was in Honolulu with his friend Lee with no acquaintances except the two greeters, Damon and Gilman, and the passenger list of the *Henry.* The members of this latter group could be of little assistance, for they were in a strange land too. Conversations between Lee and some of the local Honolulu leaders led him to apply his legal talent to pressing judicial code and legal organization problems. Lee offered to do the work if a job could be found for Bishop. This brought an immediate offer to Bishop to untangle the affairs of Ladd and Company.

On July 27, 1833, some thirteen years earlier, three young men appeared in Honolulu: Peter Allan Brinsmade, age twenty-eight, William Ladd, twenty-six, and William Hooper, twenty-four. They opened a "mercantile trading establishment," at first under the firm name of Ladd and Company. A chief interest of this group centered in a government lease of nine hundred eighty acres of land about Koloa, Kauai. The lease was signed July 29, 1835, a date usually accepted for the founding of the first sugar plantation in Hawaii. This venture, along with others including silk, castor oil, and *kukui* nut products, caused financial embarrassment to Ladd and Company; and consideration was given to selling out.

This study led to an unwise and unusual linking of private enterprise and government. Ladd and Company obtained permission under terms of a fantastic lease to occupy and develop unimproved areas anywhere in the Kingdom at a nominal rental for one hundred years. The contract was made subject to recognition of the Kingdom of Hawaii as an independent nation by the United States, Great Britain, and France. The King was more broadly concerned about the necessity of a guaranteed independence for his nation than merely a Ladd and Company contract, but this was a factor in his determination to win a clear status among nations. William Richards, a trusted adviser of the King, and a native named Haalilio were appointed special envoys to approach the United States for recognition. This was forthcoming in 1842. Great Britain followed, April 1, 1843, and France gave recognition to the new nation, November 28, 1843.

The need for capital in the Ladd and Company venture sent Brinsmade on a side trip to Belgium in 1844 to attempt leasing the rights of the company to a Belgian corporation. While he was away, the local leaders in Ladd and Company in Honolulu gave up. On April 18, 1845, Ladd and Company's assets were auctioned at a sheriff's sale and were obtained by the Hawaiian Treasury Board for $3600. Now the government became a half owner and was, temporarily at least, in private business.

By the time the *Henry* rounded Diamond Head, the Ladd and Company affairs were in such complete disorder that Bishop seemed to be a provident answer to the trying situation that engulfed both King and commoner. Basically, the Ladd and Company reputation had been made in connection with the sugar enterprise at Koloa, Kauai. Bishop had to visit Koloa in the course of working on the books of Ladd and Company and there began his acquaintance with the island which was to bring him to favor it a little more perhaps than any other.

While working on the affairs of Ladd and Company, Bishop was offered the clerkship of the U. S. Consulate in Honolulu. Joel Turrill was the United States Consul. This consulate-acquaintanceship of Turrill and Bishop was not of long standing, for Turrill left the Kingdom in 1850 and died in 1859. But in that short time the two men developed a deep mutual trust and respect. After Turrill left, Bishop sent him numerous letters of frank detail about the economic and business life and the leading personalities in the current Honolulu scene. These Bishop letters, along with a number that William L. Lee wrote to Turrill, are in the Hawaiian Historical Society's manuscript collection and constitute an important research file on the life and times of Honolulu in the 1850's. The Consulate letters in the Copy Book of General Letters for the period of September 21, 1848, to March 19, 1850, are in the handwriting of Bishop.

He had not completely given up the thought of continuing on to

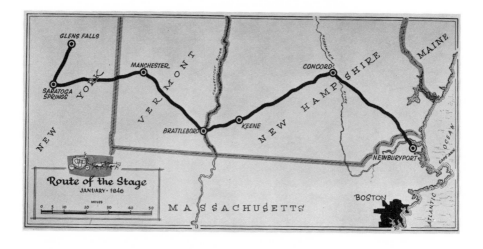

Above: Advertisement appearing in the Massachusetts and eastern New York State newspapers in December and January of 1845–1846. It was this advertisement that caught the attention of Bishop and Lee.
Below: The stage route taken by Bishop and Lee in January, 1846, from Sandy Hill, New York, to Newburyport, Massachusetts.

Left: From a daguerreotype in the Bishop Museum; taken with Lee at the time of sailing from Newburyport, Massachusetts. Bishop, 24, is pictured on the right.

Below: a prototype of the brig *Henry* aboard which Bishop and Lee sailed on February 23, 1846, on their proposed trip to the Oregon Country.

GOVERNMENT OF THE HAWAIIAN ISLANDS.

The undersigned, a native of *New York United States*, lately residing in *Honolulu Island of Oahu*, being duly sworn upon the Holy Evangelists, upon his oath declares that he will support the Constitution and Laws of the Hawaiian Islands, and bear true allegiance to His Majesty *Kamehameha III the King.*

Chas. R. Bishop

Subscribed and sworn to, this 27th day of *February*
A. D., 18 49.
Before me, *Wm Ap Jones*
Clerk
to Minister of Int.

10.

Bishop's oath of allegiance, as a naturalized citizen, to the King and to the Kingdom of Hawaii. From page 10, Naturalization Book, Kingdom of Hawaii, 1849–1850, in Archives of Hawaii.

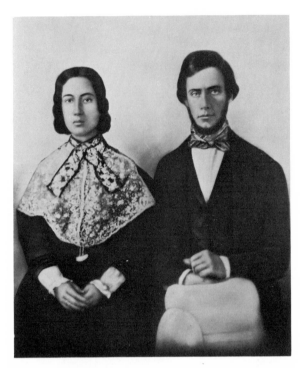

Left: The wedding picture of Charles and Bernice Bishop. From a daguerreotype given to the Bishop Museum by Mr. E. Faxon Bishop, who had received it from the New York State Historical Association.

Below: The first house at this site, the birthplace of Bernice Pauahi Paki, was a commodious thatched roof building. The house and the premises carried the name "Aikupika." Paki, father of Bernice, constructed an almost entirely new house about 1847 which was given another name, "Haleakala." The house was on King Street close to the present site of the headquarters of the Bank of Hawaii. From a painting by David Howard Hitchcock.

Oregon, although in the hue and cry of prospering traffic in Honolulu he was beginning to lose interest. Business in bills of exchange was brisk, and the interest return was high, usually 15%. Whale oil transshipping was big business between the commission merchants and the whalers. South America and California both would take all the tallow and goatskins that were available. Then the news of the rush to the newly discovered gold fields in California reached Honolulu. Wave after wave of excitement swept the island seaport. Bishop's original restlessness, dormant in his first Honolulu years, reappeared now, and almost a year to a day after gold had been discovered in Sutter Creek he joined other Honolulu citizens in an advertisement in the *Polynesian:*

January 6, 1849

Notice

The subscribers hereby give notice of their intention to depart from this kingdom, and request all persons having demands against them to present them immediately.

W. E. Gill	J. M. Stone
W. Darkem	C. R. Bishop
T. Gardner	A. W. Bush
A. Gaulet	F. Martin
Ahfou	

This advertisement was one alternative open to him, since under the statute laws of 1846–1848 nobody could leave the Kingdom without giving public notice or without procuring a passport from the Foreign Office.

But the advertisement was read by more than one Honolulan. Lee saw it and sought out his friend with the view of changing the decision. The purpose as advertised in the *Polynesian* was shortly and effectively side-tracked. Bishop's start in the direction of California was halted at Honolulu for almost fifty years. In short succession he married Princess Bernice Pauahi, was made a lifetime member of the House of Nobles, joined the Privy Council, became Collector General of Customs, helped organize the Royal Hawaiian Agricultural Society, opened a bank under the name of Bishop and Company, and generally without realizing it, laid the foundation for his leadership in the community. Much of this direction obviously came at the insistence of Lee. He would never have started for Oregon by way of Honolulu had it not been for Lee's leadership. He

probably would have proceeded to complete the voyage to Oregon
or have departed for California, had it not been for his friend.

Shortly after Lee's passing, Bishop wrote a short, informal, memorial paragraph to J. Turrill. The letter was dated June 26, 1857:

> . . . The death of our friend Lee tho' long expected, is a heavy blow, and
> has brought sadness upon the whole community. It is unnecessary for me
> to write to you of his great worth as a public officer, and a private man,
> or of the great love and respect which all persons had for him who knew
> him. . . .

Bishop recognized Lee's leadership and always respected it. There
was a strong bond of mutual trust between the two; Lee designated
his wife and his friend Bishop as executors of his estate.

There was one other individual in Honolulu during these years
who was a most helpful associate of Bishop. This was the surprisingly little known General James Fowle Baldwin Marshall, of the
Indian Agency, Hampton Institute, and Hawaii business and diplo-
macy fame, who lived a life that touched in many significant ways
the life of Bishop. This New Englander was born in Boston, Massachusetts, in 1815, and came to the Kingdom of Hawaii in 1839. He
was a friend of Kamehameha III and a member of the Hawaiian
legislature, although his fundamental role in the community was
that of merchant. It was this man who was entrusted by the King
with a secret mission to London to present and protest the Kingdom
of Hawaii's political embroilment with Lord George Paulet in 1843.
He accomplished his mission, and the independence of Hawaii was
re-established.

Marshall was attracted to many of Honolulu's charitable and
benevolent enterprises. He was deeply interested in the Seamen's
Bethel and Bethel Union Church. General Samuel Chapman Armstrong * was a member of a Sunday School class which Marshall
taught jointly with Bishop at Bethel. Marshall interested himself in
public education. He was a member of the Royal Hawaiian Agricultural Society and prepared papers on "Kauai Plantations," and
"Coolies on Lihue Plantation." Among the first officers of the Society
we find the position of vice-president filled by Marshall.

In business, he formed a partnership with Francis Johnson. Captain Brewer, founder of C. Brewer and Company, joined them; and
upon the disbandment of this firm in 1847, Marshall participated in
a second mercantile group which lasted until 1850. He owned a part

* See pp. 252–253.

of the Lihue Plantation in its early formative days, having purchased Bishop's grantor interest, May 27, 1850, and was actually for a time manager of that plantation.

Marshall eventually returned to the New England area as the Civil War broke out. He earned his general officer rank at this time, serving first as paymaster general of Massachusetts for the Army and then as director of the Sanitary Commission. The American Unitarian Association later had an Indian school in Montana, and to that he devoted himself. Then as secretary of the Emigrant Aid Association he directed the emigration of three thousand Minnesotans to the new virgin lands of Florida. All this brought him finally to Hampton Institute in 1870 where for the next fourteen years he handled the funds of his former Sunday School pupil's struggling institution.

He did not close the door on Hawaii. His close friendship of the lengthening years with Bishop was constantly renewed and refreshed. This is why he appeared on the platform as a co-speaker with Bishop when a Kamehameha Schools' Founder's Day speaker was needed on December 19, 1889. He died in 1891, and in his Will still provided for his own system of benevolences, among them a twelve hundred dollar contribution in trust to H. A. Widemann and Charles R. Bishop for "educational purposes" in the Islands. The money, at the discretion of the Trustees, was sent to the Hilo Boys' Boarding School. Bishop, of course, would never forget that it was Marshall who chaperoned his friend William L. Lee's fiancée * around Cape Horn and made the arrangements for the Sunday wedding aboard the barkentine *Leland* in Honolulu harbor. The Cooke Journal † refers to this:

March 12, [1849]: When we were going to church [March 11] it was reported that the *Leland* was coming in. At the second singing, Mr. Bishop came in and asked me where John Ii was. They went out together. After the Meeting John Ii returned saying they wanted a permit for Mr.

* Catherine Cornelia Newton was the intended bride. After Lee's decease in 1857 she married (1861) Edward Livingston Youmans, a writer, editor, and promoter of scientific education. Both Bishop and Marshall continued a frequent exchange of letters with her for the next thirty years.

† Amos Starr Cooke kept a diary (he occasionally labeled his material a Journal) and he and his wife Juliette Montague (Cooke) wrote letters covering their family life and work in Hawaii. These papers, housed in the Hawaiian Mission Children's Society library, constitute a chief source of the story of the courtship and marriage of the Charles Reed Bishops. See pp. 22–32.

Lee and Miss Newton to marry, as the latter wanted to be married before she came ashore.

It was then not only friend Lee who counselled Bishop as to where he might establish himself for a career; Marshall had a hand in it too. The years between 1846 and 1850 (Bishop's arrival in Hawaii and marriage) were touch-and-go years in Bishop's thinking. Marshall and his sister Elizabeth lived in what amounted to a foreign colony in or close to the area bounded by King, Fort, Beretania, and Alakea Streets. A short walk from his room in the Court House brought Bishop almost daily to the Marshall residence.

Rather unsung, this man Marshall, but of the respect and admiration in which Bishop held him there can be no doubt. His Unitarian philosophy, business acumen, community philanthropy, and the mutual acquaintance with General Armstrong made important impressions on the thinking of Bishop.

Having marched and countermarched on the gold rush temptation, Bishop was soon laying the foundation of his remarkable Hawaii career. He did not forget the Ladd and Company experiences in sugar at Koloa where a great potential for development existed, waiting for the right formula of intelligence and capital. He returned to Kauai again and again with new ventures in sugar.

Bishop was proposed as Collector of Customs by G. P. Judd on February 23, 1849, but was not confirmed in the appointment until March 1. Between these dates, Bishop visited the office of the Minister of Interior and there on February 27th signed an oath to "support the Constitution and Laws of the Hawaiian Islands." Citizenship in the Kingdom was prerequisite to holding public office. The action promised deep involvement for now Bishop had openly and finally cast his lot with his new native land. About a year prior to this, a Customs Commission was created with authority to act as a board for rule making and appeal regarding business at the Customs House. In the "Privy Council Reports," September 25, 1849, there appears this item:

Mr. A. B. Bates and Charles R. Bishop were appointed Commissioners of Customs in place of Mr. G. P. Judd and Wm. Paty who have left the country. His Majesty and the Council consented.

Bishop's assignment now was dual in nature since he was also Collector of Customs.

Late in 1849, the first of Bishop's acquisitions of land is noted in the "Privy Council Reports." October 8, 1849, the Minister of the Interior was authorized to ". . . execute a patent in fee simple in favor of Charles R. Bishop for Ouaoa in Hamakualoa, Maui at $1.00 per acre."

He made a good impression in his new assignment, and on March 4, 1850, Mr. Wyllie, in one reference in the "Privy Council Reports":

. . . called the attention of the Council to the excellent statistical material tables prepared by the Collector General of Customs and moved the following resolution which was passed: *Resolved* that the Statistical Tables of the duties received in 1849, as published in the *Polynesian* of 19th January and 2nd instant are highly creditable to C. R. Bishop, Esquire, Collector General of Customs.

Bishop continued as Collector of Customs until April 5, 1853, when he resigned. The "Privy Council Reports," March 2, 1853, contain this resolution:

Mr. Armstrong read the resignation of C. R. Bishop as Collector General of Customs on which

Res. 2

Resolved; That we advise the King to accept the Resignation of the Collector General of Customs with thanks for his faithful and acceptable performance of the duties of his office during his term of service.

Bishop's original appointment as Commissioner of Customs had lapsed, and nothing was done about reappointing him until his resignation as Collector of Customs was received. Another entry may be noted in the "Privy Council Reports," March 27, 1854:

Mr. Allen read the resignation of Mr. Everett as a Commissioner of Customs. Mr. C. R. Bishop was nominated by vote to supply his place.

This new appointment as Commissioner of Customs lasted through 1859. In that year the Commission was abolished. Giving up the Collector of Customs position signified the end to employee status for Bishop. He had saved his money through an almost miserly thrift and had invested his savings most wisely, albeit cautiously, in sugar ventures, land, and bills of exchange.

2

Marriage

BERNICE PAUAHI PAKI

ON JUNE 8, 1850, A MARRIAGE notice appeared in the *"Polynesian"*:

In this town, on the 4th Instant, by Rev. R. Armstrong, Charles R. Bishop, Esquire, Collector General of Customs, to Miss Bernice Pauahi, all of this place.

Princess Bernice was eighteen and Charles was twenty-eight. The wedding took place in the Chiefs' Children's School which had been started in the home of Mr. and Mrs. Amos Starr Cooke. This was both home and school to Bernice for ten years. The Cookes would have closed their school for royal children earlier had not Bernice pleaded with them to hold it open for her as a home and a school until after her marriage. Both of the Cookes were at the wedding, as were the Reverend and Mrs. Richard Armstrong, Mrs. Elizabeth Kekaaniau Pratt, and Mrs. Bush. The bride wore a muslin gown, white, with a wreath of jasmine.

We do not know the occasion of the first meeting of the royal princess and Charles. It was undoubtedly at a party held at the Cooke home and to which Cooke refers in his diary, February 25, 1847: "Have invited a party for Thursday evening. Messers Wyllie, Ricord, and Judd, Judge Turrill and three children and Mr. Bishop. . . . 25 in all." This is the first mention of any opportunity that Bishop may have had to meet Bernice. Entries in the diary indicate that he began to call at the Cooke home about once a month. Of his immediate interest in Bernice there may be some doubt. The diary states, June 28, 1847: "At 4 o'clock, all being ready, Mr. Jasper and Jane, Lot and Bernice, Mr. Bishop and Elizabeth Judd came out of Sarai's room upon the platform and Mr. Armstrong there married them (Jasper and Jane)." This first sorting linked Elizabeth Judd with Charles Bishop and Bernice with Lot. Abner Paki, father of

Bernice, wanted his daughter to marry either of the Princes—Lot Kamehameha or Alexander Liholiho Iolani. The latter eliminated himself; he was in love with Emma Rooke. Lot was free. The two Princes were the sons of Kekuanaoa and Kinau, and Emma was the niece and adopted daughter of Dr. T. C. B. Rooke. The Cookes did no "engineering" of a romance between Bernice and Charles, evidence of which is contained in a letter Mr. Cooke wrote to his sister Fanny, September 18, 1847: "We greatly hope that Lot will conduct [*sic*] as to render himself worthy of her (Bernice). If not we think she may marry Alexander who is two years younger than she."

It is most unlikely in his first three years in Honolulu that Bishop had established any ties, sentimental or other, in the light of his advertising in January 1849 that he was about to leave the Kingdom. There is ample evidence that his interest in Bernice picked up as soon as he reversed himself regarding California.

The pattern did change and a warm acquaintance and mutual regard developed between the two. The monthly calls at the Cooke home continued. The two began to attend Mrs. Fuller's Singing School on Thursday evenings.

Bishop's social life in Honolulu during 1849 is detailed in "Lizzie" Marshall's diary * and touches upon horseback rides to such scenic spots as the Pali, cocoanut grove (Waikiki), and Pauoa Valley; informal dancing with quadrilles, waltzes, and polkas; daily teas; soirees; games including forfeit, charades, and fox and goose; picnics; and exchange visits in homes and ships with officers and crew. Bishop moved in this social circle with Honolulu's leading families: Brewer, Andrews, Janion, Peirce, Thompson, Turrill, Hoffman, Castle, Vida, Dominis, Upham, Ladd, Marshall, and many more. Bernice and her Royal School people, the Amos Cookes, did not move in this circle but stepped in from time to time. Bernice was never mentioned in the Cooke diary as going out to visit without Mr. or Mrs. Cooke being included. This was a type of chaperonage insisted upon by the Cookes and welcomed by Bernice. As might be expected Bernice and Charles met frequently at the various homes or on rides and picnics according to the diary.

The Cooke diary returns us to Charles and Bernice and in barest details records the progress of the budding romance:

* This diary covers the period from June 1–Nov. 17, 1849. It is in the possession of a great grandniece of James Marshall, Mrs. Kenneth H. Wood of Natick, Massachusetts.

Wed. March 14 [1849]: Mrs. C. (Cooke) questioned Bernice about Lot & Al . . . She said, "No." This evening Mr. Bishop has called.

Fri. March 30: This evening Mr. Bishop has called and had a long talk with Bernice.

Thurs. August 16: Monday Mrs. C. received a note from Mr. C. R. Bishop respecting B. & today she replied to it and returned it. It will probably lead to a union of those two.

Thurs. August 30: Yesterday, Bernice had a talk with Gov. Kekuanaoa about his desire that she marry Lot. She told him she did not like Lot. It made (her) quite unhappy all day & she went to bed early with a headache.

Sat. Sept. 1: Mr. Bishop and Bernice have gone out to walk this evening.

Tues. Sept. 4: Saturday night we did not get to sleep till near midnight, because Mr. B. & B. did not return till 11½ 'clk . . . Mr. B. & B. have agreed to suspend matters for six months or so.

But things could be bright occasionally. Reverend Henry H. Parker wrote a paper, "Reminiscences of Mrs. Bishop's Life," and contributes his bit to the courtship:

On a bright afternoon in the fall of 1849 . . . a pretty girl stepped into a single-seated buggy on the old Punahou School grounds and rode away with a young businessman of Honolulu. The girl's name was Bernice Pauahi. You can easily guess who the young man was. . . . I can see true to life as I saw it that day the picture of that man and maid in the neat buggy, driving down the road that led to the makai gate which opened through the big stone wall into the Manoa Road now called Punahou Street.

Back to the diary again:

Thurs. September 6: Heard this afternoon that Dr. Judd was to sail in the *Honolulu* for San Francisco on his way to France and that he was to be accompanied by Lot and Alexander. The Governor, Paki and Konia sent for Bernice this evening and wish her to be engaged to Lot, so as to marry him when he shall return from France, and they wish her to decide at once without seeing him and without his saying to her whether or not he loves her.

Fri. September 7: Mr. Armstrong called yesterday and we consulted him about Bernice's *pilikia*. He thought we had taken a wise course. This forenoon B. wrote a note to Lot and requested him to call and see her and he came. She told him the wishes of their parents and said she would consent in accordance with their commands, but she knew it would make her always unhappy for he did not love her, nor did she him. After this she wrote to the Governor and said if they (the Governor, Paki and Konia) wished her buried in a coffin, she would submit to their authority. That she would as soon have them bury her as to promise to marry Lot.

Governor replied to it saying she was deceiving herself. Lot, seeing her letter to Governor, wrote saying he exonerated her from all her promises in her youth, that he would not be the means of rendering her unhappy, that he knew *he* was unworthy of her, but that there was one who was worthy, even the one she loved, and he hoped she would be happy with him. Requested to be remembered to us and that he wished he was worthy to call upon us, etc. Since this B. feels more lighthearted.

Sat. September 8: Konia took tea with us—she has been blaming Bernice because she talked so plainly to Lot.

Tues. September 11: Mrs. Dole has just come in to inquire if it is true that Lot & Bernice were married.

Sat. September 15: Mr. Bishop is visiting Bernice in the parlor.

Thurs. November 1: Much opposition with some against Mr. Bishop & Bernice being married. It comes mostly from Mrs. Judd & her family.

November 9: Bernice wrote to Mr. Bishop in such a manner to release him if he wished. It was her own thought to do so. Last evening he called but she had retired. He has called tonight besides writing to her today.

Fri. November 16: I rec'd a letter from Paki inquiring why we had let Mr. Bishop call and see Bernice & steal her heart. I devoted last evening to writing a reply & sent it this morning. I received another which I did not answer. Paki wrote to Mr. Wyllie about Mr. Bishop & he came to talk with Bernice & was so pleased with her maturity etc—that [he] went & told Mr. B. that he had made a fine choice. Mr. W. called together some of the Ministers of State & Chiefs & talked over the affair. I do not think they will oppose strenuously the match.

Mon. December 10: This evening Mr. Bishop has called & Bernice has played for him & sung for him. She has baked today.

Fri. December 21: Bernice's birthday (19th) passed off without any noise. In the evening Mr. Bishop called & Mrs. C. [Cooke] lectured him about ??

Mon. December 24: Mr. Bishop called in the evening (Saturday). At evening (Sunday) Mr. Bishop came to wait upon Bernice to the Chapel.

Mon. January 7, 1850: I fell in with Mrs. Judd and we conversed for an hour the subject of Mr. Bishop and Bernice.

Mon. February 25: This evening Mr. Bishop has called again. He calls every evening.

On this same day, Cooke wrote to his sister Fanny:

Juliette & Bernice are engaged in sewing & Mr. Bishop is reading to them from the "Life of Hannah More." Probably you are aware that Miss B. has a beau who calls almost every evening & probably will till they find a home of their own. He is a fine young man & is the Collector General of Customs. . . .

It is very apparent that her thoughts & affections are centering in him and well they may, for he is every way worthy of her heart & hand . . .

We continue now principally for Bernice's sake. She is very anxious to have us remain until she can have a home of her own.

The final events in the story are best learned from further entries in the Cooke diary:

Thurs. March 28: Mr. Bishop went yesterday accompanied by Mr. Hall to get a license to be married. He did object but said that Paki should be consulted. This morning Bernice went down there and he consented if she would wait until his house was done, say about three months, and be married there, and she said "Yes."

Mon. May 6: Miss Coffin moved into our family for a few days in order to sew for Bernice.

Sat. May 11: Mr. Bishop and Bernice have concluded to make but a very little wedding party at their nuptials.

Sat. May 25: Today Mr. Bishop wrote to Bernice that he had told Paki that he wished to be married in 10 days, and asked if his house would be in readiness. He replied to Mr. B. No! & that if he wished to be married so soon he better be married here—Tuesday, the 4th of June will probably be the day—& no foreign company to be invited.

Thurs. June 6: (Monday) That evening was monthly concert, but instead of going to it I went down to see & to invite Paki and Konia to the wedding on Tuesday evening. The latter manifested a good deal of opposition & asked which wedding? Said we had helped their daughter against them etc. etc. I drew up my artillery & we kept at it till ten o'clock. The next day (Tuesday) when Bernice and Mrs. C. found out what I had said, they felt very bad, especially when they read the notes from each, declining to come to the wedding, saying she must look to us, Mr. and Mrs. Cooke for all her *pono*.

At 8 o'clock Mr. Bishop was on the spot & bro. Armstrong married them, no stranger being present but the parson & his wife. After the ceremony we sat down to tea and at 9 o'clock they went in a wagon to Judge Andrews, where they were to board.

Mr. and Mrs. Bishop came down & dined with us & then sailed for Koloa, Kauai on the Kalama, 20 tons burden Capt. Hendley.

There was a slight touch of giddiness in the air that fourth day of June 1850. Early that morning the prospective bridegroom took a few moments to write a rare bit of detached announcement to his good friend, and former employer, J. Turrill:

. . . Please give my love to Mrs. Turrill and the children and tell her that the grass and trees in the yard are looking finely owing to the frequent showers this season. Tell her also that I would write to her, but that I am to be married this evening at Mr. Cooke's: and have a thousand and one things to do today. I hope to leave in a day or two for Kauai to spend three weeks.

Writers in commenting on the wedding mention the likelihood that the young married couple "fled" to Kauai to escape the wrath of her parents. This probably was not true. Bishop had spent considerable time on Kauai on behalf of the sugar plantations in which he was already interested, and he knew the area very intimately. He had not such acquaintance with the other islands, and it was most logical that it would be Kauai which he would suggest for the honeymoon. In 1851 the couple prolonged a visit to Kauai through eleven weeks.

Mr. Richard Armstrong, who married Charles and the Princess Bernice, had been urged not to go through with the marriage; but when Armstrong was visiting Paki one day, Bishop came to call. Armstrong placed Bishop's hand in that of Paki and left. That was the start of the reconciliation between Bernice's parents and the young people.* This version of a reconciliation differs from an entry in the Cooke diary, Saturday, August 2, 1851: "[Mrs. Cooke] Heard that Konia, Paki & Gov were reconciled to Bernice at the advice of Victoria."

The Bishops' marriage was not to be blessed with children of their own, and this stimulated several attempts at adoption. The first effort was a royal infant adopted by the Bishops and named Keolaokalani † Paki Bishop. The official date of this action was February, 1863. The baby was the son of Princess Ruth Keelikolani Keanolani Kanahoahoa and John Young Davis. He had been given the illustrious nickname *Hoku O Pakipika* or Star of the Pacific. Unhappiness filled the household shortly thereafter when on August 29, 1863, the infant died.

Another effort involved twin sisters, one of whom was named Lydia Crowningburg, High Chiefess Keomailani. The twins were the children of William Isaac Jesse Crowningburg and Auhea Kekauluohi also known as Miriam Elizabeth. One twin, Lydia, was taken at birth by Queen Emma and the other by Bernice. One day a *kahu* took Bernice's twin girl for a walk up Nuuanu Stream and slipped with the little girl on the rocks. The youngster died of injuries. Before long both Bernice and Emma wanted the responsibility of rearing the surviving twin, who, however, was sent off to England to be educated. Upon her return, she was married to Wray Taylor who had followed her from England. The ceremony was

---

* This story comes from Ellen Armstrong Weaver (Mrs. Philip H.), who had heard the story from Bishop himself years later. Richard Armstrong, was the father of Samuel Chapman Armstrong and Ellen Armstrong Weaver.

† This name is also spelled Keolaonalani and frequently shortened to Keola.

performed at St. Andrew's Cathedral by Alfred Willis, the Right Reverend Bishop of Honolulu. A family of five children resulted from this marriage. First among them was Kaiheekai III, William Edward Bishop Taylor. This boy was to become an object of the Bishops' affection and while never adopted by them was baptized as their own godson. When Bishop opened the Preparatory Department of The Kamehameha Schools, he personally escorted little William to the campus for enrollment.

Shortly before this, Bishop placed a son of his Uncle Linus Dewey Bishop of Fort Edwards, New York, G. Bradley Bishop, in the bank; and he was hopeful that this young man might eventually take over management of the bank. But tragedy struck again; and young B. Bradley died December 4, 1882, at the age of twenty-two, of a disease referred to in those days as the "galloping consumption." There were no more efforts at adoption.

The lives of the Bishops blended in a social leadership of Honolulu that was simple and humble and yet of the very highest order. Their home, "Haleakala," on King Street, was a mecca for the admirals, the statesmen, the poets, and the scientists. And yet Mrs. Bishop would patiently listen to any of her own people who constantly called on her with their troubles. Mr. Bishop was busy in finance and promotion; but his office and the whole center of his business circle was but a few hundred feet from home, and in this small area the childless pair moved to perform miracles of work and hospitality for stranger and friend.

They also travelled.* Their last joint visit to San Francisco was in 1884 when each, however, made the crossing alone: she going first to seek assistance from the medical profession and he on May 10, 1884, to bring her home. The doctors in Honolulu had advised her to travel to the Mainland for the medical help obtainable there. She left on the *Alameda* April 1, and Mr. Bishop wrote to Rudolph W. Meyer, his Molokai Ranch manager, April 19: "This morning I have a letter from Mrs. Bishop per *Zealandia*. She had a very rough passage over."

There was a not unusual alternation of hope and despair in the story of Mrs. Bishop's quest for health. A follow-up letter from Mrs. Bishop stirred him deeply and he moved swiftly. On May 10, he wrote rather forlornly to Meyer:

* See pp. 339–340.

. . . I am going to San Francisco on the *Mariposa*. Mrs. Bishop was not quite well at last report and cannot come home this month, consequently I shall go over, and may or may not return in one month. I hope to find her so well that I may return immediately in the *Mariposa* whether she comes with me or not. She will not be expecting me because she knows how inconvenient it is for me to leave home now; and she also knows that I know that she has every attention and comfort possible where she is. While I feel I shall find her better, I feel that I must go. . . .

Little, however, could be accomplished by staying in San Francisco; and the Bishops returned, leaving June 9 on the *Mariposa*, probably with a quiet understanding of the fatal inevitability of the effects of Mrs. Bishop's malignant disease. However, a line in a letter to Meyer, June 23, indicates a slight improvement: "Mrs. Bishop continues to improve in health."

They had moved into "Haleakala," upon returning but shortly changed to their Waikiki home; and these comments were made in successive letters to Meyer:

July 7: . . . On the 5th we moved out to Waikiki. Last week Mrs. Bishop was quite unwell for several days but she is now much better again. . . .

August 9th: . . . Mrs. Bishop has been quite well lately. Waikiki life seems to agree with her.

August 28th: . . . I'm sorry to say that Mrs. Bishop is not quite as well as she has been. . . .

Waikiki had proved of some relief; but, actually, none was to be found anywhere.

A most sympathetic account of Mrs. Bishop's last days is found in correspondence Mrs. Amos Starr Cooke had with her sister. On Monday, October 6, 1884, she says:

I went on Sat. with *pilu* to Waikiki to call on Bernice Bishop. She, Bernice, is not as well & her looks shocked me. I asked her how she was & she replied, "I do not know how to think of myself." She said in a low voice that there is some new trouble. . . . B. told me that when they returned they expected to live in Ruth's house. They had been altering it so it would be convenient. She has a beautiful place at Waikiki, *elegant* & nicely furnished. It was Lot's place. . . .

This letter had not been mailed yet and Mrs. Cooke added comments two days later, October 6th:

I telephoned this morning to C. R. Bishop residence, Waikiki to inquire about Bernice & whether she would like me to call on her. Mrs. Allen

[Cordie] answered, said *'Come in the morning.'* So I went. *She is failing!* . . . Talked with me freely, told me all about San Francisco operation & how she felt about it, how she suffered after it. She seems to feel willing to go or to stay as God sees best. Talked of that part of it very freely. . . . I was much comforted with what she said. She asked me to pray for her & to bid all her friends pray for she needed help from on high.

It was Mrs. Bishop's wish to move to Keoua Hale,* the beautiful palace-like home at 21 Emma Street, which her cousin Ruth Keelikolani had willed to her but two years before. Mrs. Cooke writes of seeing the Bishop entourage on its way there:

On Tuesday near night [October 9th] I met the company bringing Mrs. B. into town. She lay in the arms of a nurse, a woman was fanning her all the time. It was a mournful sight. Mr. Bishop, Dr. & several friends were with her, five carriages in all.

This was to be the last move. She passed away about noon on Thursday, October 16.

Following his wife's death, Bishop went to Molokai for a change, and he stayed with the Meyer family. Upon his return he wrote a letter of touching sentiment:

November 24: We had a smooth run down, and I was quite comfortable in the Captain's room on his lounge. I am greatly obliged to you and your family for your kindness. . . . The great drawback upon my complete enjoyment was the oft recurring thought that the one who had long anticipated such a visit and who would have been so much pleased with what I saw, and for whose sake mainly I was interested in that property, was not there, and could not even welcome me on my return home and hear from me my experiences and observations. . . .

Thus we note the conclusion of the life of the last of the Kamehameha royal dynasty. Mrs. Bishop's virtues and high human qualities have been extolled in prose and verse and oratory. Her beneficent life and works are solemnly recalled to memory every December 19, by the children of The Kamehameha Schools.

As with all members of the royal family there was much discussion of the lines of descent involved in Mrs. Bishop's family history. Mr. Bishop wrote rather aggressively on any question of genealogy of his wife and her family. Illustrative of his concern was this letter to Joseph O. Carter, November 14, 1898:

---

* The total property (building and grounds) were referred to as Kaakopua. See pp. 35–36.

. . . In the "preface" to his Report Mr. Brigham says Mrs. Bishop was descended from both Kalaniopuu and Kamehameha I. I criticised his statement and he is not pleased with me. Brigham's history names Kalaniopuu as her ancestor. Kekuanaoa, Keoni Ana and others told me— and as is generally admitted—that Kamehameha I was her G.G. Grandfather. As Kalaniopuu was uncle and not the father of Kamehameha (and was not the ancestor of Paki) I do not see how she could have descended from *both*. All that I'm anxious for is to avoid absurdities, untruths, and disagreeable criticism, or to "stir things up.". . .

Mrs. Bishop's trust in her husband was complete. She assigned to him an income-for-life interest in a long list of parcels of land in scattered locations of the Kingdom.* Bishop gave evidence of his deep affection in other ways. He dedicated the Bishop Museum to her, and it was constructed and endowed with his own funds. On The Kamehameha School for Boys' campus he erected the Bernice Pauahi Bishop Chapel and paid for its construction in its entirety. He encouraged her in her counseling of the Hawaiian people; and she in turn counseled with him in regard to the needs of the Hawaiians in politics, social life, education, and religion, and in the almost endless number of contacts he had with her people in his community life.

Some years later he wrote to his favorite "niece," Kaiulani, of a certain coach ride with Pauahi at his side. Princess Kaiulani had been visiting in France and Italy in 1895, and she wrote of her enjoyable trip through Mentone in France. This evoked a sentimental reply; and on January 22, 1896, he wrote to her in Scotland:

. . . You ask if I have ever been there. [Italy] Yes! The names Mentone and Bordighere always make my heart quicken its beating when I think of the most delightful drive of my life, made by your Aunt Bernice and me from San Nemo to Nice stopping only at Mentone for lunch February 22, 1876. We had an easy carriage with four good horses, and only the coachman. It was almost, if not quite, the happiest day in my life. . . .

He genuinely loved Mrs. Bishop. There is nowhere the slightest question of his wholehearted devotion and love for her as his helpmate. His own words addressed to a family friend, Mrs. D. C. Bates, on November 28, 1884, reveal his deep sense of bereavement:

Your kind letter of the 14th inst. was duly re'd. and I thank you, your good husband and daughter for your expressions of sympathy with me.
  When you left us I knew that in all probability you would never see my

* See pp. 165–171.

dear wife again in this life, for the cruel and relentless disease was making apparent progress, but we did not any of us expect to have to part with her so soon. I know that you all loved her, for nobody could know her at all well and not love her.

For myself I will only say that I am trying to bear my loss and my loneliness as reasonably as I can, looking forward hopefully to the time when I shall find the loved one again.

HONOLULU RESIDENCES

When the bride and groom returned to Honolulu, July 2, 1850, after a month-long honeymoon on Kauai, they boarded for a short time with Judge Andrews in town. They then moved into a newly finished little house up Nuuanu Valley. This was described by Liliuokalani as a "modest home at the termination of the beautiful Nuuanu Valley, directly opposite the tombs of the Hawaiian monarchs." This home was also owned by Judge Andrews. It took the sentimental name of Wanakakoa from a stately grove of koa trees in the *makai* ° yard. Before very long, Bishop started construction of a small cottage on Alakea Street, adjacent on the *mauka* side to the Hawaiian Theatre, which in turn was *mauka* of the original Masonic Temple on the *waikiki-mauka* corner of Hotel and Alakea Streets. The house-lot had been purchased from William French.

When they moved to their Alakea Street cottage, they did not eat there and apparently did not entertain much, at least at this time. They boarded at the home of Mr. John Ladd nearby. Boarding for many of the Honolulu families was a common solution of the dining problem of the time. At Mr. Ladd's table the Bishops would meet several other families, among them the Elisha H. Allens and the Luther Severances. It was more than a dining facility, for there was a social advantage in this boarding custom; and there was opportunity for exchange of news and views. It, therefore, performed a

---

° References are made in this book employing Hawaiian words as directions:
makai—towards the sea
mauka—towards the mountain
waikiki—towards the area known as Waikiki
ewa—towards the district of Ewa

Left: Princess Ruth Keelikolani, a half sister of Kamehameha IV and Kamehameha V,
was born February 9, 1826,
and died May 24, 1883. It
was her lands which were
willed to her cousin, Bernice
Pauahi Bishop, and which com-
prised the larger share of the
lands which ultimately became
the foundation of The Kamehameha Schools.

Below: "Keoua Hale" (Kaakopua), the home of Princess Ruth at 21
Emma Street. She died here in 1883. Her cousin Bernice, to whom she
willed her royal family lands, died here in 1884. In this house Mr.
Bishop established his residence for the ten succeeding years before he
moved to California.

most useful and important function in the leisure hours of the lives of this little circle of friends.

In the late 1820's Abner Paki, Bernice's father, had constructed a native type house on a site several acres in size on the *mauka* side of King Street, extending from about the middle of the present Bishop Street a few hundred feet *ewa*, almost to Fort Street. The house and premises were given the name "Aikupika." This is an Hawaiian word with the meaning "Egyptian." The place also carried a colloquial sobriquet, "Paki." Here Bernice was born, December 19, 1831.

A few years later, Abner and Konia Paki moved to Lahaina, Maui in order to handle his appointment as Chamberlain to the Court. The seat of Hawaiian government was at Lahaina at that time. The capital was moved to Honolulu in 1845, and Paki returned with the government party. He soon began construction of the new home on the old Aikupika site and upon completion gave it the name, "Haleakala," House of the Sun. Despite the sentimentality of the new name, Bishop used the old "Aikupika" designation in his deed of October 1, 1894, wherein he transferred the property to the Bernice P. Bishop Estate. A field stone wall was constructed around the entire area with two wide driveways. Along the rear and sides of the site, houses for retainers were built. There was also a stable. The Bishops moved into this home immediately after the death of Paki on June 13, 1855. Happily, the estrangement that existed after Bernice's marriage to Charles had given way to a complete reconciliation among all parties before Paki's passing. The young Princess Liliuokalani was a member of the family when the Bishops moved in, and another was Bernice's mother, Konia, who survived her husband by two years, passing away July 2, 1857. The retainers also remained and were the direct and personal responsibility of Bernice, who was held in high affection by all. This was, of course, nothing other than her *alii* * responsibility to which she had been trained. A tamarind tree, which had been planted at "Haleakala" on the day of her birth, had grown to be a large and beautiful spreading shade tree. In its shelter Bernice would frequently sit as friendly counsellor and arbiter among her people who came to her in trouble and need. Bishop later had this tamarind tree cut down. One section of it was sent to the Bishop Museum and another large section sawed into lumber and made into a table now in the possession of a great grandniece of his in California, Mrs. Jackson Dorn.

* Royal family.

Among the retainer families was one named Kahanamoku. In 1869, the Duke of Edinburgh visited Honolulu and was entertained at "Haleakala" by the Bishops. On the very day of the reception, July 21, 1869, a baby boy was born into the Kahanamoku menage, and Bernice, upon being asked to name the baby, suggested the name of *Duke*. His full name was Duke Halapu Kahanamoku.*

The King Street home for a quarter century was the hospitality center of the Kingdom. William T. Brigham and Horace Mann disembarked from the barkentine *Smyrniote* one day in the spring of 1864, and Brigham later described his pleasure with the friendly greeting that Mann and he had enjoyed:

Mrs. Bishop explained the many new and native dishes as I sat by her side, while the little *kahilis* waved over our heads. This proved the first of many delightful entertainments in Haleakala, at the Waikiki home, and on picnics, from the Bishop hospitality.

We had a Reading Club, and we did not hesitate to dive into Shakespeare, Schiller, Milton and each taking part, and the Bishop parlor was the most frequent place of meeting. More than once, dropping in for a call after dinner, Mr. Bishop suggested charades. . . . When the moon was full we had our horseback rides, or the king's boat and often the governor's was put at our disposal and with Mrs. Bishop, Liliuokalani and other Alii, with songs accompanied by guitars, we were rowed about the harbor. In all these amusements Bishop seemed pleased.

Many years later in thinking of a director for his new museum, Bishop looked back to that 1864 visit of the two men and remembered his fine impressions of William T. Brigham and invited him to accept the position.

"Haleakala" had a checkered career after Mrs. Bishop died in 1884. She had willed the property along with many other parcels to her husband for his use throughout his remaining years. He moved uptown to 21 Emma Street shortly after the death of his wife and thereby released the King Street property for income purposes. At his own expense he erected several brick store buildings along King Street up to the corner of Fort Street. E. O. Hall and Son, Lewers and Cooke, and Williams Brothers were tenants. Mr. Dudoit op-

* When Duke grew up he married Julia Paakonia Lonokahikini Paoa, and this marriage produced six boys and three girls. One of the children, born August 26, 1890, was named Duke Paoa Kahanamoku, who, after attending The Kamehameha School for Boys, went on to become an Olympic swimming champion and one of Hawaii's most illustrious sons. His father had served as a footman for the Bishops and his grandfather as a coachman.

erated the old residence as a boarding house for a few years; and upon his surrender of the lease, Mr. Hamilton Johnson continued it also as a boarding house.

On January 19, 1893, the U. S. Marines were called ashore to assist in maintaining order during tense government troubles and were headquartered on these premises. The upper floor of the house was used for officers, and an outside retainer's building was used for a hospital and armory. The Marines remained until April 1, 1893, whereupon Bishop leased the property to the Arlington Hotel people who remodelled the residence as the hotel dining hall. They rehabilitated it so acceptably that he almost sold the Pacific Club * on the idea of leasing it as a club site. At another time, 1895, the residence was utilized as the headquarters of operation against the dread bubonic plague epidemic. By this time, however, Bishop had turned the property over to the Bishop Estate in order that any income or returns from the possible sale of the fee might be made available for the use of The Kamehameha Schools. This transfer † was made in 1894.

On the *waikiki* side of "Haleakala" was the home of Dr. John S. McGrew. Alexander Young purchased the McGrew property and erected the Alexander Young Hotel but left enough room for opening a new street along its *ewa* side, and to this the Bishop Estate** dedicated a parallel strip. With the two halves joined, the street became a thoroughfare of respectable width extending from Hotel Street to the waterfront and was named Bishop Street. It was opened in 1900. The middle line of this street is, therefore, the old boundary between "Haleakala" and the McGrew home. Later the Bishop Estate sold the present King and Bishop corner in fee simple to the Bank of Hawaii but retained frontage on both King and Bishop Streets *ewa* and *mauka* of the bank corner.

Upon Mrs. Bishop's death, Mr. Bishop moved into the home which had been opened but a short while before, on February 9–10, 1882, by the Princess Ruth Keelikolani, its owner and builder. The celebration upon completion of the home consisted of a *luau*,†† on the ninth of February, 1882, and a reception and grand ball the

* See p. 141.
† See pp. 165–171.
** See pp. 143–145.
†† Typical native feast.

following evening. She was not to enjoy the new home at 21 Emma Street very long. She died May 24, 1883. In her Will she gave all her land holdings and property, including the home, to her cousin Bernice.

Princess Ruth's home was beautiful and spacious with drawing rooms, forty-eight by twenty-four feet, and twenty-four by nineteen feet. The ceilings were frescoed, and an Hawaiian Royal coat-of-arms in plaster, three feet in diameter, was laid into the ceilings of each of four of the main rooms. The beautiful wrought-iron gates which ornamented the two driveways, and which were never closed, may now be seen at either end of the service driveways at the Bishop Museum.

William Fessenden Allen had married Cordelia Church Bishop, a niece of Bishop's, and the two families were life-long friends. The Allens became his official hosts and lived with him at "Keoua Hale" for his remaining years in Honolulu. When he moved to San Francisco in 1894, he returned the fee to the Bishop Estate, which transferred it in 1895 to the Board of Education for $30,000. On its 4.31 acres of land the Honolulu High School was located for some years. The building was torn down in 1915 to provide a site for the newly organized Central Intermediate School.

The other home of the Bishops was the Waikiki seaside residence. This property, as with many other parcels, belonged to Kamehameha V who passed it on to his half sister, Princess Ruth Keelikolani, and from her it came into the possession of Bernice. Bishop held it as one of the lifetime properties willed to him by his wife and returned it with all the others to the Bishop Estate. The property may be identified as that occupied in large part by the Sheraton Royal Hawaiian Hotel. Originally there was a thatched-roof cottage erected by Kamehameha V, which consisted of one bedroom. The Bishops remodelled it into a large residence and added several accessory buildings. They spent many happy hours of relaxation in the gentle, dry climate of that resort area.

Residences can provide tender memories of gentle, gracious hospitality. The homes of the Bishops were centers of friendly association and will serve as eternal reminders of two happy, useful lives dedicated to the finest in cultural community life and thought.

TRAVELS

THE BISHOPS TRAVELLED a great deal.* They had been warned by Honolulu medical men to obtain a change of climate, ideally, every two years. They made many trips among the several islands of the Hawaiian chain. Mrs. Bishop had a family home in Lahaina, Maui, and friends and relatives on all the islands. She was a visitor of frequent regularity to some spots, Kona and Hilo in particular. The Bishops honeymooned on Kauai in 1850 and managed to return there virtually every year thereafter for a two to four weeks' stay.

The doctors' admonition of seeking a cooler and drier climate at intervals of two years was not lost upon these people. Their first major trip was to San Francisco and was a modest eight weeks of absence from Honolulu. Altogether they made four trips to the mainland, the second of which (1871) lasted for five months and took them into Canada and as far as Boston, with a stop at Glens Falls, New York. One of the most significant events in the history of the American West was the joining of the rails of the Union Pacific and the Central Pacific at Promontory Point, Utah, May 10, 1869. It was great news and served to stimulate travel interest in the farthest corners; and, of course, the story came to Honolulu and the Bishops. They determined to cross the United States by train in 1871. Their railroad trip started at San Francisco on the Western Pacific. They changed to the Central Pacific at Sacramento, to the Union Pacific at Ogden, and to the Chicago and North Western at Omaha. At Chicago they transferred to the New York Central and Hudson River Line. Seven days and seven nights it took to cross the continent, and the Pullman fare was $225 one way for one person.

Many notable experiences were enjoyed by the Bishops on this trip. Certainly, they enjoyed looking about his birthplace town, Glens Falls, New York. They visited all the Bishop relatives, possibly with some embarrassment since his reputation as a very wealthy

* See Appendix, pp. 339–341.

man of the "Sandwich Isles" had preceded him. Actually, the general reception of the pair upon the occasion of his first visit was only lukewarm. Their hosts in Fort Edwards were Mr. and Mrs. James Cheesman. This seemed to have created a bit of gentle eyebrow raising by socially minded local townspeople. Cheesman ran a news store and a book shop. As the Bishops were leaving the New York area on this trip, the frightening loss of thirty-three whaling vessels in the Arctic Ocean was reported. This disaster spelled the beginning of the end of the whaling trade.

On the return to San Francisco, the couple just missed the historic Chicago fire which was to signalize the start of many modern practices in building codes, insurance procedures, and methods of fire fighting. A few weeks later, in the fall of 1871, we find William Chapman Ralston, former part owner of Bishop and Company and ill fated head of the Bank of California, soliciting Honolulu leaders as part of a nationwide campaign for relief of victims of disastrous fires in the States of Illinois, Minnesota, and Wisconsin. The Chicago fire sparked this campaign; Bishop contributed $50.00.

When the Bishops returned to the Glens Falls area in 1876, their welcome was spontaneous and very generous. One stop on the trip was Troy, New York. A reference to that stop is recorded in the *Glens Falls Republican,* August 1, 1876:

Who Came to See Us

A correspondent of the Troy Times writes; "As an indication how the Centennial [commemoration of the Signing of the Declaration of Independence—July 4, 1776] brings the world together, I send you a few names and residences from the Rockwell House register, . . . Mr. and Mrs. Charles R. Bishop and E. B. Bishop [niece Emma Bernice] Honolulu, Hawaiian Islands—Mr. Bishop being prime minister, and his wife the possible future queen of the Sandwich Islands. Mr. B. is a native of Warren County."

The travelers moved on to Glens Falls and Sandy Hill. Here they were the guests of George Bradley. This visit is recorded in the July 23, 1876, issue of the *Sandy Hill Herald:*

The Husband of a Princess

Charles B. [*sic*] Bishop, who went to Honolulu from the neighborhood, with Wm. L. Lee of Sandy Hill, many years ago, is visiting here with his wife, a princess of the island. Mr. Bishop was formerly clerk in "The Old Stone Store" next door to the Herald Office, previous to his going to the Sandwich Islands. He is now a man of note in his adopted country, and it is not improbable that he may yet be the ruler of the Hawaiian Islands, as his wife is daughter of a former King of the place.

The main effort of the 1875–1876 travelling was directed to Europe. They went to Europe twice during these years. They sailed for Europe on the SS *Bothnia,* July 7, 1875, and had started on a rather ambitious circuit of visits on the continent when word was received that the Bank of California had closed its doors. The San Francisco trouble was soon over, and the party sailed for Europe the second time on the SS *Main,* arriving at Bremerhaven, November 4, 1875. This turned out to be a royal Hawaiian tour of Europe. They encountered many Honolulu friends in France, Germany, Austria, Switzerland, Italy, and the British Isles; made numerous purchases of art objects; had an audience with the Pope; and had themselves photographed in several galleries. They visited Monte Carlo but did not play at the gambling tables. This was a wonderful holiday for both of them, and the whole story lives graphically through the travel diaries kept by Mrs. Bishop, the originals of which in Mrs. Bishop's handwriting are in the Bishop Museum.

After his wife's death, Bishop made almost annual trips to San Francisco but did not venture to the East Coast again until 1889. This time, since it was the month of April and cold, he decided to try the southern train route by way of New Orleans, Mobile, Atlanta, Chattanooga, and Cincinnati. But there were other discomforts besides the cold which he could not avoid. He wrote to Damon from New York, May 19, 1889:

One day in Chattanooga and the rest of the time was being shaken and dustied in the cars.

Car travel does not agree with my health much better than steamer travel. I'll have to own up to being an old man and come to quiet and easy life.

He made two more trips, one in 1891 and the other in 1893, both to the east coast; but that marked the end of any further extended travel for him. He never again left the Bay area except to go to Sacramento or other nearby spots in California.

3

Business

THE ROYAL HAWAIIAN AGRICULTURAL SOCIETY

THE LETTER FILES, minute books, and journals of representative associations and agencies in Hawaii since early missionary days reveal clearly the marked dedication and intellectual caliber of its community leaders. Some of the recorded proceedings seem academic, even pedantic; and yet, whether their flavor arose from the scholasticism of the missionary or the pragmatism of the entrepreneur, they invariably stand forth in beautiful, flowing rhetoric, well organized and intensely applicable and pertinent to the problem in hand. This was true of the Royal Hawaiian Agricultural Society which was organized August 12, 1850. A preliminary meeting looking to the creation of such a society was held in the Bethel vestry, April 27, with Judge Lorrin Andrews, chairman, and Charles R. Bishop, secretary. William L. Lee stated the purposes of formation as, "Uniting the action of those interested in the culture of the soil, and to seek legislative aid for the mutual protection of masters and servants." *Thrum's Annual,* in 1895, a half century afterward, commented:

. . . Nothing has ever equalled the Royal Hawaiian Agricultural Society —annual exhibitions, premiums, introduction of improved varieties of plants and domestic animals. Its printed transactions are even now interesting reading.

In another *Annual,* that of 1902, further praise is heaped on the Society by the editor:

. . . The manner in which the whole subject was treated is worthy of the highest commendation, even today. Inquiries were made into nearly every branch of agricultural research known at that time: Sheep, Meat Cattle, Horses, Poultry, Trees, Cattle, Roads, Labor, Seasons, Leather, Horticultural Implements, Sugar, Tobacco, Fences, Coffee, Swine, Birds,

Garden Seeds and Flowers, Grains, Capital and Banking, Butter and Cheese, Figs, Harbors, Interisland Navigation, Arrowroot, Pests, Bees, Indigo, Kukui Oil, Salt and Analysis of Soils.

Those associated with the society were progressive, energetic men. Many of the reports are as rich in literary content, as they are in historical and scientific value, and are equally interesting a century later.

The Society continued through the 1850's before it passed out of existence. In 1919, *Thrum's* again refers to the influence and work of this Society:

. . . The introduction of Chinese as laborers into Hawaii is traceable to its [the Society's] influence and cooperation, the first shipment of 200 coming on the *Thetis,* in 1852. It inaugurated our rice growing industry, promoted wheat growing and the first flour mill, encouraged improvement of stock of all kinds and farming in general; of cane growing and sugar making; steam machinery introduced into the industry, the Lihue Plantation being the first.

It was the prime mover in the treaty of reciprocity, not the Chamber of Commerce.

Bishop's connection with the Royal Hawaiian Agricultural Society did not cease with his being "a prime mover" and in being listed as secretary. He was appointed a member of a "Committee of Ten, whose duty it shall be to collect statistics relating to the export of domestic produce etc. . . ." In the First Annual Report of August 11, 1851, he appears as treasurer, succeeding S. N. Castle, who had resigned May 31. The date of Bishop's appointment was June 30, 1851. He was *elected* treasurer August 13. At the annual meeting in June, 1852, he declined re-election but accepted membership on the Committee to Examine Exhibits and to Award Premiums at the Fair. He was also appointed chairman of the Statistics Committee. In June, 1853, his name is listed on the Executive Committee. He was well qualified to handle the statistics, for he had been Collector of Customs since February, 1849, and the compiling of statistics was widely involved in that position. He was likewise well prepared for the treasurership by the bookkeeping and accounting practices of his private business.

The members of the Society were assigned variously to subject committees. Bishop was listed on several; among them, the sweet potato committee (chairman), the fig, honey bee, and sugar committees. He presented papers on the honey bee and sugar. The report on bees was laboriously prepared and constituted a very presentable documentaion of the subject. A minor sidelight on his connection with the Society was the introduction of singing birds into Hawaii. In 1859 he imported seven linnets, on the bark *Felix*, for distribution in the hills above Honolulu.

The Royal Hawaiian Agricultural Society faded out of the Honolulu scene, but the principle inherent in its creation would not die. There followed, intermittently, other associations or companies including The Planters' Labor and Supply Company and the Hawaiian Sugar Planters' Association. None of the later associations developed their programs with greater purity of literary effort or with wider diversity in subject matter than The Royal Hawaiian Agricultural Society.

Bishop also had a close interest in the Planters' Labor and Supply Company—the first organized attempt to continue the original purposes of the Royal Hawaiian Agricultural Society. Bishop and Company was one of the firms joining in the Planters' Convention March 20–29, 1882. Incorporation was accomplished during that week. From the *Planters' Monthly,* the official publication of the newly organized Company, participation of Bishop is noted. Committee chairmanships and memberships on committees were staggered so that all stockholders (Bishop held five shares) of the Company would be acquainted with several areas of the program. As a consequence, Bishop was chairman or member variously of the Forestry, Audit, Legislative, and Reciprocity Committees. He was active in this work until 1894.

BISHOP AND COMPANY

BISHOP'S FIRST HONOLULU advertisement on January 6, 1849, announced that he was leaving the Kingdom, object: Gold Rush. His second advertisement, a series of three, was a happy sequel. It was more than the telling of the opening of a bank. He was remaining in the Kingdom; he had found a personal gold rush in the Sandwich Isles.

If his academic training had been somewhat deficient for any such undertaking as a bank, his practical experience in the general stores in New York and his government clerkship and customs office and mercantile experience in Honolulu prepared him more than commonly well. John Cook * described an initial venture of Bishop's:

Charles R. Bishop—Remember when he arrived. He started a small dry goods store on the S. E. corner of Maunakea and King Streets. There were eleven partners in the partnership and the firm name was Coday, Calhoun, Bishop & Co. . . .

Bishop and William A. Aldrich, as partners, started a general store in 1853, with the name Aldrich and Bishop. The opening of this enterprise was keyed to the completion of the new Makee and Anthon's Block—the first three story brick building in Honolulu. It was finished just in time for the firm to occupy the ground floor on the Queen Street side. The building stood at the *ewa-mauka* corner of Queen and Kaahumanu Streets.

While local trade was important, it was the trade of the whaling vessels that gave the real impetus to the new business. The journal of the partnership, written in Bishop's handwriting and covering the five years of the store operation, reflects the relative importance of whaling to the partners. When the partnership was dissolved, in early 1858, each withdrew $13,923.46 as his half share. During the life of the partnership each had paid himself $25.00 weekly as salary. Aldrich continued the operation as sole owner until 1861. Six months after the termination of the partnership, on August 15, 1858, Aldrich and Bishop renewed their former association in a bank under the name of Bishop and Company.

One of the motivating factors in the organization of the bank was the excellent paper on the need of a bank in Honolulu presented by Robert C. Wyllie before the Royal Hawaiian Agricultural Society, June 1, 1852. This was probably the most significant paper among the numerous outstanding papers presented before the membership. He enunciated the important principles of sound banking and illustrated his paper with examples of banking procedures from several financial centers around the world. He described the prevailing attitudes toward money matters in the Kingdom and the factors and problems confronting business men in the Pacific. He outlined an actual banking structure for Hawaii and gave it a name: Hawaiian Bank of Loan, Deposit, and Discount. It would have $500,000 in stock, in shares of $100 each.

* John Cook, *Reminiscences* (The New Freedom Press, Honolulu, 1927), pp. 14–15.

Wyllie's paper was timely. Business in Honolulu needed bank services. One interesting need is described in the *History of C. Brewer & Company, Ltd.**

. . . It had been customary, prior to 1858 for the merchants to store their coin in individual safes, so that when the whalers arrived they were prepared to furnish the captains with the silver necessary to pay off the crews in exchange for whalers' drafts usually drawn at ten days' sight and at from four to ten percent discount. It frequently happened that some of the whalers arriving late had to delay the "paying off" of crews until money came in again, which often took from three to five days, for the supply of actual coin in those days was very limited.

The Hawaiian Temperance Society, in 1853 and 1854, strongly advocated the establishment of a savings bank and a bank of deposit. Some of the men whose views were recorded in the minutes were among those who had emphasized the issue in the Royal Hawaiian Agricultural Society.

In the meantime there had been sporadic attempts to start a bank. The House of Representatives passed an act to charter a "Pacific Bank of Honolulu" in June, 1854, but the House of Nobles rejected it. Page, Bacon and Company, after briefly operating through an agency in Honolulu, established a bona fide branch as a partnership. It started business October 14, 1854, in a room on the Kaahumanu Street side of the Makee and Anthon's Block. The firm suspended in December, 1855. While the community regarded it as a savings bank, its tentative charter authorized it to issue notes and to deal in exchange only.

About this time William L. Lee, writing to Joel Turrill, included a brief mention of Bishop, February 26, 1855:

. . . Bishop is as usual in a flourishing condition, and he and Aldrich, next to Capt. Spencer, are said to be making more money than any one else in town. Bishop is the cautious, financial member of the firm, and Aldrich the selling member. Bishop grows every day in public esteem. . . .

It was this growth in "public esteem" which led Alexander Liholiho, upon ascending the Hawaiian throne, to invite Bishop to take the portfolio of Minister of Finance. While Bishop could not accept this appointment it was evidence of the regard with which he was held.

---

* Josephine Sullivan, *A History of C. Brewer & Company, Ltd.* (Boston, Walton Advertising and Printing Company, 1926), p. 113.

On August 17, 1858, in the same Makee and Anthon's Block where Aldrich and Bishop had done business as a mercantile partnership, the bank was opened. Bishop had now embarked on his matchless career as a Builder of Hawaii. The community's deep trust in him was the result of his simple, plain, everyday life, totally devoid of ostentation or misanthropy. The deposits listed on opening day were very gratifying to Messrs. Bishop and Aldrich: C. H. Lewis, $1300.00; W. A. Aldrich, $3176.50; W. R. Seal, $175.00; Geo. Thomas, $33.75; G. P. Judd, $3000.00. The first loan, in the amount of $4000, was made on August 26 to R. C. Janion, a forerunner of Theo. H. Davies and Company, Limited. The time was thirty-three days, the rate twelve per cent. The bank paid eight per cent on deposits of $300 or under. It is well known that the two proprietors handled the cashier and bookkeeping chores themselves. They also divided the janitor work. Their first safe was a small strong box—nothing more than a foot locker—and held an amazing variety of coins: French Napoleons; copper tokens from Italy, Chile, and China; English Sovereigns—many of them so worn as to defy identification.

The Honolulu community thought well of the banking venture. Just before the opening was announced, the *Pacific Commercial Advertiser* printed this paragraph; the date was August 5, 1858:

A Savings Bank—We are much gratified with the prospect of having a bank for savings established in Honolulu, Messrs. Chas. R. Bishop and Wm. Aldrich having associated themselves together for this purpose. The plan, however, is to have two separate departments, one for savings deposits and the other for a general banking business. The gentlemen named have ample means to ensure the enterprise being placed on such a basis as will command public confidence, and if conducted with system and liberality, cannot fail to become not only popular, but of permanent benefit to the country. No prospectus has as yet been prepared, nor site selected, but the particulars will transpire in the course of a week or two.

Three days prior to the opening, the *Polynesian* spoke happily and with its usual admonishment and advice:

Savings Bank

By referring to the advertising columns of to-day's paper our readers will perceive that Honolulu is now bound by another link of that magic chain which we call civilization, without taking much heed to its meaning, and too often without making special note of its existence or operations.

On Tuesday next Messrs. Bishop & Co. will open their Banking Establishment in the basement room, upper end of Makee's building, Kaahumanu Street, where the poor but prudent may deposit their earnings and receive a handsome interest thereon. Let none be discouraged or frightened away by a false shame. Remember that the greatest rivers are only the accumulations of small brooks and rills, and that the greatest fortunes generally commenced with a six pence. The mechanic, the laborer, the young man or young woman who can and will retain 3 or 5 dollars weekly of their wages and deposit them in a bank will at the end of five years have from $1000 to $1500 to start themselves in business with, to purchase a house or land or both, to furnish an outfit or procure a dowry.

Could the Hawaiian born proportion of our population be induced to deposit their savings in the savings bank instead of investing in horseflesh and silks, it would in our opinion prove more productive of thrift and consequent general and material comfort than aught else we know of just now; and would the "Hae" show up the affair theoretically and practically, in dollars and cents, we are sanguine enough to anticipate the happiest results.

To give the new enterprise an essential international capability, the bankers immediately signed agreements with correspondents abroad. These included Messrs. Grinnel, Minturn and Company and Messrs. Lee and Walker and Company of New York City; Tremont National Bank and Henry A. Peirce and Company of Boston; Oriental Bank Corporation of London; and Marcuard, Andre and Company of Paris. Despite skeptics, the new banking firm prospered. Despite disasters such as the destruction of the whaling fleet in the late months of 1871, it continued to grow steadily.

Aldrich was a promoter and a seller. One of his San Francisco interests was in a firm by the name of Charles W. Brooks and Company. This firm failed in 1866. Aldrich had already made trips to California, in 1864 and 1865, preparing to move there permanently. The Brooks and Company's failure forced his hand, and he rather quickly offered his half interest in the bank to Bishop, who, however, had no inclination to purchase it on his own account. He preferred operating the bank with a competent partner. He considered carefully and finally offered the partnership to a highly regarded Honolulu business and community friend, James Walker Austin, who had arrived in the Islands in 1851. The two men had entered into a close social and financial relationship that was to continue for almost a quarter of a century. They joined in many real estate ventures: buying, selling, and managing. They refereed several bankruptcy cases, among them the notable Walker, Allen and Company's closing in 1867. Their community interests were almost identical: Austin was the first secretary of Queen's Hospital and an officer of the Royal Hawaiian Agricultural Society and the Sailors' Home Society. He was a member of the executive committee of Oahu College and worked on the board of the American Relief Fund Association. He also was a very frequent and honored guest at the important lunches and dinners held at the Bishop home. Austin regretfully declined the bank partnership offer because he did not plan to reside permanently in the Islands. He left in 1872 and honored his friend by making the bank the agent of all his Hawaiian property.

Bishop now made a bold move. He booked passage for himself and Mrs. Bishop on the *Ajax* outbound for San Francisco, April 4, 1866. He called upon William Chapman Ralston, cashier of the Bank of California, and succeeded in completing sale of the partnership to him. The magnitude of the transaction is reflected in a "Balance Sheet of the Bank of California, July 11, 1866. Evening. Assetts [sic] Bishop and Company, Honolulu, $93,598.98." The Bishops returned to Honolulu on the *Swallow,* June 18. The results of this trip were to be far reaching—a banking affiliation was initiated that was to terminate only temporarily with the tragic death of Ralston but ultimately land Bishop in a top portfolio in the Bank of California.

Aldrich, with his principal Honolulu problem solved, hurried off to San Francisco on the *Comet,* July 19, and there he prospered anew. He founded the commission house of Aldrich and Merrill in 1866 at 204 California Street in San Francisco. The firm continued under this name into 1867, when Aldrich became a silent partner in a reorganization under the name of J. C. Merrill and Co. In Aldrich's obituary (he died in 1892) he was termed a "prominent capitalist of Alameda County." He was listed as a director of the Oakland Bank of Savings, the Savings and Loan Society of San Francisco, and the Merced Security and Savings Bank. He was also a member of the Pacific Union Club.

Ralston became President of the Bank of California in July of 1873. Since the geographical remoteness of Hawaii made it difficult for him to keep an eye on his bank interests there, he sold out to Bishop. For the next two years Bishop was sole owner of the bank. A Honolulu man, John H. Paty, had gone to work in 1859 as a bookkeeper in the bank and on May 1, 1875, became a partner. It was this arrangement which allowed the Bishops to start an eventful trip three weeks later to the United States and Europe in complete confidence that all would be cared for in their prolonged absence.

They had scarcely arrived in Europe, however, when on August 26, 1875, news was flashed to them by the recently completed Cyrus Field cable that the Bank of California had closed its doors. Ralston was the key figure in the Bank of California, the leading financial establishment of San Francisco and the Bay area. A few days prior to the closing, Ralston lost his life; whether by accident or design is still a matter of controversy. But when he died, the bank closed.

The travelers, including a niece, Emma Bernice Bishop, returned immediately to New York. Mrs. Bishop and the niece waited there while Bishop made a hurried and worried trip to the west coast. By the time he had arrived in San Francisco the crisis was over, and his own bank's safety had been assured.

The news of the bank closing reached Honolulu via the bark *Jalawar*, Sunday morning, September 19, 1875; and rumors excited the depositors of Bishop and Company. Later that morning Samuel Mills Damon ° was notified about an unusual crowd milling around the doors of the bank. He went down to the bank, threw open the doors, and offered anyone money for his balance on deposit. Confidence was easily and quickly restored. Bishop and Company was better prepared to weather a run than its big brother correspondent, the Bank of California. Monday morning, Damon posted this notice on the Post Office bulletin board:

The undersigned beg to assure their customers that their interests have not suffered at all by the suspension of the Bank of California. Messers Hickox and Spencer, bankers as well as Messers J. C. Merrill & Co., immediately upon receiving the intelligence of the suspension of the bank, offered to protect all drafts of ours, and proceeded to do so. All our unmatured remittances were turned over directly to Messers Hickox and Spencer. All our drafts in transit are fully covered by remittances and there will be no delay in their payment by Messers Hickox & Spencer.

Bishop & Co.

Honolulu September 19, 1875

J. C. Merrill and Company was the firm originally organized by Aldrich and from which he retired as an active partner.

Bishop returned to his wife and niece waiting in New York, and the three sailed again to Europe and continued their interrupted journey. His relief with the way things turned out was naturally

---

° Samuel Mills Damon was the son of the chaplain of Seamen's Bethel, Samuel Chenery Damon. He was first employed as bookkeeper in 1872. See p. 14.

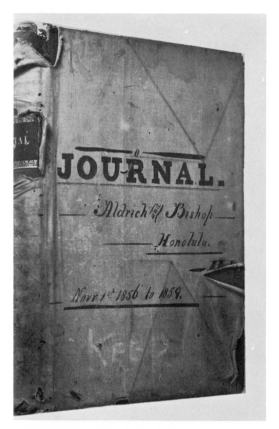

Left: Journal, Aldrich and Bishop, 1856–1859.

Below: Aldrich and Bishop Store, 1853.

Interior Office, }
May 14, 1858. }

NEW ADVERTISEMENTS.

COPARTNERSHIP.

THE UNDERSIGNED HAVE THIS DAY FORMED A COPART-
nership under the style of " BISHOP & CO.," for the purpose
of transacting a general *BANKING* business, connecting there-
with a Savings Bank, in Honolulu.   CHAS. R. BISHOP,
                                      W. A. ALDRICH.

P. S.—The Bank will be opened on the 17th inst.
Honolulu, August 12th, 1858.—15-4t

BISHOP & CO.'S
SAVINGS BANK!

THE UNDERSIGNED WILL RECEIVE MONEY AT THEIR
Savings Bank upon the following terms :

On sums of $300 or under, from one person, they will pay
interest at the rate of 8 per cent. per annum from date of receipt, on all sums that shall have remained in deposit three
months, or have been in deposit three months at the time of
making up the yearly accounts.

No interest will be allowed on money withdrawn within three
months after the date of deposit.

Thirty days notice must be given at the Bank of an intention
to withdraw any money, and the Depositor's "Pass-book" must
be produced at the same time.

No money will be paid except upon the draft of the Depositor,
accompanied by the " Pass-book."

On the first day of September of each year, after 1858, the
accounts will be made up, and interest on all sums that shall
have remained on deposit three months or more, and unpaid,
will be credited to the Depositors, and from that date form part
of the principal.

Sums of more than $300 will be received, subject to special
agreement.

The Bank will be open every day in the week except Sundays
and holidays, and on Saturdays will be open till 6 P. M.
                                      BISHOP & CO.

Honolulu, August 11th, 1858.—15-tf

CHAS. R. BISHOP.   WM. A. ALDRICH.

BISHOP & CO.,
BANKERS,

Office in the East corner of ' Makee's Block,' on
Kaahumanu street, Honolulu,

Will receive deposits,
      Discount first class business paper,
            Attend to collecting, &c. &c. &c.   15-tf

The Savings Bank of Bishop and Company was launched with a clus-
ter of three advertisements in the August 14, 1858, issue of the *Polynesian.*

great, and he so expressed himself to Elisha H. Allen,* January 2, 1876:

. . . Was I not fortunate in getting through with a little loss by the suspension of the Bank of California! It made great confusion in my affairs for a short time—gave me much anxiety, travel, and expense. But my affairs were sound at the bottom, and I had *excellent friends,* who helped me like brothers. My experience of kindness, good will and confidence is worth a great deal to me, and cannot be forgotten. There is more of virtue and true friendship among men and in mankind than many people will admit or than they know anything about. . . .

In 1878, on May 26, the firm moved into its own specially designed quarters at the *makai-waikiki* corner of Kaahumanu and Merchant Streets. The new location was about 200 feet *mauka* of the old site. No tea, no program of dedication! Characteristically, Bishop sent $25.00 to each of these benevolent societies: Ladies Strangers' Friend Society, British Benevolent Society, American Relief Fund, and the German Relief Fund. That was his way of celebrating the opening of the new quarters. A contemporary reporter's description of the new bank appeared in the May 29, 1879, issue of the *Hawaiian Gazette:*

. . . The new Banking House of Messrs. Bishop & Co., is one of the handsomest edifices in Honolulu. The building was occupied for the first time on the 22nd inst., where they are now doing business. This new banking house is a credit to the liberality and good taste of Messrs. Bishop & Co., and to the skill of the builder, Mr. Baker.† Exteriorally, the building is very handsome as well as ornamental, occupying as it does a conspicuous site in the center of the business section of the city. The inside finish is on a style commensurate with the structure itself. The carpenter work was done by Mr. George Lucas, of Honolulu, who is a first-class mechanic, and has demonstrated in this instance that for workmanship and taste, the new banking house will compare favorably with any similar building elsewhere.

The internal arrangement of the building is all that could be desired to secure convenience and comfort to the employees and the public. No expense has been spared to make this new building a model banking house, and we are sure it is a success in all the essentials of a thoroughly arranged, substantially built and well appointed establishment. It is fire-

* Elisha H. Allen served as United States Consul to Honolulu 1849–1853, and as Minister of Finance of Hawaii, 1853–1857. He was appointed Chief Justice of the Supreme Court of Hawaii, upon the passing of William Little Lee, and served in that capacity through 1877. He was Minister to the United States from Honolulu, 1877–1883.

† Thomas J. Baker, who arrived in Honolulu July 1876, was the general contractor.

proof and provided with ample and well-secured vaults and fire-proof safes, to accommodate all who may think proper to place their funds or other valuables there for safe keeping.

Reciprocity brought a towering prosperity to the Islands. Planters became overextended; and Bishop, in facing their emergency demands for financing, continued in his customary role of caution and conservative judgment. He wrote to Allen on June 16, 1879: ". . . I do not loan much money to planters directly, but loan to merchants (Agents for planters) taking the notes of the planter as collateral to those of the merchant. . . ." But he had far more on his mind in this letter. He had not advanced very deeply into the massive charities that were to mark the 1880's and 1890's for him. He had witnessed the retirement of Aldrich to a simple, well-furnished life of unworried ease; and, perhaps most of all, he had been horrified by the tragic and untimely death of Ralston and its likely relation to the tension and inescapable pressure of life as a banker. And it probably is not unfair to state that Bishop's financial relations with the Legislature and members of the royal family were distressing him deeply. At any rate he continued:

. . . I have a good business and am not *anxious* to retire, but would be willing to give fair advantage to a suitable man as a partner, if he could put in $300,000 of cash capital, pay one third now, one third in two or three months and the remainder in four, five, or six months. Or I would sell out on fair terms and retire from banking. Any party wishing to buy me out, would need to command at least $300,000 cash within a short time and to have credit also, which such a capital would give of course. The Exchange branch of the business is good, and will improve. It is a *rare chance* for the employment of Eastern capital and brains.

If you think there is no chance of your finding anybody to take up either of these opportunities, say nothing about it; and you will of course be very guarded and prudent in the use that you may make of this letter. . . .

Samuel Mills Damon answered the description of a likely purchaser; he had been a trusted employee since 1872, and while he could not consider the purchase of a bank at this time, Bishop did find in him his third partner, September 1, 1881. Paty withdrew on August 31, 1892. It was fortunate for Bishop that he had two such men as partners during this period. Paty was well qualified to look after the bank with Bishop absent so much on the mainland. Damon was very close to the monarchy and government, and his role with the people in power probably did much to assure the bank's safety during the turbulent eighties and nineties.

Bishop's greatest contribution to Hawaii's economy was undoubtedly in the few years following the enactment of the Reciprocity Treaty with the United States. He furnished funds to the government and to private enterprise. On one occasion he borrowed $500,000, at the rate of one per cent per month, from San Francisco to bolster the sugar planters. The *Star-Bulletin* carried a column entitled, "Following notes by one who knew him well." This paragraph from the column appeared in the June 7, 1915, issue:

At a crisis in the sugar industry Mr. Bishop came to its relief with the resources of his bank, in return for which the bank received a contract to handle all the exchange of the planters. This was a great advantage of the bank, although hardly to be compared with its service in saving the mainstay of the Kingdom. What the late history of Hawaii, commercially and politically, would have been had the development of sugar production been halted at that early period is outside the realm of rational speculation.

In January, 1882, Bishop and Company purchased the Hoffman property next to the bank building on Merchant Street and prepared to expand facilities. This meant another celebration in 1883, and a little story in the same column of the *Star-Bulletin*, July 7, 1915, covers that:

Mr. Bishop, although maintaining the social dignity becoming the husband of a high chiefess who had been offered the crown, was averse to anything like meritorious display. He would not stand for spending money on useless celebrations.

As the quarter century of the bank approached, one of his partners told a newspaperman that the event would probably be celebrated with a banquet at the British [Pacific] Club, but cautioned him, to get the news from Mr. Bishop before publishing it. On the question being put to the latter, it was promptly answered in the negative with the remark, "I don't believe in spending money on such foolishness."

Claus Spreckels * enters the picture in 1882. He was proposing many things to the legislature: a new coinage plan, a new bank with few restrictions, a financing plan for government money, and others. On May 4, 1885, he opened a bank which Bishop and Company absorbed twenty-five years later.

Honolulu was plagued by the usual kinds of disasters which

* See pp. 117–119.

sometimes befall great cities in the course of their history—
epidemics, tidal waves, storms, earthquakes, and fires. On April 18,
1886, the worst of three tragic holocausts* in the history of Honolulu, flamed up in a congested Chinese tenement at Smith and Hotel
Streets. The devastated area extended from the wall on the *ewa* side
of the Palace to Nuuanu Stream and from Beretania Street to the
wharves. In fighting the fire, the volunteer companies ran out of
water. Two English men-of-war sent help, but the blaze swept
through some sixty acres of improved property with a destruction
estimated at a million and a quarter dollars. The Sailors' Home was
dynamited in an attempt to stop the fire, and the Bethel Union
Church was destroyed. Less than a quarter million dollars was
recovered in insurance.

There were insurance agencies already licensed and operating in
the Kingdom. The first one, Starkey Janion and Company, was
appointed agent of the Liverpool Underwriters. This was exactly
forty years prior to the 1886 fire and but a few months before Bishop
and Lee arrived in the Islands. Starkey Janion and Company, however, was restricted in its field of operations; the company was not
empowered to issue policies. Bishop and Company, in its early
years, negotiated agency contracts with the Pacific Insurance Company of San Francisco and the Manhattan Life Insurance Company
of New York City. When the 1871 Chicago fire losses forced the
former company out of business, the Fireman's Fund Insurance
Company gave an agency contract to the Hawaii bank. This association of the two companies led to a directorship for Bishop in the
Fireman's Fund, when he moved to San Francisco. He served as
director from 1900–1915.

Bishop and Company had a fair insurance business, but in 1886,
there was still no such thing as a board of underwriters. He joined
his company with Castle and Cooke, Limited; Theo. H. Davies and
Company, Limited; and H. Hackfeld and Company as the first
signatories to a new Honolulu Board of Underwriters. Its object
was:

. . . to promote harmony and correct practices in underwriting, and to
establish and maintain just and equitable rates of premiums upon all the
property insured by its members, and also for the prevention of careless
endorsements and authorization of non-concurring policies.

* See pp. 255, 270.

Bishop believed in insurance but was not much interested in it as a personal business pursuit and never so much as attended a meeting of the Board of Underwriters. He usually sent C. O. Berger as his representative. The first meeting of the new Board was held June 16, 1886, and a constitution was adopted August 11, 1886. The directors moved swiftly. As a rate-making body of prime importance, the Board of Underwriters served well. Of recent years, with procedural changes in insurance matters in business and government, the Board's function has changed over to one largely of public relations wherein it educates the public in insurance matters and public safety.

The final chapter in the Bishop and Company story starts on August 11, 1894, when the *Pacific Commercial Advertiser* said that Samuel Damon was to be dethroned. Bishop had left for San Francisco for the last time on March 2. Rumors were flying. "Mr. Bishop," the story went on to say, "was selling out to Lilienthal Brothers of San Francisco. If Lilienthal Brothers obtain control, out will go Damon, and Godfrey Brown* will run it." Further comment on this development comes from a Honolulu author:

. . . During the summer of 1894, Mr. Alexander had protracted negotiations with Mr. Lilienthal who was co-manager with Ignatz Steinhart of the Anglo-California Bank. That seemed the logical bank to deal with because it was interested in getting Hawaiian business. Charles R. Bishop was retiring from his banking business in Honolulu and Steinhart had an option to purchase it and establish a branch of the Anglo-California in Honolulu. Although the Anglo-Californian really wanted the account of the proposed new agency its managers imposed conditions which neither Sam Alexander nor Henry Baldwin could swallow. Particularly distasteful was the idea of accepting Steinhart's brother-in-law as a partner in the new firm. The agency was to be postponed a year.†

The final action was quite different. Damon stepped in and took over as sole owner on June 1, 1895. He gave first a single personal note** for $800,000 to Bishop and later, in 1895, replaced it with fourteen notes in various amounts and due dates but with the same total. All were made by Samuel M. Damon, payable to the order of Charles R. Bishop; and all were endorsed "payable without re-

---

* President of the Hawaiian Bell Telephone Company.
† Arthur L. Dean, *Alexander & Baldwin, Ltd.* (Honolulu Advertiser Co., Ltd., 1950), pp. 44–45.
** See pp. 222–226.

course." The proceeds of the Damon note were placed at the disposal of the Charles R. Bishop Trust.

There were some touch-and-go moments in Damon's early years as owner of the bank. One of them revolved around the request that Damon felt he needed to make in order to create a desirable margin of safety in the bank operation. Three of his $50,000 notes falling due in 1909 threw too much of a shadow on his long-range plans. So he asked the other Trustees of the Charles R. Bishop Trust to approve extending them to 1914. The date of this meeting was November 19, 1896. Damon gave a little detail of the transfer of the bank as he tried to obtain Trustee approval of the extension of the notes:

The negotiations by Mr. Bishop with the Anglo-California Bank having fallen through, Mr. Bishop had expressed to Mr. Damon the wish to get the bank off his hands. In taking over the Bank at $800,000 he had assumed the liability of accounts of large amounts of very doubtful nature. . . . The sale of the Bank and the completion of the transfer had been done hurriedly at Mr. Bishop's request. He was given very little time to digest the whole of the matter.

There were four Trustees present at this meeting, and they divided—Charles Montague Cooke and Joseph O. Carter against the extension, with Charles McEwen Hyde* and Samuel Mills Damon for (and the last-named with his evident conflict-of-interest was allowed to vote). This parliamentarily sent the question to Bishop in San Francisco (he was the fifth trustee). After the discussion which chiefly involved him, Damon voluntarily resigned from his Trusteeships with the three Trusts and made a personal call on Bishop in San Francisco. A letter dated October 20, 1897, over the latter's signature, went to the Trustees in Honolulu:

In furtherance of the desire of Samuel M. Damon, that Two hundred and Fifty Thousand Dollars of his notes held by you for account of the Charles R. Bishop Trust and to come due A.D. 1909, may be extended, and made payable December 1st, 1914, I have to request that you will consent to such extension upon the terms proposed by Mr. Damon, Viz:— One hundred and fifty thousand dollars ($150,000) of said new notes to be secured by Bonds of The Oahu Railway and Land Company (Being interest at six per cent.) for a like amount ($100,000) as collateral. . . .

Even this was not immediately agreeable, but the parties concerned could not sidestep Bishop's right to amend the Deed of Trust. The notes were extended and the bank was given some valuable relief.

* See pp. 142, 146, 264, 288–289, 298–299.

Damon's resignation from the trusteeships, April 2, 1897, disturbed Bishop; and after the San Francisco conference Damon was persuaded to accept reappointments, January 11, 1898. Matters among the Trustees after his reappointment were resumed in a friendly, reasonable climate which gave years of enhanced constructive service to the purposes of the Trusts. Bishop had no continuing connection with his former Honolulu institution. Bishop and Company, in the first hundred years of its existence, experienced several absorptions of other banks and changes in management and corporate forms; but it retained the name "Bishop" in some part of any current title. It was changed to the more general name of First National Bank of Hawaii in 1960.

Bishop combined judgment and restraint with a rare sense of propriety in business relations and an uncanny ability to visualize new business and new traffic in elements and situations. This characteristic accounted for his purchases of parcels of land in Honolulu and in all the islands, as well as his reluctance to go into coffee and his willingness to go into sugar. He also had a practical appreciation of the potential constructive effects of communication and transportation which was manifested in his constant enterprise and interest in the ocean cable, good shipping lines, telephone service, and a sound currency and banking system. Some of his investments were made to push an industry, others to save an industry. And his genius was that as he pushed and as he saved, he also profited. All of this however, goes back to the fact that he was Bishop and Company. His humanity, his integrity, his cautiousness were embedded in the public image of his bank.

4

Government

CHARLES REED BISHOP AND THE ALII

MR. BISHOP'S ASSOCIATION with Hawaiian royalty began with his marriage to Princess Bernice Pauahi Paki in 1850 and continued even through the many years remaining to him after he had permanently changed residence to California. Because of his position of influence in the business community, and because of his marriage to the beautiful great granddaughter of Kamehameha I, he was inevitably closely acquainted with the weaknesses and strengths and the modesties and ambitions socially, politically, and financially of every member of the royal family. Primarily, he was the financial counsellor of each of them. He was also personal and political counsellor and perhaps was more readily accepted as a friend and adviser than any other non-Hawaiian citizen of the Kingdom. Having a quiet satisfaction in the successes of any member, he watched over the expenditures of each one in the manner of a family banker. Rebuffed and repulsed upon occasion, he never lost his interest and hope in a final outcome of good in the life of every Kamehameha. Throughout this entire relationship, that covered almost fifty years of generally enlightened rule by the several Kamehamehas, he was warmly and seriously regarded by the royal family as a dedicated friend.

ALEXANDER LIHOLIHO IOLANI—ALII

YOUNG ALEXANDER LIHOLIHO IOLANI attended the Royal School with Lot Kamehameha and Bernice Pauahi Paki. All three were

Kamehamehas. One of the two boys presumably was to marry Bernice, who gave evidence of her real affections in accepting the hand of Charles Reed Bishop. Alexander, who was destined to become Kamehameha IV in 1854, married Emma Rooke. Lot never married.

Bishop's first comment upon Hawaiian royalty dealt with Alexander and appeared in a letter to J. Turrill (formerly U. S. Consul to Hawaii) in 1857. He recorded his sadness with the passing of his closest and dearest friend, William L. Lee, and then went on to say: "The King [Kamehameha IV] behaves like a gentleman."

The pressures of the regency, including the foreign threat of invasion by filibuster, the questions of annexation and reciprocity which even at that time swirled about the royal head, were too much. The death of his son, the beloved Prince of Hawaii, was a final blow, and Kamehameha IV died in 1863. He will be remembered in part for the constructive reforms which he initiated in government. He relied to a great degree upon the intelligence and judgment of the distinguished legal mind, William L. Lee, and missed him as an adviser when Lee passed away in 1857. Kamehameha IV is likely to be remembered far longer, however, as the associate of Queen Emma in founding the Queen's Hospital.* The Bishops contributed to the first fund-raising efforts, and Bishop went on to be the leading financial director of that institution.

LOT KAMEHAMEHA—ALII (KAPUAIWA)

KAMEHAMEHA V WAS SWORN in as regent of the Kingdom of Hawaii, November 30, 1863. He was an older brother of Kamehameha IV. The House of Nobles and the House of Representatives were merged during his reign into a unicameral body. Lot was an individual of intellectual ability, well versed in foreign policy, and an independent thinker; but he was characterized also as an aristocrat and a reactionary. He was a strong monarch, and Bishop's only reference in his known correspondence was a highly favorable comment in a letter to Rev. C. M. Hyde, December 20, 1895:

* See pp. 273–277.

. . . I was interested in R. A. Lyman's paper on Kamehameha V. He was with the King a great deal and knew him intimately; and I think that he does not overestimate his good qualities. He was a strong minded, honest and patriotic ruler, and has often been misrepresented and misjudged. He had faults, of course, but they have been exaggerated by those who did not know him as well as Mr. Lyman knew him. Towards the close of his reign I knew him better and appreciated him more highly and correctly than I did in the early part of his reign. . . .

Kamehameha V died December 11, 1872. One of the interesting stories of Hawaiian royalty comes, virtually, from his deathbed. Despite strong urging he failed, or declined, to name a successor. The Constitution of 1864 provided that the direct heirs of Kamehameha V would inherit the throne or it would go to his sister Victoria Kamamalu; and if neither of these alternatives worked out, the one appointed by the King would rule. If he made no appointment the Legislative Assembly would elect some native from among the alii as successor.

Kamehameha V never married. His sister Victoria Kamamalu predeceased him. When he was urged to make an appointment he demurred and finally refused. He had tried to persuade Mrs. Bishop to take the appointment, but she declined and suggested his sister-in-law, Emma. The dying King would not consider her. Nor would he consider either of the only two other real candidates, Lunalilo and Kalakaua.

Bishop enters this bedside story a quarter century later. Liliuokalani had published her autobiography* in early 1898. In this is depicted the sickbed scene where Kamehameha V was exhorted to name a successor. She relates that Mrs. Bishop suggested Ruth Keelikolani and that the dying monarch pronounced her as unable to handle the assignment. Bishop's information on what transpired did not agree with the Liliuokalani account. He wrote of the matter to W. D. Alexander, March 23, 1898:

. . . I shall send to the Trustees under the will of Mrs. Bishop, the statements of the late Gov. Dominis and Stephen H. Phillips, and perhaps that of Mrs. Bishop as to what occurred at the death bed of Kamehameha V with regard to appointment of his successor and they will, if they approve, consent to their publication by the Historical Society, or in such other way as they may think best. . . .

* Liliuokalani, *Hawaii's Story by Hawaii's Queen* (Boston, Lothrop, Lee & Shepard Co., 1898).

The statements, except that of Mrs. Bishop, were later published.*
This action seemed agreeable to all concerned for discussion
ceased.

As for the succession, a minor battle of manifestoes broke out
between Lunalilo and Kalakaua, chiefly on the issue of genealogy.
Lunalilo's suggestion that an election be held finally won out; he
was elected, and the first man named among his advisers was
Charles R. Bishop as Foreign Minister.

WILLIAM CHARLES LUNALILO—ALII

THE DEVOTION OF the Bishops to Lunalilo was genuine. Mrs.
Bishop had been a fellow student of Lunalilo at Royal School.
Bishop, in accepting the portfolio of Foreign Minister, was
expressing his devotion and his hope for service to the Hawaiian
people. His official and private correspondence written during the
year of his foreign ministership bulks larger in physical size than any
other period of comparable length in his long life.

Bishop was "in" on many things in that Lunalilo "year." For
example, he had an opportunity to advance an important British
Royal Academy of Science research project. The planet Venus
moves between the sun and the earth in a pair of crossings with but
eight years intervening, and then 105 years must elapse before
another pair of crossings occurs, also eight years apart. An English
astronomer, Edward Halley, informed the Royal Society of England
in 1680 that Venus would make such a crossing in 1761 and 1769.
This was used as a "public" purpose to cover Captain James Cook's
proposed exploration under secret orders to discover and explore
the new unknown continent, Austral. He was to maintain the secrecy
aspect with an open observation of the Transit of Venus in 1761 in
Tahiti. The next one was to be 1874; and Bishop, in 1873, as Foreign
Minister of Hawaii under King Lunalilo, made arrangements for the

* S. H. Phillips and J. O. Dominis, *Correspondence Relating to the Last
Hours of Kamehameha V.* (Annual Report, Hawaiian Historical Society, 1898).

visit of the Royal Society astronomers who desired to use the cloud-
less skies above Mauna Loa and Haleakala for the scheduled observation of the Transit of Venus. The British astronomers came,
made their successful observations, and left, grateful for the assistance rendered and the hospitality accorded. Bishop was rather easily
and carefully performing a duty of his office. His contact with the
British scientists provided an item of experience which he would be
reminded of some years later in his founding of the Bishop Museum
and in his encouraging the establishment of an astronomical observatory.

The Pearl Harbor cession was one of the touchiest political
subjects ever to confront Bishop. It came up, attended with bitter
controversy, in his Foreign Minister year. The United States naval
authorities had their eye on the strategic Pearl River Lagoon as early
as 1846, the year of Bishop's arrival in Hawaii. William Howard,
commander of the steamer *Constitution,* flying the American Flag,
was given a permit in 1852 to investigate harbors and navigation
waters of all the islands including Pearl Lagoon.

One of Bishop's earliest acts as Foreign Minister was to receive
Major General John M. Schofield, Commander of the U. S. Army
Military Division of the Pacific and Brevet Brigadier General B. S.
Alexander of the Corps of Engineers. The S. S. *California* brought
these men to Honolulu on January 15, 1873. They came on a confidential mission for W. W. Belknap, Secretary of War of the United
States; they were to ascertain the defense capabilities of the various
ports and chiefly to study the Pearl Harbor potential. Bishop was
acquainted with all of this and he aided them materially in their
mission. To sidetrack curiosity, the two general officers visited Kauai
and at the insistence of Bishop used the government steamer
Kilauea. Bishop then wrote to the Honorable D. McBride on Kauai
to meet the two visitors at Waimea with a wagon; and he sent along
W. C. Parke, Esquire, Marshal of the Kingdom, as the King's representative.

The mission of the two Army officers gave an idea to Bishop. He
met with the Honolulu Chamber of Commerce and obtained support of a renewal of study of the subject of reciprocity (no mention
of Pearl Harbor or cession). He thereupon wrote, February 25, 1873,
to Henry A. Peirce, Resident Minister of the United States in Hawaii:

I have the honor to inform your Excellency that a Committee of the Honolulu Chamber of Commerce has waited upon His Majesty's Ministers and discussed with them the subject of a Treaty of Reciprocity between the Government of the United States and that of the Hawaiian Islands, and presented at the same time a Resolution, of which the following is a copy:

'Resolved, That the Committee wait upon the Ministers and express the strong conviction of the Chamber that a Treaty of Reciprocity is of greatest importance to the interests of the Country at the present time.

'They respectfully request therefore that His Majesty's Government obtain from the representative of the United States Government, information as to the possibility of negotiating such a treaty on any terms that His Majesty's Government would be prepared to accept.

'The Chamber of Commerce desires to express its readiness to cooperate with His Majesty's Government in promoting this object.'

You are aware, Mr. Minister, that the Hawaiian Government has for many years past been desirous of securing such a treaty as is above referred to; that two such treaties have been negotiated, and have failed of ratification by the Senate of the United States, the Hawaiian Government being in both instances willing to ratify, and the Legislative Assembly having passed the law necessary to give effect to that last negotiated.

Under such circumstances it must appear reasonable to your excellency that His Majesty's Government should hesitate to take the initiative in renewing negotiations; but, being anxious to meet the intelligent wishes of all classes of the community, they will feel greatly obliged to you if you will give such information as would offer a proper answer to the foregoing resolution. . . .

Schofield and Alexander took two months to complete their studies of the Pearl Harbor potential and then returned to the mainland. Their report was not published until twenty years later. But Pearl Harbor suddenly had become important to the United States. On July 7, 1873, Bishop wrote to Henry A. Peirce:

. . . I now have the honor to inform Your Excellency that I am authorized by my Sovereign to negotiate at Honolulu with a duly authorized representative of your Government a Special Treaty of Reciprocity between the United States and the Hawaiian Kingdom, upon the basis of the Treaty negotiated and signed at San Francisco May 21st, 1867, subject of course, to some changes and modifications the most important of which will be, to raise the grade of Sugar that would be admitted into the United States free of duty, from No. 12 to No. 16 Dutch Standard of color; and I am also authorized to include in the convention a cession for purposes of a Naval Station, of the Salt Water Lagoon (to high tide mark, and exclusive of enclosed fish ponds) known as Pearl River, in the district of Ewa, Island of Oahu, together with such a limited extent of land in and upon said lagoon as may be agreed upon. . . .

Due notice of this proposal was dispatched to Manley Hopkins, Esquire, H. H. M.'s "Charge d'Affaires" and Consul General in London. Well aware of the need to keep the home folks informed, the King and Bishop collaborated on a public statement which was published July 12, 1873, in the *Pacific Commercial Advertiser.*° It was a bold and challenging statement, the first ever made in public:

We are satisfied from various petitions and from other sources of information, that the business of the Islands is not in a prosperous condition; and we regard it as the duty of the Government to promote the material welfare of the community by all reasonable and just measures.

During the last two reigns, there were strong efforts made for a Treaty of Reciprocity with the United States, but without success. Regarding the value of such a treaty, there is, we believe, very little difference of opinion, and it is thought that an additional inducement may be wisely made by a cession of the lagoon known as Pearl River to the United States for a naval station. At present it is of little value to us, and we are of the opinion that a treaty, making the cession as one of its stipulations, may be so guarded in its terms as to protect the rights of all parties, and give strength and prosperity to the Kingdom. The United States have always been friendly to Hawaii, and we have no doubt that they will continue to be so.

When such a treaty shall have been negotiated by the Minister of Foreign Affairs, and approved by the King, it will then be submitted to the Legislative Assembly for their approval. We believe that such a treaty would impart new life to business of all description; that lands would be in demand for new agricultural enterprises, and instead of worthy and industrious men leaving the Kingdom, more of that class would be attracted here.

To advance the prosperity of this Kingdom is the purpose and policy of His Majesty's Government, and this measure, if successful, will strongly tend to promote that object; and we confidently believe that when fairly considered, and well understood, it will commend itself favorably to the public judgment.

But an old instinct against surrendering territory to a foreign country was beginning to assert itself. And the King himself was beginning to question such action:

. . . He [King Lunalilo] continued to receive Joe Carter frequently until he was taken sick; and that fact strengthens the impression that he is not heartily in favor of reciprocity *with any cession of territory;* and accounts for the other fact, that many prominent natives who have usually made the King's wishes their own, or apparently so, have spoken against cession. . . .

° "Official Declaration on Reciprocity by Charles Reed Bishop, for the King."

So wrote Bishop to Elisha H. Allen, September 5, 1873. In that same letter he gives further light on the Schofield survey: ". . . I am glad to hear that Genl Schofield still talks favorably, and I hope that he may be called to Washington, at the right time to give his opinions." October 15, Bishop again discussed the subject of cession:

. . . Rhodes, Gibson and Carter continue to be very active against the Gov't especially against those who favor cession of Pearl River, and Ward and many others encourage them. . . . I do not think that His Maj. would consent to the negotiation of a treaty at Washington, providing any cession of territory were required, and whether or not there would be any use in trying for a reciprocity treaty without cession, especially after what has transpired on that subject, you can judge of better than I can. . . .

An interesting twist to the cession story is contained in a letter from Queen Emma to her cousin, Peter Kaeo. The letter is dated October 27:

. . . During the King's illness last month Mr. H. M. Whitney and Judge Hartwell went to Doctor Trousseau to ascertain the King's exact state of health. When they found out how he was, these gentlemen a day or two after returned to the Doctor with a message for him to put before Mrs. Bishop, asking that she should accept the Throne. The Doctor called, and had a confidential interview with her, telling who requested him. Her reply to him was to tell those gentlemen she could not accept the Throne, even if offered by the King, on the grounds of affection for her husband— that she does not like to oppose her husband on the cession of Puuloa,* which she would have to do. They have already now had several disagreements upon it, the first they have ever had. She opposes cession of territory while he favours.

On November 11, Bishop brought up the subject in another letter to Allen. The King's health was not improving and opponents of the idea of cession were growing in strength:

. . . A new native newspaper has been started under Gibson's management, avowedly in opposition to the present Ministry, and is supported largely by Ward and some others who draw their living from the government, and by others opposed to the cession of Pearl River. With any cession of territory in a treaty it would hardly be *possible* to carry it through, and now, since cession has been proposed on our part it is not probable that reciprocity *without* cession could be obtained. . . .

But cession talk was halted for the time being by Lunalilo himself. He authorized Bishop to write again to Peirce, November 14:

* Pearl Harbor.

On the 7th day of July last, I had the honor to inform your Excellency, by a note of that date, that I had been authorized by my Sovereign to negotiate with a duly empowered Representative of the United States, a Special Treaty of Reciprocity, upon the basis of that signed at San Francisco May 21st 1867; and that I was also authorized to include in such a treaty a cession, for the purposes of a Naval Station, of the salt water Lagoon known as Pearl River; and I further stated, that the treaty which might be agreed upon, would be subject to ratification by the King, and the approval of the Legislative Assembly of the Kingdom, according to the Constitution.

Up to the present time, His Majesty's Government is not aware of the views or intentions of your Government upon the subject referred to, and can only judge of its disposition by the liberal views manifested in past negotiations for reciprocity in commerce, but which have not, unfortunately, been sustained by the requisite majority of the Senate.

Wishing at all times to act with perfect frankness with you, and with the great nation and friendly Government which you represent, it is my duty to state that the expressed wishes of a large proportion of the business community, as well as their own views of the desirableness of the measure, induced His Majesty's Government to make the proposition contained in my note referred to. Since the submission of that note, it has become evident that, the general feeling in that country is so adverse to the measure, that even if the United States should acquiesce in it, a treaty on the basis of a cession of territory, would not be ratified by the next Legislative Assembly. Under these circumstances, it has pleased His Majesty the King, to direct me to withdraw that part of my note of 7th July which relates to a cession of the Pearl River Lagoon and other territory to the United States, for a Naval Station, and to request you, Mr. Minister, to advise your Government of the same, at the earliest date practicable.

His Majesty's Government still entertains the opinion that a Special Treaty of Reciprocity of a similar character to that of May 21st 1867, would prove to be mutually advantageous to the United States and the Hawaiian Kingdom.

A tender personal note appears in a November 26th letter to Allen: ". . . *Every chief* in the country was opposed to it, and only the fact that I was committed to it, kept my own good wife from so expressing herself. . . ." December 7, 1873, he writes to Allen: ". . . Mrs. Bishop consoles me by saying that I ought to have known that the natives would not favor cession." Pearl Harbor was to rest for awhile; and Bishop's fears that reciprocity was impossible without cession were groundless, for an excellent treaty was agreed to in 1876 and proved to be a great financial stimulus to the Kingdom.

The Lunalilo year was a complicated and varied experience for Bishop. He was almost overwhelmed with the involved demands of

Kamehameha IV. Alexander Liholiho Iolani was born February 9, 1834, and died November 30, 1863. He reigned from
1854 to 1863. His Queen Consort was Emma. Since their
only son died in infancy, Kamehameha IV was succeeded
by his older brother, Kamehameha V.

Kamehameha V. Lot Kameha-
meha, also known as Kapuaiwa,
was born December 11, 1830,
and died December 11, 1872.
He was the son of Kinau and
M. Kekuanaoa and was a bach-
elor. He did not name a successor.

Lunalilo was born January 31,
1835, and died February 3,
1874. His reign was short,
from January 8, 1873, to the
date of his death. He was Hawaii's first elected monarch.

Kalakaua was the seventh ruler of the Kingdom of Hawaii and its second elected king. He was born November 16, 1836, came to the throne on February 12, 1874, and died January 20, 1891.

Queen Liliuokalani was born September 2, 1838, and died November 11, 1917. Her reign as the eighth ruler of the Kingdom of Hawaii was short, 1891–1893.

treaty making. Austria, Germany, Denmark, France, Russia, United States, and even little Tonga, a tiny outpost of Polynesia, were all on the treaty-making list. There was a volume of correspondence relating to diplomatic buttons and uniforms for the Hawaiian monarch's representatives in foreign courts. The business of exchanging medals, orders, scrolls, and trappings of every description, was a part of the work that he supervised. He handled plans for the entertainment of distinguished foreign representatives; many were entertained by the Bishops at their popular home "Haleakala." Claims such as the losses sustained in the destruction of the Hawaiian barque *Harvest* at Ascension Island by the rebel cruiser *Shenandoah*, April 11, 1865, were processed by Bishop. Conferring of decorations, quelling a mutiny, firing salutes on the namedays of foreign rulers, promoting steamship lines, and protecting the rights of Hawaiian seamen on foreign vessels were routine pursuits of his office.

Considerable correspondence illuminated the degrading injustices of the South Pacific labor traffic. He was highly critical of any movement in labor that smacked of slave trade, and he established and enforced sound immigration rules. In one instance he won the gratitude of Emperor Meiji of Japan for his insistence on respect for the Japanese government's policies in labor trade. It won him the Order of the Rising Sun,* First Class, the highest honor that may be conferred upon a foreigner. In a letter to Robert M. Brown, Consul General for the Empire of Japan, Mr. Bishop warned, January 2, 1874:

. . . Much as laborers are wanted here for specific industries, and families to settle as a permanent population, this Government will not approve of any steps to procure either that would be offensive to the friendly Government of Japan.

Leprosy, a community problem that obsessed him, was another subject of the 1873 year. The importation of eucalyptus trees, the handling of boracic acid, the availability of "saluting" powder, postal regulations, coffee growing, and a wide variety of subjects cropped up in his official correspondence. One of his most frustrating problems should have been one of the simplest to solve; he was never certain of routines in etiquette or protocol. As he wrote to William Martin, "Charge d'affaires" in Paris:

* See p. 107.

. . . I say to you frankly that in matters of this nature, His Majesty as well as I is inexperienced. [They were discussing whether the Hawaiian Grand Cross should have a diamond mounting for each of the potentates of foreign countries]. . . .

. . . and that much will be left to your tact and knowledge of the etiquette so that no mistakes may be made and no offense given.

The public concern with Kamehameha V's failure to appoint a successor was mild compared to the question of a successor for Lunalilo. Kalakaua was aggravating a popular feeling against any cession of land of the Kingdom. Emma was willing to step aside for the election of Lunalilo but would do battle for designation as his successor, especially if Kalakaua were involved. The conflict over succession was intensified because Lunalilo was decidedly unwell. Bishop was deeply worried. "The King is dangerously ill. Hope he gets well and appoints a successor. We don't want another election of a Sovereign," he wrote to Allen, in Bangor, Maine, September 5, 1873. Allen was a good listener, for Bishop wrote frequently to him the next three months and unburdened his worry:

October 15:
. . . The King has had a long and severe sickness, in which his lungs and throat were much affected; but he is now nearly well again, and will soon go to Kona, Hawaii, to recruit. His sickness caused us much anxiety and excited high hopes in the minds of Col. D. K.° and his friend. We have tried very hard to persuade him to appoint and proclaim his successor, but thus far without success, and he seems unable to make up his mind upon the subject. . . .

November 11:
. . . The King is not quite as well as he was a few days ago. He has a cough and rheumatism and a poor appetite. . . . *Between ourselves,* he is threatened with consumption. . . . He still declines to name a successor, and I fear that he will continue to do so. May God spare him many years! and save us from a repetition of the experiences of the past and present year. . . .

November 20:
. . . The King's health is a matter of great solicitude, and some of the physicians are of opinion that he has a decided consumptive tendency. Were he to be taken away, D. K. would probably succeed him.

November 26:
. . . He and nearly all of the Chief ladies, except Mrs. Bishop, are at Kailua, and he is reported to have improved rapidly. His sickness has had some influence (unfavorable of course) on public affairs. He has thus far declined to appoint a successor, and probably will not make an appointment, as he seems to be in favor [of] elections!! . . . Kalakaua

° David Kalakaua

has added a great deal to his popularity with the natives and with some foreigners by his opposition . . . to cession of *any* territory; and should there be occasion to elect another Sovereign, he would probably be chosen. . . .

December 7, 1873:

. . . It might save a good deal of expense and some anxiety if the King would now appoint him Kalakaua as successor. D. K. would do the best he could, no doubt, and if he were fortunate in his advisors might do very well. . . .

January 20, 1874:

. . . We were anxious to have the King return to Honolulu. . . . He refused to come, but sent the *Kilauea* back to bring another Doctor up, . . . I persuaded Mr. Hall to go up. The ev'g before they reached Kailua the King had a hemorrhage from the lungs. After much urging by Mr. Hall, the Doctors and others he consented to come, and the trip down has done him no harm. The Doctors say he may live a week or two longer, but give no hope of his recovery. . . . The public mind seems to be settled upon [Kalakaua] as the coming man, and as it is very doubtful if a majority of the Nobles would approve of any other, we have tried our best to have the King appoint him. Queen Emma, Ruth Keelikolani and Mrs. Bishop have each given him the same advice. Kalakaua has behaved in such a way towards the King as to offend him grievously, and it seems impossible for him to appoint him. He has indicated a preference for Queen Emma, tho he has not said that he wished to appoint her. He has not *named* anyone. . . .

February 3:

Several times within the last three days I have been sent for, because the King was thought to be near his end. . . . He has taken scarcely any nourishment the last four days, and his mind is "flighty." He has not appointed a successor, and now it is too late to do so. Q. E. and some of her particular friends tried very hard up to Saturday evening to get an appointment, but without success. She seems disappointed. The King never mentioned her *name* to me, nor to anybody else that I *know* of; and yet I think he had it in mind to appoint her. . . . We shall call the "Legislative Assembly," with the understanding that that means *all* of the Nobles and all the Representatives of the People, elected yesterday. . . .

Lunalilo, Hawaii's first elected King, was in office the shortest period of any of the monarchs. He died in the evening of February 3.

At an Extraordinary Meeting of the Privy Council at Iolani Palace, February 6, the customary resolutions were read and adopted, and then Bishop asked to speak:

It is quite probable that various reports regarding the appointment of a successor by the late King, will be spread abroad. I think it quite proper that you gentlemen, who occupy a responsible position, should know just what was done about that matter by the Members of His Majesty's Cabinet.

In September last on more than one occasion, I urged upon His Majesty the great importance and desirableness of appointing his successor, my colleagues also advised strongly the same way.

Again, after his late return from Kailua, the Minister of the Interior and myself, the Attorney General also being present advised him with every argument that we could command, and appealed to him to make an appointment. I stated to him repeatedly that whenever he desired to name his successor it would be the duty of his ministers to summon the Nobles without delay and that I would make it my special business to attend to it. I now say for myself and am also authorized to state in behalf of my colleagues, that His Majesty never said to me, or to either of them, that he was ready to make an appointment and wished to have the Nobles summoned, nor did he ever name to me, or to either of them any person whom he wished to appoint. . . . In justice to myself and all concerned I thought it proper to make this Statement to you, so that you might know the truth. We the Ministers do not speak for ourselves only.

The regular election of representatives had been held the day before, and the question of succession was placed in the hands of the new Legislative Assembly which voted thirty-nine to six for Kalakaua over Queen Emma. Rioting broke out and a moderate state of civil war ensued. Bishop dispatched identical emergency pleas to Henry A. Peirce, Minister Resident of the United States, and Major James Hay Wodehouse, Her British Majesty's Commissioner and Consul General, February 12:

A riotous mob having unexpectedly made a violent attack upon the Court House and the members of the Legislature, which we have not the force at hand to resist, I have to request that you cause to be furnished at the earliest moment possible aid from the U. S. Ships *Tuscarora* and *Portsmouth* to the Police, in quelling the riot and temporarily protecting life and property.

An intimate picture of Bishop's role during these stormy days is contained in a dispatch from Peirce to Hon. Hamilton Fish, Secretary of State, Washington, D. C. It was dated February 17, 1874:

Sir: I have now the honor to report what has transpired hereon and since the 12th instant. On that day the legislative assembly elected the high chief, Hon. David Kalakaua, King of these islands. . . . On the 13th instant he was installed as sovereign . . . in presence of all the officers of Government, the members of the diplomatic and consular corps, naval officers, and many other spectators.

On the announcement by the president of the assembly from the balcony of the courthouse at 3 P.M. of the 13th instant that Kalakaua was elected King, the populace received it with jeers and contempt.

The members of a committee . . . were set upon and beaten by a mob. The rioters . . . assaulted the courthouse. . . . The offices . . . were sacked and gutted, cries were heard to "fire the town." It was at this condition or aspect of affairs that I received requests from the King elect and Minister Bishop and Governor Dominis to cause an armed force to be landed from the United States vessels of war *Tuscarora* and *Portsmouth* then in port.

Peirce summarized the events leading up to the request for a landing party.

At midnight of the 12th instant I received a note signed by King Kalakaua requesting my presence at the palace at 7 o'clock the ensuing morning. On arrival there I found present His Majesty, Mr. Bishop, Minister of Foreign Affairs, Mr. Wodehouse, British Commissioner, and Mr. Ballieu, French Commissioner.

Mr. Bishop stated that the object of the meeting was to ascertain whether the representatives of the United States, Great Britain, and France then present, respectively, recognized Kalakaua as sovereign of the Hawaiian Kingdom. Each of the representatives replied in the affirmative.

Mr. Bishop then informed us that the King would be sworn into office and inaugurated on that day at 11 o'clock A.M. and he desired our presence on the occasion. The ceremony being hastened as to time, on account of the critical condition of affairs, the installation took place as arranged.

The "foreign aid" described in the early part of the Peirce dispatch was made available later in the day, after the attack by the aroused opposition. Bishop's last days as Foreign Minister were weighted with worry; but distasteful as the necessary moves were, he acted promptly and with determination to establish peace and order.

DAVID KALAKAUA—ALII

DAVID KALAKAUA REIGNED from 1874 to 1891. Bishop was sincerely hopeful that Kalakaua would succeed in his kingship. Unquestionably the newly elected regent started out in auspicious fashion. Bishop was commissioned as President of the Board of Education at the time of Kalakaua's accession to the throne and presided over the first Legislature convened by the King. He was a member of the Privy Council and a Noble in the distinguished House of Nobles.

When Kalakaua was on his deathbed in the Palace Hotel in San Francisco, January 20, 1891, Bishop was in the room. Between these two moments; the glorious day of Kalakaua's assumption of the kingship and the deep stillness of death of the Hawaiian monarch seventeen years later, runs a story which, as a statement of relationship between Bishop and the new King, is not a simple matter to elicit from the record. There were many references in the Bishop letters to the effects of the Reciprocity Treaty and the general state of economics in the kingdom, but in the first ten years practically no comment is made on Kalakaua himself. A brief paragraph in a letter to Elisha H. Allen, February 14, 1880, is the only known comment in private correspondence from the accession in 1874 to the end of 1885:

. . . The worst of it is that H. M. [His Majesty] took quite an active interest in electing some nincompoops who are mere tools of his, and has expressed some plans which are so weak and useless that he has lost a good deal of the confidence and respect of foreigners and the most intelligent natives. I think he sees his mistake and I wish he would profit by it. He has a great fancy for military. . . . His health and habits are good and his ministers seem pretty sound in their views and intentions. . . .

A combination of trends fashioned by the later advisers and Ministers of the King raised increasingly grave concerns in the mind of Bishop. He attempted, with rare affection and understanding, to stimulate higher standards among the elected representatives in the Legislature. He hoped for mature and able men among the ministers and advisers, and these hopes were fully shared by his wife. But the electorate deteriorated. The Ministers and advisers were more self-centered than community-minded; some of them could even be labelled adventurers. The ill-considered plan to construct a Pacific Ocean area political empire under the rather all inclusive title, Polynesia, to be ruled by Kalakaua, was advanced and partially carried through by Walter Murray Gibson.* Some construction of legation buildings was actually completed at Apia in Western Samoa. Tonga almost joined the negotiations, but the project collapsed because of the fanciful impracticality inherent in it. Then Claus Spreckels contributed to community uneasiness because of his silver

* See pp. 75–79.

coinage proposals and the "easy money" era stimulated thereby. Opium and the lottery were openly considered in the Legislature. Governmental pomp and ceremony reached a highly stepped-up tempo.

A strong wedge of unpublicized dispute was driving Kalakaua and Bishop apart. Mrs. Bishop shared her husband's solicitude and apprehension. So strongly did the Bishops feel about the extravagances and reckless public actions of the Kalakaua regime that they could not bring themselves to attend the Coronation or the Coronation Banquet and Ball. A gulf was widening between the Bishops and the exponents and adherents of the Kalakaua rule. To R. W. Meyer, he wrote on April 2, 1884: ". . . The King was lately in Kau and is encouraging natives and others to make a *hui** with him to lease Kamaoa—the Government lands!! . . ."

On the other hand the tendency to write a good word would not be stilled. To Meyer on April 26, 1884:

. . . You will see by the King's speech that the report about the extravagant Budget was a hoax. I told several persons that I could not credit it, but with the present state of affairs people are not surprised at absurdities. . . .

But conditions did not improve; to Meyer, December 9, 1885:

. . . It is strange that the King does not see that he and his family are being made tools of by his ministers and C. S.† But they are all looking out for large salaries, regardless of the interest of the people. . . .

A rather deplorable situation is described in a letter dated January 30, 1886, again to Meyer:

. . . What a sad thing it is that it should be possible that the people should believe that the King and his ministers should send or encourage the sending of gin to the leper settlement or anywhere else. What an example of their love for the people. . . . In my own mind I have no doubt that most of the money and gin is furnished at the expense of C. S. of San Francisco, an alien and non-resident! . . .

Lesser scandals, such as sales of offices, defrauding of the customs revenue by abuse of the royal privilege, the illegal leasing of lands in Kona and Kau to the King without auction, and the sales of exemptions to lepers, were added to the major scandals. The attempts at passage of lottery and opium bills, the $10,000,000 loan effort, the

* Group or association.
† Claus Spreckels.

London Loan negotiations, the Moreno Trans-Pacific Cable Company $100,000 subsidy, the Spreckels Bank Charter Bill, the Hawaiian Silver Coinage, and the Primacy of the Pacific Empire Building, were legislative proposals—some of them gross irregularities— chiefly voiced by selfish and dishonest advisers to the King. Such proposals reflected the inevitable march towards absolutism in the Hawaiian government. Regarding the Opium Bill, Bishop spoke at some length, vigorously and in detail, of its effects upon the people. He spoke as a legislator in the assembly* on October 11 and 13, 1886.

The Legislature of 1886 adjourned in the early fall and was considered the most corrupt and the weakest assembly in the history of the Kingdom. To Meyer, on October 18, 1886, Bishop wrote:

. . . At last the legislature has closed, and its follies, which are many, are on record. Many of the appropriations for roads and other useful things will not be spent, but the money will be used for other purposes. . . . Paihaole voted for the opium bill and probably hopes for a reward in some shape, and will get it. . . . What Rex means by putting an end to the Boundary Commission I do not know. . . .

This Legislature had approved a loan of two million dollars to be floated in San Francisco. But London seemed a better source of the money, and the Kingdom fiscal agents turned their attention to that English city. Writing from San Francisco about the London Loan, Bishop had this to say to S. M. Damon, December 4:

. . . Were it *certain* that only $500,000 would be for sale in Honolulu and that the remainder [$1,500,000] will be taken abroad in London or anywhere else, we might have no difficulty in disposing of such part as we do not care to hold at par. But the papers have published so much about the extravagance and folly of the King and his gov't and about the Loan, that it is possible that the English may not want it. If and in that case there will be a large amount obtainable at home at seven percent discount. If inquired of from London the banks here [San Francisco] will give cautious and conservative replies and their opinions will have an influence. . . .

London took $980,000 and Honolulu $771,800; and of the latter amount, C. Spreckels received a repayment of advances claimed in the amount of $630,000.

Upon returning to Honolulu, Bishop wrote to Meyer, January 7, 1887:

. . . so long as he [Kalakaua] is *King* he is entitled to respectful treat-

* See pp. 103–104.

ment, on account of his office *if* for no other reason, and all such re-marks as you mention, either verbal or written are wrong and will do harm. There is occasion for great patience and forbearance all round, so that affairs may be settled and work smoothly. . . .

May 17:
. . . We have a shameful state of demoralization in government, and those who govern are too stupid and bad to see their danger or to listen to wise and friendly counsel. . . . The King is "running" all of the departments. . . .

Storm clouds were appearing. Things were working up to a climax; a series of excerpts from the Bishop-Meyer correspondence describes the worsening situation.

May 23:
. . . It is evident that the newspapers and the enlisting of young men in the voluntary military companies is worrying and frightening the King and his ministers, but whether it will do any good or not is uncertain. . . . Any talk of revolutionary action is unwise, especially if it is serious. No doubt there is great discontent and hard feeling, and plenty of cause for it; and I fear that the King is not wise enough to "turn over a new leaf," and remove the cause.

June 13:
. . . What a pity that they [the natives] have so much of bad example in influential quarters. Unless decidedly checked Rex will go from bad to worse, and that perhaps is the shortest road to reform and general improvement.

June 21:
. . . There is still talk of a public meeting, and of making "*demands.*" I ask what they will do if Rex does not comply with the demands, and some reply, "*make him.*" I say: "You cannot *make him* comply, and it is a mistake to "*demand*" what you cannot, and do not intend to try to enforce. When they agree upon what seems to us to be a reasonable course I may take part in a meeting. . . .

June 27:
. . . It is probable there will be a meeting on Thursday of this week.
I know that to let things go from bad to worse is usually not right or wise, not right if you can prevent it without too great a sacrifice, but sometimes it is the only way of uniting the better part of the community for reform. . . . Things are tending in that direction in Hawaii Nei. There are some here, I am told, who want to make strong demands, and if necessary enforce them. *Demands* are offensive, and if made without the power to carry them out, may only lead to humiliation and trouble. Peaceable means must first be exhausted, and natives must, if possible, be made to see that what is wanted is honest government for all, in which they should be the most interested.
I do not approve of threats or demands, and I do not like a petition;

but may consent to try the last once more. To talk of the ballot box is almost taunting one with his helplessness. . . . The King has the power of absolute veto on laws and constitutional amendments; has control of all appointments, . . . His advantages over all opponents are very great; . . .

. . . Whichever way I turn affairs look discouraging to me. Demoralization is going on among the Hawaiians, and they do not realize their shame and danger. How very much they need a good leader of their own race, a man of talents, character and eloquence! . . .

June 28:
Rumor says the Cabinet were requested to resign at 2 o'clock this morning. The men were bad enough, but Rex and his system are worse.

June 28:
The report of a change in the cabinet was premature, and yet I think the King is wishing to make a change of *men*. . . . I told Kaulukou this morning that he and all other natives who had talent and cared for the welfare of their country ought to take hold with the foreigners and insist upon an honest and proper government for the good of *all* people. . . .

Bishop's forecast regarding a "meeting on Thursday of this week" was substantiated when, on June 30, the entire town closed down; and a mass meeting was held, guarded by the Honolulu Rifles. Bishop had never cared for the limelight, but upon this occasion he addressed the meeting. He could, despite his natural reserve, speak straight to a point. This had been true in the uprising against Kalakaua that was brought on by the followers of Queen Emma. It was so again in the anti-Kalakaua mass meeting of June 30, when he addressed the aroused citizens in these words:

This is unquestionably an important meeting, the most important ever held in Honolulu. I see before me mechanics, merchants, professional men. They are not here for amusement, but because they feel that the course of affairs calls for prompt and determined action. We should discuss matters in a peaceable manner, without any threats. The fact that so many men have come here shows that we do not need any threats.

I came here in 1846, became naturalized in 1849, and have lived under five kings. We thought we had really a liberal Constitution because these kings would not encroach upon the rights of their subjects; but we have found out within the last few years that our Constitution is defective, partly on account of bad advice to the King, but largely upon his own account. The King has encroached upon our rights. We have very few mass meetings, but when we have one like this I believe it means either a new Constitution or one with material reforms, which I am sure we shall have. I come here as a Hawaiian, not for any class or clique. If it was for any class or clique I would not come here at all.

. . . It is my wish to have changes made in the Constitution by the People, and in a legal way, and not by a league of foreigners with guns in their hands. A Constitution made without legal form or sanction, under duress, would have no binding force legally or morally, and might be changed again at any favorable moment. There is no confidence in the King now, and why should there be any more under a new Constitution? . . . I am told . . . there is danger of the impatient who are around. . . . It seems to me that a ball has been set in motion and a force created which cannot be properly controled. The King has so outraged public sentiment, that he has put in jeopardy the rights of his subjects.

Out of this came the new Constitution of 1887, a ministry responsible solely to the people, and suffrage for the foreigner. Now Bishop wrote again to Meyer, July 11, 1887:

. . . The King signed the Constitution without any hesitation, and will probably have no hesitation in violating it, or in signing another when he can see any personal advantage in it. He has thanked the "Rifles" and pretends to be pleased with the Constitution, and with himself for giving such a liberal law to his people!

My preference was for a Convention. It would have taken more time and cost more money, and might have failed, but I do not like Mexican methods. But since what has been done, was by honest and patriotic men, without violence, and has been accepted, I hope that we may have better government under it, and by accepting a position which I do not want, and will be a heavy tax upon my time and patience, I am showing my disposition to help. . . .

The reference here is to his agreement to return to his former position of President of the Board of Education. Perhaps one of the greatest beneficial results of this uprising was the quick arrest of Walter Murray Gibson on July 1, and his hurried sailing away forever on July 5. It was too late, this arrest and his departure, for the evil he manufactured would never die. But Gibson, perhaps more than any other, was the individual most influential with Kalakaua.

The name of Walter Murray Gibson was one which could generate an argument at any time, in the 1860's when he first arrived in Hawaii or even now, a century later. He never wanted for critics, but he also had his defenders. Even the circumstances of his birth have created an unresolved debate. He may have been born at sea in a Spanish vessel or on land at Courtlow, Northumberland, England.

One date given for his birth is January 16, 1822, one week before Bishop's, and the other is two years later.

He spent his young-man years in irregular adventuring in Central America, Mexican California, and Brazil; and from this last place he fled arrest and wound up in Sumatra. Here an overly zealous quest for personal recognition almost resulted in a clash between the state departments of Holland and the United States. The difficulties disappeared when Gibson gave up and sailed away to the island of Lanai in the Hawaiian chain. Here he promoted an ambitious colonization without success.

Bishop's first contact with Gibson was at this point, and it had to do with money. This is revealed in a letter he wrote to Gibson, September 15, 1879:

Soon after your return from the United States, I notified you that your note in favor of J. W. Austin for $705.25 dated June 20th 1868 and payable one year from date with interest at 10% was due and unpaid, and I understood you to say that you would take it up very soon. Since that time I have heard nothing from you regarding the note, and nothing has been paid either on a/c of payment or interest. Mr. Austin expected the note to be paid at maturity, and I trust that you will have it cancelled without delay.

You can hardly have forgotten that you are owing me for two years rent of the premises leased by you in Lahaina.

This initial experience was to color Bishop's feelings towards Gibson for years to come.

Subsequently, Gibson moved to Honolulu and was found first in Lunalilo's camp, then Kalakaua's. As a member of the Kalakaua Legislature he supported an opium-licensing bill, a large government loan bill, another authorizing sale of spirituous liquors to natives, one to stop segregation of lepers, and still another providing for the minting of a huge supply of coins. He held an appointment as premier from 1882 until he was forced out of office by public opinion in 1887. Bishop had resigned his presidency of the Board of Education in 1883 due to the severe strain between the government and himself, and Gibson immediately accepted the commission for that position. Gibson had not only been a guileful aide to Kalakaua; he had associated himself very closely in much of this political promotion with an adventurer by the name of Celso Caesar Moreno. This relationship was largely one of opportunism limited only by the imagination of the pair. Opium was involved, as was a million dollar cable to China, a concession for a steamship line, and an illusory scheme to educate native boys abroad.

A reference to Gibson is found in Bishop's correspondence in the fall of 1873. This was in the period of his foreign ministership under Lunalilo, and he probably had a greater awareness of Gibson's activities because of that. In a November 26 letter he wrote to Allen:

. . . You will I know, be surprised, disappointed and almost offended, when you hear that the proposal to cede Pearl River as a part of the basis for negotiation for Reciprocity, has been withdrawn. . . . The impression was general that His Majesty was at heart opposed . . . and unscrupulous efforts of Ward, Rhodes, Gibson and others was creating a strong prejudice in the minds of the natives, not only against the Ministry, but against foreigners and especially Americans which would have secured certain defeat of a treaty for cession in the Legislature. . . . He [His Majesty] finally said that he could not favor and sustain it. I wrote Mr. Peirce and we all resigned. He (the King), expressed his undiminished confidence, and requested us all to withdraw our resignations; and considering the state of his health, and that he was about to leave for Kona, we *reluctantly* consented to hold on. Mr. Judd, the Atty, Genl. is the only one to whom the service is agreeable. Mr. Hall and Mr. Sterling are both anxious to be relieved, and you know my feelings. I have not consulted my comfort or pleasure so far, and will not, so long as my health will admit that we have done the right and proper thing, under the circumstances. . . . Of course Gibson, Ward & Co. are in high glee, and I hear that Ward tells of the number of "old and influential" natives that he sent to talk privately with H. M. against cession. Is it not humiliating, discouraging and disgusting to be in such a position? Do you wonder that I wish to be free and away? But what good to Hawaiians, or anybody else, would come of my "throwing up the sponge?" Kalakaua had added a good deal to his popularity with the natives, and with some foreigners, by his opposition—which has been of a moderate but decided character—to cession of *any* territory; and should there be occasion to elect another Sovereign, he would probably be chosen.

Gibson was interested in the leper problem. In a letter to Meyer, March 17, 1884, Bishop writes:

. . . I hear Gibson and Van Gieson have been to Niu to buy or lease premises for another branch hospital for lepers—a place, I suppose, for such as one in the first stages and can pay for isolation and better fare than they can have either at Kakaako or Molokai. . . . This leprosy infliction is to be a heavy tax upon this country for many years to come. . . .

About a year later he mentioned Gibson again in a letter to Meyer, May 11, 1885:

. . . I am glad Mr. Gibson is to visit the settlement, or rather I would be glad if I had confidence in his honest and unselfish intentions. But there is so much of demagoguery and crookedness in the government business. . . . I think Mr. Gibson will see, if he is willing to see it, that the lepers can be supported better, more comfortably, and cheaply at the settlement than in the small premises here. . . .

Bishop changed the subject in another letter to Meyer, December 5, 1885: ". . . I have seen a report of sales of wool in London, and am now satisfied that Mr. Gibson's wool is better than Molokai wool. . . . Gibson had, I understand about 80,000 lbs. . . ."

In 1887 the political roof over Kalakaua's head was leaking. Gibson who had partly played flatterer to the King, had also grievously mislead him. Gibson was on the receiving end of so much criticism from the public press that he stepped in and purchased the *Pacific Commercial Advertiser*, and this occasioned a strong comment from Bishop, June 6, 1887, to Meyer:

. . . The P. C. Advertiser is now avowedly the Gov't paper and Gibson's hand is now clearly apparent, in cunning and misleading defense. I do not think it possible for the King to clear himself of the damaging charges made against him so plainly. And that he is guilty of much more not exposed or made public I have no doubt. A public meeting would call out some extreme and fiery talk, as well as some that would be sound, true and well considered. About the wisdom and advantage of such a meeting just now I am still doubtful. Vituperation, quarrels and small fights would do no good. It seems to me that things have got to be worse so as to bring about more general feeling of unity and of action before much can be done toward improvement. . . .

Bishop apparently did not think the opposition press was too helpful. There was some irregularity in the supply situation at the settlement, and supervision of this was a government responsibility. He wrote again to Meyer, June 27:

. . . I do not say that Thurston could have made honest men of Gibson and Hayselden, or could have put a stop to their wronging the lepers and the govt. for their own benefit, but he could have shown up their dishonesty in that matter beyond dispute. . . .

Things were really getting warm. On July 4, Bishop wrote once more:

. . . The change in Ministry will, no doubt, throw Hayselden as well as Gibson out of the Board of Health. I suppose you can get weight of meats, beef and mutton, furnished to lepers since 1st April last year, so as to show loss to treasury by Gibson's management. That game should be at an end.

Bishop in connecting Hayselden with Gibson did the former an injustice. Charges of malfeasance in public office against Hayselden were never proved and were dropped. As for Gibson, there are defenders who acknowledge some of his faults but who believe he was at heart a sincere and dedicated man in his dealings with the regents and others in power and leadership in the Kingdom. Those who have read his personal diaries report an impression of a worker and leader whose devotion to Hawaii was his primary and selfless purpose. But a battery of students of Hawaiian history does not so regard him. And the private pen of Bishop does not dispel the doubts. The day after the Revolution of 1887 was accomplished through a bloodless public meeting climaxing the Hawaiian League's plans on June 30, 1887, Gibson was arrested. However, he was allowed to slip aboard a sailing vessel July 5, on the eve of Kalakaua's signing of the new Constitution. Had the monarch listened to the sound, available advice of highly regarded citizens of his Kingdom, the history of his reign could have been different.

The new "Reform" legislature won by large majorities on September 12, and Bishop sailed to San Francisco. In a letter on October 7, 1887, he said to S. M. Damon: ". . . Good men here seem surprised when I tell them that I prefer a monarchial government in Hawaii with proper restraint upon the sovereign to a republic." This feeling was very important to him. His long, close relationship with the Hawaiians gave him a *kamaaina** philosophy of devotion to the native population, its welfare, and its rights, that would never dim. That is why even as he condemned Kalakaua, Bishop always held a faint though skeptical hope that Kalakaua might somehow be a good monarch and a leader of his people.

One defect of the government reform rested in the size of the supreme court. Changes were considered. One was the desirability of increasing the court to five; and the other, the matter of who would be appointed to an early vacancy. Kalakaua did not help much on this point, and Bishop's distress was evident. Further, the King exercised his veto power rather indiscreetly and usually without consulting his Ministers, and this created trouble.

No further mention of Kalakaua appears in the Bishop corre-

* One whose heart is in tune with Hawaii. (Born of the soil.)

spondence. Years later in the June 7, 1915, issue of the *Honolulu Star-Bulletin,* in the column entitled, "Following notes are by one who knew him well," there appeared this revealing paragraph:

At the angry political crisis in 1887, when an angry mass meeting with many armed men behind it was denouncing Kalakaua and his ministry, these backed by a strong military force, it was Charles R. Bishop whose counsel—added to that of the American and British representatives—caused the king to concede both a change of ministry and constitutional reform. Thus bloodshed was averted.

Kalakaua died January 20, 1891, and his sister Liliuokalani succeeded to the throne. Behind him, Kalakaua left perhaps as his most constructive legacy the Reciprocity Act of the middle 1870's. His most destructive legacy was a bitter racial rivalry. The wedge was driven so deep that the feeling of antagonism manifested itself again and again in the years ahead. It was to erupt seriously in the reign of Liliuokalani.

LYDIA KAMAKAEHA LILIUOKALANI—ALII

LILIUOKALANI WAS BORN near the present site of Queen's Hospital, September 21, 1838, to Kapaakea and Keohokalole. The parents of Mrs. Charles Reed Bishop, Abner and Konia Paki, almost immediately took the baby to their home, and Konia became her foster mother. When the lanai-enclosed residence of the Pakis, "Haleakala," was completed, Liliuokalani was in the family circle. When the Bishops moved into the home in 1855, Liliuokalani stayed on as a member of the Bishop family until she left September 16, 1862, to be married to John Dominis.

As a foster sister of Bernice Pauahi Bishop, Liliuokalani had come under the guardianship of Bishop when the Bishops moved into "Haleakala." He regarded that guardianship, of which the entire period strikingly parallels his worried watchfulness over Kalakaua, as a sacred trust throughout his life. Although he was to become increasingly disturbed with Liliuokalani's handling of her regency, he never allowed any inclination towards estrangement to become real.

After Bishop left the hushed room in the Palace Hotel in San Francisco in shocked bereavement at the death of Kalakaua, he wrote a beautiful letter of condolence and warm comfort to Liliuokalani. It is a letter of more than ordinary value for it presents a clue to the real relationship between Liliuokalani and the husband of her foster sister. There was a strong feeling of deference and affection. This letter was dated January 20, 1891:

To Queen Liliuokalani

My Sovereign and friend—

The failing health of your Royal Brother for some months past may have in some measure prepared your mind for unfavorable news regarding him, and the half masted flag of the good ship *Charleston* will have published the sad news before this reaches you, and joyful anticipations will have given way to painful apprehension and grief.

Until a week ago I thought that the King had improved in health, and no doubt the bracing climate did give him increased strength for a while, and the pleasant excitement from kind attentions of friends, and seeing new and interesting things and places kept him up, but the fatal disease was only biding its time, and when it renewed its attack was inevitable and did its work quickly, and, I am glad to say, without causing pain. He died at 2:35 P.M. today, surrounded by friends ready and anxious to do everything to promote his comfort and, if possible, prolong his life.

The care and attention of Admiral Brown could not have been more constant and tender had the King been his brother or son. And the King was not lacking in precaution and care for himself. Dr. Wood stayed with him night and day, and called in two superior physicians for consultation. Col. Macfarlane, Hooapili, the servants, nurse and friends were in constant attendance. Nothing more or better could have been done for him had he been at home. In offering to yourself, to Kapiolani and other relatives and friends my condolence and respectful sympathy, I have great satisfaction in knowing that both on the voyage and during the sojourn here in this State, nothing has been omitted which kindness and friendship could suggest to make the journey and visit profitable, beneficial, or agreeable, and that the fatal sickness did not originate after his departure from home.

I wrote to Kaiulani this afternoon, and will send her a newspaper giving particulars.

Your knowledge of affairs, and the confidence which the people have in your regard for the general welfare of the country, will make your high office with its great responsibilities comparatively easy. It is a loyal community, native and foreign, and should be united in every patriotic and righteous purpose; and I am very hopeful that it will be. That Your majesty may be spared many years to reign over a prosperous, improving and contented people, shall be my constant prayer.

> I have the honor to be
> Your obedient servant
> Chas. R. Bishop.

P. S.

On receipt of this you will not have been proclaimed as Sovereign (Queen) but you *are* virtually in that position. I write you more from the impulse of old friendship than from duty as a subject, and as it is not for official or public use, you will, I trust, pardon informalities.

> C. R. B.

At 8:15 A.M. on January 29, 1891, the Diamond Head telephones announced the appearance of the U. S. S. *Charleston* off Koko Head with the American and Hawaiian flags at half mast. The cruiser rounded Diamond Head with yards cock-billed, and shortly the body of Kalakaua was back in his native land. Before the day was over Liliuokalani had taken the oath to uphold the Constitution and was sworn in as Queen of Hawaii.

Bishop was not a member of a party or political group, but he sincerely wanted the royal government to prosper. A few days after Liliuokalani's accession to the throne, he makes the following hopeful reference to her. It was written February 5, 1891, to James Lurth of the Board of Education:

. . . The present Queen has a great opportunity for a useful honorable, and happy reign, and I seriously hope that she will improve it. By good example, by conservatism and a faithful observance of law, she will succeed, and be a blessing to her race and to the whole community.

He mentioned Liliuokalani again that day in a letter to William Brigham:

. . . The Queen (Liliuokalani) has a rare opportunity for usefulness and honor. She is old enough to be good, cautious and conservative, and I trust that she will not listen to bad advice, nor disappoint the hopes of her best friends.

Then in response to a long letter from Liliuokalani, Bishop wrote a reply.* His letter, dated March 5, 1891, is probably the finest as well as the longest letter to come from his pen. It is worded in the gentle language of a guardian; it reveals an observant, sensitive concern not only for the welfare of this distinguished member of the royal

---

* See Appendix, pp. 343–347.

family but also for the reputation and progress of the Kingdom of Hawaii.

A year passed and Bishop continued in his high hopes. He wrote to his favorite "niece" Victoria Kaiulani, April 7, 1892: ". . . The Queen is much interested in the Schools, particularly in the girls' school at Kawaiahao. She is liked and respected by the better part of the people, native and foreign. . . ." But a storm broke out suddenly on January 14, 1893. The Queen declared her intention of abrogating the Constitution. This announcement lifted the antagonisms to a plane of open strife. There had been considerable dissension among the several political factions; Ministers were changed with the calendar; opium and lottery bills were finally passed. The Queen would probably have survived all these vicissitudes of economic and racial intrigue—she was a strong, mature leader—had she not determined to rid her rule of the Constitution which had been forced upon Kalakaua in 1887 and which even then she roundly condemned.

George N. Wilcox, Mark Robinson, Cecil Brown, and P. C. Jones, conservative men of high character, were appointed to the Queen's cabinet in November, 1892. This move brought great satisfaction to Bishop, and he wrote to that effect to P. C. Jones, December 9: "I was very pleased to know that you and Geo. Wilcox had accepted office, and that you had Robinson and Brown as colleagues. . . ." He freely discussed Hawaii's sugar problem and the need of a treaty if a duty were placed upon sugar. And a week later he wrote to Jones again:

. . . The frequent changes of Ministry and other disturbing acts and reports, with the impression that the business of the country is not prospering have injured the credit of the Govt. abroad. . . .

He continued to worry. February 18, 1893, in a letter to C. M. Hyde,* he said:

. . . The laws must apply equally to natives and *haoles*, but a restricted suffrage applicable to both may be necessary or best. The Queen astonished me. . . . Much as I dread it, annexation to this country [United States] seems to be the wisest action suggested, so far for all concerned. . . .

This was really a startling position for him to take and certainly very surprising in view of his life-long hope of a sturdy, independent,

* See p. 54.

Hawaiian nation. But a fearful revolution had followed Liliuoka-lani's abrogation of the Constitution of 1887 and the proroguing of the Legislature. January, 1893, was a dark month in Hawaiian history. Bishop wrote another letter to Hyde, February 23, on annexation again:

> . . . It looks to me that the best interests of native and *haoles* will be promoted by annexation to the United States in the most liberal terms obtainable; . . . I cannot see security and permanency of Govt. in any other course.

Bishop was swinging around the continent. He had left San Francisco in the middle of February and visited Hampton Institute in Virginia, then stopped at Washington, D. C., New York, and Chicago. He was back in San Francisco early in March, 1893. Events in Hawaii had him guessing. President Cleveland's reluctance to make a decision only aggravated his perplexity. A provisional government was organized by the newly formed Committee of Safety, and its function was to contain the governmental processes until terms of union were agreed upon with the United States of America. Its action was backed up by the arrival of American troops under authority of United States Minister John C. Stevens. By coincidence these troops were quartered in "Haleakala," formerly the residence of the Bishops.

The Provisional Government arranged a treaty in Washington on February 14, 1893, but the United States Senate failed to act in sufficient time. President Harrison gave way to the newly elected President Cleveland; and he, acting with the advice of Walter Q. Gresham, Secretary of State, withdrew the treaty and decided to have a survey made of all shades of opinion in Hawaii. A special emissary, James H. Blount, was assigned the mission and left immediately for Hawaii. With all this either taking place or promising to, Bishop carried his usual worry. To Hyde, March 29, he said: "Fear that the Provisional Govt. may not be able to maintain its position and authority until it is decided what the U. S. Govt. will do makes me very anxious."

In the first of a long series of letters to W. D. Alexander * he commented September 2:

* William DeWitt Alexander, L. L. D. Born April 2, 1833, died February 22, 1913. Member of a missionary family; Instructor, President, and Trustee of Oahu College; Surveyor-General of Hawaii 1871–1901; distinguished in the history, ethnology, and folk-lore of the Polynesian race.

. . . If Mr. Gresham intends to make a careful study of the Blount's report, it will take a good deal of time. . . . Claus Spreckels . . . will, no doubt, do all he can to defeat the efforts of the Provisional Govt. . . . I suspect that some of the threatening rumors are gotten up by the royalists to worry the Authorities. . . . The Administration could greatly oblige the Americans in the islands if they would declare their views and purposes, and end the trying and damaging suspense which has now lasted more than half a year. . . .

A week later he wrote to Alexander again:

. . . .

. . . A Protectorate seems to be the form favored, and our people will have to try to make that as good as possible. . . . Hawaii under a protectorate or independent will want *liberal reciprocity* with the U. S. . . . It remains though to see . . . what kind of a government can be secured *to protect*. . . . I believe Mr. Spreckels has gone on to prevent annexation. . . . To hear him talk and boast one not knowing better might think that he carried the president, his Cabinet and the Senate in his trousers pocket!

The wobbly Provisional Government was facing possible failure. September 27, Bishop addressed another letter to Alexander, who had gone to Washington as an emissary on Hawaii's future:

. . . .

. . . If Mr. Cleveland sends a message to the Senate I am at a loss to know what it can amount to. . . . To restore the monarchy and put the queen back again may look like a simple thing to do, . . . conspiracy and revolution would be likely to occur again. . . . To wait and hang on, as the Texans did, may not be possible. We must deal with the United States Govt. in some way, for we cannot do anything with any other great power. If it is possible to make a binding and reasonable agreement with Kaiulani about the Crown lands, her allowance and general policy, etc., it may be much safer than to take a vote of the people with the chance of getting the "ex queen" back. . . .

With annexation unobtainable it seems to me that a compromise with monarchy (Kaiulani at the head if possible) is the thing most likely to lead to good order, quiet and prosperity: . . .

The next letter in the Alexander series was dated October 3:

. . . If those obstructionists in the senate would let a vote be taken on the Silver Repeal Bill, we might soon learn what we may have to expect from the Administration on Hawaiian affairs. . . .

Mr. Atherton is here. The suggestion to agree with Kaiulani and give her a chance to rule, does not find favor with my Honolulu friends.

Having read Blount's report by this time, President Cleveland seemed to have concluded that Liliuokalani should go back on the throne and a reverse trend given to the effects of the revolution. He therefore selected a new Minister, Albert S. Willis, and sent him to Hawaii with instructions to act. But Willis was powerless. The Provisional Government refused to surrender its mantle of rule. With a rather remarkable maturity the leaders of the Provisional Government had achieved a stable climate in political affairs in the Islands. Upon the occasion of Willis' visit, the government officials strongly attacked Blount's statement; and they also maintained that the United States was meddling unnecessarily in Hawaiian matters.

Bishop had a sense of prophetic understanding of men and events. He was still in San Francisco when he wrote once again to Alexander, November 1:

. . . It is not likely that the U. S. Govt. will interfere actively in the domestic affairs of Hawaii; but a message anything like what the Herald says it will be, will be a strong moral support to the Queen and her party, and may give them such encouragement as to lead to great disorder and damage.

Matters were not improving; Bishop sent a telegram on November 8, to Alexander of the Hawaiian Legation, Washington D. C.:

If reported intended action at Honolulu by U. S. Govt. is true very serious trouble not anticipated by the President may ensue. Try to communicate with and warn him promptly who will be responsible for loss of life and property which may come and which can be prevented by different course adopted immediately.

He followed this with a letter the next day:

. . . The U. S. should stand by the P. G.* until something safe for life . . . can be secured. If annexation or protectorate are impracticable at present, something else may be brought about by compromise and the friendly influence of the U. S. But to suddenly withdraw recognition and leave those who have taken part in the revolution and the P. G. to the will and tender mercies of the irritated and hungry royalists, is not what the Americans had a right to expect. There has been a good deal said about Liliuokalani in which I have not sympathized, and have not approved: . . . The present administration in Washington has kept representatives of Hawaii at arms length. . . .

Mr. Blount's way of getting information was peculiar. It was not by a free conversation or by requiring written statements, but by leading questions framed by himself, and with no cross-questioning by other counsel. . . .

See Mr. Gresham if you can, and have a *free talk with* him. They (the Prest. & Cabinet) *must want to do the right thing,* but may have

* Provisional Government.

done that which they will regret. I was not an Annexationist until after the Queen had been deposed for violating the constitution.

Earlier in the year, Kaiulani accompanied by Theophilus H. Davies, her English guardian, made a quick trip from England to Washington D. C. to see President Cleveland. The idea of the visit was urged upon Kaiulani by her guardian and his correspondents among the conservatives in Hawaii, who hoped that in some unexpected way she might serve to sidetrack the annexationists. But history was not to be so written; and Kaiulani returned to England and the continent, eventually coming home to Hawaii in 1897, feeling very much a stranger in a strange land. Bishop's concern for Kaiulani's welfare prompted a comment to Alexander, November 9: ". . . I think the withholding of all allowances for support of Kaiulani has been mean and a mistake, but they go to prove the feeling against any return of native rule. . . ."

Mr. Willis had arrived in Honolulu; and in a November 25 letter to Alexander, Bishop maintained that Willis was a bit evasive:

. . . .
. . . Up to the sailing of the "Alameda" 16th inst. Mr. Willis had not made the P. G. acquainted with his instructions and intentions—but had given out some *ominous hints* which the royalists interpret as the intention to restore Liliuokalani to power, but which the P. G., the Americans and other Annexationists *cannot* believe mean anything so bad and so unfriendly to them as that. . . .
. . . The secret and unfriendly action of the Administration so far leads one to fear the worst, . . .
It seems to me that Kaiulani and Mr. Davies captured the President and he made up his mind then. . . .
I regret that the Queen was not persuaded to abdicate in favor of Kaiulani last January. If she would now through fear or for any other reason compromise and get out of the way; it might be best to accept the Princess in her stead.
Mr. Atherton has been in to say goodbye as he is going home. He is much more hopeful than I am, and will not believe that the Queen is to be reinstated by order of the President, while *I think* that the deed has already been done. If Mr. Willis has reported to Washington and is waiting for further orders (which I do not believe) my opinion is that she will not be restored—Congress would not authorize such action.

Hon. W. D. Alexander was Bishop's principal correspondent during 1893, and the exchange continued to the middle of 1894. And so did the indecision and the frustration and the jockeying! Bishop was in San Francisco, Alexander was in Washington, and the chief trouble spot was Hawaii. Communication by ship's mail was still the fastest between Hawaii and California; between California and Washington, the telegraph. Yet despite all the lag in communication there was a close and ready awareness of current movements, trends, and actions. Bishop complained of the editorial treatment accorded the Provisional Government by the popular magazine, *The Nation.* He roundly criticized Blount and his methods of gathering information, and he was not particularly complimentary to the Queen. He was to continue to hope that she might be of a mind to rule impartially and skillfully, and yet he felt she could not now lead her country. He deplored the Opium Bill. The Lottery Bill was repugnant to him. He believed she schemed to rid the government of the Wilcox-Jones ministry:

. . . and then her purposes with regard to the constitution, . . . no doubt she knew about and encouraged the Wilcox revolt! . . . I do not think the P. G. will give up unless it is *certain* that the U. S. will use force if they resist. . . .

So wrote Bishop on December 2, to Alexander. Then a few weeks later, on December 26, another series of comments:

. . . The P. G. seems doomed to suspense and consequent expense. . . . The ex-queen has had good reason for her confidence as to restoration, and will not give it up at once . . . and she has a number of would-be office holders who are hungry, and they are advisors. Did I believe that we could have peace, security and justice under her reign, I would not object to her restoration, . . . but I do not so believe. I would prefer to try Kaiulani if it could be safely and satisfactorily arranged.

There is no doubt but that a large majority in this Country are opposed to annexation of Hawaii. Many friends of the islands are opposed to annexing detached or far-away territory . . . but what is the U. S. going to do about it? They cannot wish to see the islands go into other hands, nor to see them torn, . . . ruined by strife, mis-government or oft-recurring revolution or conspiracy. It is hardly possible that Congress will force upon the people a monarch who *did her best* to destroy a Constitution under which she was safe and could have ruled to the end of her days—but the President's friends say that the P. G. is "not a Republic," and that is pretty nearly true!

There are objections to annexation from an Hawaiian as well as from an American standpoint. . . . Abandonment in favor of Britain, though much against the wishes and feeling of Americans and the descendants of Americans, might not be so very bad for them—but the thought of being "Gobbled up" by Japan, or any of the European Powers, is too horrible to think of.

The President made up his mind *early* to restore the queen, and acted under prejudice—without, I think intending to do wrong or injury, and I think that Mr. Blount partook of that prejudice from the start, and never quite recovered from it.

I cannot think that the President or Mr. Gresham or Mr. Blount are intentionally unfriendly to their Countrymen in Hawaii, and yet by their singular treatment of them and the questions which grew out of the Revolution, they have done them wrong and harm.

Mr. Stevens was an ardent annexationist because he believed that Hawaii was drifting into disorder, and into the hands of one or other of the Great Powers. . . .

But the doldrum of charge and countercharge continued. Sanford B. Dole summarized the relative positions of the United States and the Provisional Government in his famous "Letter of Specifications" of January 11, 1894. Bishop followed this with a letter to Alexander, who was still in Washington. Bishop was departing for Hawaii the next day; the letter was dated January 29:

. . . . . .

The paper of this mor'g says that the President will instruct Mr. Willis to demand the withdrawal etc. of the letter of Prest. Dole which Mr. Cleveland and Mr. Willis have characterized as "most extraordinary.". . . Since the letter has been published it cannot be blotted out. . . . But Hawaii is at a serious disadvantage in any disagreement or misunderstanding with the U. S. Govt. . . . Annexation seems to me *very far off.* I very *often* meet men of character and influence. . . . They are afraid to begin annexing *detached* territory. . . .

With our population monarchical Govt. properly guarded and conducted is better than a republican form with free suffrage. . . . I shall go home with a heavy heart and a perplexed mind. . . .

Matters continued uncertainly for many weeks, but it was apparent that Hawaii would not be annexed while Mr. Cleveland was president. On March 15, an act was passed by the Provisional Government providing for the holding of a constitutional convention. The convention consisting largely of supporters of the philosophy of the existing government met May 30. To Alexander, on April 4, Bishop commented (he had returned to San Francisco on March 2 and was not again to return to Hawaii):

. . . . . .

. . . The natives should unite with their old friends to protect themselves against the strangers and injustice. I hope that many of them will vote to elect delegates to the Convention and that a number of good natives will be elected. . . .

It is a difficult task to form a stable Govt. under such circumstances—but as the leaders of the P. G. want to do that which is right and safe I shall hope for their success. If the leading natives are wise they will help their old friends and not be misled.

On July 4, 1894, the new Constitution was promulgated and made effective. Largely the work of President Dole and Lorrin A. Thurston, it also represented Bishop's views. This was the Constitution of the new Republic of Hawaii. To Alexander, on July 15, Bishop wrote:

. . . The situation there [Honolulu] is far from satisfactory. . . . There has been too little made of the *political acts* of the queen which led to the revolution, and too much said about her private habits.

. . . The outlook is bad in every direction. . . . The only safe thing, and the best for both countries is, *Annexation* to the U. S. under Territorial form of Govt! and next to that, a strong Protectorate applying to both internal and external affairs,—especially the former. . . . Within twenty years the statesmen of the time will be surprised and will regret that annexation was not secured, if it is refused now.

It has become *necessary* for some outside power to give stability and security to the Govt. in Hawaii. I am very sorry that it is so—but I cannot blink or change the fact.

The Bishop comments cease for many months. Opposition to the newly formed government of Hawaii simmered for a few months and then erupted. Robert Wilcox, Samuel Nowlein and a number of other opposition inspired men launched a serious and tragic attack upon the citizenry and government facilities on the island of Oahu, the night of January 6, 1895. It had all the elements of a filibustering expedition. C. L. Carter was killed in the landing and attack off Diamond Head. The leaders were captured, and the ex-Queen was arrested.

In a letter to Alexander, January 18, 1895, Bishop stated: ". . . The Govt. under the Republic is gradually gaining strength and is quite able to protect and maintain itself. Mr. Spreckels says it is not a republic and cannot stand—but it does stand. . . ." The Republic was at this very time proving his faith in its ability to stand fast in time of trouble as in the instance of this abortive Wilcox and Nowlein rebellion.

Liliuokalani was held in palace custody for a few months, after which she left for the United States. Writing to J. O. Carter, Bishop described his visit with her on her stopover in San Francisco:

. . . I called upon the ex-Queen at the California Hotel and had a pleasant chat with her. She seems to be in good health and enjoying change of climate, and will, I suppose, be going Eastward soon. I am told that some of the newspapers have taken it upon themselves to say that I am opposed to the "Dole Government," probably because they knew I called on the ex-Queen. I have not considered it necessary to publish any correction of their statements, and I do not know that her visit or journeys has any political significance or consequence. . . .

Not until May 15, 1897, does he speak again of Liliuokalani, this time to his Molokai Ranch manager, R. W. Meyer:

. . . Speaking of the ex-Queen who is still at the East, I suspect that she is supported in part by someone who is opposed to Annexation and Reciprocity. She may be willing to give her influence in opposition to Annexation, and it is possible that she is opposed to Reciprocity though I cannot see why. I believe that Captain Palmer is supported in the same way and for the same reason. . . .

Reciprocity and its high advantage to Hawaii was ever on his mind. He wrote to Rev. Hyde this same day:

There is reason for doubt and anxiety regarding what may be the action of the Congress upon the Treaty of Reciprocity between the United States and Hawaii. I cannot believe that the benefits of the Treaty will be cut off through the provision of the pending Tariff Act. . . .

McKinley had been elected President in 1896, largely on a protective tariff platform. It was this potential danger to the highly favorable Reciprocity Treaty that Bishop had in mind. Powerful interests in the United States opposed both the existing treaty and any future thought of annexation. But the course was set, and the war with Spain was the final nudge. On July 7, 1898, President McKinley signed the joint resolution of Congress establishing annexation.

Liliuokalani had remained in Washington, living in quiet, unostentatious style. She was writing the story of her life, and when this was published Bishop wrote to Brigham, March 11:

Liliuokalani has sent me her two books and I shall e'er long send them to the Museum Library. She must have had a good deal of help from Captain Palmer. It is quite evident.

The other of the two books is a line-by-line translation of the Kalakaua text of the Hawaiian genealogical prayer chant "Kumulipo." It was privately printed for a limited list of friends and scientific libraries. Liliuokalani was unable to cope with the politics of the McKinley regime and the emotions generated by the war with Spain. Seeing the inevitable threat of annexation, she decided to return to Hawaii. Her annual allowance from Hawaii was used up, and she wrote to Bishop for a temporary loan to finance the return to her homeland. On July 5, 1898, he wrote that he had made necessary provisions for the funds and advised her with regard to tickets, reservations, and sailing schedules.

The transfer of sovereignty from the Republic to Territory took place at high noon, August 12, 1898, following which, on April 20, 1900, Congress passed the Organic Act for the direction of the new Territory of Hawaii. On June 14, 1900, Sanford B. Dole took the oath as first Governor of the new Territory.

By this time Liliuokalani was resigned to the changing character of the times to which Hawaii had been introduced. She lived on in Honolulu for many years, passing away November 11, 1917. Throughout her life, Bishop had conscientiously played his role as her financial counsellor. She in turn was pleased to visit the Museum and The Kamehameha Schools, the latter particularly on December 19 each year, when the children commemorated the birthday of their benefactress, her foster sister, Bernice Pauahi Bishop. Liliuokalani was true to her deepest instincts, to her deepest love, and her deepest loyalty, Hawaii and her people. Whether her judgment led her astray or not, her "brother-in-law," Charles Reed Bishop, never lost his optimism and his hope that she might indeed succeed to a reasonable and honorable stature as ruler of her people.

VICTORIA KAIULANI—ALII

OCTOBER 16, 1875, is the birth date of her Royal Highness Princess Victoria Kaiulani. March 6, 1899, is the date of her death. In these short twenty-four years this rather frail and beautiful princess cut a sentimental swath through the hearts of Hawaiians and foreigners alike. Robert Louis Stevenson was very fond of her and composed some of his finest verse in her honor.

The daughter of Princess Likelike and Archibald Cleghorn, and niece of Liliuokalani, she was also regarded as a niece of Bernice Pauahi Bishop. This gave Charles Reed Bishop the status of uncle, a relationship of which he was very proud. His pride was in part affection; it was also summed up in his feeling that she represented more than any other royal person the conservatives' hope of re-establishing a native monarchy. The possibility that Kaiulani might assume the regency was never discussed between the two, at least in correspondence. Bishop's references to the subject were almost exclusively contained in letters to W. D. Alexander.*

Niece Kaiulani and Uncle Charles did maintain a warm and friendly personal correspondence. One interesting letter was to Kaiulani in Midlothian, Scotland, April 7, 1892:

My dear Niece,
The Queen [Liliuokalani] is much interested in the schools, particularly in the girls school at Kawaiahao. She is liked and respected by the better part of the people—native and foreign. A few like Wilcox and Bush are dissatisfied because they do not get appointed to places for which they are not fitted. . . .

[s]Charles

The above is the only letter of the Bishop correspondence in which he signed himself "Charles." He invariably signed himself "Chas. R. Bishop." He spoke his mind to her March 27, 1896:

It would surprise and grieve me were I to be told that you had gambled either at Monte Carlo or at any other place. Monte Carlo is a beautiful place, and the music there is sometimes beautiful; but it is a very sad sight to see the playing at the tables especially that by the hard-faced and bony-handed old people, men and women. . . . You are right in taking advantage of every proper opportunity for using and improving your knowledge of French and German. It is a very good thing to always have a course of study in hand systematically in addition to the usual reading, etc. etc.

It is probable that the Legislature now in Session in Honolulu will vote to give you $2000 per annum. I wish it were to be more, but I know that they have many pressing calls for money, and I hope that such a sum with your other income will meet your necessary expenses and make you comfortable.

It was not for anxiety for the return of any of the money which I sent you [he had sent her 200 English pounds at her request] that I wrote you as I did, but to impress you with the importance of carefulness about expenses and to warn you against relying at all upon borrowing. Most ladies are poor economists. . . .

* See pp. 84–88.

A little later that year, August 3, he wrote to her again: ". . . It is good to be occupied so that unprofitable thoughts may be crowded out. Your Uncle Charles is getting old and forgetful and cares more for old friends than new ones." His concern for Kaiulani's welfare was genuine. Politics in Hawaii in 1897 were boiling, and the presence of a royal princess might serve to inflame elements of the populace. The clouds of war were hanging over the youthful republic. Upon hearing of her plan to return he got off a letter to J. O. Carter, June 11, 1897:

. . . . . .

I have lately heard from Mr. Holmes and Judge Widemann that Kaiulani is intending to return to Honolulu next Fall. I hope that it is not so, but that she will remain in Europe at least a year or two more. I am confident that Mr. Davies would not advise her to return to the Islands at present.

Probably her father wants to get back and does not like to leave her behind. It is my opinion that it would be a great mistake for her to return at present, or until some considerable time to come.

He was always very fond of the Princess Kaiulani, and he poured out his affection to her in a correspondence which provides a remarkable picture of a sweet relationship between an old man and a young girl. Her passing on March 6, 1899, at the age of twenty-four, brought an untimely end to that beautiful friendship. The Trustees under the Will of Mrs. Bishop requested of Uldrick Thompson by resolution that he ask:

. . . the boys of the Kamehameha Manual School attend in a body, in uniform, the funeral of the late Princess Kaiulani on Sunday afternoon next, accompanied by the Kamehameha band and subject to the order of Major Potter who has charge of the ceremonies.

A touching tribute is found in a Bishop letter to Cleghorn, March 20, 1899. Word of Kaiulani's passing had arrived in correspondence from Honolulu:

. . . . . .

On every hand I hear expressions of sorrow and disappointment and of real sympathy for yourself, your family and the many friends of the deceased princess. You know that I was strongly attached to dear Kaiulani, and most interested in her welfare and happiness. It is sad! Sad indeed! to see such a promising young life cut off! She was the last of the young *Aliis* of high rank. By good sense and tact added to intelligence and spotless character she had made so favorable an impression on all classes of people that I was hopeful that after all the severe disappointments of late years she was yet to enjoy many years of pleasant and useful life.

The disposition lately shown by people of influence to do her justice gave promise of securing adequate means for her proper support, and it must have been gratifying to her as well as to yourself.

During all her young life you were fond and proud of the dear child and lived largely for her sake. I wish that you were at the present time fully employed in business or something of importance occupying your time and thoughts to help you to bear and recover from the crushing blow. You are fortunate in having others more or less dependent upon you. Care for them with the healing influences of time will with God's blessing do more for your relief than anything that friends can say—

With sincere sympathy, I remain, in grief,

Very truly yours,
[Signed] Chas. R. Bishop

Kaiulani's early demise prostrated the Hawaiians. A light and a hope had gone out of their lives. Her father, in clearing up her pitifully small estate, performed a very noble, unselfish act. It was not common knowledge that Bishop had presented his own wife's jewels to Kaiulani as dowry. Kaiulani had selected a few to wear and placed others in storage. Cleghorn now offered to dispose of Mrs. Bishop's jewels in any way that Bishop desired. This offer drew forth the request that they be placed safely in the Bishop Museum with cards stating how and why they came to be there.

Bishop exhibited understandable readiness when Ida M. Pope, principal of The Kamehameha School for Girls, suggested the need of a home * for graduates who were either working or going to business college or normal school. His first reaction however, was expressive of his caution and was contained in a letter to Carter, November 8, 1900:

In referring to the Kaiulani Home for girls I had not thought out the method and have not yet decided as to the best way. The girls and their relatives should do *all they can* in taking care of themselves. While I desire that the Home should have a fair trial and wish it success, I am not disposed to help healthy people to an easy or too cheap living. To provide a safe and wholesome home for good industrious young women is the purpose as I understand it; and while I would prefer to favor those for whom so much has been done at the Kamehameha School, I would not like to give them the impression that they are always to be protected. The *world* does *not owe* any (ablebodied) person a living. The Home is not exclusively for Kamehameha Girls.

* See pp. 182–183.

Time and Miss Pope served to modify Bishop's thinking. On April 24, 1903, again he addressed himself to Carter while on a trip to the Mainland:

. . . .

A late letter from Miss Pope telling me of the steps taken towards opening a new Home for girls graduating from the boarding and Normal Schools, who intend to work for an honest living pleases me very much and I have had a little talk with Mrs. Henry Waterhouse, who is enthusiastic on the subject. Such good women as Mrs. F. W. Macfarlane, Mrs. S. C. Allen and others of their class cannot do a more useful thing to their race and the community than to stir up an interest in such girls and such a safe home for them, until they can have other homes and pro-tectors. . . .

. . . .

On the same day he addressed himself to Miss Pope in highly complimentary fashion about the reported progress of the Kaiulani Home:

I am very much pleased with what you tell me has been done toward establishing the Kaiulani Home for young Women. The people chosen for officers, the location secured and the idea of starting in a small way are all good and right and I am very hopeful of success and good work. . . . Your hands and heart and time are fully occupied with girls already; many others need to be and should be in the service for their own good and the public good. . . . If Carnegie would give me leave I would help him to place some of his surplus where it would surely do good. . . . Congratulating you upon the prospect of opening a Home for the educated girls—a need which has given you much thought and great anxiety.

Bishop's interest in the well-being of young Hawaiian women resulted in a recognizable upgrading of their status. He supported many enterprises devoted to them, and the Kaiulani Home was one of the best examples. A little later, on May 25, 1905, he wrote again to Carter:

You know how greatly Hawaiian girls need friends and protectors after they leave the schools in which they have been educated, . . . it seems desirable and important that the Kaiulani Home for young women should be enlarged to accommodate a greater number and have a suitable build-ing of its own convenient locality and clear of debt or rent so as to estab-lish it on a more permanent basis. . . . This object must appeal strongly to the good women of the Islands and the management should be entirely in their hands. . . . I have had some conversation and correspondence with Miss Pope on this subject, and they know what I am willing to do.

He subsequently offered $5,000 to a group of civic-minded women under the leadership of Miss Pope, August 28, 1905. if $15,000 were raised by October 1, 1905. The funds were raised; the Kaiulani Home for Girls was opened October 16 and chartered December 15, 1905, at the Hopper estate site (presently Library of Hawaii). Two years later the present site, adjacent to the first mission homes, was improved with a $25,000 building. Bishop remembered the Home in his preparation of the Charles R. Bishop Trust deed. He authorized, under the direction of the Trustees, a maximum annual payment of $1,000 for the term of the Trust. Payments actually had begun in 1903, and when they were cut off in 1942, $33,500 had been paid in. Added to the $5,000 subscription in 1905, the total was $38,500. Hands across the years were clasped when The Kamehameha Schools were granted the temporary full use of the property and income of the Kaiulani Trust in 1950 for the purpose of housing Kamehameha girls as boarding students.

THE PRIVY COUNCIL

GROWING PAINS IN business were elementary compared to what was happening in government in the Kingdom of Hawaii. The interlacing of business and royalty drew Bishop into government with both a sense of reluctance and obligation. It was not easy for him to share business time with government pursuits; and yet, through his wife's royal family connection and his usual willingness to serve, he accepted assignments. And who can say but that he felt gratification in the many orders which were bestowed upon him or that he took pride in attending formal state functions in cutaway coat with the broad riband denoting some particular order. He was most helpful to the political needs of the Kingdom through his membership on the Privy Council and the House of Nobles. There were many commissions and ministerships and committees that demanded his time off and on; but the Privy councillorship and membership in the House of Nobles were the keys to his service.

Some of the entries relating to Bishop that were made in the Privy

Council Reports between 1849 and 1859 covered personal business transactions. Others dealt with his official life as Collector General and Commissioner of Customs.* The most significant of these items appeared in the Reports, January 10, 1859:

. . . Mr. Charles R. Bishop appeared and took the usual Oath of a Privy Counsellor [*sic*] as follows:

Oath

I, Charles R. Bishop, do solemnly swear on the Holy Evangelists, to support the Constitution; and to observe strict secrecy in regard to all matters coming to my knowledge as a Privy Counsellor upon which a special injunction shall have been imposed by the King.

[signed] Chas. R. Bishop

Subscribed and sworn to me by Chas. R. Bishop at a meeting of the Privy Council held in the Palace, this 10th day of January A.D. 1859 before me G. M. Robertson Associate Justice of the Supreme Court.

[Appointment by Kamehameha IV]

The Privy Council was provided for in the first of three Organic Acts passed by the Legislature on October 29, 1845. It started business in March, 1846, when Bishop was but a month out of Newburyport, Massachusetts. Mr. John Ricord described as a "lawyer of promising genius," had addressed the Legislature on May 20, 1845, on a ponderous subject: "Inferences of the Constitution and the Implied Powers and Duties of the King." The Constitution referred to was the first written constitution of the Kingdom and had gone into effect in 1840. Ricord suggested three successive alterations which the Legislature designated "Organic Acts." John Ricord's "alterations" were treated with the greatest seriousness. The fact that the three recommendations proposed the organization of an *Executive Ministry, Executive Department,* and a *Judiciary Department* is evidence that the islanders were groping with the rudiments of a democratic political philosophy that supplied a remarkable parallel to political discussions three-quarters of a century earlier in the halls of Colonial America. Here was the germ of the checks and balances principle inherent in the executive, legislative, and judicial divisions established in the Constitution of the United States of America.

The Privy Council was composed of the heads of the five executive departments (named in Organic Act #1 as Interior, Foreign Affairs, Finance, Public Instruction, and Attorney General), gov-

---

* See pp. 20–21.

ernors of the four islands, and a few honorary members appointed by the King. This Privy Council was an outgrowth of the old Council of Chiefs which had operated as a strong executive committee for the King. It was now modified and greatly strengthened and was to constitute a very powerful agency of Hawaiian government for some years to come. It was similar to a cabinet, in one sense, and an executive committee in another.

Under the Constitution of 1852 (the second one), the honorary members were still appointed by the King; but the power to legalize or nullify the acts of the King was added. Also, ministers and governors were now members ex-officio of the Privy Council. The powers of the Privy Council were greatly diminished in the Constitution of 1864: the King could make appointments without the approval of the Council. The power to vote appropriations during the adjournment recesses of the Legislative Assembly was granted to the Council, but this was not the source of much more than prestige. In the Constitution of 1887 the Privy Council was limited to concurrence in granting pardons, and its number was set at twenty-four. In the turmoil of 1893, and the subsequent changeover to a republic, the Privy Council disappeared.

Bishop was absent more often than present at meetings during his first year (1859) on the Council, but his record following that was probably unsurpassed by any member. His membership extended without a break from 1859 through 1892. Unlike commissions to membership in the House of Nobles, the successive rulers named anew the members of the Privy Council. Thus, Bishop was commissioned a "Member of Our Privy Council," by Kamehameha V, on December 7, 1863; by Lunalilo, on January 22, 1873; Kalakaua, on February 23, 1874; and Liliuokalani, on March 7, 1891.

Few formal actions referring to Bishop are to be found in the Minute Books. One, however, is interesting since it points up a serious concern of the day. Kalakaua appointed Bishop and four others as commissioners for the unpromising mission of devising a program to increase the Hawaiian race. In the Legislative Assembly, September 9, 1876, the Attorney General introduced a "Resolution, for the appointment by His Majesty of a Committee on 'Hooulu Lahui,' or increase-of-the-race matters." The Privy Council picked it up on November 11, when His Excellency W. L. Green introduced the Legislature's resolution:

Whereas; It is the expressed desire of His Majesty the King, to arrest the decrease of the Hawaiian People and to devise means for the increase of the Original Stock in these Islands. . . .

Therefore, be it Resolved; That His Majesty in Privy Council may appoint a commission of at least five discreet and well known persons of this Kingdom to devise ways and means by which to arrest the decrease and decay of the Original Hawaiian Race. . . .

Commissioned;

H. R. H. Prince Leleiohoku
His Ex. W. R. Castle
Hon. C. R. Bishop
Rev. H. H. Parker
Rev. M. Kuaea

Nothing resulted from the committee on the "Hooulu Lahui," assignment. Some years later Kapiolani linked an informal organization known as the Hooulu Lahui Society to her maternity home project.*

Bishop's Privy Council membership was to offer a stability and steadiness to royal finances, which in turn generally tended to keep the economics and the politics of the Kingdom in a fairly even balance. It was not always true, notably in the Kalakaua era when Bishop felt so ineffectual that he and Mrs. Bishop left for a two-year jaunt to America and Europe shortly after Kalakaua's assumption of the kingship. Participation in Privy Council proceedings was a significant key to Bishop's constructive financial assistance and orientation of the members of the two kingly dynasties of Hawaii.

THE HOUSE OF NOBLES

Bishop was contemporary with the American missionaries although not one of them. There were striking parallels in the ideals and practical working ideas of both, particularly in a shared concern for the general well-being of the Hawaiian rulers and lesser nobility. In his role of counsellor he undoubtedly kept the royal dynasties steady in administration. It was his opportunity for more than thirty years to advise the regents as a member of the Privy Council and to

* See p. 279.

have a hand in legislative deliberation as a member of the House of Nobles. He was, therefore, in a strong counselling position in both the executive and the legislative branches of the government simultaneously for a long period of time.

The first written Constitution (1840) provided for a House of Nobles and a House of Representatives in a legislative branch of the government. A law in 1850 empowered the Ministers to sit in the House of Nobles. The Constitution of 1852 provided that the King would appoint the Nobles for life, and the number of Nobles was limited to thirty. The House of Nobles was also authorized to sit as the Court of Impeachment. In the Constitution of 1864, the Nobles and Representatives were directed to constitute themselves a unicameral legislative body. The title of the new body was officially given as Legislative Assembly, and at this time the number of Nobles was reduced to twenty. In the Constitution of 1887, many changes were introduced as far as the Nobles were concerned: their number was increased to twenty-four; they were to be elected for six years and not appointed for life; they were required to satisfy a property qualification and to have a residence record of three years in the Kingdom; and they were to be paid no salary.

The Minute Book of the House of Nobles carries an entry, October 3, 1859, "Extraordinary Session" at the Palace in Honolulu, which states: "The Chancellor administered the oath to Mr. Chas. R. Bishop." Kamehameha IV had appointed him a member of the House of Nobles. Bishop saw action immediately, although in a minor capacity, by being appointed a member of a committee of three to notify the King that the House of Nobles was in session. He was made a member of another committee of three to reply to the King's request for approval of the Prince of Hawaii as heir and successor to the throne. The 1860 session lasted sixty-seven days, and Bishop was present at all meetings.

Late in this session, on June 20, an entry shows that: "A message was received from the Representatives [House of] transmitting a Bill passed by them, entitled 'An Act in Aid of Queen's Hospital Corporation.' The Bill was read a first and a second time and referred to a select committee consisting of Messrs. Gregg, Bishop and Armstrong." This was the beginning of Bishop's long association with Queen's Hospital. He was on numerous other committees during his freshman legislative year in the House of Nobles; and a list is quite informative: Civil Code, Pilotage, Protection of Foreign Diplomats, Seamen's Desertion, Board of Health, and others. The next session was in 1862, for the House of Nobles was now on a biennial basis. It lasted seventy-eight days, and Bishop attended most of the meetings.

Two years later, Kamehameha V promulgated a new constitution which was to surprise the critics and remain in force for twenty-three years. Bishop received a renewal of his commission as a member of the House of Nobles, this time at the hands of Kamehameha V. It was dated August 20, 1864. No later commission was granted; this one was for life.

A list of the sessions with his committeeships shows the extent to which he was able to be of service to the Kingdom:

1864 Member Foreign Relations Committee
     Chairman Finance Committee
1866 No committee activity for Mr. Bishop.
1867 Chairman Finance Committee
1868 Chairman Finance Committee
1870 Chairman Finance Committee
     Chairman Foreign Affairs Committee
     Member Commerce and Manufacturing Committee
1872 Chairman Finance Committee
     Member Foreign Affairs Committee
1873 No committee activity. The entire session was devoted largely to amending the Constitution. Bishop was also Foreign Minister for Lunalilo and could not give much attention to legislation.
1874 Bishop was elected president of the Legislative Assembly. He presided seventy-three days out of eighty-four.
1876 Mr. and Mrs. Bishop were on an American and European tour.
1878 Chairman Foreign Relations Committee. Bishop contested with Godfrey Rhodes for the presidency of the Assembly and lost.
1880 Bishop and Rhodes had another contest, and Bishop won.
1882 Bishop lost to Rhodes this time.
     Chairman Foreign Relations Committee.
1884 Chairman Education Committee.
1886 Bishop lost out to John S. Walker in the voting for the presidency of the Assembly.
1887 This was the year of an extraordinary session. Kalakaua accepted a new constitution.

The House of Nobles lost its distinctive traditional aura in 1887. The new Constitution reduced it to a routine political body. Comment is not available about Bishop and his continuation as a Noble. He is not listed among the Nobles after 1887, and it may be assumed that as the basis of membership changed from being appointive to elective he dropped out of the picture.

There is no verbatim secretarial record of the proceedings of the Legislative Assembly except for one year, and that record is in a volume called *Hawaiian Hansard for 1886*. Several summaries of Bishop's speeches are printed, of which two on the Opium Bill demonstrate his intuitive understanding of threats to the public welfare:

124th Day, Monday, Oct. 11

Noble Bishop thought that after what has been said by the Attorney General and the member for Molokai, it did not seem necessary to add anything to receive the non-passage of the bill. The first bill was bad enough, but this one was so stupidly defective and so manifestly dishonest that it should not be necessary to say anything against it to condemn it. The original bill had the excuse to offer of being something worth while for the revenue it promised, but this one is destitute of even that excuse. As it reads it only gives $30,000 for a few years license. It is hypocritical to pretend that it confirms the use of opium to persons suffering from disease. No one is going to pay $30,000 to provide opium to be used as a medicine. The proviso that the certificate of a physician must be obtained is put in as a mere blind. It is well known that the result will be that certificates of physicians will be for sale right and left by both native and foreign doctors. There will be no difficulty in getting certificates. License was tried in years past both for the sale of opium and the sale of awa. The bill says somebody is to have a license. Who is to have it? There are chances for a job in this business at the very beginning. Let the Minister give the license to whom he will, it will be believed that he got more for it than the price of the license. It will subject him to suspicion and temptations both at the same time. No doubt those who give out the license would make money out of it. It is useless to pretend that the opium habit would not spread among the Hawaiians. Such was the case years ago. Natives were getting more into the habit of using the drug. He could not believe that the representatives of the people were willing to pass a law that would increase the sale of opium among the Chinese and among their own people. They cannot dodge their responsibility. They know that it will lead to these effects among their own people. Would any intelligent Hawaiian after voting for this sort of thing dare to say he was in favor of increasing the nation [sic]. If they pass this bill they should drop that motto and adopt one more honest. If he knew that not a single Hawaiian would use opium under the bill, he would still be opposed to it. There are thousands of Chinese who are kept from the use of opium by the present law and who would be drawn into it by this bill being adopted. It is admitted to be the most difficult habit for a man to break off. He would not believe that the members of this legislature would for any amount of money take the tabu from the opium and see it spreading among the people. He hoped they loved the people they represented better than to be guilty of any such action. He believed the bill would be killed right here. . . .

126th Day, Wednesday, Oct. 13

Noble Bishop could not help feeling sorry for those members who support this bill. It is evident that they feel themselves in the way; hence the weak, silly, childish arguments which they use. No it is perfectly evident that there is an influence exerted here which they know they ought to resist. We know that in past years, when opium was licensed, the holders of licenses were constantly running to the Customs officers and police complaining that they had paid their money, but that others were bringing in the article at the same time. Another thing more important than all this is that, while opium was licensed, it was used more and more, every year by the natives of this country. It may not be possible to keep it entirely away from old opium smokers, but we can keep it away from those who have not acquired the habit. The natives frequent Chinese houses and stores, and it will be absolutely impossible to keep it from them. The proviso that it must not be sold to natives and Japanese gives it the appearance of respectability, but it really amounts to nothing. Young people will learn the habit partly out of curiosity, and the habit once fixed upon them they cannot be rescued from it. If it is to be licensed, as much as possible should be got for the license. That is the only argument brought in favor of the bill, and up till this morning no other argument had been pretended to be offered. . . .

The Opium Bill was passed by the Legislature and signed by the King. Bishop, despite this setback, spoke with a powerful voice in the public forum. The legislative deliberations in which he participated faithfully for almost thirty years show the mark of his thinking. This was a major channel of Bishop influence upon the direction the economic and political history of the Kingdom was to follow.

HONORS AND AWARDS

The Kamehamehas, from the Conqueror to Kamehameha V, did not indulge in much pomp and circumstance of royal court pro-

cedure. Gradually, through a political and social evolution inter-
larded with a window-dressing pressure of regal styles and fashions
observable among the representatives of foreign nations in Honolulu, a structure of kingly routine, etiquette, and custom began to
evolve. Kamehameha V actually gave the cause its start in 1865,
when on April 11, he established the Order of Kamehameha I. In the
decree establishing the Order, he said that he was:

. . . Desirous to cultivate and develop among our subjects the feelings
of Honor and Loyalty to our Dynasty and its institutions—and it is our
wish to confer honorary distinctions upon such of our subjects and
foreigners as have rendered or may hereafter render to our Dynasty and
people important services. . . .

There were three grades of appointment: Grand Cross, Knight
Commander, and Knight Companion. Shortly after publication of
this royal thesis, several persons, among them Bishop, were appointed to the Grand Council, Order of Kamehameha I. The Grand
Council and Executive Council were the media through which
Kamehameha V and the succeeding rulers were to announce their
appointments and generally guide the rather innocuous procedures
of the Order. In the minutes of this Council, dated May 7, 1874, we
read:

It pleased His Majesty to commend that Honorable C. R. Bishop K. C.
[Knight Commander] should be one of the Executive Council in the
place of deVarigny who has left the Kingdom permanently.

The recommendation was in the voice of Kalakaua.

In the minutes of the Grand Council of May 28, 1874, we read the
following directions:

His Majesty the King was pleased to appoint Messrs. Bishop, Dominis
and Harris a committee to take into consideration the subject of exchange
for foreigners and commanded them to prepare any correspondence that
might be necessary.

The Secretary was likewise advised to deposit all funds he might have
at the bank of Messrs. Bishop & Co., to be used for the advantage of the
Order.

It also pleased His Majesty at the above meeting to propose the name
of Chas. R. Bishop as a proper person to be promoted to Knight Grand
Cross which was approved by the Executive Committee.

Herein lies the beginning of the campaign Kalakaua was to wage
with increasing intensity to give color, drama, and ceremonial display to his person, his court, and his Kingdom. Bishop had just

finished a period of service under Lunalilo, as Foreign Minister, and was well prepared to guide correspondence concerning the exchange of decorations, royal amenities, salutes, and the like. In the order of business, the Executive Council of the Order and the Grand Council would meet alternately but with no stated or regular intervals. Bishop was present without missing a meeting throughout the life of the Order. On April 11, 1877, he was appointed "Chancellor of the Order with the rank of Knight Grand Commander."

Kalakaua was not content with perpetuating the Order of Kamehameha I; his ambitions would be served even better with an order carrying his own name. Consequently, in commemoration of his election to the throne, he established the Royal Order of Kalakaua, September 28, 1875.

Article 1 stated the purpose: "The Order of Kalakaua is hereby established for the recompense of distinguished merit and services rendered to the State, or Ourselves or Our Successors." Kalakaua was becoming meticulously regal, even to the capitalizing of his possessive personal pronouns. Article 2 provided that the "Reigning Monarch shall be Grand Master of the Order." Four grades were set up in Article 4; viz., Knight Grand Cross with Cordon, Grand Officer, Knight Commander, and Knight Companion. Subsequent articles of the decree provided variously a meeting each 12th day of February, a fine of $20.00 for an absence, and fees running from $50 to $150 for anyone appointed to one of the grades.

On November 11, 1875, Bishop was made a Knight Grand Cross of the Royal Order of Kalakaua; and in the minutes of October 16, 1876, we find him appointed a member of the Executive Council. His attendance was almost perfect at both the Executive and Grand Council meetings of this Order, for he missed but one in the eight years of his association.

This was not the end of the Kalakaua royal orders. There were to be three more. On September 12, 1882, Kalakaua issued a decree establishing the "Crown of Hawaii"; January 31, 1883, the "Order of Kapiolani"; and December 16, 1866, the "Order of the Star of Oceania." These orders were drafted by Walter Murray Gibson, and Bishop had little or no connection with any of them.

Mrs. Bishop was also the recipient of honors and awards. The collection of crosses, stars, cordons, ribbons, medals, pendants, and brooches in the several Orders presented to either Mr. or Mrs. Bishop by the Hawaiian monarchs is housed at the Bishop Museum.

Other honors came to Bishop. One was a citation from the emperor of Japan, dated February 3, 1882. This was the Grand Cordon of the Imperial First Order of the Rising Sun. Another was the Order of Franz Joseph (1849) of Austria. Mexico honored him with the Order of Our Lady of Guadalupe. From Bavaria came the "Quis et Deus" decoration. Baden sent the "Für Ehre und Wahrheit." The Order of Frederick (1830) came from Würtemberg. There were many others.

The Honolulu press gave slight attention to news of honors of any kind. The decrees of the monarchs were published as business-of-government, but news items and editorial comment regarding them seldom appeared in the papers. Bishop's faithful attendance at the Council meetings of the Kamehameha I and Kalakaua Orders was probably in no facetious sense due to his dislike of paying a $20.00 fine for each such absence but rather to a strong feeling of obligation to public service.

5

Interests

SUGAR IN HAWAII

BISHOP'S CHIEF BUSINESS specialty, aside from Bishop and Company, was sugar. He was interested in the Hawaiian Immigration Society because of sugar. That Society evolved from the Chamber of Commerce.

He was also deeply interested in communication and continually pressed for the successful laying of a Pacific cable. However, he maintained but a passing interest in some of the utilities. He evinced some reluctance to move into the local telephone and electric light services. He was downright suspicious of the railroad, and yet it was the railroad (about which he later changed his mind) that contributed so heavily to the fantastic growth of sugar.

The Lihue Plantation was one of the earliest major starts in the raising of sugar cane in the Kingdom of Hawaii.* Henry A. Peirce obtained a charter in 1849, for a co-partnership under the name of Henry A. Peirce and Company, "to buy lands, cultivate cane and manufacture sugar at Nawiliwili, on the Island of Kauai." The original money was supplied in the following distribution: Henry A. Peirce, one-half or $8000; William L. Lee, one-quarter or $4000; Charles R. Bishop, one-quarter or $4000. Again William L. Lee's fine hand in leading Bishop to a decision to remain in Hawaii is seen in this modest but important participation in a sugar plantation.

Bishop was "in and out" of the Lihue Plantation Company. On December 14, 1850, he conveyed his grantor interest to his friend James Fowle Baldwin Marshall. This new co-partnership was changed again March 1, 1852, when Lee conveyed one-half of his grantor interest to Bishop. A share at this time was figured as

* The earliest of record was the sugar effort of Ladd and Company, see pp. 15–16.

one-eighth of the ownership. On March 15, 1853, Bishop conveyed a sixteenth interest in Lihue Plantation, which was half of his holdings as of that date, to E. O. Hall. In January, 1853, J. F. B. Marshall had sold half of his interest to William A. Aldrich. This was at the very time that Aldrich and Bishop were forming their mercantile agency. So the two men held shares, one-sixteenth by Bishop and one-eighth by Aldrich. William L. Lee passed away in 1857, and his share of Lihue Plantation was taken back by the surviving partners. Their shares were then redistributed on a basis of fourteenths instead of sixteenths. Bishop conveyed his one-fourteenth share to William Hyde Rice on February 15, 1861. Then he re-entered Lihue Plantation by acquiring a fourteenth share on December 12, 1861, but this time in the name of Bishop and Company. On May 14, 1867, A. F. Judd conveyed a one-seventh interest to him. On May 4, 1877, V. Provost sold him a fourteenth interest. He now owned three-fourteenths, with Bishop and Company on the list for one-fourteenth. After Mrs. Bishop's death, needing money for his growing San Francisco financial ventures, Bishop began to rid himself of Lihue Plantation stock. On September 27, 1887, the record shows a transfer of two-fourteenths to C. M. Cooke for $100,000 with the condition that the money in San Francisco exchange was to be raised in twenty-four hours.

W. H. Rice, who was to become one of the stalwarts of Kauai and to found one of the great families of the Kingdom, obtained his first job from Bishop in 1867. His wage was $25.00 a month, and his work was running cattle on Lihue Plantation. About 1887 another young man destined to become a leading citizen of Kauai, Paul Isenberg, was working for Lihue Plantation. When the suggestion was made to Bishop that Isenberg's salary be raised, it brought the rejoinder: "No, no, wait till he asks for more." In 1890, Paul Isenberg, who must have obtained money somehow if not in a raise in salary, purchased Bishop's last two shares of Lihue for $100,000. This closed out the Bishop interest in Lihue.

When whaling followed sandalwood into an economic limbo, it was sugar that held the limelight; and it was sugar that sweetened the Bishop and Company balance sheet. The Civil War gave increased impetus to sugar prosperity in Hawaii, which produced 750 tons in 1860, 5,000 tons in 1865, and 9,000 in 1869.

In 1867, through the failure of the important firm of Walker, Allen and Company, Bishop was drawn into his only Oahu sugar venture.

As early as 1858, Warren and Levi Chamberlain, sons of missionary Levi Chamberlain, had discussed starting a sugar plantation in the Waialua area on Oahu. In 1864 they formed the Waialua Plantation, using lands of the Manual Labor School and some adjacent holdings of their own. Their efforts might have been successful had not Walker, Allen and Company gone into voluntary bankruptcy in January, 1867. The firm held several liens on their plantation. At a meeting in the Court House in Honolulu, the creditors elected C. R. Bishop, Esq., and J. W. Austin, Esq., as assignees for the estate of Walker, Allen and Company. Through his role of Assignee and because of an interest in the distressed property, Bishop arranged for W. C. Parke to bid in for him; and the sale was completed at $4750. Bishop was but briefly, an Oahu plantation owner. He sold out to O. R. Ward in 1870. This plantation was finally absorbed in the giant Waialua Agricultural Company.

The United States was a natural and almost exclusive market for Hawaiian sugar but the step-up in Hawaiian sugar production alarmed some of the interests in the United States, and a high tariff was imposed shortly after the conclusion of the Civil War. Sugar thereupon moved temporarily to markets in Australia and New Zealand, and this revived reciprocity talk.

Hawaii was feeling the pinch of the high U. S. tariff. Bishop explained to the Austrian Consul, March 18, 1873: "Our consumption of refined sugar here is too small, and the high tariff on such sugar in the United States too great an obstacle to make it possible for us to make any other than 'raw' sugars." And on May 27, 1873, to the Consul at Sydney, he wrote: "I am satisfied that our sugar planters have lost by not sending more sugar to your port during the last six months, instead of shipping to San Francisco. . . ." Then he wrote to Consul Severance in San Francisco, June 8, 1873: ". . . The shipments to Sydney may be rather late in season but will probably give better returns than they would had they been sent to California or Oregon."

The pressure was mounting. Hawaii's planters preferred shipping to San Francisco. It was closer than Sydney or Wellington, and the planters' harvest in Hawaii was better suited to the timing of the market demand in California. So on July 7, 1873, to Manley Hopkins, Lunalilo's Consul in London, went this bit of news:

. . . the low prices for sugar that have, during the six or eight months last past, ruled in our principal markets is embarrassing our planters and discouraging enterprise. Therefore His Majesty's Government had determined to again open negotiations with the United States for a Special Treaty of Reciprocity, partly upon the cession of Pearl River for a Naval Station, provided such a treaty can be agreed upon as will seem to His Majesty and His advisers to be safe and clearly for the interest of the nation. . . .

Evidence of the troubles that the plantations were having, and Bishop's concern for them, is noted in an Amos Starr Cooke letter to his sister Fanny, September 4, 1873:

. . . It has been only through the forebearance of Mr. C. R. Bishop that we have kept up for months past. For a while we got no returns, the plantations must have their $10,000 per mo. to be kept in operation.

Bishop commented to Elisha H. Allen on October 25, 1873:

There is nothing new from Washington, upon the subject of Reciprocity; and in the meantime the people are very much influenced against what appears to me to be their best interests. . . .

He was referring to the opposition of the Hawaiians which was developing to any cession of Pearl River.* Then to Allen, on November 20, he wrote:

Col. Steinberger professes to be on intimate and confidential terms with President Grant. I do not see much of him or have much confidence in him but I tried to impress him with the fact that our sugars are now going mainly to the Australasian Colonies, and that trade, our purchases will gradually tend in that direction; that reciprocity would secure the principal part of our trade to the U. S. and that we buy fully up to our means. . . .

By January 7, 1874, Bishop was frustrated. He wrote to Allen:

My own opinion is that we have no chance of getting a reasonably fair reciprocity treaty with the United States at present. No doubt Senators Hamlin, Sumner and many others who have always been friendly to Hawaii and to yourself personally, would favor us; but I think that the present Administration is indifferent, if not really opposed to the measure. . . . Of course we want reciprocity and with prosperity could do much more for the benefit of all classes and especially for the sick, the ignorant and the poor; but we can do tolerably well as we are; and no good comes of so much croaking and exaggeration of our difficulties. . . .

Kalakaua had sent Allen and H. A. P. Carter to Washington in the fall of 1874, and after a few weeks he followed with a large party of government officials and court retainers. The total effect of this

* See pp. 60–64.

mission was the passage of a Reciprocity Act which received the Hawaiian Legislature's approval in April, 1875. But the Enabling Act had not been passed. Allen and Carter therefore returned to the capital later to help that along in any possible way. January 2, 1876, Bishop again wrote to Allen from Rome:

. . . I don't envy you the care of watching the U. S. Congress in the matter of the Treaty. It seems to me that the passage of the necessary Act at this Session is very doubtful. The Democrats are strong, and are not disposed to help the President or Republican Senate to carry out their measures; and each party seems to outdo the other in appearing to be virtuous, and especially in the one virtue of economy. . . .

These were rather strange words for the thrifty banker; but his mind was on reciprocity, and governmental economy at this juncture did not seem important. But apparently he was more pessimistic than he needed to be. On May 10, 1876, he wrote happily to Allen from London:

In this day's "Times" I read, "The House of Representatives has ratified the Hawaiian Treaty"—and I take the few moments which I *have* to spare today to write you a note of congratulation. You have worked so long for the treaty, that the *victory* aside from the advantages which you hope that the country and individuals will reap, must give you great satisfaction. . . . Now there will be a breeze at Honolulu, . . .

It had not actually passed, and on July 4, he wrote again to Allen expressing great concern that the Senate was now delaying action. But his current fears of the Enabling Act being passed over at this session of Congress was unfounded. The Enabling Act was passed and went into effect, September 9, 1876. Sugar immediately stopped moving to the Pacific Southwest and returned to United States markets in phenomenal increases. Sugar production was doubled between 1877–1880. In 1890 it was ten times the tonnage of 1874. Plantations increased from thirty-five in 1874 to sixty-three in 1879.

Bishop reacted quickly to the news from Washington. He owned a large fee of fertile land in Kau, a remote district of the island of Hawaii at the far opposite end of the island chain from Kauai, where his sugar interests had chiefly centered. He gained the interest of C. Brewer and Company officials, and talks ensued regarding a plantation utilizing the Kau land as a base. Peter Cushman Jones, Jr., a Honolulu banker and capitalist, was invited to act on behalf of C. Brewer and Company and Bishop. On November 15, 1876, Jones

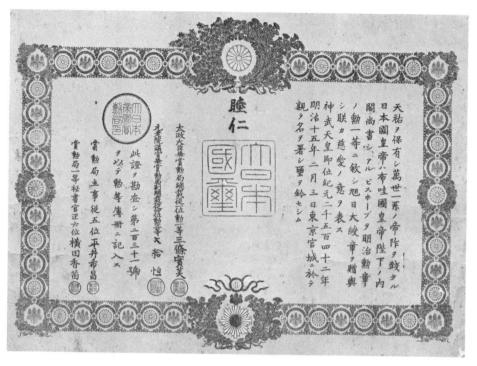

The scroll accompanying the Award of the Order of the Rising Sun, First Class, to Charles Reed Bishop by the Emperor of Japan, February 3, 1882.

filed a petition for charter of the Hawaiian Agricultural Company. The charter was granted December 22, 1876. The signers were: "Chas. R. Bishop, Jon O. Dominis, H. A. P. Carter, P. C. Jones, Jr., J. D. Brewer." At the first meeting the above named signers, who were also the stockholders, elected Bishop as President and Director and approved the purchase from Bishop of the "property conveyed to the company by deed dated December 29, 1876." The stock (par $500) was held in this distribution: Charles R. Bishop, 110 shares; R. A. Lyman, 20 shares; and John O. Dominis, 20 shares; J. D. Brewer, P. C. Jones, Jr. and H. A. P. Carter, representing C. Brewer and Company, were listed with a total of 90 shares.

Bishop was elected President and Director at the first meeting and re-elected to the same positions for successive annual terms through 1893. The story of his fourteen years at the helm of Hawaiian Agricultural Company is a saga of its own. Before the initial planting had been completed, a drought set in. Even the manager recommended discontinuance of sugar planting. A railroad was proposed and had developed to the point of having locomotives and rails and other equipment on board a freighting vessel bound for the landing in Kau, when it was decided to sell the materials and drop the idea. When things were at a low ebb—a mortgage in the amount of $120,000 had been taken at 12% interest per annum, a note for $42,000 had been signed, assessments had been levied against stockholders, and still no mill, boiling house, or tramway had been installed—Bishop, in the company of Albert Francis Judd and P. C. Jones, Jr., made an inspection visit to the plantation in Kau. Upon their return the Directors employed a new manager and stepped up the program of improvements. Finally, the plantation began to prosper.

Bishop owned 110 shares of the original stock offering. His first sale of any of this stock was mentioned in a letter to Allen, January 1, 1878: "I don't want any Princeville * stock. I have sold 30 shares of my Hawaiian Agricultural Company stock and now own 80 shares which equals a one-third ownership."

Through successive capital stock issues he added substantially to his holdings. When he left for San Francisco and a transcontinental tour of the United States, April 12, 1889, he wanted funds for financing prospective Bay area transactions. He left instructions

* Princeville was a cattle ranch venture up along the eastern side of Kauai.

with Samuel M. Damon to sell 871 shares of the Hawaiian Agricultural Company stock at no less than par. Damon offered the odd lot of shares to C. M. Cooke at $105 (par $100), and Cooke accepted the offer almost too quickly for Bishop's mental comfort. He wrote Damon, July 24, 1889:

Regarding the sale of my shares in the Hawaiian Agriculture Company, I will say that I hardly anticipated such prompt and decided action. My letter to Mr. Jones was more in the nature of an inquiry than of authority to sell but friend Jones and yourself gave it a more liberal interpretation, and I think you were right. I wanted to sell out at the best price obtainable not below par, and I approve of your action. The question now is, what to do with the money to make it safe and yield a moderate income.

Two more sales of stock, each to C. M. Cooke, finally took Bishop out of Hawaiian Agricultural. In June, 1893, Cooke purchased five hundred shares and in January, 1894, two hundred fifty more. The price was at par of $100 or $75,000.

With the passage of the Reciprocity Act, sugar planters moved rapidly to open new plantations and extend old ones. Some of them moved too rapidly causing a severe strain on plantation financing, and here Bishop and Company played the role of economic lifesaver to the Kingdom economy. Bishop wrote to Allen, June 16, 1879, from San Francisco:

I had hoped to induce parties here to invest in plant or loan money on them, or in some way furnish capital; but have not been successful. . . . A number of plantations are now partly finished and are being furnished with machinery, which will take off the first crop in 1880, and begin to pay back. They want money with which to complete their works and take off the crops now growing and looking well. No *entirely new* places are projected, except the large works of Mr. Spreckels and are not likely to be until a renewal of the treaty is secured. . . .

One agency which was overextended was C. Brewer and Company. The Hawaiian Agricultural Company was the strongest asset of the agency, for it was on solid ground financially. This was not the case with other Brewer enterprises and need for reorganization was apparent.

One of Bishop's most useful "saves" was his participation in a reorganization of that agency. In *A History of C. Brewer and Company,** this explanation appears:

* Josephine Sullivan, *op. cit.,* pp. 145–147.

. . . In the fall of the year (1880) H. A. P. Carter returned to Hawaii. He felt keenly the great burden under which the house was laboring. He persuaded Charles R. Bishop, the banker, to join the firm as a silent partner. Accordingly, Bishop advanced $100,000 and took the firm's note for three years, at ten per cent per annum. No partnership articles were ever signed, but the understanding was that for this advance he was to have five twenty-fourths of the profits. Jones [Peter Cushman] later said; "Considering the time and the circumstances this was a very helpful act on the part of Mr. Bishop, and helped to tide us over a very critical period." The money and credit which Bishop then furnished were absolutely necessary for the preservation of the business because of the hard times and the heavy financial drain placed upon the firm by the plantations. Welch & Co. [a San Francisco investment agency] could not do more than it had already done. At the end of the year 1880 the books showed a profit of $21,600, of which $4500 was paid to Bishop, . . . [In 1881 it amounted to $12,500 and in 1882, $10,000] . . .

Eighteen hundred and eighty-two was the last year for C. Brewer & Co. as a firm, for the incorporation took place as of January 1, 1883. Mr. Carter had been anxious for some time to withdraw part of his funds from the concern. Mr. Brewer's interest had never been settled, and in the interest of his widow and children the amount due them should be paid. Chief Justice Harris was the father of Mrs. Brewer and fully understood the condition of affairs, and was very lenient with us. It devolved upon me to solve the problem and after conferring with Harris, Carter, Bishop and Andrew Welch, who first suggested the incorporation of the business, we decided to adopt this plan. Mr. Bishop agreeing to take $140,000 of the corporation, provided we would take 400 shares of Hawaiian Agricultural Company at par. Mr. Welch also agreed to take $100,000 of the stock, putting in the mortgages he held with us. Mr. Harris died before the business was incorporated, but Mrs. Brewer approved of the plan, taking the amount due the estate of her husband in stock of the corporation. The amount of property was $550,000, but not one dollar was asked for by the members of the old firm for good will.

The agreement made with Mr. Bishop to take in 400 shares of H. A. Co. Stock, which at that time was upon a dividend-paying basis, turned out to be a very valuable asset of the corporation, for that estate has paid good dividends every year except one since we took it in as part of our capital. In January, 1883, application was made for a charter for C. Brewer & Co., for a term of fifty years. The charter members were H. A. P. Carter, P. C. Jones and J. O. Carter, and on February 7th the charter was signed, and the corporation duly formed. The first officers were: President and Manager, P. C. Jones; Secretary and Treasurer, J. O. Carter; Auditor, Henry May; directors, Charles R. Bishop and H. A. P. Carter.

The stock in the original incorporation was held by the following individuals:

H. A. P. Carter	1350 shares @ $100	$135,000.00
P. C. Jones	1200 "	120,000.00
C. R. Bishop	1400 "	140,000.00
Andrew Welch	1000 "	100,000.00
Estate of J. D. Brewer	300 "	30,000.00
Henry May	250 "	25,000.00
	5,500 "	$550,000.00

Thus, Bishop was the largest stockholder at the time of incorporation. He was elected a Director in 1883 and reelected each year through 1892, when he disposed of the last of his interest in C. Brewer and Company.

The name of Bishop was destined to be associated with C. Brewer for many years. Eben Faxon Bishop,* a cousin once removed, had been urged by Bishop to try his fortunes in Hawaii. Young Faxon answered the call, arriving in 1883, and promptly went to work as a junior clerk in the newly incorporated firm of C. Brewer and Company.

Several plantations in the Castle and Cooke chain, among them, Haiku, Waialua, and Papaikou, were facing some problems in financing operations. Samuel N. Castle, in writing to Hon. W. R. Castle, October 4, 1879, speaks of a Bishop and Company proposal wherein San Francisco money (Jones and Co.) would be employed:

. . . We understand Bishop & Co.'s proposal [on behalf of San Francisco parties] to be, an immediate advance of $26. per ton on the estimated crop for 1880. Our note to be given for the sum advanced and the said crop to be pledged or mortgaged for the payment and one fourth of the proceeds of the said crop to be applied to cancel this loan as the sugars go forward, and the proceeds of the other three-fourths to be drawn against to meet expenses and other uses.

Following the sugar crisis were other years when the price of sugar was news. On March 13, 1886, Bishop wrote to R. W. Meyer on Molokai:

The late news from Washington is not favorable to our interests, but as nothing had been decided I am hopeful that nothing much against us will be done. Sugar is low all over the world, and prospect of improvement not bright at present.

On May 3, 1886, in another letter to Meyer, his gloomy spirit had not brightened much:

* See pp. 318–319.

Sugar has again advanced a little in price. The House of Reps. in Congress is understood to be in favor of abrogating the Treaty and it is believed that the Senate and the Cabinet are opposed to abrogation, and in favor of changing the Treaty, so as, to get something more for their side. Just what the new provisions will be, or how they will be received here by the King and natives it is too soon to say or express any opinion.

Claus Spreckels, a businessman of extraordinary ability, enters the Bishop story about this time. Spreckels had been among the first from the Mainland to come to Hawaii because of the Reciprocity Treaty. He had ingratiated himself with the politicians of the Kingdom and achieved a special intimate acquaintance with the royal family and certain leading citizens. The instrument for building Spreckels' sugar empire was a partnership by the name of Irwin and Company. He started the Oceanic Steamship Company, worked out details for minting a huge supply of Kalakaua coins, promoted a large sugar enterprise on Maui through an "influenced" land deal, introduced an overly liberal bank law, and so on. While Spreckels' sugar deals probably disturbed Bishop, the pressure applied upon the monarchy, not only in sugar activity but also in many items of business enterprise, probably outraged him. In a letter to Meyer, December 9, 1885, he writes:

. . . The election of the former members or of any Govt. candidates means extravagant appropriations, probably increase of taxes and subjection to Spreckels and Gibson. It is strange that the King does not see that he and his family are being made tools of by his ministers and C. S.

This was the first mention of Spreckels in any of Bishop's correspondence, and it rather coincides with the turning point in Spreckels' influence in the Kingdom. The *Hawaiian Hansard* has this entry of the proceedings of the Legislature, September 30, 1886, referring to the Spreckels loan:

. . . Noble Bishop said when this (loan) Act was up before, he favored the idea of borrowing $1,000,000. His remarks on that occasion corresponded with those of the Minister (Gibson) this morning. There was only one feature in the amendment that met his approval, that limiting the amount we are to go into debt. The amendment he proposed at the time, would have accomplished all the good this one can possibly do, and would have saved us some mortification and possibly some money. It is proposed to borrow $2,000,000, on the negotiating of which we have to pay off a debt which is not pressing at all. The loss will be at least $50,000, and probably more. The original bill provided that no commission was to be paid in any money applied to pay off bonds of 1882. That is left out of the present act. People here ought to have the opportunity to take up the bonds if they are willing to do so. He thought his Excellency's remarks about the advisability of the whole debt being held by one strong party was a new idea of public debt. The way in which the whole thing is being done is really humiliating.

It was not necessarily this speech of Bishop's that turned the tide against the Spreckels loan and started the government towards making a "London Loan," but it was an indication of the way sentiment was running. He got off his usual thrice-weekly letter to Meyer, October 2, 1886, "The Legislature is still going on its insane course. Mr. Spreckels is here to look out for his interests."

In a letter to Damon, October 7, 1887, he wrote:

. . . Mr. Spreckels expects to make himself the most popular man in the U. S., if not in the whole world by introducing beet culture for sugar making in all parts where vegetables grow well; and as he claims to have secured the control of certain necessary patents for manufacture, he will have the advantage over all others, and will be "Sugar King" not only of the Pacific Coast but of the whole Republic!! The American Refinery is to be nowhere and of course Hawaiian planting will be as badly off as the Refinery! He has talked a great deal of big brag to Atherton. . . . If sugar business in Hawaii is to be ruined by the beet culture, Mr. Spreckels ought to be willing to part with his lands and plantation at a loss figure and the Haw'n Com'l Co. should do likewise. I am more afraid of the reduction of duties than I am of beets, though the latter may not compete strongly with our cane.

Bishop, with his weather eye out on congressional trends, commented to Meyer, November 26, 1888, "Gen'l Harrison is elected president, I'm sorry to say. What Congress will do about tariff changes nobody can say with any certainty."

April 23, 1889, he wrote to Damon. The price of sugar was high and things seemed a little brighter:

. . . Geo. Macfarlane . . . and W. H. Bailey have had several talks with Mr. Spreckels who went east on the 20th, about Waikapu and Wailuku stocks, and he (Mac.) has made an agreement with Bailey, which the latter or P. C. Jones may explain to you, to run for 3 months, within which time they hope to make a favorable sale to Mr. Spreckels. . . . If he sells we shall get our pay from him, and if he does not, and we take the Waikapu stock or keep what we have got we should insist upon the option which is too liberal towards him being closed, so that we may know what we own and do as we like with it. . . . Mr. Spreckels and others have formed a large Co. Capital $5,000,000 for

Beet sugar business. Spreckels holding controlling interest, and will expand about $5,000,000 this year and so on as opportunity offers.

On May 1, 1889, Bishop wrote:

I think Geo. Macfarlane started east yesterday. He and W. H. Bailey are working together to make a good sale of a part or all of the Wailuku Plantation and the remaining half of Waikapu to Mr. Spreckels but they want it kept *quite secret.* Some of them may have spoken to you about it, but if they have not, do not mention it. Whether or not Mr. Spreckels has authorized anybody to buy in Honolulu or here I do not know.

Spreckels continued to be a subject for Bishop comments in letters to Alexander but these ceased in 1894. When careful study is given to the manifests of the port of Honolulu, both outbound and inbound for the years 1882 to 1894, it is curious to discover the rather large number of trips when Messrs. Spreckels and Bishop were fellow passengers. There may be no more than pure coincidence in the timings. One notable trip possessed of much good humor was one when the two were aboard the *Zealandia,* April 17, 1882, out of San Francisco bound for Honolulu. A few weeks later, the *Hawaiian Gazette,* July 18, carried this story:

. . . Crown vs Spencer
Upon information and belief the undersigned charge the defendant in this action, Frank Spencer, alias "Snorkey," "Bill the Bruiser," "Red Handed Mike," and "Jesse James," with the following crimes and misdemeanors, to wit: Grand Larceny, Petit Larceny, and Breach of Promise, that upon the day and date hereinbefore mentioned, he did with intent and malice, and against the peace and dignity of the Crown, steal, purloin, and cowardly filch, one silver watch, the property of Capt. Webber, of value unknown, constituting Petit Larceny; one gold watch and chain, value s'teen dollars, the property of Mrs. Slade; and that he has willfully entangled the maiden affections of the plaintiff in the third count, Agnes Young, and thereafter indignantly refused to marry her.
(Signed) Charles R. Bishop
Claus Spreckels

This was one of the few times when Messrs. Spreckels and Bishop were to be together on anything. Be that as it may, the contribution of Spreckels to the advancement of sugar in Hawaii was substantial. That his rather domineering personality and his "short cut" operations were a part of it was unfortunate. One more sugar venture *

* Arthur L. Dean, *op. cit.,* pp. 31–32.

remained for Bishop; a second multimillion dollar sugar plantation on Kauai:

> . . . Most important sugar plantation of 1883–1899 period was the Hawaiian Sugar Company of Kauai. Early in 1888 Wm. Renny Watson leased from Gay and Robinson a large area of Makaweli land. March 5 Mr. Watson wrote to Henry Baldwin from Honolulu inviting him to come in on the new venture. He had provisional subscriptions from James Campbell, C. R. Bishop and others.
> Watson went to Europe—decided against organizing a British Co. Alexander, Baldwin, and Walsh talked with Watson in Europe. The upshot was that a charter of incorporation was granted October 30, 1889 on a petition signed by Wm. Renny Watson, Henry P. Baldwin, E. M. Walsh, Charles R. Bishop and George W. Macfarlane.

Bishop had returned to Honolulu August 23, 1889, and therefore had ample time to develop his position in this deal. The authorization for capital stock in this new Hawaiian Sugar Company was set at $2,000,000 with permission to increase to $5,000,000. He subscribed for 400 shares of the stock at $100 par value. At the preliminary meeting on November 1, 1889, he was elected a Director.

A leading aspect of this entire project was the construction of the Makaweli Mill to handle Gay-Robinson sugar cane. A custom-designed lot of machinery was required, and an agent was dispatched to England to supervise the manufacture and shipping of the special equipment. The new plantation company ran into many problems, some of them involving close personal and family interests of satellite managements; others concerned such projects as the diversion of river waters for irrigation available in the Hanapepe-Waimea area, and labor availabilities were a pressing worry. The plantation surmounted all these obstacles and went on to become a good sugar producer. Bishop did not remain long on the stockholder's roster. While a member, however, he attended every meeting in 1889 and 1890, many of which were held in his banking offices. He was re-elected a Director a second time, and shortly thereafter, because of the pressure of San Francisco business, withdrew partly in favor of two cousins, Charles H. Bishop of Kauai and E. Faxon Bishop.

Bishop made many references to sugar and reciprocity in later correspondence running through March of 1913. He revealed again and again his understanding of the significance of assistance to the Hawaii sugar industry and that such assistance had to assure stability throughout the extremely long growing periods of cane. The economic history of Hawaii would have been written in drastically different language had it not been for Bishop's foresight and wisdom in solving the problems of the sugar industry.

THE HAWAIIAN IMMIGRATION SOCIETY

It was the Royal Hawaiian Agricultural Society which took first notice of a need for "cheap" labor to supply the large-scale plantation labor requirement. The discussants were men of high principle and had sound understanding of the racial and cultural problems of the Kingdom, as well as its economic needs. There were three distinct concepts, in the minds of various groups, of the nature and purposes of any immigration program for the Kingdom. One group wanted a cognate type of immigrant. Another was interested in "population," and a third had no other concern but for efficient, cheap labor. Elsewhere in this section a quotation from Bishop employs the expression, "workers only." Despite his rather strong talk about "workers only," there can be no question about his stand generally. He was witnessing the uninterrupted and tragic decline of the native race, and he would willingly support any constructive tactic to reverse that trend. The plantation labor problem, however, was only worsened by this decline in the Hawaiian population, and the need for adequate help was pyramiding. He could, therefore, be expected to support the planters' efforts to obtain an economic advantage in the world market by using the best cheap labor available.

The Society employed Captain Cass of the bark *Thetis* to bring in 180 Chinese coolies who were engaged for five years at $3.00 per month including passage, food, clothing, medical costs, and housing. Kamehameha III tried to repatriate all the Pitcairn Islanders to Hawaii, but Great Britain would not agree to that. Some years went by with growing demands from the plantations. On December 30, 1864, a Board of Immigration was established. The following April, Dr. Hillebrand went on a tour of the west Pacific countries, stopping at China, India, and the Malay Archipelago. In July he rounded up 500 Chinese coolies and sent them to Hawaii in two vessels. Bishop and Company frequently acted as agent for allocation of imported labor. An entry in the Waialua Plantation Journal (Levi and Warren Chamberlain) on May 13, 1867, notes this practice:

[Levi] reported having obtained 15 Chinamen thro Bishop & Co. and that he has started them off.

In June, 1868, the Legislature took up the subject and heeded the pleas of an earlier Legislature. It authorized the Board of Immigration to "re-people" this country with eighty-four Manahikis from Reirson's Island and Humphrey's Island. Later that year Hillebrand sailed the bark *R. W. Wood* from Danger Island with forty-two Bukabukas aboard, but none of these stayed. Kamehameha V, on July 30 of this same year, appointed Bishop a member of the Board of Immigration effective during the absence from the Kingdom of C. deVarigny.

Walter Murray Gibson was most insistent that the Malay Archipelago could supply good workers. Nothing came of this. He tried populating Lanai with a colony of white workers, and that failed. Prior to this in 1868 Eugene Van Reed, Consul General to Japan, sent 148 Japanese workers. Almost all the unexceptional racial strains had been tried out. Reciprocity as a treaty relationship with the United States was gaining momentum. Whaling had all but sounded its death knell. Oil had just been discovered in Pennsylvania and Kingdom prosperity was on the rise. The native Hawaiians were regarded as most desirable on the plantations; but their population was decreasing, even as the plantation demands were growing; hence the feverish push for immigrant labor. At a meeting of the Honolulu Chamber of Commerce on October 29, 1872, the subject of immigration was on the agenda, and a few of the members stayed to discuss the organization of an immigration society or company. The Hawaiian Immigration Society was quickly formed according to a report of the secretary, July, 1874, which reads as follows:

In accordance with a resolution of the Honolulu Chamber of Commerce, setting forth that it is the opinion of this Chamber, that an Association should be formed for the purpose of aiding the immigration of laborers and populations into the Hawaiian Islands, the Hawaiian Immigration Society was established November 6, 1872, and the following organization of officers took place:

S. N. Castle, President
W. L. Green, Vice-President
W. M. Gibson, Secretary
C. R. Bishop
J. C. Glade
With the above ⎫ Executive Committee
officers ex officio ⎭

As Foreign Minister under Lunalilo, and reflecting the sense of urgency of plantation drives for immigrant labor, Bishop wrote a detailed letter of inquiry to Robert M. Brown, His Hawaiian Majesty's Chargé d'Affaires and Consul General for the Empire of Japan at Yokohama, January 2, 1874:

. . . .

The supply of laborers is still short, and our planters and others who have employed Chinese and Japanese, are generally partial to the latter, and would gladly give employment to able-bodied young men and to their wives, if married, on sugar plantations . . . for not less than three years. Five years would be preferred, because for the first year at least, the services of such men—not understanding the language used by the employers, nor the work to be done—are of very little value.

As the Hawaiians have many characteristics similar to the Japanese, and are well disposed towards them; and as our laws and public sentiment guarantee to those serving under contract—whether native or alien —full and equal protection, Japanese laborers, if disposed to emigrate at all, can find no better country to go to than these islands; where the climate, proximity to Japan, and general conditions are favorable for them.

About six dollars per month for good men, with lodging, food, payment of personal taxes ($5 per annum) and payment of passage one way, and possibly both ways, on a contract for five years, would, I suppose, be considered fair to either party. Some of our planters would prefer to furnish land to be cultivated on shares, giving from 20% to 50% of the product of sugar or of its value, . . .

Much as laborers are wanted here for specific industries, and families to settle as a permanent population, this Government will not approve of any steps to procure either, that would be offensive to the friendly Government of Japan.

This inquiry was ignored, and almost another decade was to pass before Hawaii was successful in clearing negotiations for contract laborers from Japan.

Kamehameha V died a few weeks after the establishment of the Society. The public distraction with his demise and the agitation surrounding the selection of a new regent sidetracked action about immigration. Bishop, however, in his customary cautious role had urged that this group:

. . . not be precipitate in subscribing money and forming a company, unless sure of where to go and what to go for. The planters will not aid in a scheme merely looking to population. Our object must be to get workers only. I prefer the Chinese but still am of the opinion our first move must be to Japan.

This statement was made at the meeting of October 29, 1872, when the first discussion on immigration took place and, in a sense, constituted a slight restraining sentiment after Gibson expounded on the entire field of immigration and advocated the formation of an immigration company. As a part of the directive of that preliminary meeting, Bishop joined Messrs. Green and Glade in drafting a preamble and resolutions; and these were adopted two years later at a second preliminary meeting, November 1, 1874, without the "company" idea. Bishop then stated in the discussion which followed:

The conditions of this country were not the same as were found in England and the United States. We must cultivate entirely for a foreign market to pay for our importations. We import all our building material, and all our clothing and drinks. We cannot go back to the times of Kamehameha I and live on poi and wear a *malo*. We cannot export taro and beans; and it is idle to parcel out small lands to be settled as small independent farms, but as adjuncts to large planting operations.

On March 10, 1874, King Kalakaua gave Bishop his second appointment as a member of the Board of Immigration.

A listing of the major immigration efforts and successes, many of which clearly resulted from the Reciprocity Treaty of 1876, gives a valuable picture of the racial amalgamation which years later was to create a cultural conglomerate the likes of which the world had never seen and which in many ways was to satisfy all three ideologies of immigration supporters:

Portuguese: *1878.* Dr. Hillebrand engaged 180 from Funchal, 418 from Madeira, and 332 from the Azores.
    1882. Hon. H. A. P. Carter negotiated an immigration convention in Portugal, and 6000 arrived in the Islands over the next six years.
Polynesians: *1878 to 1884.* Nearly 2000 Polynesians were brought in, mostly from the Gilbert Islands, and including some black Melanesian cannibals. This migration did not work.
Chinese: *1866.* There were 1200 Chinese here.
    1878. The total was 6000.

1880. Despite interruption by a small pox epidemic and efforts by the Board of Immigration, more than 26,000 Chinese came into Hawaii between 1880 and 1890.

Northern European: *1880.* The Board of Immigration sent Captain L'Orange to Norway. On February 18, 1881, 392 Norwegians went directly to the island of Maui.

German: *1881.* One hundred twenty-four came from Bremen for the Lihue Plantation. In October, 1882, 183 arrived in Honolulu followed by 595 in 1883.

Swedish: *1881.* Two hundred twenty-three Scandinavians arrived May 14, 1881, from Drammen on the *Musca.*

Japanese: *1884.* Under a new agreement with the Japanese government, February 9, 1885, 956 came. This was but the first of well filled ship's manifests—groups of workers thronged in from the farms and rice paddies of the land of the Rising Sun.

Whether the Hawaii Immigration Society or Bishop's part in it can be praised as noteworthy or effective is rather doubtful. The economic pressure brought cheap labor from several parts of the world in more or less steady streams. The Royal Hawaiian Agricultural Society and the Honolulu Chamber of Commerce, of course, had some share in the labor traffic. The Planters' Society, a successor of sorts to the Agricultural Society, did much to promote immigration.

Bishop was always insistent upon fair treatment even to his dislike of the use of what seemed to him to be degrading names—coolie, for example. As Foreign Minister, he wrote to Edward Reeve, Esqr., H. H. M.'s Consul General for the Australian Colonies, on February 11, 1873:

The outrages that have been committed in the "Labor Traffic" of the South Pacific, and especially the massacre on board the *Cart.* . . . is shocking to every right minded person. . . . The subjects of Labor and Immigration are matters in which His Majesty, His Government, and the community generally feel a deep interest . . . our experience in promoting immigration from Polynesia has been far from satisfactory.

To C. E. DeLong, Minister Plenipotentiary of the United States, Yedo, Japan, he wrote on March 17, 1873:

. . . It is unfortunate both for the laborer and the employer, for Japan and for Hawaii that all engagements to emigrate under a contract . . . is called "Coolie Trade" and indiscriminately condemned. . . . Japanese men and women can find good employment, fair pay and good treatment in this country, as laborers on plantations, in mechanics shops and as house servants, and this Government will give them full protection in all their rights. . . .

To Manley Hopkins, Esqr., N. N. W. Chargé d'Affaires, Cornhill, London, Bishop writes on February 15, 1873:

. . . You will be quite safe in assuring the Dutch Consul General that the number of people that we would be able to induce to emigrate from the dependencies of his Government in the East Indies would make no perceptible difference in the population of those islands.

To Edward Reeve, he wrote again on March 15, 1873:

I have placed in the hands of His Majesty and others your "Scheme" for the Introduction of Immigration from the Samoan Group. . . . It is not probable that the Samoans would emigrate on any terms . . . even if they were *willing to come.* . . . It is painful to notice that the people of that group are becoming more and more demoralized through their foolish strife. . . . The opinion prevails in the Community that Japanese are the most desirable immigrants within our reach; and at *present they* are not allowed to leave their country in any considerable number.

A letter to Elisha H. Allen, April 3, 1878, states that: ". . . [the] ship "*H. W. Carlton*" Captain Harkness, from Hong Kong, with over 300 Chinese went ashore on the west end of Molokai in the night—and was lost. . . ."

By way of contrast, R. W. Meyer, who constituted a sounding board via correspondence for Bishop, received this humorous message, June 27, 1885:

There is nothing in the Japanese contracts about hot water but they think a great deal of hot water for bathing or washing themselves, and obliging them in that way and in other ways peculiar to them helps perhaps in keeping their employers out of hot water.

To W. D. Alexander, he wrote on October 3, 1900: ". . . The question of labor for the plantations causes some anxiety and is a warning against too great expansion."

This is not the whole story of immigration to Hawaii. It does outline the main facts of Bishop's connection with it. An inescapable facet of this subject was his status as a planter. He was not only a community leader in such agencies as the Chamber of Commerce and the Immigration Society; he was also heavily committed in sugar investments. In relating his thinking to the three schools of thought regarding the purposes of encouraging immigration to the Kingdom, it is apparent that he supported all with perhaps the greatest emphasis upon immigration cognate in racial background and efficient and cheap plantation ability in type.

THE HONOLULU CHAMBER OF COMMERCE

THE CHAMBER OF COMMERCE of Honolulu, the second oldest organization of its kind west of the Rocky Mountains and the only one under the American flag to be chartered by a king, was officially launched October 15, 1850. It was known as, "The Hawaiian Chamber of Commerce." William L. Lee had a hand in the chartering. Bishop was not among the twenty Honolulans who signed the charter; but his future partner in trade and banking, W. A. Aldrich, was a signer. Chambers of commerce have a way of ballooning with the enthusiasm of prosperity. They also can wither from the lack of nourishing traffic. The Hawaiian Chamber of Commerce was no exception to such variables and extremes. Business was good in 1850, and Kamehameha III had declared Honolulu to be a city and the capital of the Kingdom. California was still in its feverish gold rush mood. The volunteer fire department, the health department, and the mail service were established; and this was the year of the founding of the Chamber of Commerce. But the following year, 1851, was the first of seven depression years, and the Chamber almost passed out of existence.

The first significant incorporation of the Chamber of Commerce was in 1871. Bishop was a signatory to the incorporation papers. Again the organization declined, only to come to real life finally in 1883. In this rechartering, he was elected President. He continued as President for the next eight years, except for one term. Towards the end of his chairmanship he experienced the usual difficulties in attempting to make a resignation stick. In the Minute Book of the Honolulu Chamber of Commerce, No. 1, pp. 117–119, the following item regarding the annual meeting appears August 15, 1888:

Mr. Schaefer nominated the Hon. C. R. Bishop and gave his reasons for so doing and trusted that he would accept the office if elected. Mr. Bishop said that he had been president before, but had resigned for what he thought good reasons, at the time. If the members desired him to occupy the position again, he would not refuse.

At a similar meeting, July 15, 1891, another entry was made:

Letter from Hon. Chas. R. Bishop tendering his resignation as President of the Chamber read by the Secretary. Remarks were made upon this resignation by different members, when the motion was made, seconded and unanimously carried that the Resignation of the Hon. C. R. Bishop be not accepted, and the Secretary is instructed to so inform him.

As President, Bishop attended regularly and discharged his committee assignments conscientiously. His interests in the Chamber of Commerce rested chiefly among foreign relations, immigration, and the currency. The experience as Foreign Minister in Lunalilo's reign (1873) had alerted him to the dangers and difficulties which might confront and beset the Hawaiian Kingdom in its struggle to achieve stability. One of these was immigration, which was closely yoked with sugar prosperity.

The chief subject value of the record of the meetings rests in the application of Bishop's hard currency philosophy to the financial affairs of the Kingdom. The unprecedented prosperity in the years immediately preceding the 1883 rechartering of the Chamber had created an easy-money climate. Economically speaking, there was some danger of debasing the currency. To this problem the stalwarts of the Chamber of Commerce addressed themselves, and it was at this point that the experience of Bishop was called on to safeguard the Kingdom's economic life line—its currency. He knew its flexibility and its fluidity. He was aware of its limitations and uses; its relation to credit, trade, exchange and shipping, and buying and selling.

Silver had always been the popular medium of exchange in Hawaii. The history of silver in Hawaii is a story of American, Russian, French, English, and other nations' coins. In 1850 there were one hundred different silver coins in circulation in Hawaii. Sometimes silver commanded a premium, sometimes the market was glutted. In 1880, the Privy Council levied a ten per cent import tax on silver. Smugglers brought it in. Then in 1883, the Kalakaua government created consternation in trade circles with the new dollar, half dollar, quarter, and ten-cent silver coins. In fact, this proposal revived the dormant Chamber of Commerce and was a basic reason for its rechartering. Walter Murray Gibson was designated the coinage agent for the Kingdom and was to receive a fourteen per cent commission on the million dollars' worth of Kalakaua coins which he would bring in duty free.

It was at this point that Bishop and the Chamber of Commerce made a study and presented certain recommendations. One is noteworthy as a key recommendation:

Limit the importation of silver to internal requirements of the Kingdom and withdraw from circulation all silver coins other than new Hawaiian coins or U. S. silver coins and ship them abroad at the expense of the treasury.

The essential principle in the recommendation was adopted by the Legislature, and government coinage in Hawaii was for all time at an end. Standard silver coins of both the United States and Hawaii became the only legal tender in silver in Hawaii. As the changes were made and the currency "settled down," there was a reduction in circulation of silver by almost half. The circulation of gold was increased, and the rate of exchange was cut drastically. This currency reform, of course, did not occur overnight. On February 21, 1885, Bishop wrote to his ranch manager on Molokai:

Our currency is still in an unsettled condition. The only thing we can get is Treasury Certificates or silver. If Mr. Raupp can only pay a part in gold we must take the remainder in Certs. or silver.

And on April 30, he wrote again to Meyer:

Silver may be at a large discount by and by so that in selling to butchers it is not safe to engage positively to take silver at par, but so long as silver can be readily disposed of in exchange for gold or its equivalent at nor over 5% disct. I would not insist upon full pay in gold. The state of the currency is very unsatisfactory, so that it is necessary to be on one's guard about promises for the future.

Years later on July 29, 1896, in response to an inquiry from J. O. Carter, Bishop made a statement relative to the great debate on silver that was raging in the political houses of America:

You ask me, "how would free coinage of silver affect our Island interests?" I believe that the free coinage of silver, 16 to 1, without an international agreement with England and other great powers, would be very damaging to the interests of the Islands as well as to the interests of this country. Anything that greatly disturbs the business of Great Britain or this country, especially in matters of currency, by which confidence is unsettled, is always widespread and damaging in its effects.

The rechartered Chamber held almost forty meetings during the period of November 9, 1883, to March 11, 1885. Thirty-two of them dealt with the currency problem. Towards the end, about eight of them were devoted to banking. On May 23, 1884, a bill was introduced at the behest of Spreckels that drew the fire of Bishop. This was an act to permit the incorporation of a Hawaiian National Bank. The idea of competition in the Honolulu banking field did not trouble him; but this bill would allow almost universal business powers, several categories of tax exemptions, and many special privileges. Bishop joined S. M. Damon and Paul Isenberg in the preparation of a reasonable and constructive substitute bill. The Legislature passed the alternate banking act on August 11, 1884, and Spreckels opened his bank, May 4, 1885. This bank was later absorbed by Bishop and Company.

Bishop's chief connection with the Honolulu Chamber of Commerce came during certain of the Kalakaua years. There was a strong element of leniency in his evaluation of Kalakaua's financial operations, and throughout this consideration he assumed a dignified, constructive comportment. Few people realized that the tragedy of Mrs. Bishop's illness and decease was concurrently being enacted and must have called upon all the mental reserves that he possessed. Notwithstanding his personal grief, Bishop, with prudence and foresight, provided leadership in resolving currency and banking issues for the solid economic good of Hawaii.

THE PACIFIC CABLE

THROUGHOUT HIS LIFE in Hawaii, Bishop was constantly advocating good steamship lines to California, Australia, New Zealand, and the Orient. He had little financial interest in shipping concerns, but he was mindful of the value of a good, reliable ocean transportation service. When it came to communication, he was unusually vocal. The story of the cable and the many attempts to lay one between the West Coast and the Islands always seemed to end in complete frustration; and because of the public fretting and fussing it seemed as though next to reciprocity, the people in Hawaii wanted a cable more than anything else.

Cyrus W. Field had overcome almost insurmountable difficulties and failures in finally leading a group of English and American capitalists into the successful laying of an Atlantic cable. The task lasted from 1857 to 1866. The world was startled with this story; and it resulted in a rash of Hawaii-to-California cable projects, none of which was to succeed until John W. Mackey formed the Commercial Cable Company, later the Postal Telegraph Company, and offered to lay such a cable using all American terminals, with no subsidy and at low rates for government messages. His plans worked, and the first message went through the cable, December 28, 1902.

The announcement of the laying of the Atlantic Cable came to Bishop as he was on his first trip to America with Mrs. Bishop. He began commenting in his letters then, and he was to refer continually to the need for a cable for 35 years. He appreciated the practical worth of the virtually instantaneous transmission of information for government and industry alike.

Field followed his Atlantic triumph with efforts aimed at organizing support for a trans-Pacific cable to Hawaii. It was a futile quest. The Hawaiian Legislature met frequently to discuss the subject; and over the years it passed four separate cable acts, the first in 1874 granting "free use of roads, facilities for terminals, and exemption from port charges and duties." Bishop was a prime mover in this and the succeeding acts. An "Act to Encourage Telegraphic Communication between America and Asia" was passed by the American Congress. In 1884 the Hawaiian Legislature offered a $20,000 subsidy. The names of Celso Caesar Moreno, Leland Stanford, Mark Hopkins, Zephaniah Swift Spalding, J. A. Scrymser, and many others appeared in the cable quest down through the years.

The American State Department and the Senate's Committee on Foreign Affairs had spoken on cable matters from time to time. Numerous foreign governments wanted a share in the cable business. Subsidies, exclusive grants, protests, lawsuits, promises—all were part of cable history. Chambers of commerce and corporations marched, and as often countermarched, on the trail of the elusory cable.

On November 15, 1890, the Hawaiian Legislature passed a new act authorizing an exclusive franchise and an annual subsidy of $20,000 if the cable were laid by January 1, 1894. Bishop joined a newly organized California corporation in the company of William Alvord, S. T. Alexander, Alfred S. Hartwell, Hugh Craig, and others; and the group sent Hartwell to Washington where he almost obtained an additional subsidy of $200,000 annually and a franchise. Congress failed to take action, and the Hawaiian Legislature was persuaded to extend the franchise to January 1, 1895. However, at this time politics in Hawaii became revolutionary, and all activities relating to cables were suspended. Other efforts destined to failure followed, until the end of 1902, when Mackey closed the cable circuit and enabled communication from the Hawaiian Islands to the mainland United States to become an accomplished fact.

The participation of Bishop in cable matters was almost casual from a personal investment view. His real contribution lay in the constant nudging of his friends in government and business—he never allowed the subject to rest. A typical comment on the problem is contained in a letter which went forward to W. D. Alexander, on January 18, 1895, after he had removed himself from the earlier cable corporation affiliation:

About the Cable, I fear that there may be too much objection in Congress to giving the British Co. a lease, and that from Congress we shall get nothing but talk, and may be left without any cable! Congress should provide a cable as our people have long wished might be done, or let somebody else do it. The Republicans are so intent on opposing Mr. Cleveland and damaging the Democrats for the sake of party and power that they let public interests, financial, commercial and political go to "the dogs!"

THE TELEPHONE AND THE ELECTRIC LIGHT

BISHOP WAS NOT usually inclined to rush into anything new; but when he learned of the practical success of the original sets of telephones, first on a Maui plantation in 1878 and only months later in Honolulu where Samuel Wilder linked the office in Iolani Palace with the office in a lumber yard, he went to work. The Hawaiian Bell Telephone Company started the first service, December 30, 1879, and boasted an inventory of thirty instruments. Bishop was chairman of the first meeting to organize the company and was listed as a member of the Board of Directors. The service rendered, however, was unsatisfactory and costs jumped. Bishop soon removed himself from his director's role.

A rival organization named the Mutual Telephone Company was organized August 16, 1883. The new company encountered financial difficulties and Bishop was "present by invitation" at several of its Board meetings in 1887 and 1888 to work out a solution; a $35,000 mortgage was granted by Bishop and Company on all of Mutual's properties to be repaid in installments at seven per cent per annum. On September 11, 1889 Bishop was elected Vice-President and a month later took thirty-five hundred shares of Mutual stock at $10 par value and cancelled the mortgage. He was re-elected Vice-President each year through 1894 (at the board meeting of September 29, 1893, he was elected Director and Vice-President).

Following several false starts, a merger of the faltering Hawaiian Bell Telephone Company with the Mutual Telephone Company was completed in September, 1894. After one of the earlier attempts at merger, Bishop commented to Samuel M. Damon (May 30, 1889): "I'm surprised at the difficulties in making a union of the telephone company. There are cats and dogs in both companies."

As for the introduction of the electric light into Honolulu, Bishop was at best only lukewarm. Until 1858, when he organized Bishop and Company with Aldrich, he and his Honolulu fellow citizens had seen the use of *kukui* nut oil, wax candles, and a crude kerosene employed for lighting. In that year, C. O. Berger introduced the first gas lamps and held a contract for many years to light Honolulu's streets. In 1886, Berger proposed an installation of the new electricity for lighting, and Honolulu Iron Works proudly housed the first dynamo—that company had an abundance of fuel on hand. In the Legislature a lively debate was going on regarding the merits of electricity as a source of municipal lighting, appropriate hours for the lights to be burning, and the proper location of light standards. Bishop entered this discussion, and the report of the legislative proceedings, September 17, 1886, contains his opinion:

Honorable C. R. Bishop considered that, it was not so much the brilliant light in one place and darkness in another they wanted as a light spread over the city. The wisest thing to do would be to wait and increase the present number of lights.

What he had seen and what the Legislature was discussing was the small number of bright lights that had been turned on in the presence of a huge crowd of onlookers in the vicinity of Palace Square.

Progress in electric lighting moved swiftly. Bishop even found the question raised in his own Kamehameha Schools plant, where William Oleson and Theodore Richards ultimately received approval to install generators for campus power and light. For a while, he was reluctant to permit electric lines to be installed in the chapel at the Schools. He gave as his reason that there would be no necessity for lighting since evening meetings would not be held. But he had his way with the Museum. No lighting for more than half a century! "No museum has occasion to be open at night."

OAHU RAILWAY AND LAND COMPANY

BREWSTER, MASSACHUSETTS, was the birthplace of Benjamin Franklin Dillingham. His youthful ambition was sailoring; and this brought him to Honolulu, on the bark *Whistler,* where a prolonged visit developed as the result of a broken leg.* The temporary stopover was extended to a life-long stay in the Islands. He obtained a job as a clerk in a hardware store and shortly joined Alfred Castle in purchasing the store. This was 1869, and the new store was known as Dillingham and Company.

An ill-timed optimism about the effects of reciprocity almost brought disaster to Dillingham. The story is in a Samuel N. Castle letter to his son James, November 17, 1876:

. . . Mr. Dillingham, when East, under the feeling that reciprocity would stimulate business at once bought much too largely for the market. He forgot my cautions, oft repeated about buying and bought twice as much as we could safely do. If he had found on his return a very active & enlarged market, he might have paid, but he found it unusually dull, and pay day, could not wait. After spending sleepless nights from mental anguish approaching insanity he came to me and after I had suffered too, mentally I went to Bishop & Co. and through his [CRB] help I now hope to bridge the chasm though perhaps all I have as well as C & C's may suffer. . . .

Bishop did step in, and all involved weathered the crisis. Dillingham's optimism was justified by subsequent results, but the dark

* Dillingham broke his leg in a collision with a break (a high-set four wheel vehicle with a seat in front for the driver and another behind for the footman) while out on a horseback ride. He was removed to the Marine Hospital where he was visited frequently by Emma Smith, whom he later married. She was the daughter of missionary Lowell Smith.

days of late 1876 and early 1877 left permanent shadows on the principals involved.

Dillingham left this firm in 1889 and embarked upon a program of railway building, artesian well digging, and subsequent sugar plantation promotion which left his business and banking acquaintances aghast. His railroad was called "Dillingham's Folly." The purpose of the railroad was merely secondary to the reclamation of thousands of acres of arid and apparently profitless land. Today, while the railroad has been superseded by the truck, the thousands of acres of reclaimed land are among the most highly productive in the sugar cane world.

Bishop made use of Dillingham's practical advice on problems of his own. Long before the railroad and sugar plantation projects, he wrote to R. W. Meyer, November 29, 1884:

I have inquired of Dillingham . . . and others about a boring apparatus for finding water. None of them know of any such contrivance. In some places where there is no stone they put a steel point into a piece of iron pipe and drive it down, adding new lengths as they sink it, and when they find water put a pump in and let it remain, adding a windmill. They do that in California in some parts. Dillingham employed some of the well borers to sink a well with a hand machine. . . . He thinks it would be cheaper and more satisfactory to have a well or wells *dug* and shored up or not according to circumstances.

After experimenting with well digging Dillingham arrived at the concept of supplying artesian water for reclamation of the dry Oahu lands. But his railroad had to be first, and we find a further Dillingham reference in a Bishop letter to P. C. Jones, December 9, 1892:

If Mr. Dillingham succeeds, as he now hopes to since Gen'l Willey * has reported favorably on the securities for the bonds of the O. R. & L. Co. [Oahu Railway and Land Company] it will help a good many people in Honolulu, and may help the Gov't in making a loan on reasonable terms. No more money should be borrowed than is absolutely necessary. I take it for granted that the legislation asked for by the O. R. & L. Co. has been had, though there was some unreasonable objection made to it when first proposed.

The specific legislation referred to, House Bill 189, was interesting: it authorized validation of past and future mortgages and other conveyances of its franchises by Oahu Railway and Land Company.

Only a week later Bishop again commented on the Dillingham enterprises to Jones:

* General H. J. Willey was sent to Honolulu to make an examination of the railroad for his company, the Lancashire Investment Company.

If Mr. Dillingham succeeds, as he now thinks he will, it will be a help to Honolulu in a financial way and it may open the way for a loan to the Gov't. Mr. Campbell will hardly be so harsh and short sighted as to press Mr. D. or the O. R. & L. Co. while there is a possibility not to say probability of Mr. D's success. Gen'l Willey's report is favorable.

He viewed the early Dillingham efforts with his customary caution and found it difficult to warm up to the soundness of the economic prospects of them. General Willey's review of the railroad plans was a favorable factor in lining up the Bishop support beginning to be evident in the letters to Jones. But Bishop was still not certain. In a letter to J. O. Carter, dated January 9, 1895, he says:

Mr. Dillingham sent me a "Prospectus of the Oahu Sugar Company" which contains some large figures. I am sorry that the condition of the Sugar market and business are very much against such an undertaking. The present prospect for sugar planting is not favorable. . . .

Otto Isenberg told him that "Paul Isenberg and Mr. Hackfeld and others will likely start a large plantation in Honouliuli," and this elicited a comment from Bishop in a letter to Carter on September 28, 1896:

. . . [It] will be good for the railway and our friend Dillingham. If the latter succeeds and comes out ahead after all his trials and hard work I shall be very much pleased on his account and for his creditors and friends.

Dillingham started many projects while his massive attack on the sugar problem was under way. On June 4, 1897, Bishop wrote to C. M. Hyde:

You do not say in what way Mr. Dillingham wants to utilize the Fish Pond adjoining the Prison. He is fertile in schemes and enterprises, and I am sure that the Trustees will consider well any proposition that he may make. . . .

By July 12, there was some pressure regarding the fish pond, for again in a letter to Hyde, he observed:

Regarding the selling of the old Kaawa pond to the Railway for $7,000 . . . I should prefer . . . to wait and . . . consult Mr. Damon. . . . I notice that Mr. Dillingham offers to pay for the old pond $7,000 in Railroad bonds; How safe the Railroad bonds are of course I do not know. . . . I prefer a mortgage on the property.

I am glad to know that Mr. Dillingham is disposed to give employment to the Kamehameha boys.

Dillingham had written a letter to Bishop, under date of June 29, offering to lease Kawailoa which still had some years to run under a lease to James Campbell. But Bishop referred him to the Trustees in Honolulu in a letter dated August 2. The pond project was, therefore, still dangling; but he had a word of hopeful suggestion about Dillingham when he wrote Hyde on August 4:

Were I Mr. Dillingham's advisor, and did I think he would be likely to follow my advice, I would say to him, "You have had great success in starting, or helping to start, another large plantation at Ewa; now do not branch out again in any similar enterprise, but snug up and reduce obligations now existing."

It is doubtful if Hyde showed the letter to Dillingham. Fundamentally, the advice was sound; but Dillingham was a titan whose dreams were customarily translated into works.

Henry Holmes, secretary of the Board of Trustees of the Bishop Estate, had warned Bishop of the Railway's power under its government franchise to take property for its own use and was speaking of the Kaawa pond. Said Bishop on August 27:

. . . I hope that the Trustees may be able to sell the old pond, at a good price, on long time, taking their note and mortgage at a lower rate of interest (if necessary) than they have usually paid.

I know that Mr. Dillingham is very enterprising and sanguine and that he had remarkable success in lately getting the new plantation started in Ewa; which has and will make use of a large amount of spare capital; but I do not believe that he can repeat that or anything like it in Waialua, or that his undertaking it will be advantageous to him or to his creditors. . . . If he is depending on annexation, he may be disappointed, for that is by no means certain; and if it fails, reciprocity as under the present treaty, will not continue very long.

Bishop seemed to have overlooked his own days of somewhat similar overextension in new enterprises; but he was growing older—he was almost eighty—and was drawing the cloak of caution and reserve more closely about himself.

S. M. Damon comes into the Dillingham discussion in the Bishop correspondence about this time. A portion of Damon's personal notes to Bishop, in the amount of $150,000, were involved in the purchase of the bank and were up for payment. Bishop offered to endorse an extension if the Charles R. Bishop Trust would not. But he also suggested that the Trustees accept Oahu Railway and Land Company bonds as security, if offered by Damon for two-thirds of the $150,000 in personal notes, in the event they would not extend on one of the first two alternatives. This was the first real admission on Bishop's part of the likely soundness of the Dillingham investments. As a matter of fact, a heavy traffic in loans on Oahu Railway and

Land Company bonds was developing. The Trustees of both the Bishop Estate and the Charles R. Bishop Trust were solicited frequently on behalf of short term loans and other financing.

Bishop came to respect Dillingham's foresight. He wrote to Mr. Henry Holmes on October 1, 1897:

. . . . . .

I gladly accord to Mr. Dillingham all the credit he deserves for his enterprising spirit, unceasing industry and persistence. He has qualities which I greatly respect, and I am anxious for his success. The amount of his obligation has disturbed the minds and been a burden to some of his friends for a number of years past, and is still sufficient to cause anxiety.

Bishop's worry about Oahu Railway and Land Company bonds seemed to have evaporated by mid-year 1898. On August 3, he wrote to Carter:

Mr. Allen says that there is no intention or probability of extending the Oahu Railway beyond Kahuku, and he has great faith in the bonds of the Company as an investment, and from what he tells me of the present business of the road and the present and prospective improvements along the route which contribute to the earnings, I am favorably impressed. There is scarcely a possibility of a competing line of railway.

The Kawailoa lease was effected in August, 1898, and the Dillingham interests obtained a substantial boost to their economy. The details of the lease were worked out by Damon, and they reveal a "first" for that type of lease and set the pattern for the entire leasing fraternity in Hawaii. Bishop commented about the novel terms in a letter to Carter, August 25:

The plan of leasing the Estate lands as suggested by Mr. Damon in the offer to Mr. B. F. Dillingham seems to me wise and just, especially for large tracts and long time, i.e., to take a share of the gross income, with a minimum fixed. . . .

He was still a bit apprehensive about the railroad promotion even a year later. He confided to Carter on November 28:

. . . What you tell me of the genesis of the Waialua Agricultural Company is interesting in what seems to be its extravagance, if for nothing else. That is the spirit which is evidently abroad in the islands. How long it will continue to go "to and from and up and down," and the result thereof, remain to be seen. I hope that no one will get hurt.

In two letters to Dillingham, he expresses his appreciation for a picture and added in the first his not unusual admonition that the "people of Hawaii will not be in a hurry to undertake any more new plantations until the labor question and some other important matters which concern them are settled." In the second letter (he was writing under date of December 27, 1902) he must have been anticipating a little of the New Year's Eve atmosphere for he remarked, "I thank you for two neat little ties and wish you and your family a very happy New Year of 365 days and six hours." He added an historical note, "You are in at the landing of the Cable, which will we think be accomplished today."

The years passed, and a combination of the mellowing nature of Bishop and the very real business success of Dillingham called forth this comment, March 28, 1904, in a letter to Carter:

Our friend Mr. Dillingham, like all the others interested in planting, has been greatly disappointed in the price of sugar, this year. I hope that he will return soon, improved in health and braced up with a large stock of his usual hopefulness and courage. He has remarkable energy and ability and deserves success.

And finally when writing to Carter, November 13, 1905, it was obvious that he had come to respect Dillingham's Waialua Agricultural Company project: ". . . Plantation and other great improvements seem to be of the right kind, that is, those made during the last two years, the value of the bonds must have improved also." He used the Oahu Railway and Land Company bonds as collateral and in payment of obligations, rather generously over the years. He came to have great faith in Dillingham's enterprise and judgment. The two became close and excellent friends.

A FRATERNAL ORDER AND TWO CLUBS

International Order of Odd Fellows

BISHOP WAS NOT much of a "joiner." He was initiated in the Excelsior Lodge No. 1, I. O. O. F., about the time he opened the Bishop and Company bank in 1858. This may have come from his wish for the special kind of personal security probably obtainable at the time only through membership in some benefit society.

Gilbert Watson was a passenger on the Brig *Henry* along with Messrs. Bishop and Lee on the eventful and stormy trip to Oregon by way of Honolulu in 1846. Watson, like the others, was bound for Oregon and like the others elected to remain in Honolulu. He was the physician mentioned as one of the features in the Brig *Henry* advertisement soliciting passengers for this trip. He had in his possession a dispensation from the Grand Lodge of Odd Fellows of the United States which authorized him to organize a lodge of Odd Fellows at any place he might settle. Captain Kilborn and the second officer of the Brig *Henry* were also Odd Fellows. The three organized Excelsior Lodge No. 1, on December 10, 1846. Anthony Ten Eyck was Noble Grand, Marshall Johnson was Vice Grand, Gorham D. Gilman, Secretary, and Charles Brewer, Treasurer.

The record shows that "Chas. Reed Bishop, #152, age 36, Honolulu merchant, was initiated August 31, 1858, took his first and second degrees on October 5, and the third and fourth, November 2." The minutes do not reveal much "work" by Bishop. During his membership he is listed variously as Vice Grand, Noble Grand, Past Grand, and Grand Standard Bearer. He at least took part in the ritual.

There were certain financial advantages inherent in membership. According to the rules of the Order, death benefits were paid if a wife passes away. On October 21, 1884, it was "moved and carried that funeral benefits be paid to Bro. C. R. Bishop, Ent., to thirty dollars as funeral benefits." The lodge turned out in full regalia and took its appropriate place in the procession at the funeral of Mrs. Bishop. A letter of condolence, "to Bro. C. R. Bishop was ordered."

He finally withdrew from both the I. O. O. F. and the Polynesian Encampment and described his reasons for doing so to J. O. Carter in a letter from his residence, the Occidental Hotel in San Francisco, January 6, 1897:

It is so long since I have had anything to do with the I. O. O. F. except to pay dues, that I do not think I could work my way into a lodge of either branch of the Order; and as I do not intend to again reside in Honolulu there seems to be no good reason why I should continue to be a member of Excelsior Lodge or of Polynesian Encampment. If it is in order I hereby authorize you to apply in my name or on my behalf for withdrawal cards or letters from both lodges mentioned and if this is not in proper form please advise me that I may do all that is proper. It is not probable that I shall apply for admittance to any lodge in this country.

This association with the Odd Fellows was his only effort in the direction of a fraternal or benefit society. He was never a member of a Masonic body.

The British Club

On the purely social side we find Bishop closely identified with the British Club for a period of over twenty years; June 2, 1874, was the date he joined; December 31, 1895, the date of his resignation. When the British Club applied to the Privy Council for a charter on March 11, 1879, Bishop as a member of the Council steered the request through to approval. He was listed at the time as the owner of five shares of club stock. When he joined he paid an "entrance" of $20.00 which entitled him to two of the three hundred shares by which membership and ownership were held. In the reorganization of the British Club in the year of chartering, 1879, the capital was set at $6000 with authority to increase to $20,000. In the original capitalization, 120 shares were sold at $50.00 each. Twelve of these shares were in his name, the maximum allowable to any member. Dues were $7.50 per half year, and his dues-paying record was untarnished. The Club at one time considered leasing the old King Street Bishop home, "Haleakala," sometimes called "Paki," and more recently "the Arlington"; but this deal was not completed. This search for club facilities was made in 1892 and was occasioned by another reorganization of the Club which also involved a change of name. The old and revered German Club was merged with the British Club under the new name, Pacific Club. This reorganization was officially confirmed on September 3, 1892. Bishop was in San Francisco but his proxy was recorded for the twelve shares which he still held.

In his twenty years of membership Bishop introduced but a handful of guests, and those from among his business acquaintances from San Francisco. He probably never felt completely at ease in the Club for he was associating chiefly with college graduates and for the most part a much younger set. Perhaps his strong interest in and his close relationship to the royal family was a slight barrier. He did, however, ask W. F. Allen, his host over the years at 21 Emma Street, to entertain many of his visiting friends on his behalf at the Club. This was Bishop's only venture in a social club membership until he joined the Pacific Union Club in San Francisco in 1891.

The Social Science Association of Honolulu

The Social Science Association of Honolulu was organized by Rev. C. M. Hyde.* In Haverhill, Massachusetts, he had been a member of the Social Science Association, a group of men who met once a month to discuss topics affecting the general wellbeing of society. After becoming acquainted with the community leaders in Hawaii, Hyde invited a number to meet and form the Social Science Association of Honolulu. The first meeting was February 27, 1882.

Bishop was elected to membership January 21, 1886; and this item in the minutes described the action:

The rules were suspended by unanimous consent and Hon. C. R. Bishop was elected to membership.

He is recorded as a guest of William O. Smith at a meeting on January 14, 1884. A. Francis Judd † presented the essay that evening; his subject: "Hawaiian Currency." This was a controversial subject in the Chamber of Commerce and on the floor of the Legislature, and W. O. Smith felt Bishop would be interested in listening to Judd's essay.

Bishop continued on the roster through 1892. The Minutes show him as host in 1887, 1888, 1889, and 1892; and the meetings with him as host were held in his home at 21 Emma Street. No record is found of any essay which he might have prepared. This is a little odd since one requirement of membership is that each member present a paper as his name comes up on the roster. The Association was one of his most cherished fellowships, and his attendance was invariably regular when he was in Honolulu. Part of his interest stemmed naturally from his deep affection for Hyde, his close associate and adviser. Hyde continued as secretary of the Association almost until the day of his death in 1899.

It is more than a coincidence that Mr. Bishop's closest associates were usually listed in the same community activities. All of Mrs. Bishop's Trustees were members of the Social Science Association as was William B. Oleson, first principal of the Kamehameha School for Boys.

* See p. 54.
†Chief Justice of the Supreme Court of Hawaii.

6

Fruition

THE BERNICE P. BISHOP ESTATE
and
THE KAMEHAMEHA SCHOOLS

THREE GREAT TRUSTS carry the name of either Charles Reed Bishop or Bernice Pauahi Bishop. They constitute a group of legal charitable instruments which, chartered under the laws of Hawaii, give affectionate and sincere expression to the generosity and devotion of their creators. There is some confusion in the titles of the trusts, their purposes, and identity of the correct creator. The B. P. Bishop Estate was established in the Will of Mrs. Bishop and provided that her personal royal lands be placed in a foundation to erect and maintain The Kamehameha Schools. The Bernice Pauahi Bishop Museum Trust was endowed with the personal donations of cash and land of Mr. Bishop. The Museum was erected in his wife's memory. The Charles R. Bishop Trust was established by Mr. Bishop with his own personal funds and is chiefly a foundation of the Museum.

Thirty-four years of happily married life ended for the Bishops when Bernice succumbed in October of 1884. Perhaps in all of Bishop's long life, no obligation was held more highly or was more faithfully discharged than the one placed upon him in his wife's Will establishing The Kamehameha Schools and its foundation, the Bernice P. Bishop Estate. Over the years, he had added his touch of good, practical management to a surprisingly long list of community agencies which also had received a thumping assist from his personal resources. He volunteered scholarships to many individuals, his charities were numerous, and he devoted much of his thought and energy towards the establishment of the Bernice Pauahi Bishop Museum. This last was a solemn gesture of dedication to his wife and was initiated and supported from his own funds. But it was his wife's major project of schools for the children of her race which was to become his ascendant burden, and he never veered from his purpose to place the foundation and the institution on the high road of professional achievement and financial security.

At the outset, Mrs. Bishop held title to certain royal family lands; but upon the passing of her cousin, Princess Ruth Keelikolani in 1883, she was suddenly confronted with considerably more than a tenfold addition to her holdings. Ruth had not achieved great stature in intellectual or cultural matters, nor, perhaps, had she aspired to any prominence in these fields; but her action, as set forth in her Will written in Hawaiian and translated by John E. Bush, would bring everlasting glory and honor to her name, for hers constituted the bulk of the lands * that went into the B. P. Bishop Estate, the foundation of The Kamehameha Schools:

I, Ruth Keelikolani, being in sound mind and disposing memory, God helping me with a clear understanding; and being desirous of directing the manner of disposing of my Estate after my death: Therefore, I do hereby make, publish, and herewith declare this instrument to be my Last Will and Testament.

. . . I give and bequeath forever to my beloved cousin (kaikaina) Bernice Pauahi Bishop, my entire Estate, both real and personal, from Hawaii to Kauai, all of said Estate to be hers.

. . . I do appoint Charles R. Bishop and Rudolph W. Meyer to be my Executors of this my last Will and Testament.

(Signed) R. Keelikolani

The above written instrument consisting of one sheet was on this 24th day of January, A.D. 1883, signed and published and declared by the said Ruth Keelikolani as and for her last Will and Testament in the presence of us, who at her request and in her presence and in the presence of each other signed our names as witnesses thereto.

(Signed) Alexander Mackintosh
(Signed) Thomas Brown

Admitted to Probate June 22nd, 1883.
(Translated by Jno. E. Bush).

With one ninth of all the land area of the Kingdom in her name, Bernice embarked upon a careful study of the disposition that might properly be made of her wealth. She had the fruitful example of

---

* Princess Ruth was, next to Mrs. Bishop, the last of the Kamehamehas and had large holdings of kingdom land, some acquired in her own name from the Great Mahele and others by inheritance through Victoria Kamamalu and Governor Kekuanaoa.

THIS ANCIENT HAWAIIAN SANCTUARY (PUUHONUA)
WAS PRESERVED THROUGH THE FORESIGHT OF
CHARLES R. BISHOP WHO ADDED IT TO THE
BISHOP ESTATE. WITH THE COOPERATION OF THE
STATE OF HAWAII, THE TRUSTEES OF THE
BERNICE PAUAHI BISHOP ESTATE HAVE DEDICATED
IT TO THE PEOPLE OF THE UNITED STATES AS A
MONUMENT TO THE ACHIEVEMENTS OF THE
POLYNESIANS WHO FIRST DISCOVERED AND
SETTLED THESE ISLANDS.

Bronze Marker at Hoonaunau

From an early photograph. The building to the left is Bishop Hall, class-
room for The Kamehameha School for Boys. In the center is the Bernice Pauahi Bishop Museum and to the far right, The Kamehameha
Schools President's home.

Queen Emma and Kamehameha IV, who applied their royal acres and personal energies to a hospital for Honolulu's native sick, and the idea of Lunalilo, who placed his royal acres behind the founding of a home for Hawaii's aged. The banker and his princess discussed many plans. Bishop refers to alternate ideas in two communications: one was in the nature of an official statement and was addressed to the Trustees Under the Will of Bernice Pauahi Bishop, April 6, 1910:

When Mrs. Bishop made her will she had considered two schemes for using the income on the residue of her estate for the benefit of the people of her country, giving to either plan the name of Kamehameha, and intending that in the advantages from her benevolence those of her race should have some preference.

One scheme was to establish two schools, one for boys and one for girls, in which they would receive a good education [Mr. Bishop employed the language of the Will itself in this portion of the statement] in the common English branches, with instruction in morals and in such useful knowledge as would tend to make good and industrious men and women, and the other scheme was to establish one or more hospitals.

She chose the former, partly, I think, because of the existence of the Queen's Hospital.

In one other letter he replies to a question by S. M. Damon on this same point, October 9, 1911:

In yours of March 24th you ask me; "How did Mrs. Bishop and yourself and others come to the conclusion that the lands of Kamehameha, the Estate of Mrs. Bishop and your own gifts should all be directed toward the education of Hawaiians? My wife and I had talks about the disposal of her estate, after proof of Keelikolani's will and up to the date of her (Mrs. Bishop's) will, October 31, 1883, but nothing was said about my property. She wished to establish an institution bearing the name Kamehameha, for which name she had high respect and preference, and a hospital or hospitals and schools for boys and girls were mentioned, and in consideration of the Queen's Hospital already established, in which Kamehameha Fourth and Fifth and Queen Emma and the government had shown so much interest [he might have referred also to his own interest in Queen's Hospital for he was the key community figure in that institution for many years], it was decided that schools should be preferred, not for boys and girls of pure or part aboriginal blood exclusively, but that that class should have preference; that is they should have the first right, provided, of course, that they took advantage of the opportunity and complied with the conditions and rules of the Will and of the Trustees of the Estate. . . . Owing to the critical condition of Mrs. Bishop's health the will and codicil were somewhat hurried, but that it was intended to give full power to the executors can hardly be misunderstood. She no doubt had given more thought to the matter than I had. I did not promise to do anything for the Kamehameha Schools out of my estate, but being interested in her plans and wishes and because of her very generous gifts to me in life interest in some of her property, I decided to carry out her wishes regarding the schools and promised to do something toward a Museum of Hawaiian and other Polynesian objects, of which she and Queen Emma had some already in hand, but not on an extensive scale. After the time came for the establishment of the Schools and in order to accomplish something quickly without sacrifice or embarrassment of her estate, I soon reconveyed to her estate the life interests given by her will and added a considerable amount of my own property on Oahu, Hawaii and Molokai. . . .

The late David Oleson, son of the first Kamehameha principal, William B. Oleson, told me that his father was principal of the Hilo Boys' Boarding School in the early 1880's and had advised with Mr. and Mrs. Bishop about a school to be named Kamehameha. Agreement had been reached on four basic principles for conducting the school: it should be in Honolulu, Christian, the children should learn to write and speak English clearly, and it should be a practical school teaching the children to lead useful lives.

General Samuel Chapman Armstrong was in Honolulu in 1880 and had visited the Hilo Boys' Boarding School, long an object of his study and support. He had drawn on the Hilo school experience in establishing the Hampton Normal and Agricultural Institute. It was almost inevitable that the programs at Hilo and Hampton would appeal to the Bishops. Armstrong spent a good deal of time at the Bishop home while in Honolulu, and the 1880 talks gave a sense of direction to the planning of The Kamehameha Schools.

It was not only Armstrong who advised strong emphasis on training in vocations for the Hawaiian youth who would soon be served by the projected Kamehameha Schools. Rev. C. M. Hyde * had a pipeline right into the Bishops' minds and hearts, and training of native boys and girls in trades and home management was a chief interest of his. A new Teachers Association (public schools) held its first meeting at Lahaina, in January 1883, and its second in Honolulu, in January 1884. At each meeting Hyde spoke on the same subject: Industrial Education. Clearly, the program of studies that was to mark Kamehameha for sixty years had its start in the collective advice of Oleson, Armstrong, and Hyde.

An eminent jurist, Francis March Hatch,† was invited to prepare

* See p. 54.
† Hatch was not only a distinguished lawyer, he served as Hawaii's envoy to Washington during Cleveland's administration.

Mrs. Bishop's Will. Two originals in longhand were prepared by Hatch and signed by Mrs. Bishop. One copy was given to Henry Holmes and the other to Samuel Damon. The Holmes copy finally found its way into the files of the Probate Court.

The first meeting of the Board of Trustees, consisting of Charles Reed Bishop, Rev. Charles McEwen Hyde, William Owen Smith, Samuel Mills Damon, and Charles Montague Cooke, was held the evening of April 9, 1885, at Keoua Hale (21 Emma Street), with Bishop being chosen chairman for the evening. This was the first recorded meeting in the Minute Book of the Trustees. A good deal of financial and legal work had been tended to in the interval between the date of Mrs. Bishop's passing, October 16, 1884, and the night of the first recorded meeting.

The official date of the Trustees' appointments, fixed by the date of Mrs. Bishop's death, was October 16, 1884. With the finances and business affairs still in process of organization, the Trustees did not meet again after the April meeting until August 6; and at Bishop's invitation, they gathered around a board table in the upstairs room of Bishop and Company. This continued to be the meeting place for some years. At this meeting the all-important question of a site for The Kamehameha Schools was on the agenda. Damon immediately suggested Palama. He had been given the beautiful Moanalua Garden area as an outright gift in fee simple by Mrs. Bishop and was watching with some trepidation the low economic-level housing construction creeping *ewa* towards his beautiful hills and valleys. A sizable pair of campus sites as envisioned in The Kamehameha Schools proposal could stand athwart the march of low-cost housing, and his Moanalua could flourish and stand undisturbed beyond the Kamehameha buffer. And it worked out that way—for a time. At the next meeting, December 9, 1885, Bishop was elected President of the Board. Two weeks later, in addition to reviewing and adopting the "Prospectus for The Kamehameha Schools," the Trustees decided on the Palama site. Considering the factors of community growth as foreseeable at that time, it may be considered a wise site selection. The climate was exceedingly favorable for operating a school; and although the site was solid lava, the ground was comparatively level. King Street was a very unimportant, narrow, dirt road bisecting the campuses of the boys' and girls' schools but presented no problem then, to the school operation.

Bishop was fortunate in the availability of Robert Lishman, a contractor who had been invited to the Islands by King Kalakaua in

1875. His work on such projects as the Judiciary building, Captain Cook monument, Kamehameha I statue, and Lunalilo mausoleum was impressive. He and an expert stone mason named William Mutch were selected time after time on community projects in which Bishop held an interest. Mutch eventually became superintendent of buildings and grounds for The Schools.

At the suggestion of Bishop, lava that was quarried and dressed in individual pieces was utilized in the construction of the first important building, Bishop Hall, on the campus of The School for Boys. This was the first of several, including the first two units of the Bishop Museum quadriform and the Bishop Memorial Chapel. The lava was obtained from previously school-owned property, about two blocks *mauka* of the Houghtailing and School Streets intersection. The quarry was named the Yoachim Quarry after one of the Portuguese foremen. So highly regarded was this type of stone for exterior surfaces that the Trustees were called on by Central Union Church, the Hawaiian Lodge #21 of the Masonic order, and Punahou School, for permission to quarry lava stone from the same source. Permission was granted to each agency to take all that was required for building for $200 except that the price to Punahou was $100 (Bishop was donating the Punahou building). All of these agencies, including the Bishop Estate, supplemented the Yoachim Quarry stone with some of a whitish color from Kapena Falls in Nuuanu Valley. The stone was all dressed by hand labor; and yet, at prevailing prices, the cost was low.

The full story of the respective benefactions of Bishop and his lovely Hawaiian Princess has never been set forth in print, and it is an interesting tale in terms of the contributions of each. Mrs. Bishop held title to a vast share of the total acreage of the Kingdom of Hawaii. She derived a small income from rents of some of this land. At the January 22, 1886, meeting of the Trustees, Messrs. Bishop and Damon, who were executors of Mrs. Bishop's Will, turned over $18,705.19 in cash in settlement of the finances of her estate. The lands, except for surveying and clearing of titles, were intact. The assessed valuation of the 375,569 acres of land was $474,000 as of December 31, 1885. Much of the land Mrs. Bishop willed to her husband for a life interest. Many parcels were assigned likewise for a life interest to relatives, retainers, and friends; and the balance was placed in trust to construct and maintain the two Kamehameha Schools.

Bishop had witnessed the way the several states handled their educational lands made available under the Morrill Act of 1862, which set aside 30,000 acres in each state. He saw that the states which sold the land lost a valuable heritage. He also witnessed the basic trends of land ownership in the Bay area of San Francisco emerging to make land the best long-range investment. Therefore, he was well prepared to advise his wife regarding the desirability of retaining her lands and inserting in her Will the clause restricting the sale of her lands except for certain conditions.* This single provision proved to be the strongest insurance for perpetuity in progress and growth that could have been devised. Had it not been honored from the start The Kamehameha Schools might not have the tremendous potential they now enjoy.

Bishop, in writing to the Trustees, April 6, 1910 (he had been asked by Henry Holmes to answer some questions), said:

Being anxious that the Schools should be established as soon as practicable and maintained in a manner worthy of the generous purposes of their founder and to leave no opening for insinuation that I was personally profiting by the delay, I used all that I had received from the Estate in personal property in building Bishop Hall, the Preparatory, a part of the School for Girls, and the Chapel, and turned over some of my own lands and gave up all the properties † from which I could have taken the rental for life. . . .

The policy of not selling land was insistently and regularly reaffirmed by Bishop. His first comment on the subject appeared in a letter to Theodore Richards, October 6, 1894: "I have no respect for the economy of anyone who would expend and reduce the *capital* of the estate, although the trustees have the authority in the will to do so." To Hyde, November 7, 1896, he writes:

The capital of the B. P. Bishop Estate should not be any further reduced as there can be no better security than the lands owned by it. They should not be *sold;* but they should be leased in large tracts or small lots and for long term at just and fair rates of rent, such rate as one can with good conscience insist on prompt and full payment of. . . .

The last quotation may be considered an original statement establishing the land lease principle that later came into wide use throughout Hawaii. Among the United States of today, the system is unique to Hawaii; and it can readily be traced to the feeling enunci-

---

* J. Garner Anthony, *Wills and Deeds of Trust* (3rd ed.; Honolulu Printshop of Hawaii Co., Ltd. 1957), p. 24.

† See pp. 165–171.

ated by Bishop in that letter. He had but the day before written more specifically to Carter:

I am glad to know that the Trustees are opposed to selling the land at Waialua or any other valuable lands belonging to the Estate, and the talk about public interest in the matter does not impress me favorably. I have heard a good deal of that kind of talk, which seems to me pure cant. The objects to which the income of the Estate is devoted seem to me to be in the public interest. At any rate, it is our duty as Trustees to protect the interests committed to our care. The Estate cannot have any better security than the real estate which it owns. . . .

He wrote to Henry Holmes on September 2, 1897:

I am as a rule strongly opposed to selling the lands of the estate of Mrs. Bishop, and in consenting to a sale of the Molokai property am making an important exception to that rule for reasons that seem to me good. . . .

Carter was a frequent target of these "don't sell the land" exhortations. Once, on January 11, 1906, Bishop insisted, ". . . The more I think that the best security for the estate and the support and perpetuation of the schools is in its real estate, even if it pays but quite [*sic*] return. . . ." Another letter was dispatched with the date line, September 27:

If the lots can be leased on a *net* rental of four per cent . . . on long lease to desirable tenants, I would say hold on to the lands and make the leases. Even three per cent *net* may be better than taking the risk of investments in such bonds and mortgages as are now obtainable in Hawaii! The right to make investments outside the territory should be seriously considered. . . . If the Estate can own real estate in California without being subject to taxes upon it in the Territory I would be in favor of some purchases of favorable terms.

The long leases to the plantations are now the best investments existing. . . .

He was impressed with results of the leasehold arrangement, for even in the few years remaining to him, the corpus or capital structure of the estate was substantially enhanced; and the income available from new and adjusted leases showed a remarkable and steady climb. His only reaction to this development and growth on the part of the estate, and one which almost overshadowed his sense of satisfaction about the whole thing, was his constant recoil from the reports indicating that spending was eternally keeping pace. His utterances regarding the desirability of the leasehold process were paralleled by his regular and frequent complaints about expenses of

present school activities and the ever-recurring rush of newly proposed projects in education.

While "not selling the land" was but a strong admonition, it was
carefully observed. The real job of the Trustees was to establish two
schools, one for girls and one for boys; and the Will stated Mrs.
Bishop's intentions clearly. The boys' school was to come first;
consequently, we find a group of boys assembling October 3, 1887,
for a first day of school with formal and official school opening
exercises on November 4, 1887. The school was called the Manual.
For a principal, the Trustees had looked no farther than the Hilo
Boys' Boarding School, where William Brewster Oleson,* a new
Englander, had happily and very adequately acted as principal
since 1878. Oleson was absent from his Hilo post for nine months in
1881, and upon his return he pitched into an expansion program
which attracted Bishop's attention. In the Bishop Estate Minutes of
January 22, 1886, an entry states; "Dr. Hyde inquired if the trustees
could not make some definite proposition to Mr. Oleson. Not
ready."

Bishop was ready however. He got off a note to Oleson, February
1, 1886—advance warning of an impending offer: ". . . I further
hope that matters will so arrange themselves in your mind and to
you, that you will be ready and willing, to take hold and build up
the Kamehameha School for Boys. . . ." On February 26, 1886,
Oleson was officially recognized in the Estate Minutes with an offer
of a position as principal at a salary of "$3000, a dwelling and
pasturage." On April 15, 1886, the Minutes show an acceptance by
Oleson, and he came on to Honolulu that summer to start work on
selection of students, preparation of courses of study, recruitment of
staff, and construction of necessary facilities. The Trustees met
regularly once a month, and the records show that Bishop attended
every meeting in 1886 except one, in December, and every meeting
in 1887 except two, in September and October. He was in San
Francisco upon both occasions. During his absence in the fall of
1887, it looked as though the opening would be marred by the tardy
arrival of certain of the new teachers. He explained to Damon,
October 7: "Mr. Oleson and all of you will be disappointed by the
new arrival of the teachers, whom ere this you know will go in the
Mariposa, three weeks behind the time when they should have
been there."

* See pp. 171–173, 241.

They did arrive late, and this accounts for the postponement of the opening exercises to November 4. The *Mariposa* docked in Honolulu, October 28; and the teachers were whisked up to Palama by horse and buggy. They had a week at their disposal to orient themselves and to prepare the very new students for a public opening ceremony of the Manual. The formal opening must have been exciting. Princess Liliuokalani and other members of the royal family were present. The Minutes of the meeting of December 2, in which the above item was recorded, contain some other interesting passages:

Board. For breakfast the boys have had bread, poi, beefstew and coffee; for dinner bread, poi, salmon and occasionally bananas; for supper, bread, taro, or sweet potatoes, beef stew, milk and occasionally sugar cane. Sunday noon, the meal consists of bread, rice, sugar and milk.

Mrs. Bishop's birthday was December 19; and the first opportunity that presented itself for a Kamehameha Schools observance was December 19, 1887, a few weeks after the opening of the Manual. Bishop had returned from the mainland a few days earlier and was the one to whom all turned for a keynote of commemoration. Before an interested audience of Hawaiian royalty, fellow townsmen, and the new and rather small and select student body of the Manual, Bishop presented a stirring address:

The Trustees of the estate of the late Hon. Bernice Pauahi Bishop, deeming it proper to set apart a day in each year to be known as Founder's Day, to be observed as a holiday by those connected with the Kamehameha Schools, and a day of remembrance of her who provided for the establishment of these schools, have chosen the anniversary of her birth, the 19th of December, for that purpose, and this is the first observance of the day. If an institution is useful to mankind, then is the founder thereof worthy to be gratefully remembered. Kamehameha I, by his skill and courage as a warrior, and his ability as a ruler, founded this nation. Kamehameha II, abolished the tabu and opened the way for Christianity and civilization to come in. Kamehameha III gave to the people their *kuleanas* and a Constitutional Government and thus laid the foundation for our independence as a nation. Kamehameha IV and Queen Emma were the founders of the Queen's Hospital. Kamehameha V was a patriotic and able sovereign and Lunalilo was the founder of a Home which bears his name. All these should be held in honored remembrance by the Hawaiian people.

Bernice Pauahi Bishop, by founding the Kamehameha Schools intended to establish institutions which should be of lasting benefit to her country; and also to honor the name of Kamehameha, the most conspicuous name in Polynesian history, a name with which we associate ability, courage, patriotism and generosity. The founder of these schools was a true Hawaiian. She knew the advantage of education and well directed industry. Industrious and skillful herself, she respected those qualities in others. Her heart was heavy when she saw the rapid diminution of the Hawaiian people going on decade after decade, and felt that it was largely the result of their ignorance and carelessness. She knew that these fair islands, which only a little more than a century ago held a population of her own race estimated at 300,000 or more, would not be left without people; that whether the Hawaiians increased or not, men from the East and men from the West would come in to occupy them; skillful, industrious, self-asserting men, looking mainly to their own interests. The hope that there would come a turning point, when, through enlightenment, the adoption of regular habits and Christian ways of living, the natives would not only hold their own in numbers, but would increase again like the people of other races at times grew faint and almost died out. She foresaw that, in a few years the natives would cease to be much, if any in the majority, and that they would have to compete with other nationalities in all the ways open to them for getting an honest living; and without legal preferences for their protection, that their privileges, success and comfort, would depend upon their moral character, intelligence and industry. And so, in order that her own people might have the opportunity for fitting themselves for such competition, and be able to hold their own in a manly and friendly way, without asking any favors which they were not likely to receive, these schools were provided for, in which Hawaiians have the preference, and which she hoped they would value and take the advantages of as fully as possible.

Could the founder of these schools have looked into the future and realized the scenes before us this day, I am sure it would have excited new hopes in her breast, as it does in my own. If the Hawaiians while continuing friendly and just toward those of all other nationalities, are true to themselves, and take advantage of the opportunities which they have, and are governed by those sound principles and habits in which they have been instructed, and in which these youths now present are here being taught day by day both in precept and example, there is no reason why they should not from this time forth, increase in numbers, self-reliance and influence. But, on the other hand, if they are intemperate, wasteful of time, careless of health and indifferent as to character; if they follow those evil examples of which there are so many on every side, then nothing can save them from a low position and loss of influence, in their own native land, or perhaps from ultimate extinction as a race. But let us be cheerful and hopeful of the best and see to it that from these schools as well as from other good schools shall go out young men fitted and determined to take and maintain a good standing in every industry and occupation in which they may engage. The schools are to be permanent and to improve in method as time goes on. They are intended for capable, industrious and well-behaved youths only; and if Hawaiian boys of such character fail to come in, other boys will certainly take their places. We look to those who may be trained in the Kamehameha Schools to honor the memory of the founder and the name of the schools by their good conduct, not only while in school, but in their mature lives as well. So long as we are in the right, we may reasonably trust in God for his help; let us always try to be in the right.

In the ten minutes' delivery time of this first Founder's Day address, he expressed Mrs. Bishop's whole philosophy underlying the establishing of her charity; and, certainly, he was also speaking for himself. Founder's Day was not officially adopted as a Kamehameha memorial day until set into the Minutes at the June 15, 1888, meeting of the Trustees.

The Manual was scarcely launched before Bishop realized an educational need that had not been covered in the plans set forth in Mrs. Bishop's Will. There were many of the younger Hawaiian boys homeless for one reason or another with no school or home for them. Consequently, in the May 18, 1888, Minutes, a start is made:

Mr. Bishop stated that he would build at his own expense, and present to the Estate, the school building for younger boys, the Trustees to have charge and management of the school and he submitted plans of the building.

Mr. Cooke moved, seconded by Dr. Hyde that the Trustees accept for the Estate the very generous offer of Mr. Bishop with thanks, and pledge themselves to maintain this school in accordance with Mr. Bishop's wishes as a department of the Kamehameha School for Boys.

Thus was launched a second unit in the Kamehameha group, with Miss C. A. Reamer in charge. October 29, 1888, the Preparatory Department was opened; and on Founder's Day, December 19, it was dedicated. Upon this occasion a Lieutenant Robert Crawford and Bishop shared the rostrum and gave addresses. A year later, Bishop was on the platform again and this time shared the speaking honors with his life-long friend, General James Fowle Baldwin Marshall. Included in his Charles R. Bishop Trust deed was a mandatory provision that the sum of $200 be allowed toward the expenses of the annual Founder's Day celebration. During this time, the proposal was made that the Trustees "take the Kawaiahao Seminary as the Girls School. . . ." This was only one of several proposals of mergers that came to the Trustees over the years, and this one was rejected as indeed all were.

Mrs. Bishop's provision for a girls' school was almost overlooked in the rush of firmly establishing the boys' school and the Preparatory Department. It was discussed briefly in the meeting of February 21, 1890. The secretary recorded this:

. . . Some discussion took place about the kind of school for girls . . . no decision was made . . . but it seemed to be the opinion of the Trustees, that a school to teach employment, such as cooking, dressmaking, care of house etc etc for older girls, would be preferable to a preparatory for young girls.

But a school for girls was ever in Bishop's thoughts. Founder's Day had had its fifth commemoration, and he could see that the boys' school was well launched. The Trustees' Minutes of December 30, 1891, reflect his concern:

The President feared that the establishment of the Girls' School was being lost sight of. Very little provision had so far been made for this important trust and every additional improvement carried out at the K. S. for Boys delayed the day when its execution would be undertaken.

Two years were to pass and the goal was still not in sight. In the Minutes of May 6, 1893, an entry states that:

Mr. Bishop gave it as his opinion that commencement on the Kamehameha School for Girls should not be thought of for the present. . . .

This was a reference to current political events, which reflected his deep feelings regarding his adopted land. The following item appears in the Minutes of the same meeting, May 6, 1893. The shaky and tottering Provisional Government had just been created a few weeks before, and the very future of native Hawaiians was in social and political jeopardy:

The President said there was one matter upon which he would like to express his views, whatever was the outcome of the present state of political affairs he hoped the Hawaiian flag would always be the flag of the Kamehameha Schools. It was always to be remembered that these were the Kamehameha Schools; the Hawaiian flag was the flag of the Kamehamehas and it ought to be displayed at the School on all anniversaries and occasions when flags were usually displayed.

The Schools have faithfully and carefully observed this injunction. An American flag flies at the top of each of the Kamehameha flagpoles; and on all Sundays, holidays, and anniversaries, an Hawaiian flag is raised to a position immediately below.

The Trustees voted to commence the School for Girls in 1894. On November 17, 1893, the Trustees are recorded as going "out to Palama . . . to select a site for the [Girls] school. . . ." Ida May

Pope,* principal of the Kawaiahao Seminary, was employed to head
the school. On February 28, 1894, Bishop, in Honolulu for a short
time before his permanent move to San Francisco, attended his
next-to-last meeting with the Trustees. At this time, a site was
selected *makai* of the boys' school campus and across King Street.
The plans for the first buildings were reviewed and adopted; ground
was broken March 13. Miss Pope left about this time for a mainland
trip to recruit teachers and purchase needed furnishings and equipment. Bishop offered some of the furnishings of his palatial, 21
Emma Street home to the girls' school. On August 17, 1894, he
offered $5,000 for the building fund if it were needed. The total cost
of the project was estimated at $65,000. The Kamehameha School
for Girls was opened with some fanfare and a considerable audience
of Hawaiian royalty and Honolulu friends, December 19, 1894.
Thirty-five pupils constituted the enrollment on this date. By now
the exact cost could be computed; and exclusive of the donations of
furniture, the figure came to $94,908.98. Bishop noting this made
available as a gift an additional $20,000. Due to the wood frame
construction and the ease with which the ground could be prepared,
the project was readied in only a few months.

One other department almost came into being about this time.
Theodore Richards proposed the organization of a normal school.
The idea was discussed in a Trustees' meeting, December 6, 1893.
Bishop was not in town. Richards was invited to the meeting to
report a conference with President Dole, chairman of the Government Advisory Council, which was concerning itself with a reorganization of the Board of Education. "A Kamehameha-managed school
for teachers would," in Richards' opinion, "commend itself to the
Board of Education because of its cheapness. It also would give
Hawaiian teachers an equal competitive opportunity with others for
government teaching jobs." The Trustees questioned the propriety
of this, especially since the government would be closely associated
in management and control in such an arrangement. No action was
taken, but the discussion certainly gave stimulation to the early
planning recently started on the projected girls' school.

On March 16, 1894, the Trustees considered ". . . the advisability
of making the Preparatory School a model or normal school for the
practice class of the Manual. . . ." They decided to establish a
normal class strictly under Kamehameha auspices. J. L. Dumas was

* See pp. 181–183.

employed as instructor and he immediately moved a little too fast for Bishop's mental comfort. Dumas contributed an article to a local paper, *Holomua,* August 12, 1894, entitled "A New Departure." In this, Dumas stated that "Hawaiians not graduates of or students not connected with Kamehameha School, are invited to join the normal class." This evoked, beyond the quotation from Dumas' article which Bishop placed in his letter of August 28, 1894, to Richards, a usual admonition:

It may not be necessary, but you will permit me to advise you against making any departure from the usual order in the schools or incurring any new expenses or making concessions to first bring the matter before the trustees and secure their approval and authorization in such definite form as to prevent any possibility of misunderstanding or blame.

Nothing much came of the normal class activity but it was the forerunner of the government normal school which opened shortly thereafter, causing the Kamehameha normal class to be dropped.

Economy at the Schools

Bishop's letters in the 1890's, and until a year before his death, dwell on two or three basic themes as regards the welfare and future of the schools. A chief theme was economy. This was closer than a second-nature theme with him—it was his first nature. One time he expressed himself strongly to Theodore Richards, February 8, 1895:

. . . The expenses have been very large, and with so many persons under pay I fear that they are likely to continue heavy. When I think of the large income of the Estate and what I have added to it in money, lands in Kona and Honolulu and Molokai and the rents given up, the present debt gives me a chill. Money which comes easily is usually spent freely —often too freely. I do not like to find fault, but I do wish to have all proposed improvements and changes well considered before spending the money, in short, I ask for real and constant economy.

Richards fired a quick reply back to Bishop, who replied in return, March 5:

I am satisfied that you have no idea of being careless or extravagant as to the expenses of the school under your charge. . . . In nearly everything we do, in matters of State, Church or School, the business-man's view of the dollar and cent aspect has an important place. . . .

But admonitions continued to flow, and everyone in Honolulu in any major position related to the Estate or the Schools became the object of the economy emphasis; Bishop wrote to Richards on May 17, 1895: ". . . I would be less unwilling to try some experiments were the Estate out of debt and in funds." He wrote to Carter, September 18: "In observing the Founder's Day, it is not intended that it shall be made expensive by any great demonstrations or feasts. . . ." Again he wrote to Carter, November 5: ". . . I think it is desirable to have whether in business or in a matter of the Estate, a *reserve* to meet contingencies. . . ." To Hyde, Bishop writes on November 6: ". . . Is it not wise for us to finish what we have under way both in the Schools and the Museum, and to snug up affairs, before we branch out into anything new?"

It was not by coincidence that this concentration of the barrage was delivered within a few days to several different key Honolulu figures. Bishop was truly alarmed by the rapid build-up of expense, and he expressed his apprehension to Richards on March 9, 1896:

The large expenditures for various things and the large overdraft of the Estate at the Bank is a source of constant irritation and regret to me, and no watchfulness and pain should be spared to get back again into a proper condition. . . . I never intended there should be any debt except possibly as a temporary incident for a small sum. To deliberately increase that debt . . . would be little short of a crime. . . . Improvement should be made gradually, according to needs and *means*. . . . My contributions to the Estate were intended to protect the capital and prevent debt.

The Bishop worry about the ever present possibility of a financial statement out of balance is nowhere better expressed than in this note to Carter, August 30, 1899:

I am more anxious than I am willing to express, to see the expenditures for the schools and their premises brought and kept within the net income from rents and interest, as they certainly should be. To see property sold and the proceeds used in any way other than as an investment hurts my feelings. Unnecessary ornamentation and improvements should be postponed until they can be paid for out of surplus revenue. I fear that I shall never see the balance in the account on the right side, and I hope that in my last days I may not be haunted with the ghost of a doubt as to the wisdom of devoting the estate to the establishment of such schools. Good work has been done and I hope that by wise management and control it may continue and improve for *centuries* to come. An example of true economy without haste or waste will be a good object lesson in that community.

It was not unusual to find him writing emphatically about economy to the principals—they were logical targets, because their support of their own educational programs was a powerful factor in the schools' spending. He wrote to Uldrick Thompson, who relieved Richards as Principal of the Manual, October 11, 1899: "The question of protecting and managing the estate wisely and for the future prosperity and perpetuity of the schools occupies my thoughts a great deal." A little later, March 21, 1902, Charles Bartlett Dyke, Principal of both the boys' and girls' schools, received a letter:

. . . An impression has prevailed in the community that the income of the Estate was so large that there was no necessity for economy, or caution in expenditures or privileges, and that carefulness on the part of the Trustees might properly be called meanness!

If the Kamehameha Schools are to *endure* . . . the yearly expenditures must soon be brought down and kept *clearly within* the net income of the estate . . . there should be the beginning of a reserve fund out of possible surplus to provide against unlooked for accidents and demands. The capital of the Estate which is the endowment of the schools, must be protected and preserved. . . .

The Kamehameha Program of Studies

Bishop never aspired to the role of educator, yet he was forever engaged in a voluntary and strong support of numerous educational enterprises. Given a practical common sense chance to evaluate both the needs of youth and the economic requirements in terms of educational preparation for living in the Kingdom of Hawaii, he developed a few basic principles and did not hesitate to enunciate them.

In a long letter to Theodore Richards, October 25, 1893, he goes into some detail on education at Kamehameha:

Self control and discipline should be inculcated, and you cannot have any military training, and keep it up without some "fuss and feathers." Look at all the trapping and showy colors in the military organizations. . . . Order in the rooms and cleanliness in person and apparel need to be carefully looked after. . . . If the *teachers* can bear the *noise* of the practice of beginners on wind instruments, I do not know that I have any objection to a band, if it does not take the place of work or singing.

He believed in outdoor trips, and writes to Richards, May 17, 1895:

. . . I spoke to Mr. Oleson about taking the boys out into the country for the purpose of studying trees, plants, birds and so on. Such expeditions are good not only for the boys but the teachers also.

The dairy and agricultural school I must say that I am doubtful about. If it is undertaken I am fearful it will cost more than it will be worth, and prove a disappointment.

To Hyde, he expatiated on music, February 16, 1898:

. . . I am afraid that the teaching in music and some other branches in the Girls' School is of too high or ornamental a character for the best good of the girls. Any teaching or style of living that does not take into account the relationship, homelife, opportunities and probable future of the students, especially in Hawaii may lead to disappointment and misery.

Uldrick Thompson heard from Bishop under date of June 2, 1898, stating some thoughts on the school:

. . . We know that the object and aim of the school is to train and equip Hawaiian youth for good and useful living, with correct ideas as to industry, economy and self helpfulness. . . . It is my wish that the Hawaiian young men should make themselves handy, if not skillful, in many ways, so that they may hold their own in the strong competition of workers of other races. Intelligent and honest industry with *inexpensive* habits of living is their necessary equipment.

His correspondence with Thompson was filled with advice on teaching the virtues of thrift, economy, and good habits of work. He also expressed pleasure with reports sent to him from time to time concerning the progress in the agricultural courses. He did not have much faith in this subject at Kamehameha, but his distrust was based on the costliness of preparing the sterile rocky soil on the school grounds and the need for irrigation. Yet, when Thompson had successes, Bishop could spare a reserved appreciative commendation–October 7, 1899:

I am not going to question your calculation of income for milk, (at the high price of *ten* cents per quart) bananas etc., for I'm pleased to know that you hope to do so well, and I shall be interested in the result. . . . The instruction in Agriculture etc, should be mainly such as can be put in practice and made profitable by the students after they leave the school, and when they have no "rich estate" behind them to pay the bills.

When Perley Horne came on the scene some years later and first held the new title, President of the Kamehameha Schools, he was addressed by Bishop. The date was March 9, 1908:

I quite agree with Mr. Oleson in his remarks about agriculture at Kamehameha. The soil there is too poor and too rebellious—as they say of some of the ores—and water too scarce and costly to make farming a success or possible at any reasonable outlay. He is right too as to the importance of a thorough knowledge and correct use of English in the schools.

He enlarged upon the common subjects again to Horne, March 3, 1910. Bishop was eighty-eight years old, but his logic and incisiveness would have been a credit to a far younger man:

Drill and practice in English and mathematics need to be thorough and constant. So long as they find employment in the schools as teachers they must, of course, have good instruction in the ordinary studies of the common schools in order to fit them for such employment.

My impression is that one of the errors of the present system of the schools is having too many kinds of lessons. For the teachers the change from one subject to another breaks up the monotony and is restful, but does it not lead to superficiality in the pupils?

. . . Training for character, good habits and health are of the very highest consequence.

In the October 9, 1911, letter to Damon quoted above, Bishop states:

The schools are doing good work now, and I do not see at present any necessity for any considerable change in the system. Thoroughness in teaching both in the academical and in the manual branches should be kept up and in the discipline and moral influence there should be no letting down.

He still was advising two years later. On March 22, 1913, he addressed himself to his cousin, E. Faxon Bishop, a Trustee of the Bishop Estate:

It may or may not have been a mistake to drop the tailoring which used to be taught and practiced at Kamehameha. I do not know of anything that the young men are more likely to follow than to follow the trade of tailoring, if they will fit themselves to be good workmen. I believe that a moderate amount of knowledge in that line would, to say the least, do them no harm. The prejudice against that trade is rank folly.

He was supporting an outmoded item in the vocational education list. However, he was still expressing his normal reaction to any change in the vocational education program which might seem to weaken the potential training ground for growth in character, habits of work, and a usable trade skill.

His whole thesis of unfailing emphasis on the value of work, discipline, and good teaching was not different from the growth and experience in these qualities in his own life. Such emphasis has been a guiding principle in the subsequent work of the Trustees and has characterized the climate of the Schools for three quarters of a century.

Who May Attend Kamehameha?

There is a wealth of research available regarding Mrs. Bishop's intentions in the matter of the admission of students at Kamehameha. In her Will we find these passages, and they contain all that governs:

. . . to erect and maintain in the Hawaiian Islands two schools, each for boarding and day scholars, one for boys and one for girls. . . .
    . . . and to devote a portion of each year's income to the support and education of orphans, and others in indigent circumstances, giving the preference to Hawaiian of pure or part aboriginal blood.

Even this juxtaposition of two excerpts unrelated in the Will may be misleading, and a clarification of it will be found in the references which follow. The Prospectus prepared by the Trustees immediately after Mrs. Bishop's death, in an early meeting, contains direct statements of explanation of her intentions:

. . . While they will be conducted with special reference to advantages to be afforded to Hawaiians by preference, as the will requires, they will not be exclusively Hawaiian . . . the noble minded Hawaiian chiefess who endowed the Kamehameha Schools, put no limitation of race or condition on her general bequest.

Regardless of what the Prospectus and the Will may say, there was an unshakeable assumption on the part of the Hawaiian people that Kamehameha belonged to their children; and in all his years Bishop never deviated from a full and generous support of that assumption. He wrote to Hyde, February 11, 1897:

There is nothing in the will of Mrs. Bishop excluding white boys or girls from the Schools, but it is understood by the Trustees that only those having native blood are to be admitted at present, that they are to have the preference so long as they avail themselves of the privileges open to them to a reasonable extent.

A more general confirmation of this position appeared two years later in a letter to Carter:

The great work of The Schools is in building character and establishing habits of industry, order, self-helpfulness, and ambition. Character building and preparation for successful struggle with the conditions of life which they cannot avoid and which belong to the common people who are obliged to earn their living were the objects and the class which the founder of The Schools had in mind.

To Damon, he wrote on February 20, 1901, and this letter was spread on the Minutes of the Trustees:

Considering the understanding and the past policy of the Trustees, I think that Mr. Thompson was justified in declining to admit a boy to the school who had no Hawaiian blood in his makeup. According to the reading of Clause 13 on Page 8 of the Will as published, the preference to Hawaiians of pure or part aboriginal blood applied only to education of orphans and others in indigent circumstances; but it was intended and expected that the Hawaiians having aboriginal blood would have preference, provided that those of suitable age, health, character, and intellect should apply in numbers sufficient to make up a good school, and provided, of course, that they should observe the rules and meet the conditions as to payment, etc. made by the Trustees. Education of the natives was the first, but not the exclusive and perpetual purpose of the Founder of The Schools. . . .

The boarding schools in Hilo and Lahainaluna were in large degree held as examples, with expected improvements of course. The Schools were intended to be perpetual, and as it was impossible to tell how many boys and girls of aboriginal blood would in the beginning or thereafter qualify and apply for admissions, those of other races were not barred or excluded.

In a Founder's Day address he included a mention of the admissions policies:

If the advantages provided to be enjoyed on such exceptional favorable terms were not appreciated and availed of by the natives, they would be opened to others. . . . It was wise to prepare for and admit natives only, and I do not think the time has yet come when it is better to depart from that rule. The natives, however, have got to try to hold their own in competition with races whose habits of life are comparatively inexpensive and who can thrive on moderate wages.

. . . If the youth of native blood fall off in numbers, or stand off in any improper way the youth of other races will be taken in, of course, on terms suited to the conditions which then exist.

As to white boys exciting emulation in the school, I am not impressed. There is a pretty free admixture of the blood of a number of races there already.

The Trustees received another comment on admissions from him; March 10, 1909, was the date of the letter:

The Trustees of the Kamehameha Schools, owing to conditions peculiar to the country, and the pecuniary circumstances of the aboriginal Hawaiians, who are to a degree to be preferred to all other races, are caused expenses which would not apply to other countries.

On April 6, 1910, he wrote a long letter to the Trustees, commenting on an opinion rendered by Henry Holmes on certain points in

Mrs. Bishop's Will. The first paragraph is one of general summary:

When Mrs. Bishop made her Will she had considered two schemes for using the income on the residue of her estate for the benefit of the people of her country, giving to either plan the name of Kamehameha, and intending that in the advantages from her benevolence those of her race should have some preference.

He was more specific and more emphatic in a letter to Damon, October 9, 1911:

It is decidedly my wish that the native Hawaiians of pure and part aboriginal blood shall, in sufficient numbers to form convenient and efficient schools, take advantage of the preference given them by the Will, with the understanding, of course, that they be obedient to the rules and conditions made by the Trustees under the Will; if they do not do so, they cannot expect that others not of their class shall be permanently excluded. So long as the number of applicants keeps up as it has done so far, it seems to me better that the young people of other nationalities should not be admitted.

It is obvious that Mr. and Mrs. Bishop were in complete understanding as to her purposes in providing for the education of boys and girls of native Hawaiian stock. The course set by Mrs. Bishop and strongly adhered to by her husband in the thirty years remaining to him after Mrs. Bishop's passing has become firmly established.

Thoughts on Being a Trustee

Advice was given freely by Bishop. Many were the comments on how the Trustees should conduct themselves, their obligations under the Trust instrument, how to keep records, how to approach new proposals, and what to do in a host of situations. Mrs. Bishop had started it off with the charge that, "my Trustees should do thorough work in regard to said schools as far as they go." To Hyde, Bishop wrote on November 6, 1895, a letter filled with long distance advice: ". . . The Deed gives wide discretion to the Trustees, and I have no doubt but that they will use it cautiously and wisely."

He was considering a trustee setup for the Museum Trust and wrote his views to Damon, January 27, 1896. Therein is contained a key to much of the thinking that motivated him in the manner in which he prepared the Charles R. Bishop Trust and advised his wife with regard to her estate. This letter is quoted [*] in the chapter

[*] See pp. 195–196.

dealing with the Bishop Museum. On March 19, 1897, he wrote to Hyde:

There is one point which I consider important in conducting the affairs of the various Trusts, and that is that there should be a perfect understanding between all of the Trustees, so that each may know and have a voice in all that is done or proposed.

Again he wrote to Hyde, April 29:

It is my purpose to resign all my Trusteeships as soon as possible after I confer with Mr. Damon, so that someone residing in Honolulu may be appointed in my stead.

Dated May 15, another letter to Hyde states:

It is unfortunate that so many (trustees) should be unavoidably absent for a considerable time, all at once, and I hope that after the return of Mr. Damon and Mr. Allen, and when someone shall have been appointed in my place, there will be no resignations for many years to come.

On October 13, he sent his resignation to the Trustees of the Estate of Mrs. Bernice Pauahi Bishop in these words:

It being important and desirable that the Trustees of the Estate of Mrs. Bernice Pauahi Bishop should be residents of Honolulu, and as I am now a permanent resident of this City of San Francisco, I hereby tender my resignation as a Trustee under the Will of the late Mrs. Bernice Pauahi Bishop. . . .

An aside on Trustee qualifications is noted in a letter to Carter, August 30, 1899:

God bless the women. Do not think of appointing a woman on either board as trustee. It is not necessary nor would it be wise or right to do so. This is not disrespectful to the sex or any individual.

Bishop's Land Benefactions for Kamehameha

Bishop's contributions to The Kamehameha Schools included all lands willed to him in life interest by his wife and certain lands acquired by him on his own account. The total value of his direct cash gifts to the Schools approximated the value as appraised for probate of the 375,569 acres in Mrs. Bishop's estate. The demands of the newly organized School for Girls, as well as the expanding cost of the School for Boys and the Preparatory Department, constituted a worrisome problem. To meet the requirements for operation and capital outlay from estate resources would have meant selling off most of the valuable acres in Mrs. Bishop's holdings. To provide additional income from rents and leases, he began turning back to the Estate his life interest lands willed to him by Mrs. Bishop, together with some of his own.

Bishop thus surrendered the rentals on all the parcels, consisting of 29,069 acres of her lands and 64,619 acres of his lands, which would carry a conservative gross rental value of one million dollars over the twenty-one–twenty-five year surrender period. The value of Bishop's own properties at the time of transfer to the B. P. Bishop Estate may be set conservatively at one million dollars. Thus his total benefactions to The Kamehameha Schools, consisting of direct cash contributions, rents, various incomes available from the returned land holdings, his own transferred properties, and the land pieces themselves, were close to two and a half million dollars.

The transfers of land returned were recorded in seven deeds, the first of which was dated February 1, 1890, and the last, February 14, 1895. Bishop's life interest property transfers were recorded in the following deeds: Deed Number One, February 1, 1890; Deed Number Four, April 27, 1893; Deed Number Six, October 1, 1894; Deed Number Seven, February 14, 1895. Transfers of his personally owned properties were made by deed as listed below. Deed Number One included both life interest and his personally owned items. All other deeds were of his ownership and included: Deed Number Two, March 23, 1891; Deed Number Three, May 19, 1892; and Deed Number Five, April 27, 1893.

Among the properties turned over to his wife's estate were several of historic importance. These included the home sites of the Bishops (Haleakala) and Princess Ruth (Keoua Hale) and the *ahupuaa* * of Honaunau in South Kona, Hawaii. This last named area is devoted to coffee, grazing, and forest reserve. There were 7120 acres in the original tract. This good-sized piece of coffee and grazing land belonging to the estate of Levi Haalelea was auctioned off to

* Land ownership in Hawaiian history started with the several districts into which any island would be divided. A *district* was a large area representing the domain of a high chief. A division of a district was called an *ahupuaa* and usually constituted the domain of a lesser chief. It was a strip of land frequently wedge-shaped (due to the rough pie-shaped configuration of an island) extending from the sea to a mountain ridge. An *ili* was a division of land usually a step in status below the *ahupuaa*. There might be two or more in an *ahupuaa*. A *kuleana* was a small land claim within another's land. These terms are still used for geographic boundaries in legal land papers in Hawaii.

Charles Kanaina (Father of Lunalilo) in October, 1866, for $5,000. Kanaina was unable to raise that sum and on April 1, 1867, the court accepted Bishop's offer in the same amount. Contained within this tract was the sacred City of Refuge. Having in mind that Mrs. Bishop's grandmother had lived close by at Keei, and that the spot possessed an unusual religious significance in Hawaiian history, the Trustees of the B. P. Bishop Estate, on April 30, 1959, deeded a parcel of 164.42 acres which included the City of Refuge and related contributory living sites to the people of the United States. A bronze plaque describing this gift was dedicated on March 26, 1962.

Two other transactions were of notable and historic interest. Bishop owned the valley of Waipio on the island of Hawaii. On June 6, 1881, William C. Parke, Administrator and Commissioner, having been ordered to sell the real estate of Charles Kanaina, deceased intestate, offered for sale at public auction to the highest bidder for cash the *ahupuaa* of Waipio; and at this sale, Samuel Parker of Mana, Island of Hawaii, became the purchaser, for the sum of $18,000, and he conveyed the property to Bishop by a deed dated June 22, 1881. On May 19, 1892, in his Deed Number Three, Bishop conveyed the *ahupuaa* of Waipio to the Trustees of the B. P. Bishop Estate, who were to apply the rent, income, and profits of the said premises to the maintenance and improvement of the Bernice Pauahi Bishop Museum. When the Museum Trust was established, the Estate Trustees transferred title to this Waipio property, and the Museum building and its contents, to the new Trust. This was a Deed of Trust dated October 13, 1896.

The other transaction was the transfer of the Molokai properties. Bishop owned 46,500 acres of ranchland on the island of Molokai. In Deed Number Five, dated April 27, 1893, he transferred title to that acreage to the Bishop Estate. This was called the *ahupuaa* of Kalaukoi. He also had a life interest in the *ahupuaa* of Kaunakakai and owned several leases of Crown lands. All of these properties were conveyed to the Trustees, effective October 1, 1893, and recorded in the Estate Minutes, December 6, 1893.

He had been awarded the *ahupuaa* of Kaluakoi under Royal Patent 3146 (Grant) in 1875. The *ahupuaa* of Kaunakakai came to Mrs. Bishop through her cousin Ruth Keelikolani as a part of the Kamehameha lands distributed in the Great Mahele of 1848. The Crown leases had been granted to Bishop, by the Commissioners of Crown Lands, in indentures dated January 1, 1888, to round out the property for ranch purposes. There were about 100,000 acres in the entire area. When Mrs. Bishop inherited the ranch property on Molokai she employed Rudolph W. Meyer, a German immigrant who had married High Chiefess Kalama, as her ranch manager. This appointment was made upon the advice of her husband who then placed Meyer in charge of the entire ranch properties on Molokai.

The Friend, in its February 1894 issue, speaks glowingly of Bishop's decision to donate to The Kamehameha Schools the properties commonly referred to as the Molokai Ranch:

No citizen of Honolulu has done more in a charitable way than has Hon. C. R. Bishop, and now another of his princely donations has been made that almost eclipses his former ones. He has deeded to the Kamehameha School all his property on the island of Molokai.

This property which extends from five miles east of Kaunakakai to the western end of the island, and from the seashore to the *pali* back of the leper settlement, and up to the mountain top, consists of about one half of the total area of the island, or close to 150 square miles of territory. . . . In addition to the above Mr. Bishop has also donated $20,000 towards erecting the buildings of the Kamehameha Girls' School. . . .

The ranch story goes back much earlier than 1894. We find him writing most frequently to ranch manager Meyer, who also made occasional trips to Honolulu on ranch business and usually stayed with Bishop. There was a constant exchange of views and ideas about ranch affairs.

Meyer sent cattle over to Honolulu in a continuous stream for fattening and dressing for the market. Along with cattle went pails of peaches, turkeys, crocks of butter, legs of mutton, and whole lambs. The pantry at 21 Emma Street had a weekly delivery of Molokai Ranch produced or processed food. In a larger sense, this Meyer-to-Bishop food train routine was prophetic of what would happen on a major scale years later when the populations of Honolulu and Oahu would explode and land costs would drive the gardeners to the other islands to establish themselves as community marketbasket suppliers. But this arm's length direction of the ranch increasingly irritated Bishop. The cattle became sick, the market did not favor the Molokai Ranch sheep (undoubtedly because the strain was inferior), mynah birds were spreading the lantana pest by carrying the seeds over newly cleared land, help was hard to locate and equally hard to retain, droughts affected the grazing land, cattle prices were never steady for any length of time, paddocks needed fencing—the troubles were really normal and routine, but they were worrisome. Bishop wished to transfer the responsibility for the ranch management to other shoulders. He was planning his final departure for San Francisco for the early part of 1894 and, therefore, determined to deed all of his Molokai properties to the Trustees of his wife's Estate. He did so in the deed dated April 27, 1893, to be effective October 1, 1893. The transfer was not recorded in the Minutes until the meeting of December 6, 1893.

Molokai Ranch matters went along smoothly enough for the next four years when letters from Meyer and Hyde started a new trend of thought. To Meyer, Bishop wrote on May 15, 1897:

The frequent droughts on Molokai are a great drawback to the prosperity of the ranch, making everything uncertain. . . . I notice that you killed off a large number of wild goats, and I wish it were possible to kill all the deer, for they are about as bad as goats and have done great harm in destroying young trees. There is so much competition in the sale of cattle to the Board of Health that you will need to join with some of the competitors and take a low price.

The other letter was addressed to Hyde, a week later:

. . . Yes, the profit from the Molokai Ranch this year is surprisingly small, or as our friend Meyer might say, "enormously small." When an opportunity offers to sell that property for a good price, I trust that it will be taken advantage of.

He was no longer directing the ranch affairs but was still a Trustee of the Bishop Estate; and when he saw the ranch income dwindling and read of troubles besetting the ranch, which were not at all unfamiliar to him, it was logical that he would suggest selling it—the proceeds could be reinvested and a safer and surer income would result. This is ultimately what occurred and was perhaps the only major financial transaction resulting from his direction which present hindsight would classify as a mistake. It was one of the few major exceptions to the "don't sell the lands" rule that could be considered costly; and he had difficulty in persuading the Trustees to sell the ranch. By August 11, when he wrote to Henry Holmes, he was willing to sell for "not less than $100,000." Meyer had passed away and his removal from the ranch scene as manager created additional problems for the Trustees. An inventory had to be made, and George Campbell was selected for that purpose. A ranch manager had to be located, and this was not to be a short and easy search. Bishop did say to Holmes in that letter, that "should the property be sold, the proceeds should be *entirely* treated as capital, and invested or used in such way as to bring in *revenue.*" Over the next several weeks there was a lively exchange of correspondence between Bishop and the Honolulu Trustees. Holmes questioned the propriety of selling in view of the instructions in the Will, and this provoked a comment, August 27, 1897:

. . . I wish it were possible to sell the property for its value and to re-invest the money in some way to make the income more certain and less difficult to manage and in a manner clearly "for the best interests" of the Estate. It is now such a mixed property of fee simple leases and tenant at will, with the forests dying out and the pest of Lantana threatening, and so much to do in the matter of fencing and procuring water, it makes me tired to think of it. . . .

Then Bishop approached Carter; and in a letter written on September 1, he suggested a price of $125,000 to $150,000—the larger sum if an artesian well were to be dug and water brought to the land. He actually signed an agreement of sale with Alfred W. Carter and so notified J. O. Carter on September 2. This unilateral action had to have the agreement of the other Trustees. J. O. Carter, for one, declined to join in approving the agreement of sale. Alfred W. Carter was his nephew, but it is unlikely that the relationship affected him. He did not think the Trustees should sell. Then Bishop returned to Holmes, and on October 1, 1897, he said, "I am in favor of selling the Molokai Ranch property, but not for less than $150,-000. At present I know of no other property belonging to the estate that I would be in favor of selling. . . ."

By this time, he had sent off his letter of resignation, dated October 13, 1897. The idea of resigning probably was not induced by the Molokai Ranch talk. The resignation was officially written into the Minutes as of January 3, 1898. The Trustees, on December 24, 1897, wisely referred the question of the Trustees' power to sell lands to the Circuit Court, and four days after the effective date of the resignation an opinion was handed down which had a far-reaching effect, for it affirmed the right of the Trustees to sell real property subject to the annual review of the master of chancery of the accounts of the Trustees.

The ranch was sold at a Commissioner's Sale, February 2, 1898, for $251,000, to a group consisting of Arthur D. McClellan of Boston and Judges Alfred W. Carter and Alfred S. Hartwell. The original suggested figure of $150,000 was used as the upset price, but the auction (a method of selling that Bishop did not believe in) went higher than his fondest hopes. The sale was conducted by James F. Morgan, auctioneer, on the steps of the Judiciary Building. Bishop's only comment, in a letter to Hyde, February 4, 1898, was terse but implied an obvious satisfaction: ". . . The sale of the Molokai property turned out well. . . ."

It is an interesting speculation to state the probable size of the mistake. The income from operation of the ranch for one year at the present time is far greater than the gross sales figure for which the ranch exchanged hands in 1898. However, it was Bishop's judgment; and it cannot be said that the Estate suffered a loss, or if it did that it is measurable, since the proceeds invested well and properly have served The Kamehameha Schools.

Some Selected Biographies

Several stalwarts organized and administered The Kamehameha Schools in the early years. Without such people as William B. Oleson, Theodore Richards, Uldrick Thompson, and Ida M. Pope, the true direction of Mrs. Bishop's Will and Mr. Bishop's purpose might have been lost. Each of these administrators and teachers has written a chapter in the Kamehameha history.[*]

WILLIAM BREWSTER OLESON

The first principal of The Kamehameha School for Boys, William Brewster Oleson, was born in Portland, Maine, September 9, 1851. He attended the University of Maine and Oberlin Theological Seminary and was brought to Hawaii as principal of the Hilo Boys' Boarding School, September 1, 1878. He held that position, with a break of a year about half way through, until July 1, 1886, when he was called to The Kamehameha Schools.

Bishop knew of him through earlier correspondence. On February 3, 1885, he wrote to Oleson regretting his inability to make a large capital fund contribution as a memorial to Mrs. Bishop. Oleson was a somewhat insistent solicitor, for another reply to a second appeal is noted, July 30, 1885:

The Hilo School has been a good and very useful school in the past and is said to be an excellent school now, and I am sorry to see it crippled for

[*] Others, like Hyde and Carter, are referred to frequently throughout the text and, therefore, are not treated individually.

want of money but it is out of the question for me to promise much help at present, for I do not intend to promise more than I can perform. It is fortunate that there are so many other schools in which the Hawaiian boys can get a fair education . . . and within a year the Kamehameha School for Boys should make a beginning.

But he softened that rather strong statement by asking, "Would it be of much use for me to offer to give five hundred dollars provided others will give $2,000 in addition within six months making the whole $2500 to help you through another year?" It was but a few months later, February 1, 1886, that he really began to loosen the purse strings when he offered $2000 to the Hilo Boarding School if the gift would be matched. In that same letter,* which had been addressed to Oleson, a firm expression of hope that Oleson would be ready and willing to take hold and build up The Kamehameha School for Boys was stated. On April 15, the compact was signed.

On July 1, 1886, Oleson arrived in Honolulu to take charge at Kamehameha; there were no school buildings, equipment, students, faculty—even the site for the main building had not been selected. His background and training, which included newspaper work, wholesale grocery business, teaching, and preaching, fitted him admirably for the many facets of the task of organizing and opening the Manual Department. Oleson was an excellent principal; but in a few years his health began to break, and since a young New Englander named Theodore Richards was on the staff as a teacher and had considerable promise as an administrator, Oleson asked the Trustees to be relieved. The resignation was dated November 20, 1891, but the Trustees obtained a postponement of it until July 1, 1893. The statement of resignation is a simple pronouncement:

To the Trustees of the Estate of Mrs. B. P. Bishop
Gentlemen:—
It is with sincere regret that I find it necessary to announce my resignation as Principal of Kamehameha School, to take effect not later than July 1, 1893. This step has been under consideration for several years. It has been delayed only by my desire to see the school thoroughly organized in the right direction before my connection with it ceased. I am led to this decision by the growing conviction that I am physically unable to carry the responsibilities of the position much longer. I am warned that I shall incapacitate myself for the radical change in life which I must sooner or later make, if I continue much longer in my present position.
I make this early announcement of my resignation, partly to afford the Trustees ample time to choose my successor, and partly in view of any

* See p. 241.

possible bearing it may have on the questions of enlarging the course of study in the school, and of locating the proposed school for girls. My views are well-known as to these two particulars, and I do not wish that any one's opinion or vote, with reference to either of them, should in the slightest be influenced by the presumption that I am to remain in the school.

It gives me the keenest pain to thus announce my decision. I would not make it except that I am fully persuaded that the interests of those who are dependent on me demand it.

I wish to put on record my recognition and appreciation of your confidence in me, in first appointing me to the responsible position for which I have never felt myself competent, and in sustaining me so generously in all the difficulties of these years of organization.

Uldrick Thompson was to describe him thus, years later:

Competent or not, he was a busy person and one of extremely wide and varied talent; he virtually wrote the curriculum for each of the shops, preached on Sundays, taught classes, handled the discipline, acted as nurse, father, and mother to every boy, attended every baseball game, and was interested in every moral problem of the island, and took a very active part in political matters.

Oleson can easily be termed one of Kamehameha's greatest leaders—certainly, one of its builders. He was called upon by his successor for advice, chiefly by mail, for the next several years. He returned to Hawaii to give the Founder's Day address in 1902 and stayed on to make an examination of the Schools.

THEODORE RICHARDS

The second stalwart of Kamehameha's early days, Theodore Richards from Wesleyan College, was started on his way to Kamehameha as successor to Oleson by General Samuel Chapman Armstrong. Richards was directing Camp Chocorua for boys * on an island in Lake Asquam, New Hampshire. This was in the summer of 1889. Upon returning to Everett House in New York, he wrote Richards, September 30, 1889, offering him "a position as teacher in the Kamehameha Schools near Honolulu at a salary of eight hundred dollars a year besides board. . . ." Richards packed up and started for Honolulu, arriving a few weeks after Thompson on October 13.

The circumstances of Oleson's resignation have been related, al-

* This camp enjoys the distinction of being the first boys' camp established in America.

though one point of significance might have been overlooked. The year 1893 was one of political turbulence in Hawaii. Inevitably the Hawaiian students at Kamehameha offered potential human timber to feed the uneasy flames of public prejudice. Oleson's sympathies were with the annexationists while Richards' inclinations were strictly those of a non-interventionist. The community tensions of the first days and weeks of 1893 wore upon Oleson, and he repeatedly urged Richards to return from his mainland study and relieve him of the trying responsibility of directing the "Manual." Richards did return from his mainland trip earlier than originally planned and took over the helm as principal of Kamehameha, July 1, 1893. Fortunately, the discretion and insistence of Richards were strong enough to contain the more excitable students, and the school survived the Revolution and its aftermath primarily because it did not get into it.

Bishop wrote the letter offering Richards the principalship, March 10, 1892, more than a year before the transfer was to be effective. The interim year had been suggested by Richards for a visit to the United States to study, visit schools, and recruit teachers. The year was valuable to him and the Schools. Upon his return, he introduced a good many educational ideas and submitted many requests for physical changes—almost too many and too rapidly for Bishop. One proposal was for a school band, another for dress uniforms, and still another for lighting the dining hall and dormitories with electricity. The Kamehameha Schools took on a new face and tremendous growth under Richards' guiding hand. He moved as fast as the rather reluctant trustees would permit.

Bishop advised Richards, September 25, 1894, on many Kamehameha matters, among them the expenses of Keliinoi and King * at Oswego Normal School. Bishop paid the full expenses of Charles E. King and Samuel Keliinoi through a three-year teachers' course and rejoiced in the successes of each when they returned to the islands. An interesting comment on Kamehameha students returning to teach at their Alma Mater was made by Bishop in a letter to Carter, on April 23, 1896:

I wrote to Mr. Richards a few days ago and gave him to understand that I thought Keliinoi and King were doing well in their places, and it was better for them and for the people that they should continue where they are, and that omitting to employ them at Kamehameha cannot rightfully

* Both were members of the Kamehameha Schools first graduating class (1891).

be construed as an affront to them or their race, and that no such idea should receive the least encouragement from anybody.

Other matters treated by Bishop included the relation of wages paid to work performed and admissions policies. One comment is of particular interest:

It is better to have a limited number of boys who will learn, and out of whom men can be made than to take in a larger number including stupid or lazy or vicious boys who would demoralize others, get little or no good for themselves and do no credit to the schools.

Music was an integral subject in the Kamehameha program from the opening day. It was Richards, however, who started the choral music tradition; and this was one educational area where Bishop, who usually was never outwardly enthusiastic about anything, gave way to expressions of high praise. It was at this time that the music of a Yale song was introduced with the new words as "Sons of Hawaii," the official Kamehameha Schools' song.

Bishop wrote voluminously to Richards in this period. His comments dealt with political unrest, the need for good work habits among Hawaiians, the personality and disposition problems of Brigham * (Richards tried valiantly but could not get along any better with Brigham than had Oleson), the Revolution, and all varieties of current talk. He was pleased with Richards' handling of the students during the so-called Wilcox Insurrection and said so, February 8, 1895: "Your management of the students during the excitement has been wise and proper. They should see that you and the Trustees are their friends and the friends of law and order." A little later, March 5, 1895, he offered more praise:

I am so far satisfied, I might say pleased with your management of the school, the changes you have made, and with the interest which you take in the improvement and welfare of the young people under your charge, that I could easily forgive somewhat of what might strictly be called extravagance, if you had erred in that direction. . . .

He said it in a slightly different way to Carter about a month later, April 4, 1895:

I am so well pleased with Mr. Richards, especially with his disposition towards Hawaiians and his wise and just conduct during the late troubles, that I reluctantly criticize his business methods and what seems to me to be uncertain economy.

* William Tufts Brigham, Director of the Bernice P. Bishop Museum. See pp. 186–204.

Richards' next major projects were an alumni association and a well outfitted and equipped dairy and agricultural school. Much favor was found with the alumni project, and improved Fort Street property was turned over to the alumni for a clubhouse. The sum of $300 annually was ordered to be paid to the Alumni Association from the income of the Charles R. Bishop Trust. For the dairy and the agricultural course, Bishop could not work up any deep fervor. He complained that the soil about the school was far inferior to what Richards supposed; the water supply for irrigation was uncertain; and the milk would "cost more than champagne." "Let me warn you against impatience and too rapid changes," repeated Bishop. Richards won this battle for the dairy although it was not a rosy victory. He wrote a full letter to Bishop, February 26, 1896, detailing his financial successes with the dairy; but he concluded by saying rather plaintively, "I can afford to await justification although the constant battling for the department which the trustees have seen fit to impose upon me, is a trifle wearing. . . ." He reported in this letter that the alumni lease of the Fort Street property for a clubhouse was far from settled; he hoped the Kamehameha chapel idea would continue to show progress and was delighted at the comparative freedom the Schools were enjoying in visiting the Museum "without fear of insult or frigid intolerance." (Brigham was away from the Islands on an extended tour.) He went on to say:

I have always maintained that the Museum could and should be most valuable to the school—as a laboratory for the study of the history of this country. It is incomparably the best, which might be said of the study of life in general.

The Board of Trustees was not a full board these days; and it became, to the discomfort of Richards, an unsympathetic restriction on certain school matters. He complained of the treatment he was receiving at the hands of the short board—there were only three members present at meetings, and two of these discounted his efforts. He finally took a leave of absence and went to the United States, stopping over in San Francisco for a long personal conference with Bishop who, in writing a letter to Hyde, July 29, 1896, said, ". . . I had a long and pleasant talk with Mr. Richards yesterday. . . ." Hyde was the third Trustee who generally gave support to Richards.

Then came a time in the spring and summer months of 1897 when there were but two Trustees in Honolulu. Since two of the absentees were in San Francisco, and Bishop had not as yet resigned, Richards suggested that the Trustees might hold a meeting in San Francisco and sent an agenda for consideration. But tension was mounting between him and a faction on the Board, and the friction became unpleasant for all concerned. Bishop, who actually was quite appreciative of Richards' progressive ideas and really believed his business judgment was growing to be sound and worthy of support, could not, however, very well fail to join the Trustees in the usual collective action. He was troubled about it, and he wrote to Hyde, August 2, 1897, ". . . I would always give due consideration to any suggestion of Mr. Richards, and try to satisfy him in everything that is reasonable. . . ." And he wrote to Richards on August 11, ". . . I am much pleased with the success which you report for the past year, and with the 'good feeling' which has prevailed." But Richards decided to resign.

It can easily be seen that Richards' administration was marked by good accomplishment and varied troubles. He had to operate during the political turmoils of 1893, 1895, and 1898. The cholera epidemic required cool, skillful handling. He did many things as principal of the Manual. He coached and played on the first championship baseball team and organized the glee club, the school band, and the camping program. He introduced the school dairy and the hospital, organized the first normal class in the islands, and started the alumni association on its way with a clubhouse. The chapel was finished during his regime. The girls' school was established during his principalship. Possibly more than all of these, the Richards family, including the father, Theodore; his lovely wife, Mary Atherton Richards; and the infant children, gave every student glimpses of an ideal home life. The home was on the campus and always open to the students.

The letter of resignation was dated January 21, 1898, and was addressed to the "Trustees Under The Will of Mrs. B. P. Bishop." The letter contains no glance backward over the Kamehameha years; rather, it expresses a straightforward, reverent prayer for all the future may hold:

Jan. 21, '98

To the TRUSTEES UNDER THE WILL
of Mrs. B. P. Bishop,
Gentlemen:—

I have the honor to present to your body my resignation of the Principalship of the Kamehameha School for Boys to take effect as soon after the closing of the present School year [July 1, '98] as may be.

The increasing hold that Kamehameha has gained in my interest and affections was at first in conflict, but has now become fully reconciled with a sense of duty leading me out into another field of work.

I shall leave with the highest hopes for the Institution so admirably adapted to do an increasingly grand work; a growing respect and love for the boys whose future is so promising, and an honest belief that the present teaching force will be able, under *GOD*, to accomplish better and higher things than we have yet done.

My present purpose and expectation is to make this my last half year the best I have ever known in the school, and I am

Yours very respectfully
[signed]   Theodore Richards

On February 14, 1898, Bishop expresses his real disappointment at Richards' decision to resign:

Your letter . . . of your resignation . . . came to me as an unwelcome surprise. . . . I know, as do the trustees and friends of the school, and you know too, that under your principalship Kamehameha School has greatly improved. . . . Your sincere friendliness to the Hawaiians . . . has also won and held my appreciation and admiration. . . .

Since the resignation was to be effective June 30, 1898, Uldrick Thompson was selected by the Trustees as Principal.

For another half century, Richards was to continue old community ties and establish new important interests. But he was ever mindful of the great potential of The Kamehameha Schools and over the years acted as informal adviser and critic.° A year after Richards' resignation, Bishop wrote to Uldrick Thompson, October 11, 1899: "Just why so many boys are lately entering or wishing to enter Kamehameha School I do not know. . . . I suspect that Mr. Richards has advised them to take advantage of the opportunity. . . ."

Richards continued to expand his community horizon. He asked Clive Davies to call on Bishop in San Francisco with plans for a Hotel for Men and a request for support. Assistance for the Hawaiian Board of Missions was also solicited. The Honolulu Boys Brigade was organized with Richards as President. Somewhat later, he interested himself in forming a women's hat-making enterprise to employ Hawaiians. In some respects, the Kamehameha experience was a springboard to ever-widening circles of dedicated effort on behalf of the people of Hawaii. Frequently, however, he turned his creative gaze back upon his beloved Kamehameha. His son-in-law,

---

° It was my pleasure to meet frequently with Richards, 1946–1948, and discuss Kamehameha matters at great length.

Frank E. Midkiff, had become President of the Schools in 1923; and Richards addressed a letter to him, January 3, 1924:

. . . I respectfully suggest that you get the permission of the trustees to canvass this matter in the interest of Hawaiian boys living in Honolulu to see whether it might not be wise to start a day school. It is doubtless true that your country boys make greater progress, but the city boys are as real a problem. . . .

No provision for day students was to be made for twenty years, but credit for the suggestion belongs to Theodore Richards.

ULDRICK THOMPSON

". . . Mr. Thompson is, in his quiet way, a teacher. . . ." Thus, Bishop wrote of Uldrick Thompson to J. O. Carter, July 31, 1894, a tribute which in simple terms characterizes perhaps the greatest teacher Kamehameha ever had. He served the Schools for 33 years. The date of his engagement as a teacher was July 3, 1889, and he arrived early in the fall of that year but a few weeks before Richards started work. He thus was to know both Oleson and Richards. In looking back upon the contributions of the two associates to Kamehameha, he seemed to feel that while Oleson was somewhat of an autocrat—and an autocrat was likely needed in the organizing years—Richards was a somewhat stronger school man and consequently was better prepared to continue and enlarge the work of the Schools. But in all this, Thompson himself was modest. He was a workhorse. When Richards was about to replace Oleson in 1893, the Trustees gave Thompson the vice-principalship. When Richards resigned in 1898, Thompson was made principal. He was not too well fitted for administrative work, so he gave way to Charles B. Dyke in 1900 and again took the re-activated position of vice-principal. When Dyke resigned suddenly, March 24, 1904, Thompson was made principal ad interim but became a teacher again when Perley Horne was appointed as the first President of the Schools. To Richards, Bishop wrote, February 14, 1898:

Regarding your successor I have no authority and will not say much. I have a high opinion of Mr. Thompson as a teacher and have no doubt as to his being worthy of the high regard expressed by yourself and the principals. . . .

Upon assuming the principalship, Thompson wrote expressing his desire to keep Bishop informed on school matters. There ensued another prolonged exchange of correspondence that pointed up the fine, friendly, and mutual respect which the two men entertained for each other. Thompson made himself very popular with Bishop at the outset when he described the work the new agricultural teacher, T. F. Sedgwick was doing: "Fortunately for all concerned, the Trustees do not intend to furnish much financial aid to the work. We expect to work for all we get,—in the soil, not on the Trustees. . . ." On August 29, 1898, Bishop responded:

I like what you say about the farming which is to be at Kamehameha. . . . What you say about Mr. Sedgwick is certainly encouraging. It does not matter much what the business or profession is, it's the *man* at the head who will make it *succeed*, if there is any success in it. Anyone can make a handsome show by free expenditure of money, and yet it may be only a costly failure. . . .

He worried a little about the possible lack of a strong disposition on Thompson's part to run the principalship. He wrote Thompson a letter, October 18, 1898, in which he gave some typical Bishop counsel:

No doubt you are kept busy. I hope that you have the faculty of keeping others busy, in their places and up to the work. A good overseer or manager does not do the work with his own hands. The Captain of a vessel does not and should not do the work of the officers or crew; and neither ship, military company or large school can be carried on under debating society rules. I do not know the habits or dispositions of your assistants; but I know that you are amiable and conscientious, and I fear that if you are too easy and non-assertive some of them will impose upon you and your discipline will not be "up to the mark."

He had by now found a kindred spirit in Thompson. Another letter, January 11, 1899, contained more Bishop sentiments:

. . . The young people—and older people too if necessary—should be taught to make or pay for their own fun and entertainment, and not expect so many advantages and privileges at some one else's expense. Self-reliance and respect for the rights of others are important factors in an education.

His advice was always to the point. In a letter under date of November 10, 1899, he wrote Thompson:

Of course it is not expected that the principals of the schools or any of the teachers should give much study to the affairs of the estate or interfere in the management, but they can and should have a general knowledge of the resources and expenses, and be thoughtful to not embarrass the trustees by asking for or suggesting outlays which cannot be afforded and may reduce the value and income of the estate. . . .

A little story with local color is appropriate here. "Grant" was one of a span of horses originally in the Bishops' stable on King Street. Bishop gave Oleson a two-seated carriage along with the horse for official school transportation. "Grant" was thought to be thirty years old in 1889 and was finally turned out to rest in 1897. In a letter to Thompson, May 17, 1900, Bishop writes a bit sentimentally:

. . . Faithful old "Grant" has held on well and deserves a pension. Were I at hand I would give him some oats and sugar, or a "mash," which might suit the condition of his teeth better than oats.

Thompson, in his thirty-three years at Kamehameha, both as an administrator and a teacher, left an impact for good citizenship and work ability among the graduates that was to be felt constructively for years. "Mr. Thompson is in his quiet way, a *teacher.*"

IDA MAY POPE

The first principal of The Kamehameha School for Girls was Ida May Pope. This New England girl was placed under contract as the organizing principal, March 2, 1894, to take effect July 1, 1894. While this arrangement was being made, the Trustees decided to locate the girls' school in Palama on the *makai* side of the boys' school campus across King Street. The main building was staked out on February 14, 1894, and the foundation started March 16. The girls' school was formally opened December 19, 1894.

It was at Kawaiahao Seminary that Miss Pope gained valuable experience for the Kamehameha assignment. She had arrived in the Islands in 1890 to teach at Kawaiahao. Later she became principal. From this position Bishop took her to Kamehameha. For the next twenty years she directed the growth of the School for Girls and established its traditions, policies, and customs.

Bishop held her in high regard. In a letter to Henry Holmes, September 2, 1897, he said, "She is an able woman and I have great respect for her, and would be willing to pay her fully as much as has been paid to any other female teacher. . . ." And on May 2, he wrote to Carter: "Miss Pope is properly regarded as being remarkably superior for the position she holds. . . ." One time, however, she made a proposal for a companion preparatory department for little girl boarders, and about this time she had been suggested as a possible Trustee for a vacancy on the Board. Bishop wrote to Carter, November 22, 1899, of his concern:

. . . .

The idea of a Preparatory Dept. attached to the Girl's School should not be entertained. The fact that good Miss Pope "cannot see why" this and that new thing, all costing money, to say nothing of other reasons why not, cannot be undertaken, makes me doubt her fitness for the position of trustee. But *possibly* the responsibility of the position, with some experience, might open her mind to the wisdom of going a little slow.

Nonetheless, Miss Pope's energy was limitless, and her vision was inspired. She did not become a Trustee of the Bishop Estate, but she would never relax in her mission of helping Hawaiian girls. "Perhaps the trustees would consider taking over the Kawaiahao Seminary," she proposed. This institution with a fine record of service to Hawaiian girls had not fared too well in the years following Miss Pope's departure. But Bishop quickly and emphatically discouraged this proposal in a letter to her, March 22, 1901:

. . . If Kawaiahao Sem'y is not in the right place, owing to changed conditions around and near by, a better place should be sought for. The school as an independent institution has done good work and should be kept up. I am interested in it as you know, and would be sorry to see it fail, but would be more sorry to have the Trustees of the estate take it over or assume any responsibility for it.

She still refused to stop trying. Seeing the need of Hawaiian girls who were going on to work or to school from Kamehameha for "a safe place to go to," she joined Charles Bartlett Dyke, principal of the Manual and supervisor of all the Kamehameha units, in a letter of suggestion for a home for Hawaiian girls. Kaiulani was suggested as a name. Fortunately, the request was not based on an affiliation with Kamehameha but on an independent home basis which could be supported by interested friends.

The Kaiulani Home was opened and has enjoyed many decades of full service to the cause it represents. Miss Pope thus had three monuments: Kawaiahao Seminary, The Kamehameha School for Girls, and the Kaiulani Home for Young Women. Her impact upon the home life of the Hawaiian families is impossible to measure; but it undoubtedly has been profound and significantly good, especially because of her love and training of future wives and mothers.

She was a highly esteemed person among Honolulu's leaders.

When Bishop's ninetieth birthday party was celebrated *in absentia* on Thursday, January 25, 1912, at the Roof Garden of the Alexander Young Hotel, she was invited to present a statement. In a measure, she repaid his deep confidence in her as she spoke:

In his giving, Mr. Bishop signifies that he is well aware that, "history teaches that the hope of a nation lies in the masses." Education in the democracy of the modern industrial type must take account of industry, hold as model the 'simple' and self-supporting life, be guided by ideals which emphasize doing rather than being served, to the apothesis of work rather than of leisure, to the higher aims than that of mere wealth accumulation.

He recognizes fully the imperatives of democracy: that education is "applied learning" and the inefficiency in women is as great a danger to the state as quackery in medicine. That the educational program stands for adjustment to environment, specialization of vocational training for girls as well as boys, for pathological demands, for religious and ethical training, and that for cooperative efficiency civic knowledge is necessary.

The aid given the various institutions of Hawaii by Mr. Bishop are not gifts that come from a restricted view of educational ideals. Long is the list of institutions that have received and are receiving benefits from this discerning man for the uplift of girls of many races in this cosmopolitan community.

He has made richer and fuller the life of girls that come from the home of wealth, and he has made life worth while for the lowly sister.

The Bishop stride through the history pages of Estate and Schools is taken with advice and counsel freely addressed in every direction. The lives of a host of planners, builders, and educators were drawn in the wake of this mild-mannered man to emerge in the creation of an institution clearly destined to be one of the world's distinguished halls of learning.

THE BERNICE PAUAHI BISHOP MUSEUM

THE BERNICE PAUAHI BISHOP MUSEUM was a unique benefaction of Mr. Bishop, intended as a permanent memorial to his wife. Museums sometimes eventuate as the broad expression of an individual's early, inarticulate, personal instincts to collect. It was undoubtedly so with him. He virtually lived with the rather extensive collection of irreplaceable objects brought together by Mrs. Bishop, not only from Hawaii but also from the farthest corners of the Pacific. He also saw artifacts such as feather capes and feather helmets in museums and in the hands of private estates all over the world, yet carelessly regarded. To find primitive art works such as calabash, *kapa,** and mat being ruined by exposure to the natural elements was a disturbing sight for Bishop, and the problem of the preservation of such items weighed upon his mind.

Other factors were probably influential in the gradual development of the museum idea. He was a member of the House of Nobles and the Privy Council when legislation was adopted establishing a National Museum. The date of adoption of the Act was July 29, 1872, when Kamehameha V was regent. An appropriation of one hundred fifty dollars was made for the first year of operation. An interesting feature of the 1872 Act was its preamble:

Whereas, we as a nation, have taken our position among the civilized and enlightened nations of the earth, both in respect to capabilities in self-government and in the facilities as we enjoy in our high and common schools in the diffusion of popular intelligence; and whereas, a national museum, representing the archeology, literature, geology, and national history of our kingdom would be but another form of school for the education of our youth, as well as a repository for reference to the scientific world at large; and whereas, every succeeding year is rendering it more difficult to gather from the archives of the past the mementoes and relics of our early existence as a nation, as well as the prehistoric age of these islands.

Therefore be it enacted that the board of education be authorized to establish a national museum in some suitable government building or apartment to be provided by the minister of the interior, in which should be collected and preserved such articles illustrating the subjects named as might come into its possession from time to time, either by gift or purchase; and the board be further empowered to frame such rules and regulations in connection with the museum as it might deem best adapted to receive its permanency and efficiency as a repository for reference in the various branches of service represented therein and cause such rules and regulations to be published for the benefit of the public; and to employ such means as might be placed at its disposal from time to time in such manner as best to further the object's proposal.

When Bishop became President of the Board of Education under Lunalilo in 1873, the new National Museum in Aliiolani (Govern-

* Hawaiian spelling of *tapa.*

ment House) came under his direction. In 1874, five hundred dollars was appropriated to the museum for the next two years. The appropriation was continued in 1876, and in 1878 an additional six hundred dollars was set aside for the services of a curator. On November 8, 1875, a notice appeared in the paper:

The Hawaiian Museum is ready for visitors and will accept gifts. Museum Room, Government House. H. R. Hitchcock, curator Hawaiian Museum.

It was on the lanai of this museum room in Government House that Allen Hutchinson, the artist, was modelling a clay bust of Kalakaua when stray shots fired in the "Wilcox" Revolution created a disturbing background to his work.

Another impression that probably added incentive to the dormant museum idea in Bishop's mind was the exhibit * sponsored for the benefit of the Honolulu Library and Reading Room Association. This was a very ambitious project with a beautiful souvenir catalog of the several exhibit divisions, one of which was largely devoted to Mrs. Bishop's artifacts of Hawaiian and general Polynesian culture.

Little happened about a museum in the next few years. Bishop had been forced out of the presidency of the Board of Education. He made several rather long trips to the Mainland and was deeply involved in the planning and construction of The Kamehameha Schools. He also was occupied in building the Bishop Home for young girls. About the time of the construction at Kalaupapa, the museum idea began to emerge. The secretary of the Bishop Estate made this entry, December 2, 1887:

Mr. Bishop stated that it was his intention to build a Museum on the school premises to be called "The Bernice Pauahi Bishop Museum," and asked consent of the Trustees, to do this, and the privilege of using what material may be on the premises.

On motion of Mr. Carter, recorded by Mr. Cooke, permission was given to Mr. Bishop as asked. Mr. Bishop showed plans of main building and they were discussed at some length.

Some urgency was prodding Bishop from another angle. The William F. Allens were in charge of his 21 Emma Street home, where he had moved the large number of costly kahilis and many other valuable artifacts comprising Mrs. Bishop's collections. Mrs. Allen had the burdensome charge of these things in the great establishment built for Princess Ruth, and it was entirely sensible that she be relieved of the care for them.

* See p. 246.

In *Thrum's Annual* for 1916, William Tufts Brigham, the Director of the Bishop Museum, reviewed the circumstances and events of his first months in Honolulu when he returned for the second time in 1888. In the article he mentioned his initial reluctance to assist with the Museum development:

I had, before I came to reside in these islands in 1888, some correspondence with Judge S. B. Dole and Dr. C. M. Hyde concerning this Museum, but when I found it was to be simply a mortuary chapel, as it were, of relics, I lost all interest in it, and devoted myself on my arrival at Mr. Bishop's request to collecting material and making photographs for a History of Hawaii, and for two years with Mr. Acland Wansey, I scoured the group for facts and views; then finding that my old friend, Dr. W. D. Alexander was already engaged in writing such a history, I gave up the plan. . . . I decided to continue the practice of law. . . . Mr. Bishop . . . asked me to arrange the collection in the finished building [Museum]. This I agreed to do. . . .

On December 12, 1888, Bishop wrote to him and made overtures towards a Museum connection, although it was secondary to the idea of preparation of a manuscript on Hawaiian history:

I would like to have you undertake the writing of a comprehensive, authentic and finished History of Hawaii and also to assist me with my museum, though how much there will be to do with the latter is uncertain now. You could at least assist me with advice about collecting and arrangement of interior of buildings and contents; and I might want you to help me actively in these matters.

. . . I do not feel like pledging to you four thousand dollars per annum for two years, but I will promise $3000 for one year, and at the same rate for any part of another year that your work may require with the understanding that during the whole time you will give me such advice and assistance about my museum as you can without interfering too much with your history work.

Thus did the dream begin to achieve reality. It was inevitable that he would turn to Brigham as he thought of establishing a museum. He was impressed with Brigham's whole scientific approach, his apparent practical and matter-of-fact personal qualities, and his unusual fund of general knowledge. Bishop's first impressions were gained from the round of initial visits that Brigham made at the Bishops' home on King Street in the company of Horace Mann, son of the distinguished American educator, in 1864. Harvard University had requested the two men to explore the islands in the interests of botany and geology. They travelled throughout the islands from

May 4, 1864, to May 18, 1865.* In 1880, Brigham interrupted his New England legal career with a quick trip to Hawaii to make a special study of an expected eruption of Mauna Loa. He visited with the Bishops on that trip.

The history of Hawaii was worked at, but it never became anything more than a subject for annoyed comment by Bishop. A few years later, on August 30, 1894, he wrote to Carter:

No wonder that you are surprised at my assisting him to become a historian of Hawaii! Before doing so I consulted Mr. Dole who knew him intimately, and spoke about his extravagant speeches etc. etc.

Mr. Dole thought him capable of doing the work well, and that under the responsibility of writing history and in the quiet of his study with nothing to excite him, his writing would be very different from his talk. I forget whether I consulted Mr. Alexander or not, but I requested Mr. Brigham to submit to Messrs. Dole and Alexander whatever he might write before publishing, and he made an objection to that. To admit that I made poor use of my money and effort does not help anything now.

Whether the history of Hawaii was the real purpose in Bishop's mind in commissioning Brigham or whether it was the organization of the Museum, probably cannot be known. For him to have approached the Museum idea indirectly was not in character, so it may be assumed that he really was interested in a history and the Museum was of secondary importance at that time.

Brigham had been on a trip to Australia and had received Bishop's proposal in Sydney. Having agreed to write the history of Hawaii, he looked for a photographer to assist in the research and quickly located an assistant, a fellow passenger on the *Zealandia* outward bound from Sydney to San Francisco. This man was Acland Wansey, a native of Quirindi, Australia. Years later when Wansey was asked to relate the circumstances of his employment and what he remembered of the early days of the Museum, he said:

. . . We landed in San Francisco on December 23rd (1888). . . . I studied photography with a photographer and we set to work to get things ready for our return to the Islands in February, 1889. For a few months we lived with Judge Dole on Emma Street. . . . About the latter part of 1889 when Mr. Bishop lived on Emma Street, we went to his home and looked through most of his collection stored there. . . . On one occasion I remember perfectly well when we were at the Emma

* Mann's research was published in the Proceedings of the American Academy of Arts and Sciences, September 11, 1866.

Street house photographing that Mr. Bishop spoke about a place to keep his collection as it was risky keeping them in a wooden building. We all went down to the Judiciary Building and examined the room upstairs, it was found too small and unsuitable and might easily be entered by thieves. Then it was proposed to build a museum where the old house was. . . . Mr. Bishop seriously thought of building there [Aikupika-Haleakala grounds].

Wansey did not remain on the picture-taking assignment very long. He returned to Australia in April, 1890, but was lured back for two more years in 1897. He would probably have stayed on at the Museum until retirement, but his wife's illness compelled him to return to Australia. A substantial number of the plates illustrating the early publications issued by the Museum are products of Wansey's acquired skill and technique.

The new Museum was to have none of the trappings or attributes of a great institution. It was to be merely a means of safeguarding Mrs. Bishop's collection of Hawaiian and Polynesian antiquities. All of 1888 was spent in considering materials, methods of employing the workers, architectural aspects, and the acquisition of other collections. Bishop was in Honolulu throughout this year and gave himself freely to settling the innumerable problems attendant upon starting the ambitious project. Contractor Robert Lishman and stone mason William Mutch were available. Construction started in the spring of 1889. There is confusion as to the official founding date. *The Friend* reported it as being open on June 27, 1891, and a few months before, March 1, *The Pacific Commercial Advertiser* carried a news item about the opening. Uldrick Thompson, in his *Memoirs*, sets the opening even earlier, December 19, 1890. This last date was somewhat official in nature and was so set because it was Mrs. Bishop's birthday. Brigham, however, was installing cases and arranging exhibits all through 1891. Since the institution was never formally dedicated or officially opened the Museum authorities have designated December 19, 1889, as the founding date.

Mr. W. F. Smith, of the firm of Smith and Freeman of San Francisco, was the architect. On a transcontinental trip of the United States in the spring of 1889, we find Bishop writing back to Smith about the "degree of pointedness of the main tower, the materials for interior wall finish, the desirability of tiles against nicely laid cement for the floor," and so on. The original building, called the "Museum Hall" and consisting of the Hawaiian vestibule, *kahili* room, a picture gallery on the second floor, and the present entrance foyer, was operated by the five Trustees of the B. P. Bishop Estate.

About the time this first building was occupied, Brigham proposed building an annex. First mention of this was as early as September, 1891. It was brought up again in July, 1892, and in October Bishop agreed to supply the necessary funds. February 28, 1894, the annex, now named "Polynesian Hall," was finished at a cost of $50,499.80, and Bishop paid for it as he had for the original Museum building. On November 5, 1894, it was suggested the dedication be set for December 19, and that it be a joint Kamehameha Schools-Museum program. Brigham objected strenuously and promised he would not attend. He went off to Australia to collect specimens and left a helper, Kealoha, in charge. But the dedication went off smoothly enough, and the second Museum unit was in use. Just before the Polynesian Hall was finished, J. O. Carter wrote him that the mechanics were out of the Museum, whereupon Bishop replied: "I'm thankful that the mechanics are out of the Museum and that my credit is still fairly good. It was beginning to look as if they were to be a part of the *permanent* collection!"

Through 1897, much of the correspondence dealt with the plans for still another annex building. Bishop, in favor of delay at least until 1898, wanted to employ William Mutch on a cost basis rather than to ask for tenders from a list of contractors. He had considerable faith in Mutch's honesty. Again, Bishop wrote of building specifications, fire doors, fire walls, creosoted koa cases, tree plantings, and the like. The annexation issue was on the public mind, and the uncertainties and effects of possible annexation upon Hawaii worried him. This accounted for his recommendation for delaying the new building. However, when the annex finally was started in January, 1899, the work was not given to Mutch; it was let out in competitive bidding, to the distress of Bishop.

A contractor named Arthur Harrison received the award to build in the bid amount of $62,000. Mutch's figure was $96,500. According to Uldrick Thompson in his Reminiscenses of Kamehameha, the building was opened on December 19, 1899; but this was incorrect. The annex was not finished until September 28, 1900, and was not dedicated until November 24, 1903, when it was officially named "Hawaiian Hall."

No sooner had this project been completed than Brigham laid a set of plans for a new building before Bishop, who in turn referred the matter back to the Trustees. Little came of Brigham's current proposal, but Bishop did offer $50,000 towards the cost of a combined workroom and store room. The project dawdled along for a while, ending up as a temporary building housing a workroom. The next large permanent structure was the addition on the *ewa-mauka* corner, "Paki Hall" dedicated April 20, 1911.

To the nucleus of the Hawaiian and Polynesian antiquities which constituted his wife's collection, Bishop added many more by means of negotiation, trade, gift, and purchase. From around the world there were assembled gradually collections of *kapa*, mats, calabashes, feather work, stone implements, and a host of other categories of exhibit items. Queen Emma's collection had been donated to Bishop in a codicil to her Will, dated November 19, 1884. A passage from the Minute Book of the Queen's Hospital, dated September 15, 1886, describes how her priceless antiquities were legally saved and channelled into the personal possession of Bishop:

To carry out the Codicil of the Will of her late Majesty Queen Dowager Emma Kaleleonalani which not being witnessed according to law, could not be admitted in the Probate Court. This Codicil intended to make over or set apart for, a Museum to contain similar collections of the late Hon. Bernice Pauahi Bishop and others, all the antiquities and curios forming a part of the possessions of Her Late Majesty Dowager Queen Emma. To carry out this disposition of the testator would now require the joint consent of the residuary legatees of the Will, i.e., Prince Albert Kuniakea [sic] and the Queen's Hospital, and for this purpose therefore the Board of Trustees would have to give its consent, provided the disposition meets with its approval.

On motion of Hon. A. L. Cleghorn, recorded by Hon. W. C. Parke, the Hospital Board of Trustees unanimously adopted the following resolution:

Resolved that the Secretary and Treasurer are hereby authorized to execute for the consideration of one dollar on behalf of the Queen's Hospital a Deed of Trust from Alex J. Cartwright, Executor of the Will of the late Dowager Queen Emma Kaleleonalani conveying to Charles R. Bishop and his successors and trustees the Hawaiian curiosities which belonged to the said Dowager Queen and which she intended should be so conveyed as indicated in the Codicil of her Will signed November 19, 1884, it being understood that such curiosities are to be placed with other native curiosities which belonged to the late Bernice Pauahi Bishop and with others which may be added thereto, at an institution or museum for preservation.

This action was suggested to the Queen's Hospital Trustees by Bishop, who eventually turned over the Queen Emma collection, along with Mrs. Bishop's and other collections of his own, to the Bishop Estate Trustees in a Deed of Trust, March 23, 1891.

Other collections of a general nature came to the Museum from J. S. Emerson, George H. Dole, Eric Craig, and Oahu College. The Mann and Brigham collections of Hawaiian plants, Professor H. W. Henshaw's bird collection, the American Board of Commissioners for Foreign Missions' Pacific Area collection, the Hawaiian Board of Missions' own collection of Hawaiiana, and the Government Museum's prized collection were also acquired. A bill to effect transfer of the Hawaiian Government Museum Collection to the Bishop Museum was passed by joint resolution of the Hawaiian legislature groups, July 19, 1898. The resolution was dated July 7. Sanford B. Dole, who was President of both the Museum Trust and the Republic of Hawaii, was in close touch with the current volatile political situation. He advised instant removal of the collection from the government repository to the Museum. The artifacts were moved July 19. Other collections were added and a few of them warrant listing: the field efforts of R. C. L. Perkins, who collected jointly for the Royal Society, the British Association for the Advancement of Science, and the Bishop Museum; the J. L. Young collection from Rapanui and Tahiti; and the William R. Castle collection of Australian implements. A Museum item dated January 23, 1894, mentions:

. . . Bishop's gift of the splendid collection of shells made by the late Andrew Garrett. This is one of the choicest private collections in the world.

Another item, dated June 30, 1896, states:

To him [Bishop] the Museum is also indebted for the addition of over 1500 specimens for an Herbarium including 20 and more new species now first brought to the notice of students of botany.

Bishop had been approached about purchasing several stamp collections and had rather steadfastly refused to acquire them, partly because the asking prices were too high and also because he was never quite convinced that stamp collections were properly common or customary items for a museum. However, when the Thomas M. Thrum stamp collection, under the title "Hawaiian Postage and Revenue Stamps, Postal Cards, and Envelopes," became available, he authorized a payment of $5000. Thrum wanted $6000, so Samuel Damon put in a thousand dollars of his own to cover the balance and presented the collection to the Trustees of the Museum, February 10, 1899.

In a letter to Damon, May 2, 1889, Bishop mentions his apprehension about being overcharged for artifact purchases:

. . . J. S. Emerson . . . is going to Australia and New Zealand by and by and I have a lot of duplicates . . . which I would like to have him exchange for other native things. . . . Probably he expects to get a lot of things to sell to me at a large profit! He has "struck a bonanza" in me. . . .

This was to be a typical reaction again and again, and he always worried because he was engaging in a commerce of which he knew no rules of supply or demand. He was quite excited about locating rare objects for inclusion in the Museum, and he commented on the availability of a feather helmet, an old sled, Lillie Richard's antiquities, the American Board of Commissioners for Foreign Missions' collection, and other possibilities, in his correspondence.

William T. Brigham had worked very diligently on manuscripts relating to Hawaiian history and geography and had offered considerable advice to Bishop while the Museum was building. Shortly after the opening of the Museum, Brigham wrote, August 6, 1890, requesting appointment as curator, effective February 17, 1891, for two years at an annual salary of $2500. He outlined his suggestions very carefully and very fully. By way of reply, on August 18, 1890, Bishop stated:

The building for the Museum is a part of the Kamehameha School premises and with what is intended to be put into it, is virtually the property of the same estate, and under the control of the same trustees as the school is; but as I have paid the cost of nearly everything constituting or connected with the Museum so far, and intend to pay for all additions— except such as may be loaned or contributed, I shall no doubt really control so long as I may wish to do so.
    I have concluded to give you that appointment. . . .

This was to signalize the initiation of a stormy relationship. He was called upon again and again to hold Brigham in his position. There was a real forecast of trial and tribulation in a letter he directed to Brigham, October 14, 1890. Brigham was not appointed curator officially as yet. He was, however, constantly hovering about not to say almost haunting the Museum:

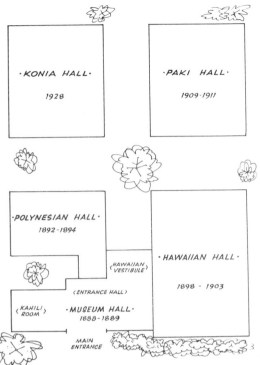

·KONIA HALL·
1928

·PAKI HALL·
1909-1911

·POLYNESIAN HALL·
1892-1894

·HAWAIIAN HALL·
1898 - 1903

(HAWAIIAN VESTIBULE)

(ENTRANCE HALL)

(KAHILI ROOM)

·MUSEUM HALL·
1888-1889

MAIN ENTRANCE

Bernice Pauahi Bishop Museum

Left: Plot plan—Museum.

Below: The Bernice Pauahi Bishop Museum, Palama, Honolulu, founded by Bishop as a memorial to his wife.

Your letter of the 13th inst, was rec'd this morning, and although I do not think its tone and tenor are altogether what they should be, I shall reply to it without unnecessary reference to the past.

It is not my purpose now to say anything to Mr. Damon about your unfriendly comments upon his actions and character, and I hope that all others will be equally considerate; but I cannot curtail his authority in my absence. He does not pretend to be scientific and is not likely to object to anything reasonable and proper, but will, I trust, be prudent in expenditure of funds. If you cannot treat him with perfect respect, and submit to his control in matters pertaining to the Museum as you would to me, it will be useless for you to think of going on with that work.

. . . I appreciate your talents and knowledge. . . . it will be vain for me to aid you, unless you control your speech, more than you have done. . . . In this small community you know that reported imprudent talk spreads quickly, and may become very damaging.

In intimating that you are imprudent in speech, and I might add hasty with your pen, I am not judging you from my own experience alone, but upon that of other friends also, who may not be so frank with you as I have been, lest you should take offense.

Bishop then left on the *Australia* November 21, for an extended tour that was to take him to Europe. He returned in December, 1891. While away, he continued his close contact with affairs in the Kingdom. He wrote his classic letter * to Queen Liliuokalani in March, resigned for the second and final time from the presidency of the Board of Education in April, and wrote voluminously and in great detail about the Museum. He also made a present in the form of a deed of gift to the Trustees. In the Minutes of May 1, 1891, this passage is recorded:

Mr. Damon read to the meeting the Hon. President's deed of gift to the Trustees for the benefit of the Kamehameha Schools of his lands in South Kona, including the *ahupuaa* of Honaunau and Kahauloa Nui, and of the articles and things in the B. Pauahi Museum [sic] at the Kamehameha School for Boys. . . . Mr. Brigham was employed by Mr. Bishop as Curator of the Museum . . . [at a] salary of $2500 per annum, which Mr. Bishop promised to continue to provide. The Museum contained many curios, etc., belonging to the Estate of Queen Emma and to the Hawaiian Government and it was Mr. Bishop's wish that the responsibility attached to the possession of these should be assumed by the Trustees, henceforth. . . .

The Museum was not only a repository for antiquities, it might also be described as a visual aids resource for students of The Kamehameha School for Boys and the Preparatory Department. In

* See pp. 343–347.

his Biennial Report as President of the Board of Education in 1892, Bishop states: "The Bishop Museum, in connection with this establishment [Kamehameha Schools] will remain a monument to its founder, and will prove a benefit to many a student for generations hence. . . ." Friend Hyde spoke of Mr. Bishop's purposes in starting the Museum at the Founder's Day exercises, December 19, 1894, of The Kamehameha Schools:

It was Mr. Bishop's desire in locating the Museum on these premises to perpetuate what of public interest, of national interest, of personal interest there is in this extensive and unique collection of Hawaiian antiquities and relics. Heredity and environment are two potent factors in the development of races and individuals. It is Mr. Bishop's desire that these memorials of the past shall furnish suitable instruction and intensify patriotic enthusiasm in the Hawaiian youth of both sexes brought into these buildings, under these influences, for education and training, and as such they properly form a part of the equipment of these schools.

That Bishop was proud of the Museum there can be no doubt. He wrote to his favorite ward and "niece," Victoria Kaiulani, on April 7, 1892:

. . . I think you will be pleased with the little museum at The Kamehameha Schools. . . . When your old "uncle" is dead and gone I hope that you will continue to take an interest in it for the sake of your dear friend and "aunt" whose name it bears. . . .

The Museum had up to this time either been a personal and direct concern of his or in his absence, of Samuel Damon. The deed of gift placed the Museum and the Schools in a semiparallel and equal position—two agencies or institutions with the same set of Trustees and yet, although integrated physically in the same campus, they were not thought of as being administratively one. On June 17, 1892, the following items appear in the minutes:

In answer to Mr. Cooke the treasurer said that the Bernice P. Bishop Museum trust account would be kept separate and spent from the ordinary estate account.

The President said that when he conveyed his Kona lands to the Trustees it was with the intention of making provision for the endowment of the Bernice P. Bishop Museum at the Kamehameha School for Boys. The deed, however, contained no such trust and was simply a conveyance of those lands upon like trusts for the Kamehameha Schools as those contained in the will of Mrs. Bishop. To repair this omission—to provide for the endowment of the Museum—he the President, had executed the deed of gift—which he delivered to the Trustees—of the land of Waipio.

. . . after July 1, 1892, he would no longer bear the expenses of the Museum. . . .

He followed the gift with another $30,000 in 1893, for the endowment of the Museum. The receipt made out to Bishop by the Trustees was dated March 1, 1893, and practically nailed down Museum policy:

Received from Charles R. Bishop the sum of Thirty Thousand Dollars on account of a legacy given by him in his will to the Trustees of the Estate of Bernice Bishop in aid of the Bernice Pauahi Bishop Museum. And we agree to safely invest said amount and to use the income only in procuring objects belonging to and illustrative of the life habits and customs of the aboriginal inhabitants of the Islands of the Pacific Ocean and of the natural history of said islands and in the care preservation and improvement of the said Museum.

There was now a definite trend towards a separation in fact of the Museum and the Schools. The Trustees' agenda was frequently beginning to be divided between Museum items and Schools items. On August 10, 1895, a major step was taken. Hyde was in the chair of a B. P. Bishop Estate meeting and announced "not for publication" the decision of Bishop to establish the Charles R. Bishop Trust.* It was to have a separate bank account. Its properties and investments were to be handled independently of the Bishop Estate. The advantage to the Museum of this move was significant. A vehicle was provided not only for carrying out Bishop's bequests but also for handling endowments and income which ultimately would contribute the major share of the Museum operating budget. The initial result of the action led to an unfettering or disentanglement of the Museum operation from that of the Schools.

On November 22, 1895, the B. P. Bishop Estate record shows:

On motion of Mr. Damon it was resolved to open a separate set of books of account and to keep distinct the *minutes* of meeting of the Trustees of the Bernice P. Bishop Museum Trust but the business of the Trust was to be done at the B. P. Bishop Estate Office.

That move was but one of a series that was leading to a definite separation of the Trusts. Bishop wrote to Damon, January 27, 1896, and discussed the qualifications of trustees for a separate Museum Trust and his own purposes in even establishing a Museum:

For most things to be managed, I do not believe in large Boards, for the responsibility is so divided that it is likely to lead to neglect, or to be left

* See pp. 223, 225, 231.

to one or two members. . . . It seems to me that five trustees, all residents of Honolulu, are enough for the Museum, and I would have no objection to have one of them appointed by the Executive of the Government, and perhaps one by the Justices (in majority) of the Supreme Court. There are good men who take an interest in the Museum as a Museum . . . and who at the same time are so unbusinesslike in their habits and ideas of economy and finances that they would, left to themselves, wreck or embarrass almost any establishment. . . . Would the Government and the Court think of that and act accordingly!

I started with the idea of making an Hawaiian Museum, but with little hope of making it nearly a complete collection even in that line, and with the belief that the building first erected would be quite sufficient for its accommodation. Pretty soon I saw that it should include all that could be procured and paid for with the money that I felt like using for such a purpose, belonging to any or all of the Polynesian Islands, and later still I concluded to make a final widening of the scope and take in the objects belonging or relating to all or any of the *Islands* of the *Pacific Ocean,* and stretched the point to include Australia, with the determination to have nothing to do with any other continent. With this limitation I think that the Museum will be unique, interesting and have a scientific value . . . a sort of hodge podge collection of things that may be interesting and valuable in their proper place, gathered from far and wide is not what I want.

He followed up his letter to Damon with one to Henry Holmes on February 12, 1896:

I have received your letter of the 1st Inst. with printed copy of Mrs. Bishop's will and several documents accompanying it, and after considering them, I have come to the conclusion that you are so well acquainted with all matters connected with said will, the property of the Estate of Mrs. Bishop, the Kamehameha Schools, the Bernice Pauahi Bishop Museum and the conditions on which the property has been conveyed to the Trustees of said Estate for the establishing and support of the Museum, and with Hawaiian laws and courts, that you are more competent to make the proposed Deed for placing the Museum on a somewhat more independent basis. . . .

. . . Having faith in your ability, knowledge and carefulness, I do request you to undertake this work. . . .

The idea of making the Museum a mere showplace for Polynesian antiquities has long since passed. . . . As to the number of Trustees, I am now inclined to make it seven, to include five Trustees of the Estate of Bernice Pauahi Bishop, and two others to be appointed by Justices of the Supreme Court or highest Court of the Country. Whether it is wise or not to provide that those two Trustees should be nominated by a majority of the five Trustees, I submit to the latter for their consideration. As the buildings of the Museum are on the property of said Estate by permission of the Trustees, and others in time are to be added, it may be necessary or at least prudent to have a lease or some formal writing, confirming and extending these privileges. . . .

. . . to confine the collection to things connected with the Islands of the Pacific would make the Museum unique and give it scientific value . . . it is my purpose to build at least one more large annex. . . . I may be able to provide for two. . . . It is my wish and purpose . . . to establish an aquarium and biological laboratory under the same authority as the Museum. . . .

The next step occurred in a meeting of the Bishop Estate, June 1, 1896:

The chairman presented a draft deed of trust prepared in anticipation of the separation of the Bernice P. Bishop Museum Trust from the B. P. Bishop Estate and for the purpose of declaring the trusts of the Museum and of conveying the Museum property to the new Trustees of the Museum.

This was the Deed of Trust which Bishop had charged Holmes with preparing. The draft Deed of Trust was sent with notes and comments for his consideration and approval. On July 23, 1896, the reply came asking that a proposed Marine Aquarium and Biological Laboratory be included. He also indicated his purpose to provide another large annex to the Museum and his desire that Sanford B. Dole and Henry Holmes be the additional two Trustees. Upon reading this letter the Trustees voted to adopt the draft Deed of Trust as amended by Bishop and enclosed with his letter the new Deed of Trust of the Bernice Pauahi Bishop Museum.

An indenture was presented at the meeting of October 13, 1896, conveying the Museum building to the new Trust, and a statement of purposes was set forth:

a. a scientific institution for collecting, preserving, storing and exhibiting specimens of Polynesia and kindred antiquities, Ethnology and Natural History, and books treating of, and pictures illustrating the same, and for the examination, investigation, treatment and study of said specimens and the publication of pictures thereof, and of such investigations and study.
b. Marine Aquarium and Biological Laboratory

The first meeting of the Trustees of the new Museum Trust was held October 28, 1896, in the back office of Bishop and Company. At the next meeting, December 9, 1896, Bishop was elected President and Sanford B. Dole Vice President; and the latter occupied the chair for a time. This marks the start of the Bernice Pauahi Bishop

Museum as an independent institution. The court authorized the transfer of the Waipio lands and a $30,000 collection of six percent government bonds to the new Trust. Bishop added to the financial relief of the Trust by forgiving a $4560.10 obligation of the Museum to Bishop and Company. Additional endowments contributed later by him included:

February 15, 1896	$8000 collection of American Board of Commissioners for Foreign Missions [Boston]
February 12, 1897	$50,000 note of Mr. and Mrs. B. F. Dillingham secured by fifty $1000 Oahu Railway and Land Company Bonds
March 12, 1897	2 lots and buildings on Merchant Street
April 9, 1897	$50,000 note of S. M. Damon
	$9,300 note of James I. Dowsett
March 11, 1898	$18,000 Charles R. Bishop Trust
December 7, 1900	$72,000 notes, mortgages and shares in Oahu Railway and Land Company

In the matter of occupying the premises in the heart of The Kamehameha School for Boys campus, Bishop and the other Trustees were of several minds. In April, 1897, as the next annex was being considered, the problem arose again. Brigham wanted to fence the premises as a kind of oasis, but Bishop, in a letter to Carter, April 29, said:

It is so well understood that the Museum buildings and everything connected with them, are to have a place in the School premises and be treated with the same consideration as if they were School buildings, and as a large majority of the Trustees of the Museum are also Trustees of the B. P. B. Estate, it seems to me hardly necessary to have a lease. There certainly needs to be no fencing off. . . .

In June, 1897, the Trustees of the Estate refused to lease the site of the Museum or adjoining ground. Some years later, Bishop (1903) expressed his hope that "the Museum would acquire a lease on the Museum premises and the necessary land immediately adjoining." On January 8, 1904, the Museum Trustees signed a lease from the estate Trustees for the Museum site and immediately adjoining land at a gross term rental of $500 for 99 years, effective February 1, 1904. A final major move was made when the property on which the buildings were constructed plus some twenty-odd acres of adjacent estate land were deeded in fee simple to the Museum Trust (1958).

Bishop was interested in a Marine Aquarium and Biological Laboratory. He had seen one in Leipzig and another in Naples years before, and he needed little encouragement from Messrs. Hyde and Brigham to provide one for Honolulu. The Museum Trust was written up to include it. The City of Honolulu even went so far as to earmark a stretch of harbor edge just *waikiki* of the present Aloha Tower as a site for Bishop's dreams. But the practical side of his nature asserted itself; he was rather heavily obligated from contributions to the Kamehameha Preparatory buildings, the several additions to the Museum, and some major gifts to Punahou. He also had just established his Charles R. Bishop Trust. When Brigham returned from a European trip and spoke a little too strongly about the aquarium, Bishop was moved to complain in a letter to Carter, October 13, 1896:

I regret that Mr. Brigham should talk so extravagantly about what he or I or anybody else will do about the Aquarium. His remarks about how much I will expend, are entirely unauthorized. I have mentioned no sum, and it would be impossible for me to furnish the large sum which he mentions. . . . He has picked up a great deal of valuable information, and he is very able; but he will be Brigham to the end.

He weighed the matter carefully throughout the rest of that year. A close San Francisco scientist and friend, Louis Agassiz, talked with him about an aquarium and agreed to draw up a complete plan, but nothing came of this. David Starr Jordan, another distinguished scientist in the Bay area, was approached by Bishop in the summer of 1895. He tried talking Jordan into a Honolulu visit at the end of 1895 to check on possible sites and to talk with the Trustees and Brigham about it. But the eminent Doctor was working on the first volume of his research on fishes, to be published by the Smithsonian Institution. He promised a complimentary set of his books on fishes which Bishop indicated would be turned over to the Museum. Brigham in the meantime had inflated the aquarium idea into a grandiose and costly dream, and Bishop again urged Jordan to visit Honolulu and "assist in planning something which would be quite as good and yet much less costly." This did not materialize either, whereupon he turned to Brigham with a letter February 12, 1897:

Since I wrote you on the 10th of November, nothing has occurred to change my purposes regarding the Aquarium. Like other Yankees, I suppose I should be disposed "to beat all creation" in this matter, but your ideas as to what is wanted, and your estimate of cost for establishment and support, so far exceed my present ability that nothing more need be said about it now.

He closed the project out in a letter to Jordan, December 14, 1897:

I have given up the intention to establish an aquarium and biological laboratory in Honolulu; because the cost would be beyond my means; but there is much other scientific work which can, and should be done in connection with the Museum.

He was alert to the value of an aquarium and was happy to read in the Honolulu press that one was actually started and so commented to J. O. Carter, September 2, 1903:

I am pleased to learn that an Aquarium is to be established and maintained at Waikiki by some of the public-spirited citizens, largely I suppose, by the R. T. & L. Co.* or those largely interested in it. No doubt it will be interesting and instructive. . . . It has seemed to me a rather too heavy and troublesome undertaking for the B. P. B. Museum, and I am glad that others can and will undertake it.

Brigham, having been unrewarded in his campaign for an aquarium as a gift from Bishop, turned to other community sources and finally realized his objective.

Bishop's studied concern for the preservation of antiquities of Hawaii took another twist about this time. He communicated his wishes in this instance to Henry Holmes, one of the Museum Trustees, February 22, 1897:

.   .   .   .   .   .

There is another matter in which I feel much interested, which sooner or later may call for the expenditures of some more from the Museum or the Trust fund. . . . I mean the acquisition and control of the Heiaus and Puuhonuas, of Pakaalana in Waipio, of Honaunau in Kona, and perhaps the one on the Islet of Mokuola in Hilo Bay, and any others of interest and worth preserving. It should not cost much to acquire all of these, for they are of no utility to the present owners. Once in the control of the Museum they could be protected perpetually.

Please be good enough to make a record of this in your record book so that it may not be overlooked. . . .

Holmes, upon reading this proposal, reflected upon the responsibility of government in such matters and undertook to prepare legislation covering the acquisition by government of these historic sites and monuments. No permanent commission on historic sites and monuments was formed, but the Legislature took some cog-

---

* Rapid Transit and Land Company.

nizance of the matter. In 1898 it passed a law authorizing acquisition of sites and monuments and appropriating $2500. A few were acquired at that time, and the authority to do so is still on the books.

Bishop resigned his trusteeship on October 13, 1897, on account of permanent residence abroad. Sanford B. Dole * was elected President of the Museum Trust. This man was a stalwart among the great leaders of Hawaii and had time, in spite of government crises, to act as Trustee of the Museum. He was more than an amateur in science. Bishop liked him and upon one occasion extended him an invitation to make the Founder's Day Address at Kamehameha. This was December 19, 1898.

Upon assuming the trusteeship, Dole became involved in the Brigham debate; but he seems to have been the only one of the Trustees, after Hyde's death, who could maintain an "even keel" relationship with Brigham. Partly in frustration and partly in bluff, Brigham had resigned; and on July 9, 1897, his resignation was accepted. Acland Wansey was installed as curator while a search was instituted for a replacement.

There was a serious question as to whether a reconciliation between the Trustees and Brigham could be accomplished. Bishop accordingly discussed the directorship with David Starr Jordan who immediately recommended Dr. Leonhard Stejneger, a distinguished scientist from Washington, D. C., with whom Bishop proceeded to correspond privately. Stejneger had been chiefly responsible for the study leading to the International Seal Fisheries Treaty. He was a distinguished ornithologist. In order to consider the position, he made a trip to Honolulu to study the Museum. Other names were added to the list of candidates: J. D. Seabury, A. M. Mellis, Robert Law, and a fourth suggested by George Munro—R. C. L. Perkins, one of the Museum's most diligent and skillful scientists.

Basically, the problems besetting Brigham lay deep within his own emotional nature. In this "crisis" of late 1897, he wrote in a mood of swift anger to Bishop that he had already "destroyed large baskets full of photography and letters," and said when he left Honolulu he would "destroy everything I have relating to the Hawaiian Islands." Bishop's comment on this was more in a vein of sadness than anything else. To Henry Holmes under date of October 20, 1897, in addition to quoting Brigham's statements, he said:

* Ethel M. Damon, *Sanford Ballard Dole and His Hawaii* (Palo Alto, California, Pacific Books, 1957).

. . . He is treating me with ingratitude, and yet I regret he could not come to an agreeable understanding with the trustees and continue his work. I have no revengeful feeling toward him, but am exceedingly sorry that so capable a man should behave so unwisely, to the injury of himself and his friends.

Brigham made a quick emergency trip to San Francisco to lay his case before Bishop, arriving but a couple of days after the above-quoted letter to Holmes was dispatched. A friend of Brigham's, a Mr. Whealan, also appeared in Bishop's apartment to join in the pleading. Brigham had with him a draft of a letter to be sent to President Sanford B. Dole, outlining his acceptance of all of the conditions set forth by a reluctant group of the Trustees in Honolulu. He did ask for a change in title of position from curator to Director. Bishop described all this to Holmes a week after the first letter and wrote most sympathetically and with understanding:

. . . My feeling about Mr. Brigham is, that in order to get on with him peaceably and get the best service he is capable of, it is necessary to make large allowances for his peculiarities, and not to be easily offended with him. . . . There are great artists in various lines, professors, poets, doctors, etc., who are so different from the man of ordinary common sense. Mr. Brigham seems to be that kind of man. . . . After all that I have written on this matter I wish to add that I shall be much pleased if the trustees of the Museum will accept Mr. Brigham's letter to Mr. Dole as a basis of reconciliation and a step toward an engagement as director. It is highly important and desirable that the action should be unanimous. . . .

After much verbal skirmishing, and with the strong recommendation of Bishop, Brigham was reinstated, effective January 1, 1898, with the title of Director and on condition that he would not conduct any visitors about the Museum without the express approval of the Trustees. A little later, October, 1901, Brigham was in trouble again. In the meeting of October 11, 1901, Mr. Smith informed the Board that he and A. W. Carter, when in San Francisco, had both talked with Bishop who said he would never again lift his voice in favor of Mr. Brigham. Matters came to a head in December, but by a vote of 4–2 Brigham was retained.

A by-product of this Brigham-created-tempest was the resignation of Henry Holmes. This action also troubled Bishop. Holmes had been a friend of long standing and a trusted associate in many of the Bishop enterprises. He had shared in the preparation of Mrs. Bishop's Will, maintained a watchful management eye over Bishop and Company banking affairs, had written the original draft of the Charles R. Bishop Trust deed, and had acted as Trustee of the Museum Trust through its early organizing years.

It was not that Brigham did not like people, although he was prejudiced against the Hawaiian boys at Kamehameha (and admitted it); but rather that he loved to work, arranging exhibits, identifying specimens, doing a dozen kinds of research in preparation for writing, and he did not relish interruptions. His caustic tongue, however, embroiled him with almost everyone with whom he came in contact. He criticized the Kamehameha students and apologized for his remarks. A Catholic bishop demanded that the Trustees remove him for remarks about Father Damien, attributed to him by museum visitors. He tried his level best to hold the visitor days at the Museum to one or two a week and for limited hours. Foreign boat days were important opportunities for passengers to visit the Museum, and even these visitors were ignored or barred. Frequently, when a ship entered Honolulu harbor a "closed" sign appeared on the outside entrance of the Museum. This evoked a comment from Bishop in a letter to J. O. Carter, June 25, 1898: "It should not be difficult or inconvenient for respectable passengers in steamers calling at Honolulu to see the Museum. Many *have been* disappointed."

In many ways, the story of the Museum is the story of Brigham. He was a superior organizer; he was a driver, and his contribution was magnificent in terms of the birth, the growth, the organization of materials, the acquisition of collections, and the program of publications. Bishop could see through Brigham's thick smoke screen of indifference to people and evaluate his contribution for what it was worth. Brigham ranted and roared his determined way, first as curator and then as Director, for about thirty years, retiring in 1920. After his visit in Hawaii with Horace Mann, in 1864, he had returned to Massachusetts, passed the bar examination and for the next twenty years practiced law and taught school. He taught botany for one year at Harvard and then embarked on a botanizing expedition to Australia. Bishop, as has been related, reached him by mail on this trip and started him on the museum road. His work on the Bishop Museum brought him world renown. Columbia granted him a doctorate in science. He was a Fellow, Royal Anthropology Institute of Great Britain and Ireland; Fellow, Imperial Academy of Science, St. Petersburg; and a member of the American Academy of

Art and Sciences. But the tribute that probably gave him his greatest satisfaction came from the pen of the donor of the institution which Brigham had served so ably—Charles Reed Bishop. It was in the form of a letter, dated January 25, 1912, written by Bishop on his ninetieth birthday:

I wish to . . . express my satisfaction with the good work you have accomplished. The Museum is far superior to anything that was anticipated by her whose name it bears, or to anything which I had hoped to accomplish when the first building was erected. The size of that building, supposed to be sufficient for purposes then contemplated, compared with the present structures, gives an idea of the superiority of the Museum over what was then expected to be accomplished. I am proud of the Museum as it now stands, and I am sure that you must be pleased with the excellent work done in which you have had so large a part. I consider myself fortunate in having been served by your ability and devotion.

Museum-related Subjects and Scientists

BIRDS AND THE HONORABLE WALTER ROTHSCHILD

The English ornithologist, Walter Rothschild, had several bird hunters at the monumental task of collecting on the island of Laysan and on all of the islands of the Hawaiian chain. Among his collectors were R. C. L. Perkins and Henry B. Palmer, both of England. Among several new species collected was a *moho* bird, discovered by Palmer on Molokai and subsequently obtained there also by Perkins. This was one of some fifteen new species discovered and was named by Rothschild *Moho Bishopi* in honor of Bishop, who had been instrumental in supplying necessary guns and dogs to the collectors. Bishop, in turn, had offered certain duplicates of the rare *mamo* and *oo* to Mr. Rothschild. In other instances he sent photographs, Museum publications, and the like. So helpful, indeed, was Bishop to the project, that Rothschild expressed his gratitude in the preface of his two-volume treatise. The first mention of Rothschild by Bishop appears in a letter to Brigham, December 19, 1892, hoping that Rothschild would part with some of the duplicate skins to help complete the Museum bird collection.

Part I of Rothschild's book came out in September, 1893, and a copy went to Bishop. The manuscript with pictures and plates was ultimately published in two large volumes, between 1893 and 1900, under the title, *Avifauna of Laysan and the Neighboring Islands with a Complete History to Date of the Birds of the Hawaiian*

Possessions. In the letter accompanying Part I, Rothschild offered duplicate skins of twenty-one birds for the Museum collection.

After several years of no word from Rothschild, Bishop was pleased to hear from him in September, 1899, that he had:

. . . sent off a box containing specimens of all the species got by my collectors in Laysan; I hope shortly to send you the third and concluding parts of my book. I would have sent the birds sooner but kept them for comparison until the manuscript of my book was complete.

This message Bishop quoted in an excited letter to Brigham, September 29, 1899. The two Rothschild volumes rank with the best ever prepared on the ornithology of Hawaii.

R. C. L. PERKINS

Frequent references to R. C. L. Perkins, of the University Museum of Zoology, Cambridge, England, were made in the Bishop correspondence. He was first mentioned in a letter to Brigham, December 19, 1892: "Has . . . Mr. Perkins secured a specimen of the *Mamo* or of the wingless bird?" A little later Bishop suggested to Brigham that he supply a gun and a dog to Perkins, and again he hoped Perkins would return to the Islands and collect for the Trustees. He considered Perkins to be a rare collector, much superior to Wilson or Palmer. On March 29, 1895, he wrote to Brigham that he was attempting to share in Perkins' collecting, which was being done for the English societies. And only a few days later, he revealed one of his own special interests in collecting areas, in a letter to Carter:

. . . I am indifferent about the collecting of the insects of the country, but quite anxious to fill out our collection of birds.

I have written Dr. Hyde on the subject of employing or joining with others in the employing of Mr. Perkins to collect for the Museum.

Bishop wrote to Hyde on December 17, 1895:

I shall return to you the pamphlet of Mr. Perkins, describing the Birds of Hawaii, because it or one like it, in fact everything that he writes on the subject should be in the Museum. He is a wonderfully keen and energetic naturalist, and I think we can rely upon everything he says or publishes.

The first hint of a slight jealousy of Perkins on the part of Brigham appears in a letter which Bishop wrote on January 22, 1897, to Hyde:

You know that Mr. Perkins is about to leave the Islands. He is thoroughly scientific, and may have some views about the Museum and what should be its aim, that may be of value, and that he may be willing to express to you and the other Trustees. He may not be willing to oppose openly any of Mr. Brigham's for he is very modest and loves peace.

Bishop wanted to arrange for Perkins' return, but the scientist had to remain in England for some years to work up and publish the results of his visits. Perkins was also a collector of shells and insects. His work in all these fields was highly regarded by Bishop. But the jealousy came to the surface, as was apparent in an April 19, 1897, letter to Brigham:

Regarding Mr. Perkins (whom you repeatedly characterize as a "boy" and who is a number of years older than Horace Mann was when he came to Honolulu:) you know that he does not pretend to know everything, and would not presume to compare himself with yourself in general knowledge, scientific or other. He does know, I think, some things very well. . . . It was not expected that he would overhaul the whole Museum, but I thought that his opinion on such matters as he does understand, might be of value. He is entirely friendly to you and to me. . . .

Perkins wrote in June, 1897, that he would be kept at the work on Hawaiian things for two more years and wondered if the Trustees would share the publication costs on *Hawaiian Creatures*. Bishop immediately lost some of his enthusiasm for Perkins, but he kept the door open and inquired of the likely costs.

The gentle Perkins-Brigham feud was continued. In a letter to Hyde, January 22, 1898, Bishop writes:

Is it not quite important to get a man soon who can carry out the work so well begun by Mr. Perkins? Mr. Perkins' communications are worth preserving on file—and Mr. Brigham's may be wanted for defense!

Perkins wrote he was probably coming to the Islands at the end of 1898 to make a special collection of a few insects. Brigham was having one of his personality battles; and Bishop in a letter to Hyde, February 16, after expressing the hope that Brigham would be reasonable, wrote:

. . . I think that he is jealous of those who possibly may be employed or who give advice about the Museum. He showed that spirit toward Mr. Perkins, and as to Entomology, in which Mr. Perkins is so much interested, he is disposed to poo poo it.

Bishop himself wrote to Perkins, May 25, and suggested the hope of getting instruction and advice, if not actual collection work. Perkins advanced his schedule and arrived in the Islands about the time of his letter from Bishop. A little later Perkins began to hint of his desire of doing some work for the Museum. But on July 5, Bishop wrote to Hyde:

. . . It now appears that the B. P. Bishop Museum can hardly expect any further service from him [Perkins] in the way of collecting, unless he should be engaged *permanently*, which is not likely while Mr. Brigham remains in charge. To assist in working up and publishing the results of his work in Hawaii so far is no doubt wise.

Brigham never acknowledged the merit of Perkins' work, and yet the Trustees participated financially with the English societies in the publication of his works. The R. C. L. Perkins work is detailed in the scientific series entitled, *Fauna Hawaiiensis.* Mrs. E. Faxon Bishop recalled that Perkins taught at the Pauoa Public School for a short time and was considered a superior teacher with a "wonderful memory and a keen mind." He was understandably nicknamed "Birdie."

Alvin Seale

Bishop suggested Alvin Seale as an ornithologist. Seale was but twenty-five years old when he was suggested for employment at the Museum, March 6, 1899. He had worked his way through Stanford University collecting and preparing bird skins for museums. He had filled orders for the American Museum of New York City, the British Museum, and the Zoological Museum in London and had excellent letters of reference from them all. He would work for $50.00 per month and room and board. Brigham did not think too well of his lack of experience, and so commented; but Bishop was fairly insistent. Seale, in the meantime, went East and studied bird preparing at the Field Museum and came back to San Francisco with the warm encouragement of Professor Loomis of the Academy of Sciences. This was in July and August of 1899. Bishop urged Brigham to consider Seale for Laysan and the neighboring islands. Brigham agreed to hire Seale at $75.00 per month plus transportation and collecting expense. Seale sailed on the *Moana,* November 1, 1899. In a series of four letters to Brigham, Bishop commented: December 11, 1899: "I'm pleased to know that Mr. Seale has made a good impression. . . ."

February 3, 1900: "Is there a vessel going to Laysan Island in the Spring, and would you advise sending Mr. Seale there?"

May 10, 1900: "Mr. W. O. Smith will report what he did in Washington towards getting passage for Mr. Seale on a Gov't vessel to Guam if he is to go there. I do not know enough about the birds on that island to be quite sure it would be profitable to send Mr. Seale there."

October 2, 1901: "Mr. Seale is thorough and conscientious in all that he undertakes to do and quite skillful in some lines. The Trustees may decide to send him to the southern islands to collect for the Museum."

Mr. Seale had successfully continued his employment for a long time, considering the circumstances; but tempers rose, and the formula relationship between Brigham and employee operated again. Seale had gone to Guam and the Marquesas and the Society Islands. While the shipments of specimens were acceptable, apparently the reports were not. At any rate, Seale was not re-engaged. He had turned in a highly creditable quality and quantity of specimens, both of birds and of fishes; and the Museum collections today are the better for them. Seale is mentioned once more in the Bishop correspondence, in a letter to Carter, May 25, 1905:

Mr. Seale who is now an Assistant Fish Commissioner and is working at Stanford would like to go for exploration and collecting in the Islands of New Guinea, Bougainville and others, but I can hardly recommend him to the Trustees; partly because Mr. Brigham thinks so poorly of him for such an expedition. He has some valuable qualifications but as Dr. Jordan says, is deficient in education.

It is likely that the deficiency in education referred to was the lack of a doctorate degree. Seale's work is considered by competent opinion to have been of high quality.

FEATHER CLOAKS

Bishop was constantly on the lookout for featherwork, and through numerous acquisitions he created a kind of featherwork-center status for the Musuem. People hurried to him with offers of cloaks. He never failed in his travels to look up all known capes, robes, and helmets in any exhibit hall or museum. The featherwork pieces constituting the initial collection of the Museum were outstanding, but there were others scattered around the world. The second, and one of the finest, of the Museum publications was *Hawaiian Featherwork*, printed in color and prepared by Brigham. Bishop was very proud of this publication. Brigham made a thorough study of the subject, including an inventory and description of all listed capes.

The first mention of featherwork in the Bishop letters was on July 23, 1891, to Brigham:

The cloak and helmet show very nicely in the photograph you sent me, and you will be pleased with the . . . cloak I bought in London. In the Louvre collection in Paris—the Marine department, it is called—I found the name Sandwich on only three things: a very high helmet in quite good order, and two helmets without any feathers.

He comments again, January 17, 1893, to Brigham:

You say Mr. Read has obtained two more feather cloaks. Does he describe their size, colors and condition, and say whether or not they are for sale, and the price? Perhaps they are obtained for the British Museum, though they were quite well supplied with such things before.

On June 11, 1895, he writes in another letter:

. . . Mr. Damon has written me about a small feather cape belonging to Peterson, and has mentioned a high valuation, somewhere from $500 to $800. I am curious to know why this cape is so much more valuable than the one I purchased in Boston for $100. What is the difference?

A few months later, January 17, 1896, he again mentions featherwork:

I send you . . . a leaf of "The Field" of August 11, 1894, in which you will find reference to the Oo and to an old cloak for sale. If convenient you can look at the feather cloak if it is still for sale, but I do not care to buy all of the old cloaks, except at a *very low* price, for the Museum is now about furnished with such specimens. I gave thirty-five pounds, about $175, for the large one I bought in London.

Bishop was not quite as reluctant to pay a price for a feather cape as he sounded. He was always happy whenever an additional cape or cloak would find its way into the museum list.

The Bishop Museum, in its research on Hawaiian capes for a proposed *Occasional Paper*, asked Bishop to solicit Liliuokalani's consent to measure and photograph all of the capes in her possession. On December 21, 1898, he acknowledged the request to Brigham:

About photographs of feather cloaks, etc. I am pleased to know that you have received so many, and had I known when Liliuokalani was here lately that she had possession of some feather work that you wished to have photographed for historical purposes I would have applied to her. . . . I was not aware that she was the *owner* of any cloaks, but supposed that she had some capes.

He thereupon wrote to Liliuokalani in Washington, D. C., and asked her permission to have her featherwork items photographed. The letter, dated January 21, 1899, describes the scope of the proposed publication:

. . . At great pains the Museum has secured photographs, measurement, form and description of figures, of nearly all the featherwork (Hawaiian) in the museums of Europe and America; and these institutions and private owners have kindly aided in this interesting object. Photographs of some of the cloaks have been handsomely printed in colors in Vienna.

. . . the favor which I ask of you is that you will permit Mr. Brigham, who is a skillful photographer, to photograph, measure and note the colors of all of the genuine Hawaiian feather work—cloaks, capes, etc. that you possess, and I give you my promise that these shall be dispatched and every possible care used, so that not the least harm shall come to your treasures. . . .

He reported in letters that same week to Brigham, Carter, and Hyde that he had written to the ex-Queen. The Museum had collected information on all known Hawaiian feather work in private hands and museums around the world and needed the Liliuokalani data to make the publication complete. But Liliuokalani owned very little of this kind of material. She offered the loan of the few pieces she owned and referred him to the Queen Dowager Kapiolani, who had some of the finest capes known. This touched off a long, fruitless effort to obtain those items from Kapiolani, who declined permission to photograph. In the meantime the *Memoirs of the Feather Work* was published, and a Mr. Dall brought a copy to Bishop. He promptly got off a letter to Brigham, October 11, 1899:

. . . The Memoir is a very valuable and very interesting work and a great credit to yourself and the Museum. I shall have much satisfaction in showing it to my friends.

A few weeks later he suggested giving copies to Princess Kawanakoa and "Cupid" [Kuhio] and to Stanford and California Universities. He was proud of this publication. He had seen the excellent papers from other museums and societies and was thrilled that at long last his little cultural empire was able, in the publication field, to hold its head up with the others. His interest in capes never flagged; on April 2, 1909, he observed to S. M. Damon: "The acquiring of the feather cape from the heirs of Lady Franklin is noticed in the San Francisco Chronicle of this morning." To Brigham he added another word a month later:

I had heard about the "Lady Franklin" cape, lately acquired, and I am glad to know it is large, and in excellent condition. It seems to me that Mr. Austin is behaving foolishly about the cape received from him. He values it, apparently, at more than it is worth.

The net result of the Museum activity on behalf of Hawaiian capes, cloaks, and helmets was the accumulation in good order and in excellent condition of the largest and finest collection of such feather work in the world.

FISHES

Almost all of the ornithologists collected fishes in addition to birds, and most of them collected insects. This was true of Perkins and Seale, who had done a large share of the collecting for the Museum. One Mr. Thompson had not only collected fishes but had also developed a special color spray for dramatic effects in mounting them. Bishop was never much interested in the collecting of fishes as a Museum activity, but he allowed the work in this area to be moved along. He told Brigham, October 27, 1894:

. . . .

I do not envy the Stanford University its collection of Haw'n fish. The Academy of Sciences also has quite a large collection. Of course they lose their colors unless kept in the dark. I would not build room for them. There are plenty of them in other *large* collections and in the sea where the fungus, ants, etc. cannot destroy them.

His humor was typical Bishopian and he sprang another little joke in a letter to Brigham, March 3, 1904:

. . . After Mr. Seale's return from Guam I received a little fish, moulded and colored by Mr. Thompson I suppose and named after me. Now I have another namesake. I am satisfied to know about them without meeting them in their resorts.

ALLEN HUTCHINSON

Brigham read an article describing some statuary located in the Australia Museum that was modeled by a roving sculptor named

Allen Hutchinson. The statuary story entitled, "Hawaiian Family Group," appeared in the December 1, 1889, issue of the *New Zealand Illustrated Magazine*. Hutchinson had modeled Indians in Canada, Hawaiians in Australia, and aborigines in Australia; and it was this type of exhibit which Brigham felt would effectively illustrate the Museum's anthropological and ethnological story of the Polynesians. The Bishop Museum was, at the very moment of Hutchinson's arrival in Honolulu, about to open its first building unit.

Hutchinson's coming to Honolulu also happened to coincide with the arrival of the *New Zealand Illustrated Magazine* carrying his story. He came without a commission of any description but cheerfully set himself up in the small Museum Room of the Government Building and started to model. He shortly agreed to give a lecture on sculpture before an audience in the YMCA, and during the course of the evening he requested a volunteer from the audience to sit for him. William T. Brigham was named by acclamation for the sitting, and great praise was given Hutchinson for he modeled a very acceptable "rough" bust in forty-five minutes. The sculptor had "arrived." He was so taken with Honolulu that he remained for eight years, except for an interlude in New Zealand to do the Maoris for the Partridge Museum and a second visit to Australia for more Hawaiian subjects for the Sydney gallery.

In the course of his time in Honolulu he did "portraits" or busts of Judge McCully, Alice Cooke, Henry Carter, William Auld, C. M. Hyde, Sanford B. Dole, Lunalilo, and many others. He was working on a bust of Kalakaua on the lanai of the Government House, July 30, 1889, when the Wilcox Revolution was staged. He continued his modeling during the morning of that eventful day but retired from the scene in a hurry when one of the bullets of a revolutionist hit the bust upon which he was working. This bust was cast in bronze at the behest of the Kalakaua Monument Association, a group which shortly thereafter dissolved. Hutchinson was not paid for it. The Kilohana Art League featured it in an exhibition in 1896. After the exhibition closed, Hutchinson, about to depart for Australia, offered it to the Museum. He did leave in June, 1897, and offered another bust to the Museum—one of Bishop. He would accept $85.00 for it; but there were no takers, and it is in the Museum today along with another, a copy.

Hyde had been behind the campaign to have Hutchinson do that plaster bust of Bishop. He persuaded the Punahou and Bishop Estate Trustees to pay a commission of $500 with $225 for expense money to Hutchinson to go to San Francisco and do the job. This exchange of plans between the two trustee groups started in March, 1895. On April 19, 1895, Damon, who had seen Bishop in San Francisco, reported to the Bishop Estate Trustees that "Mr. Bishop did not make any objections to the plan."

Brigham's scientific fancy was stimulated by his acquaintance with Hutchinson's skill and growing reputation. He greatly desired that the Museum have some of the sculpture, and to obtain it he needed Bishop's approval. So he added his support to the idea and wrote urging him to allow Hutchinson to model a bust of him. If the result were acceptable, perhaps approval of a Museum sculpture program might be more readily obtained. The reply was not long in coming, June 11, 1895:

About the bust to which you refer. I have neither said or done anything. Of course it is pleasant to act according to the wishes of my friends. I am not likely to go to Honolulu very soon, and do not know where to go here to have such work done. I have made no inquiry and would not know.

July 19, 1895, this item appears in the Estate Minutes:

Charles R. Bishop consented to sit for the busts by Allen Hutchinson— take sittings from Mr. Bishop and make two busts in plaster—one for Oahu College and one for Trustees of the Estate of Mrs. Bishop. . . .

The completed bust was delivered to the Museum where it was shown to the public on Founder's Day (Kamehameha Schools), December 19, 1895. All must have worked in accordance with Brigham's preconceived plan for to Hyde, Bishop admitted his pleasure, January 16, 1896: ". . . [I am] glad that my friends think the bust is a good likeness. . . ."

Brigham did not delay his follow-up and he prevailed upon Hyde to write promptly to Bishop. On February 14, Bishop responded with his usual frankness:

. . . Your letter came . . . in which you call my attention particularly to the matter of statuary. . . . I have not Mr. Brigham's letter before me, but I think he said the several groups, six perhaps, would cost about $300 each. I am under no obligation to Mr. Hutchinson, and would not feel it my duty to undertake any of this for his benefit. If the Trustees agree that these groups are desirable for the Museum, and that Mr.

Hutchinson is the man to do the work, and can make a fair agreement with him as to the cost and the time for doing the work, I will favor it. . . . If a fair bargain can be made with Mr. Hutchinson to undertake one of the groups . . . I will pay for it. . . . He must not be paid more for this one than would be the proportionate cost of a large number. I think he puts rather a high value on his work. . . .

. . . .

The real obstacle in Bishop's thinking was his inability to measure the dollar value of Hutchinson's work. This uncertainty was indicated in another letter to Hyde, March 7, 1896: ". . . I have dread of doing any business with Hutchinson . . . but must leave such matters in the hands of the Trustees who are on the ground."

While this transaction was under way, Hutchinson was asked to do a pair of medallions, one of Mrs. Bishop (facing right) and one of Mr. Bishop (facing left). The bas-relief of Mrs. Bishop was cast in bronze by "Founder Whyte and DeRome S.F." and was placed in the wall over the royal pew in Kawaiahao Church. The bas-relief of Mr. Bishop was never cast. The plaster model is in the Bishop Museum.

Then the Trustees on March 19, 1896, authorized two busts of Mrs. Bishop to be made. Upon hearing of the Trustees' action, he wrote to Hyde, March 30, 1896: "If he does not make a better likeness of Mrs. Bishop in the bust than he has in the medallion he sent me, I shall regret that we ever made a contract with him." In June, 1896, on the fifteenth, he wrote:

I hope that Mr. Hutchinson will succeed in making a bust of Mrs. Bishop that will be satisfactory and pleasing to those who knew her well; otherwise it would have been better if he had not undertaken it at all. In choosing a photograph for his guidance I certainly would not have selected one taken when she was a young lady, nor would I perhaps have chosen one after she had grown so stout as she was towards the end of her life. I should however prefer the latter to one of the former.

The busts of Mrs. Bishop were finished in August, 1896. One copy went to the Bishop Museum, the other to The Kamehameha School for Girls. Bishop's busts, two of them, are in plaster in the Museum. These are dated 1896. The Trustees did not like the busts of Bishop and ordered them taken out of the exhibition hall and put into storage.

The Museum in the meantime had contracted for several groups of figures of native Hawaiian types. This evidence of Hutchinson's handiwork was very pleasing to all who visited the Museum, and it was so reported to Bishop. All in all, the campaign to obtain some Hutchinson figures had succeeded famously.

In June, 1897, Allen Hutchinson wound up his work in Honolulu and moved on to Australia. Bishop was not to see Hutchinson's "Poi Pounders," "Tapa Makers," or the "Bark Stripper." Museum visitors, however, commented favorably about them and he was satisfied.

One aside in the Hutchinson story: The ailing and restless Robert Louis Stevenson arrived in Honolulu, September 20, 1893, for what was to be his last visit. He remained but five weeks and then sailed back to Samoa. During his short sojourn he summoned Allen Hutchinson to San Souci to model not only a bust, but his right hand. Stevenson liked Hutchinson's work, and he wrote to Stephen Colvin a day before departing for Samoa: ". . . I am being busted here by party named Hutchinson. Seems good." The Stevenson bust was exhibited in the New Gallery Summer Exhibition, London, in 1895.

AMERICAN BOARD OF COMMISSIONERS FOR FOREIGN MISSIONS

Organized in 1810, one of the Board's early foreign fields was the Sandwich Islands. A veritable parade of "companies" of missionaries was organized and dispatched, beginning with the First Company in 1820. These missionaries were to develop a climate of spiritual dignity and racial concern for the people of their mission to an extent and in a degree probably unmatched anywhere in the history of any church and community anywhere in the world. The American Board eventually sent missionaries to all Polynesia, and one by-product was the piling up in a storage room in Boston, Massachusetts, of a huge collection of artifacts of the native cultures from all over the Pacific Polynesia area. Bone and stone implements and utensils, mats, baskets, masques, *kapas,* jewelry, memorial drums, and a great variety of other things made up the collection.

Bishop knew of the American Board collection, but it was not until 1887 that he first wrote requesting the collection as a loan. The attitude of the American Board was negative. In the Minutes of the Prudential Committee of the American Board of Commissioners for Foreign Missions this appears:

1887—March 22—The committee to which was referred the request of Mr. C. R. Bishop of Honolulu, for the sale of the Hawaiian curiosities now in the Museum of the Board, reported recommending that the Board do not sell but should loan to Mr. Bishop these articles, to be deposited in his Museum at the Sandwich Islands, until such time as the Prudential Committee shall ask for their return. After discussion the report was recommitted for further consideration.

Bishop tried again a year later, and another entry in the Minute Book of the Prudential Committee tells the story:

1889—July 9—A renewed request was presented from Mr. C. E. [sic] Bishop of Honolulu, that the Hawaiian antiquities now in possession of the Board be permanently loaned for deposit in Mr. Bishop's museum at Honolulu. The Committee declined to assent to the request.

A rather disarming acceptance of the second denial was sent to Judson Smith, secretary of the American Board. This was dated August 28, 1889:

. . . Your very friendly and complimentary letter of the 2^d inst. was rec^d by me on my arrival here on the 23rd idum [sic].

Although the decision of the Prudential Committee is against my request, and proposal, I am much obliged to the members of that Committee for again considering the matter of loaning the Hawaiian Curiosity [sic] in the Mission rooms in Boston to the museum which I am trying to establish here. There are a few things in that collection unlike any others procurable, which I would very much like to have, but since the deliberate opinion of the Committee is opposed to parting with them on any terms, it only remains to me to thank the Com. for kindly entertaining my proposal.

But he would not give up. The Prudential Committee noted another appeal:

1891—November 3—The request presented again from Hon. C. R. Bishop, through Mr. Peter C. Jones, for a loan to Mr. Bishop's museum at Honolulu, of various articles from the Hawaiian Islands, now in the Cabinet of the Board, was considered. The Committee did not give assent to Mr. Bishop's request.

He waited a few years and then wrote to his lifelong friend and associate, Gorham D. Gilman in Boston, and solicited his aid. This was November 6, 1894. This time the Prudential Committee considered the request more seriously, and events moved rapidly:

1894—November 20—A letter from Charles R. Bishop of Honolulu, to Hon. Mr. Gilman of Boston, renewing a request for articles from the Polynesian Islands, now stored in the Board's Museum, was presented by Sec. Smith and was referred to a special Committee with a suggestion from the Cabinet concerning the provision of more suitable quarters for the Museum and the use of its present room for the Prudential Committee. The Committee were Messrs. Webb, Burr, Ellison, Hopkins and Boynton.

1894—December 26—The special Committee appointed to consider the request of the Bernice Pauahi Bishop Museum of Honolulu for a loan of certain articles now in the Board's Museum, reported the following resolution: *Voted.* That at the request of the Trustees of the "Bernice Pauahi Bishop Museum" established at Honolulu, all of the articles now in the Board's Museum, and belonging to the Board, which originated in the Hawaiian or the Micronesian Islands be loaned to the Trustees of the said Museum for the purpose of being exhibited in their Museum. The conditions of the loan being as follows, viz.:

First: That all of said articles shall be labeled as "Loaned by the American Board of Commissioners for Foreign Missions."

Second: The said Trustees shall bear all the expense of packing and removing the articles.

Third: The said Trustees shall execute an agreement satisfactory to the Executive Officers of the Board to return the articles to the Board in Boston free of charge if at any time the Prudential Committee shall require it. . . . The report and its resolutions were laid on the table for the present.

1895—February 12—The question of the Museum and its loan to the Bernice Pauahi Bishop Museum at Honolulu was taken from the table, and the recommendations of the Committee presented Dec. 26, 1894, were adopted.

At this time, unaware of the pending Board action, he wrote to Museum Director Brigham, February 8, 1895:

. . . It is still doubtful about our getting the Boston Collection of the American Board of Commissioners for Foreign Missions though I think that the majority on the Board are in favor of it. The full Board of Commissioners has not acted yet so far as I know. If they found that the Museum building was to be used as a fort they might conclude that Boston would be the safer place for the collection. . . .

He had word from Gilman that the American Board was now in a lending mood and he quickly wrote, February 21, 1895:

I have recd. through the kindness of G. D. Gilman Esq. the copy— furnished by you—of the vote of the Committee in regard to the loaning of articles from the Board's Museum to the Bernice Pauahi Bishop Museum in Honolulu, and I shall have much pleasure in forwarding the same to my associate Trustees who will gratefully accept the Collection on the terms voted by your Committee. These articles originally from the Hawaiian and Marquesan Islands will make a valuable addition to the Collection now in Honolulu, and help toward making it the most interesting, if not the largest, collection from those groups. I desire to express my thanks to the Committee for their liberality to those who have interested themselves in behalf of the Museum. . . .

Gorham D. Gilman, who was quite instrumental in bringing the negotiations to a head for his good friend, dropped a line to him at the Museum, April, 1895:

We have at length got the curios on their way back to native land— Kalakaua not being on hand to receive these ancient personages. I presume there will be no Kukui torches burned or white and black pigs immolated on their way to the comfortable quarters you have provided for them.

The Prudential Minutes record the sequel to the loan:

1895—May 21—The chairman of the Committee was authorized to sign, in behalf of the Board the contracts with the Trustees of the Bernice Pauahi Museum, Honolulu, and Hartford Theological Seminary, Hartford, Ct., concerning the Board's collection of curiosities.

1895—December 31—A communication was received through Dr. C. M. Hyde, making an offer of $8,000, under certain terms for certain Hawaiian antiquities now in possession of the Bernice Pauahi Bishop Museum. The communication was referred to the Finance Committee to consider and report.

1896—January 14—The Finance Committee reported on the proposal of the Charles R. Bishop Trust to purchase articles loaned by the Board to the Bernice Pauahi Bishop Museum, recommending that the Board's title to all of said articles be transferred to the said Museum on the terms and conditions proposed by them, viz.,—$3,000, to be paid down, and $5,000, to be paid on the first of June next. The report was accepted and its recommendations adopted.

Despite the "loan" aspects of the initial transaction, the American Board could readily use missionary funds; and the Charles R. Bishop Trust offers totaling $8000 for a clear title to the collection were accepted. Within the year, 1896, the collection was added to the others in the Bishop Museum. One more comment rounds out the story. Bishop wrote to Carter, August 15, 1896:

Construing the terms of the C. R. Bishop Deed of Trust strictly in reference to the $3000 and $5000 payments for the Collection received from the A.B.C.F.M., the Deed from the Board may not be quite perfect, but I do not see what different form of Deed the Board could really give. Believing that not a single article in that Collection will ever be called for or claimed, and trusting to the honor of the Board to protect and remunerate the purchasers in case anything should be lawfully claimed, I think it safe to accept the Deed and pay the $5000, and I have, therefore, on the 13th inst. paid the $5000 to the Rev. Walter

Frear, (Who is the general agent for the American Board of Commissioners for Foreign Missions for the Pacific Coast,) in a draft on Boston payable to the order of Frank H. Wiggin. The Bank of California has charged cost of the draft, $4990, to the account of Bishop & Co.

The fine hand of Hyde should be credited at all points in the negotiations with the American Board. His was the original inspiration. Gilman as final negotiator was of especially great value because of his residence in Boston and the opportunity for personal contact with the Prudential Committee.

Publications

Important publications included the Fornander manuscripts which Bishop purchased and turned over to the Museum. He consulted William De Witt Alexander regarding the method of preparing the material for publication; in a letter to him, January 18, 1895, he wrote:

At present I do not feel like putting the Fornander manuscripts into Dr. Emerson's hands for preparation for publication. If he would look them over and after consulting with you let me know what is to do, and what the cost would be. I will then, at the proper time decide about it. . . . In publishing the Fornander manuscript would it be necessary or desirable to translate into English? or would a good deal be printed in Hawaiian or some in both languages? In what form should it be put finally? None of these things would bring any return in *money* worth mentioning. . . .

By December of that year he broadened his discussion to include Hyde and commented to him, December 20, 1895:

Whenever the right person will undertake the translating and editing of the old manuscripts which I purchased from Fornander, and do it for reasonable compensation, I want to have it done. Of course it must be well done or not at all. Those Meles, etc., which have already been translated, whether published or not, should be collected and combined with the others. . . .

He followed this letter with another a week later to Alexander. When he got a notion he moved:

About employing Dr. Emerson to edit the ancient Hawaiian Manuscripts, I have just written to Mr. Damon who will confer with the other trustees and yourself. Just what there is to do and how much it should cost, I do not know; but I hope that Dr. Hyde will make the necessary inquiry, and that the Trustees of the Museum will be able to make a satisfactory arrangement with Dr. Emerson.

The letter to Damon was explicit, written the same day, December 27, 1895, as the above-quoted letter to Alexander:

Professor Alexander writes me that Dr. Emerson will soon be through with some work that he is doing for the Government, and he is recommended to me as the best person to undertake "editing ancient Hawaiian Mss." You know that I bought a lot of old *meles* etc., from Mr. Fornander, which is now in the possession of Prof. Alexander, and which should be translated and arranged, and sooner or later printed, perhaps in book form. And there is other of the same or similar character which I suppose should be combined with mine . . . after collecting, translating and arranging . . . get an estimate for printing. . . . As it belongs to the Museum I wish to have it under the control of the Trustees. There are some people whom I like in a way, but with whom I dislike to have any business relations. Some mechanics, some merchants and others have regarded me as a full fledged goose to be picked, and the plucking pleases them more than it does me. I would like to employ Dr. Emerson to do this work, on fair terms, say, up to the point of publishing. . . .

Great store was set on the Fornander manuscripts by Bishop, and accordingly, May 20, 1907, he released the collection to the Museum Trustees:

I, Charles R. Bishop, the undersigned, now residing in the town of Berkeley, State of California, being the owner of the Manuscript Collection of Hawaiian Legends, Chants, etc., known as the Abm. Fornander Collection, and which has been in the keeping of Hon. William D. Alexander of Honolulu, Territory of Hawaii, during a number of years last past, I now donate the entire collection to Sanford B. Dole, Henry Holmes, Joseph O. Carter, Samuel M. Damon, William O. Smith, Alfred W. Carter, and Eben F. Bishop, of said Honolulu, the Trustees of the Bernice Pauahi Bishop Museum. . . .

On June 17, 1907, he acknowledged a letter from Alexander:

. . . I received from Mr. S. M. Damon copy of your agreement (in my behalf) with Mrs. Emma M. Nukuina, for the translation of the Fornander collection of Hawaiian Legends etc, which agreement I approve, with many thanks to you.

The Fornander Collection of Hawaiian Antiquities and Folk-lore was published under that title and edited and annotated by Thomas G. Thrum,* but Bishop was never to see it in print. The Museum published the collection in three successive Memoirs, Volume IV,

---

* Publisher, *Thrum's Hawaiian Annual.*

1916–1917; V, 1918–1919; and VI, 1919–1920. Bishop passed away in 1915.

Inseparably meshed in the Fornander manuscript story is the marching in and out of two of the several Emersons who were in Hawaii in the 1890's. One was Joseph S. Emerson, whom we first encounter in a Bishop letter to Samuel Damon, May 2, 1889. These were the embryonic days of the Museum, and this Emerson was going to Australia to add to his store of artifacts of Polynesia. The J. S. Emerson Collection which was to be years in the gathering was ultimately purchased by the Museum in December, 1906.

Another Emerson (Nathaniel B.), was under consideration over a long period of time to translate the Fornander manuscripts, and he eventually did. He also translated the David Malo manuscript at the suggestion of William D. Alexander. David Malo's work was known under several names: "Moolelo Hawaii," "Archeology," "History," and "Antiquities." It was eventually published with the title, *Hawaiian Antiquities.* Upon completion of the translation Emerson sent a copy of the table of contents to Bishop and inquired if he would finance the publication. A price of $300 was offered; and Bishop, in making the offer, stated that it would become the property of the Museum if the Trustees wanted it. Brigham was not too impressed with the translation; there were errors in it, and the work was not complete. Emerson set to work again and on March 30, 1898, offered the complete translation with notes to Bishop; but this time the Museum Trustees put up the money and on July 25, 1898, acquired title. Bishop only requested that the published work be dedicated to Mrs. Bishop.

November 9, 1901, the Museum Trustees finally authorized Emerson to prepare an index for the "Translation of David Malo's Archeology," for $200. They also asked William D. Alexander to revise it and to add an introduction for $300; and they gave him another $250 to carry the work through the printing stage. It was actually published * in December, 1903. Bishop was satisfied to have the Malo manuscript published and so wrote, July 29, 1898, to Hyde: "I am glad that Emerson's book has been purchased, if too much has not been paid for it. If there are many corrections or changes that would improve it they should be made *now. . . .*" Finally, in one of his last letters, on December 29, 1909, he wrote to Brigham:

* David Malo, *Hawaiian Antiquities* (Honolulu, Bernice P. Bishop Museum, 1903).

No doubt you have a copy of our friend Dr. Emerson's book, "Unwritten Literature of Hawaii" Emerson's greatest achievement. This, with the Fornander collection of Meles and myths will, I think, satisfy the demand for that class of literature.

FINAL GESTURE

One of Bishop's last great moments of satisfaction was expressed to Trustee William O. Smith in a letter of June 25, 1909:

I have received your letter of the 15th instant enclosing a copy of the proposition of the Massachusetts Institute of Technology and the resolution adopted by the Trustees of the Bernice Pauahi Bishop Museum by which five hundred dollars per annum for five years is pledged toward the maintenance of a Geophysical Observatory and Research Laboratory to be established at the volcano of Kilauea on Hawaii.

A broad interpretation of the deed of trust authorizes the Trustees of the Museum to make the pledge as stated and, though the sum is liberal, it is not so large, I hope, as to interfere with expenditures needed for other purposes.

The information and material which will be furnished by the Observatory and Research Laboratory may have large value and help to enhance the public interests in the Museum.

It is pleasing to have relations with the Massachusetts Institute of Technology and the scientists and scholars connected with it.

Thus the venerable Bishop—he was eighty-nine—closed the door on his science-laden past. He had contributed generously to the scientific knowledge and research of Hawaii and the Pacific area. He was no scientist himself; but his unwavering support of Brigham in holding him to the post of museum builder, and his generous contributions of land and money as well as his ever-watchful supervision over the finances of the Museum, virtually guaranteed the emergence of the Bernice Pauahi Bishop Museum as an institution of world renown.

THE CHARLES R. BISHOP TRUST

BISHOP, UPON SETTLING-IN at San Francisco in 1894, quickly found it difficult to manage his many interests in Hawaii because of the dissatisfactions arising not only from the lag in correspondence but also from the very nature of the correspondence itself. People were faithfully clamoring that he continue with his many responsibilities, even though he was 2500 miles away, a ten-day ocean trip. The Trustees of the Bernice P. Bishop Estate developed a reluctance to decide certain matters without his expressed opinion as a Trustee. It was, therefore, a practical necessity that he devise some instrument such as a special trust deed, primarily for handling his many bequests, but also for guiding and handling the far flung and rather complicated Hawaii matters which he had left behind and yet which he could not in conscience cast adrift.

On August 1, 1895, about a year after his final arrival in San Francisco, he prepared such a Trust deed, named it the Charles R. Bishop Trust, and dispatched it to the Trustees of the Bishop Estate in Honolulu. This Trust deed answered his immediate purpose of providing direction for his charities and philanthropies, and ultimately constituted the back-bone of the Bernice Pauahi Bishop Museum financial structure. It emerged as a monument to his conscientious sensitivity to community efforts in Hawaii. The document proposed the utilization of the Trustees of the Bernice P. Bishop Estate.

On August 12, 1895, the Trustees of the B. P. Bishop Estate, with Messrs. Hyde, Damon, Cooke, and Carter present in meeting, accepted the new Trust deed. On September 4, 1895, C. M. Cooke was elected President and Bishop, Vice-President. September 4, 1895, can be accepted as the date of the founding of the Charles R. Bishop Trust. The momentum of the anticipated relief picked up so rapidly that within five years Bishop had almost eliminated himself from the Hawaiian scene, except for incidental and personal correspondence. He was, however, to remain a voluminous correspondent, and to write letters up to the day of his death.

The Trust deed specifically provided for the support of the Bernice Pauahi Bishop Museum and included funds for any new community enterprises which might come within his permissive directive in establishing the Trust. Under the provisions of the Trust, the Trustees decided to assist Kamehameha Schools' students with partial fee scholarships, and students in other schools, particularly those programmed for the education of Hawaiian girls. They assisted certain churches. They lent assistance wherever a need consonant with Bishop's intention might suggest itself. Bishop foresaw clearly the future needs of the Museum since he not only provided the many discretionary "assists" in all directions but insisted upon the "mandatory" provision for the memorial (Museum) to his wife.

The foundation of this Trust was a personal note given by Samuel M. Damon in 1894, in the amount of $800,000, this amount being the sales price of the Bishop Bank. The single capital fund note was replaced on April 4, 1895, with fourteen promissory notes: two for $50,000 each, and four for $25,000 each, each payable June 1, 1900; and four for $100,000 each, and four for $50,000, each payable June 1, 1905. All called for 4 per cent interest. Under the Charles R. Bishop Trust deed of August 1, 1895, these promissory notes aggregating $800,000 were assigned to the Trustees as the corpus of the Trust. Some of the notes were exchanged for Oahu Railway and Land Company bonds at 6 per cent interest. Others were exchanged for 6 per cent Olaa sugar bonds. Some were the source of funds for the payments of major bequests as listed in the Trust deed. Some money went into the repayment of advances made by Bishop in building the Bernice Pauahi Bishop Memorial Chapel. But the bulk remained as the basic capital structure of the Museum. He directed that "The Trustees shall not suffer the Trust Fund to become less than $500,000."

He was acutely aware of the Museum's problem. He wrote Hyde on January 22, 1897:

You will have to excuse me from adding anything to my contribution to the Historical Society. I have not altogether given up the idea of establishing an Aquarium, though I may come to that conclusion. I now think that all that can be saved and accumulated from the Charles R. Bishop Trust should be saved that it may be used for the Museum in any branch or department that may be connected with it. . . .

In 1897, a second annex was approaching the final drawing stage. The outreach of scientific study was calling for more scientists, special cabinets constructed, treatises published; and money was needed faster than he was willing to award it from the proceeds of the notes. There was an overdraft at the bank in January of 1897. These expenses were due chiefly to the enthusiasm of Brigham, who had been talking strongly of an aquarium, a marine laboratory, and other interesting projects; and they caused Bishop to apply the brakes. He requested that virtually all the awards to schools, seminaries, churches, and other beneficiaries be placed upon a "discretionary basis;" that the spending be watched carefully; and that the trustees remain within available income. In a letter to Henry Holmes,* he wrote:

To pay off the debt of the Museum, and forever after keep out of debt, should, I think be the aim and settled policy of the Trustees. No new thing calling for money should be undertaken without funds in hand or immediately available. Nothing can be done about an aquarium, etc., at present, and if anything is to be done in the future worth undertaking, it is necessary that the fund of the Museum shall be carefully guarded and the income husbanded for that purpose, and a very considerable sum will need to be drawn from the C. R. Bishop Trust. In the management of that Trust, it seems to me that the Museum should be given preference over every other object mentioned in Sub-Division 8th of the Deed. The Trustees have large discretion and can cut off or reduce expenditure for kindergartens and night schools, and playgrounds. With such help from the Trust, added to what I may be able to furnish, it may be possible to add to the Museum such an Aquarium and Laboratory as will attract scientists of high class, and be a credit to all concerned. Of course the Museum proper is first to be made what we wish it to be. . . .

In the provisions of the Trust deed originally dated August 1, 1895, but amended on July 24, 1897; December 14, 1897; November 22, 1904; April 8, 1910; June 27, 1914; September 4, 1914; and October 5, 1914, we see the unfolding and modifying processes of change at work. In the First Section he authorizes the delivery of one promissory note in the amount of $50,000 to Cordelia Church Allen, wife of William F. Allen. After Mrs. Bishop's death, he moved into *Keoua Hale*, the 21 Emma Street palace which Ruth Keelikolani had willed to Mrs. Bishop in 1883 and which, in turn, Mrs. Bishop had willed to her husband in 1884. Here he set up housekeeping in dignified, hospitable mood and invited the Allens to be his resident hosts. This arrangement lasted until 1894, Bishop's departure year; but the Allens stayed on for some years. It was from this house that the furnishings gathered in the United States and Europe, particularly in France and Italy, were distributed in part to The Kamehameha Schools, the Bishop Museum, Punahou School, and to such relatives as the E. Faxon Bishops and others. It was in gratitude for a life of long friendship with the Allens and their unfailing assistance as his official hosts at the Emma Street home that he made the $50,000 bequest. The Second Section of the Trust deed merely refers to the extension of due dates of the Damon notes, possibility of prepayment by Mr. Damon, and the application of income. In the

* See p. 200.

Third Section, Bishop begins the detailed list of benefactions. There are many:

Mills School [Mills Institute]
Hilo Boys' Boarding School
Young Men's Christian Association of Honolulu
Queen's Hospital
American Relief Fund
Honolulu Library and Reading Room Association
Hawaiian Evangelical Association
Maternity Home
Night Schools in Honolulu

The Fourth Section provides:

Out of my balance of interest remaining in the hands of my said Trustees, as soon as such balance is ascertained, they shall pay the Hawaiian Historical Society ° the sum of Two Thousand ($2000) Dollars.

The Fifth Section deals first with the maintenance of the tomb, monument, and grounds of the Royal Mausoleum. Both Mr. and Mrs. Bishop are buried here. The care referred to in the paragraph is mandatory upon the Trustees.

"Founder's Day" at The Kamehameha Schools is a second mandatory provision. $200 is set aside for this annual ceremonial. Each December 19, children of The Kamehameha Schools march into the Royal Mausoleum; group themselves in front of the brown granite marker over the Kamehameha crypt; and proceed with a dignified, sincere tribute to their benefactress, Bernice Pauahi Bishop. It was in his mind that the mandatory annual payments of the $200 would serve to preserve the memory of Mrs. Bishop in the minds and hearts of the succession of students passing through the doors of Kamehameha.

In a letter to Hyde, December 28, 1896, Bishop expressed a desire to assist Hawaiian girls between the ages of six and fourteen at St. Andrew's Priory and Sacred Hearts Academy in the amounts of $250 for each school under the terms of the Fifth Section. The Trustees started out with $300 in 1897, increasing this to $600 in 1948 for Sacred Hearts Convent with a final payment in 1954, making the total contribution $19,700. The $300 was increased to $1160 for the Priory in 1948, and the payments were concluded also in 1954 with a total of $23,217 having been paid for operating aid. In both schools

° See pp. 248–251.

the monies were in payment of tuition and board for Hawaiian girls who were students.

Hyde was a member of the Board of Trustees of the Charles R. Bishop Trust and was able to link the gift with the need. He suggested Makawao Female Seminary on Maui and Kohala Girls' School on the Island of Hawaii.

Paragraph Four of the Fifth Section provides half scholarships at the Kamehameha Schools for students whose parents are unable to pay the full fees. Scholarships of this type were awarded annually in totals averaging $500 from 1896 through 1947. The Trust made available about $25,000 in these supplemental allowances. As the Bernice P. Bishop Estate income increased it was no longer necessary to draw such scholarships from the Charles R. Bishop Trust and the requests were cut off. It was within the discretion of the Trustees to do this.

Free kindergartens, with special reference to those maintained for Hawaiian children of pure or part aboriginal blood, were granted the sum of $600 annually for the life of the Trust—this also at the discretion of the Trustees. Payments began in 1895 and ended in 1954 with a total of $35,700 having been paid into the Free Kindergarten Association. In the annual "Calendar" of the Association, the grant was called the "Charles R. Bishop Annuity." This substantial support led to an unusual recognition. His name was listed in the first annual report and is still carried in this wise: "Hon. C. R. Bishop, Honorary Member."

The earliest mention of a kindergarten is in connection with F. W. Damon's Chinese project of September, 1892. Damon was interested in Chinese boys, and opened a kindergarten in the Chinese Mission on Fort Street. Bishop had given money in 1892 to Damon partly on account of the kindergarten in the Mission. In 1893 the Woman's Board of Missions for the Pacific Islands opened four kindergartens specializing in several racial groups: Portuguese, Japanese, Hawaiian, and one for children of all other races. By 1895, the work was exceeding the capacity of the Woman's Board of Missions and the "Free Kindergarten and Children's Aid Association" came into being. This coincided with the creation of the Charles R. Bishop Trust, and the new kindergarten organization was included. Writing to Hyde, November 30, 1895, Bishop said, ". . . You know that I am interested in the Kindergarten, and you know to what extent I have undertaken to aid it. I would not wish to discontinue the aid to the Kindergartens in Honolulu on any account. . . ."

Paragraph Six provided $1500 for the salary of a chaplain at The Kamehameha Schools. This provision was not always adhered to nor was it often needed.

The graduates of The Kamehameha Schools were few in number in 1895, had no organization, and probably had not thought of an association until the provisions in Paragraph Seven were published. To the Alumni Association or Social Club for those who had attended Kamehameha Schools not less than two years, the sum of $300 was allowed on an annual basis. The payments from 1897 on have been made with fair regularity and total in excess of $25,000.

To three churches, Central Union, Kawaiahao, and Kaumakapili, an annual sum of $100 was provided. Bishop's connection with Kaumakapili was rather slight, but it was the "second" native church in Honolulu and would normally come within the purview of his concern. Kawaiahao and Central Union were different. Under the Trust deed, even with a minor provision of $100 annually, the total sums from 1895 to 1954 reached $6000 for each or $18,000 for the three.

Paragraph Nine provided payments to the Kona Orphanage of Kailua, North Kona, in unnamed amounts. The school was for a time called the Hawaiian Orphanage and Industrial School and survived only as long as Miss Alice Beard was its manager. Payments started in 1903 and continued through 1907 for a total of $2250. The other institution mentioned in this section is the Kaiulani Home for Young Women in Honolulu. Annual payments for the Kona Orphanage and the Kaiulani Home were limited to $1000. Beginning in 1903, the Kaiulani payments were $500 but were increased to $1000 in 1907. These payments ended in 1942 when the Home could no longer fulfill its purpose of housing Hawaiian working girls or college students. But even with the termination of payments in 1942, the Kaiulani payments amounted to $33,000.

Section Six makes two cousins of Bishop his personal beneficiaries. To Charles H. Bishop of Lihue he gave $15,000 and to E. Faxon Bishop of Honolulu, $10,000. Paragraphs Three and Nine of the Sixth Section include $25,000 for the Honolulu Library and Reading Room Association, $18,000 for Queen's Hospital, $25,000 for the Hilo Boys' Boarding School, $20,000 for the Hawaiian Evangelical Association, $5,000 for the Young Men's Christian Association, $3,000 for the American Relief Fund Association, and $5,000 for the Maternity Home. In Paragraph Ten, the American Board of Commissioners for Foreign Missions at Boston, Massachusetts, were to be paid $3000 and $5000 upon transferring title to the collection of antiquities and articles to the Trust created by the Will of Bernice Pauahi Bishop. In Paragraph Eleven The Schools' chapel was subsidized in the amount of $60,000. Oahu College (Punahou School) was to receive $50,000 under Paragraph Twelve. This institution was very dear to Bishop and probably came close upon Kamehameha and the Museum in his interest and affection.

There was however an important change in his thinking and could he have arrived at the conclusion expressed in the following passage at the time he was advising his wife about the construction of her Will, there might have been some notable broadening effects of her philanthropy. This was in a letter to Carter, October 3, 1901:

Were I to make the C.R.B. Trust over again or amend it I think that instead of providing for any of the Kam graduates to enter Oahu College, I would place the sum provided in the hands of the trustees to be used in assisting such graduates in *any* school at home or abroad, in their discretion. I take much interest in Oahu College, hoping that those who have enjoyed advantages there and who have abundant means will endow it generously and see to it that it is maintained as a *first class* school so that it shall be of great value to the present and coming generations; but it may be that in some instances native Hawaiians, assisted, could do better elsewhere.

The benefactions now cease except for an open provision in Section Eight where the Trust deed reads:

. . . $100 per annum in the support or partial support of indigent persons, such persons being Hawaiians either of pure or part aboriginal blood. . . .

Under the authority granted here the Salvation Army Boys' and Girls' Homes began receiving monies in 1910 up through 1953, and the sum of $28,516 was realized by the Homes during this time. The Honor Loan and Trust Association, especially established to assist needy and deserving students at the Normal School, benefited in 1902 and 1903 with small allowances totalling $500. Bishop was not impressed with this association nor with a companion project for a home for such students on the campus. He wrote to Carter, May 9, 1902:

. . . There are many "worthy objects" that one would like to help if one had the money to spare, so many that one has to pick and choose. The name "Honor Loan & Trust Association" would give the impression that the recipients of loans would expect to repay at some time, as should be done.

Much as I would like to see more done for Hawaiian girls after they finish at school, I know that the B.P.B. Estate cannot contribute at all, and I have come to the conclusion that it would not be prudent to allow a "Home to be located on Estate land near the Kam. Girls Schools or to have it under the care of the principal or teachers of that school. There would be great risk of its falling into financial difficulties and of annoying efforts to get support or aid from the estate. The Trustees have their hands full now, so full that I am anxious.

Another interest of the Trust for indigents was the Boys' Brigade. Theodore Richards made a direct appeal to Bishop, and the enterprise was given $1750 over the years from 1901–1904. Still another attempt to assist indigents was the Free Eye and Ear Dispensary which received payments totalling $500 in 1899–1900. While infinitesimal in size and importance, their nature enriches the picture of the Bishop philanthropy. He made one more provision in this Eighth Section, this one personal:

. . . also to pay me during my life such sum or sums of money not exceeding $500 per month, as I may from time to time direct. . . .

He never called upon the Trustees for any such payments until but a few months before his death. He wrote to the Trustees of his Charles R. Bishop Trust on September 14, 1914, of his concern that he be personally self-sufficient:

In 1913 I made distribution of a large portion of my property to my heirs and friends and objects in which I was interested. Since that time there have been many important changes in values of bonds, stocks and other properties, causing a large falling off in income from securities, including those retained by me. There is at present no prospect of improvement in their values, showing that I parted with a larger amount than I could afford at the time.

I have no extravagant habits to be corrected by closer economy, but it is quite possible that with increasing age my necessary expenses may be enlarged. Under the circumstances I feel that I have good reason for taking advantage of my right reserved in the deed of trust so that my income may be supplemented during the remainder of my life and save me from granting the right to draw from the income of said Trust at the rate of $5000.00 per annum, in monthly or quarterly payments, as I may request. I may not need to ask for so much every month or quarter, but omitting to do so should not change my right to demand it. It is my purpose to pay all my debts out of my own property and I hope that I may be able to return to the Trust a considerable part, if not the whole sum or sums, that I may receive from it.

He followed this with a cablegram on September 21, asking that the annual payment to him be set at $6000 instead of $5000; and on October 6 he requested an actual advance on this account of $1500 to be paid on January 5 and then followed this up with a request for $500 monthly thereafter. These payments were made to the month of his death, June 1915. So faithful to the letter-writing habit was he that he wrote on May 11, 1915, an acknowledgment of the Bishop and Company's draft for $500 received but the day before. He died four weeks later.

The other provisions of the Trust deed are administrative in detail. Bishop lived long enough to visualize the solid impact of his Trust upon the life and direction of the charities and educational and religious organizations of the Islands. He was slowly able to direct an increasing proportion of the Trust's income to the growing Museum; "slowly," because each of the other community beneficiaries had an intrenched interest in its own share of the income and had based its program upon that income as definite and undoubtedly perpetual, even though the Trust deed earmarked such payments as "discretionary." By 1954, however, all such payments had at least temporarily ceased; and the Museum operation had benefited accordingly. Through the lengthening days of the Trust, the Museum had more and more come into its own financially. Little money found its way into the Museum treasury the first eight or nine years, and even when the flow started in 1904 it only amounted to $2500. But as the years elapsed, greater amounts were paid to its account. The monies were used for salaries, insurance, special project grants, and publications. Over the half century of annual payments made from income, starting in 1904, the books show a total well above $950,000. Since the Trust is a permanent legal structure, the future would seem to be bright as far as income is concerned. In the creation of this little-known Charles R. Bishop Trust, Bishop most thoughtfully and carefully eased his concern for the best possible continuation and extension of the community interests which he singly or together with Mrs. Bishop had nurtured, and in some way provided for while living in Hawaii. He was a benefactor's benefactor.

7

Beneficiaries

OAHU COLLEGE AND PUNAHOU SCHOOL

ARTHUR C. ALEXANDER, a Trustee of Punahou School,* stated at an anniversary meeting: ". . . It can be safely said that Punahou School would never have attained its present standing if it had not been for Charles R. Bishop. . . ."

Arthur Floyd Griffiths, a former President of Punahou, spoke at a ninetieth birthday party for Bishop:

. . . [He] has given freely to Punahou . . . because he believed that the education of the young people of Hawaii was the surest way to promote the prosperity of the land he loved so well. He believed in a Christian education which develops strength of mind, skill of hand and character. . . .

Peter Cushman Jones, a Trustee of Punahou School, speaking at the same birthday party delivered a long, friendly tribute and said in part:

. . . Mr. Bishop became a trustee of Oahu College in 1867, and remained as such until he left the islands. . . . In 1874, I, having been elected a trustee, had the privilege of an intimate acquaintance with Mr. Bishop, for seventeen years, and I can say that I think he was the most valuable man on the board. He was always at the meetings, made valuable suggestions, and acted wisely and well upon all matters that came before the trustees for discussion. He was a member of the finance committee and watched carefully—in fact, I never knew a man so wonderfully exact in looking after the details of business as was Mr. Bishop. . . .

Bishop was elected to the Board of Trustees of Oahu College, along with Samuel N. Castle, June 10, 1867. The election was not legal, however, until the names could be submitted to "The Pru-

* See p. 236.

232

dential Committee" of the American Board of Commissioners for Foreign Missions in Boston. On December 5, 1867, notice of the "ratification of the election of Messrs. Castle and Bishop as Trustees of Oahu College" was reported to the Board of Trustees.

His first association with the Punahou campus were the Saturday afternoons when he and William L. Lee went to play "bat and ball" with the students, in the 1850's. His acquaintance reached across the threshold to management status in his new affiliation as Trustee. He served on numerous committees: one to study the establishment of a primary school; others on education, insurance, land purchase, and penmanship. Almost from the date of his election as Trustee, he served as Chairman of the Finance Committee. In 1885 he was elected Vice-President of the Board and held both the finance committee chairmanship and vice presidency by re-election until his "final" resignation in 1897. His record of attendance at those Trustees' meetings which were scheduled when he was in the Islands was without a blemish.

Many years were to elapse before his "systematic pattern of giving" was to affect this School. Punahou had its fortieth birthday in 1881. This was an auspicious event, and he gave the first of what were to prove to be the most generous gifts ever to befall this institution. This initial gift was in the amount of $5,000. He was in a strategic position to analyze the problems of growth of Punahou and through his close, almost daily association with its leaders could easily judge where he might apply aid. On October 12, 1883, announcement was made of his second gift. This was an offer of $15,000:

If a sum of $15,000 or more is raised in cash between this evening and the first of June next, I will give $15,000 towards a scientific department for the college to erect a building and procure chemical and other apparatus for the same.

The Trustees raised $18,000. The Bishop Hall of Science was erected in 1884. On October 15, 1888, a third gift was announced. He would give $36,000 to endow the presidency of the college, and "others" were to give $12,000. This requirement was met and P. C. Jones, treasurer of Oahu College, received the $36,000. On June 20, 1891, Oahu College celebrated the Semi-Centennial of its founding, and we find Bishop down for $50,000 with the usual string attached—the Trustees and friends of the school must raise another $50,000. This was his fourth gift and had been presented to the Board of Trustees, April 3, 1891, via Samuel M. Damon. A few weeks earlier, February 23, he had been appointed chairman of the Committee on Finance for the Semi-Centennial.

It may be that the generosity represented by this gift prompted a special response for on June 1, 1891, "Dr. Hyde moved that the articles in the museum at Oahu College which are desired for the Bishop Museum be transferred to the B. P. Bishop Museum." This motion, recorded in the Minute Book, was adopted. May 22, 1893, the Minute Book speaks of the next major gift: "Mr. Cooke reported on the donation of Charles R. Bishop to Oahu College with conditions . . . $50,000." This was to provide for scholarships. In the Minute Book for June 8, 1893, another entry appeared dealing with this gift in some greater detail:

C. M. Cooke was called upon for a report. He stated that Mr. Damon had made known to him, on the 31st last, that C. R. Bishop had donated $50,000 to Oahu College—on account of a legacy given by him in his will. . . . This was designed for technical education—the mechanical trades, tree planting, budding and grafting—for night or day classes in technical, commercial education.

Bishop proposed changes including a business education department but was not successful, largely because the nature of the corporate structure held the Trustees apart from school policy and operation. Still, he endeavored to strengthen the business department and to develop a realistic vocational business course. These rather ineffectual efforts may not have succeeded because it was 1893, the year of the "changing governments" in Hawaii, and also because of the priority he was giving San Francisco in his current plans.

In March, 1894, as he was nearing the close of his service in watchdogging Punahou's finances, he made his seventh major capital gift—this one for $123,000. The specified use of $50,000 of this sum was to build Pauahi Hall, thus honoring his beloved late wife. The deed of Trust, listing the specified conditions of use and certain named securities, was dated February 26, 1894. He resigned in 1894 after more than a quarter century of devoted work as a Punahou Trustee. He was re-elected for a few more years *in absentia*, and it bothered him. He wrote to C. M. Hyde on July 26, 1897:

I notice with interest what you write about Oahu College, its endowment, good work, etc., and notifying me of my reelection as a

Trustee. I am pleased with the compliment paid me by my reelection, but would really prefer that someone else had been elected in my stead, only because I think that all the Trustees should reside where they can attend the meetings and take part in the care of the College.

By the time he moved to California in 1894, most of his principal capital contributions for Punahou had already been made. He prepared the Charles R. Bishop Trust deed wherein no mention is made of Punahou; but he was still not finished with his giving. During the 1875–1876 European trip, he and his wife purchased a modest collection of oil paintings, some originals and copies of others which they had commissioned. This collection was divided into two parts, one of which went into the home of the Bishops on King Street and later was moved to the 21 Emma Street home. It was thence widely distributed by the W. F. Allens, who were the recipients of the contents of that home when Bishop moved to California. The other part of the collection was presented to Punahou, March 19, 1895, and included:

Geovanni Tiepolo, "Finding of Moses"
Guido Remi, "Aurora" (copy)
J. G. Stone, "Turkish Poulterer" or "Street Scene In Constantinople"
T. Hill, three North American landscapes: "The Wasatch Mountains," "Vancouver Island," and "Alaska Scenery."
Luigi Ademolli, six etchings of scenes from Homer's "Iliad."
Engravings of Washington, Shaherbeine and his friends Evangeline, Dante, and Beatrice.

The Punahou Preparatory School, after much debate, had been moved to the Punahou campus in 1901. Bishop donated $5000 at this time in six scholarships for his favorite charges—the Hawaiian boys and girls—who might be assisted in attending Punahou. And in July, 1903, he made an eighth major gift: $50,000 along with some "old tramway stock." Out of this transaction came the Charles R. Bishop Hall. But he would not authorize parting with the $50,000 without a struggle. He had warned J. O. Carter, May 9, 1902:

It has been my wish and is so still that there should be no hurrying about paying the $50,000 to Oahu College, for considering what I have done for that institution it has seemed to me that others, those who have personally or through their family enjoyed advantages from the old school should have a chance to give it a lift, and that they might see the necessity and advantage of action sooner if I held back for a while. The trust saves $2000 per annum by waiting, and the money will all be wanted.

Even in his deep twilight years his memory did not falter. Included in the Seventh Section of his Will, probated shortly after his death in 1915, was this provision:

I give and bequeath to the trustees of Oahu College . . . $10,000, and my Twenty-nine First Mortgage Six Per Cent Gold Bonds of West Sacramento Company . . . to be used for the improvement of the Bishop Hall of Science Building or to found scholarships at the college, or for both purposes.

The bonds were worth $8700. His total dollar-giving to Punahou and Oahu College can be estimated at well over $350,000. This sum is not large in modern currency, but at the time of the gifts the sums were substantial. He was the greatest benefactor of Punahou School.

The names Punahou and Oahu College have been used almost interchangeably in this sketch. Confusion has arisen over the years. Punahou opened its doors in 1842 on a Missionary Station area which bore the name, "Punahou." In 1857, however, a charter was issued in the name of Oahu College. Classes which were started in the name of Oahu College, thereafter, were discontinued in 1900. It was this grafting of the name Oahu College to that of Punahou School that caused the confusion. The Trustees finally put an end to it by officially adopting the name of Punahou in 1934.

The story of Punahou is a wonderful tale of outstanding and distinguished personalities in educational leadership. It is a tale of the successful achievement of its graduates throughout the world and in Hawaii and of an affection for their alma mater that is rarely encountered even in colleges.

President Griffiths was quoted at the beginning of this section with regard to Bishop's significance to Punahou. On Bishop's ninety-third birthday President Griffiths generously gave a valedictory on his life and works; it was to an assembly of students at Punahou, January 25, 1915, and in a sense it was truly valedictory since it was to constitute a last expression of public praise. Mr. Bishop died five months later:

I cannot let this occasion pass without reminding the students of the great debt that Punahou has to Mr. Bishop. He has given generously in money. . . . He has given freely of himself. Although he is not a graduate of Punahou no one has had more interest in its welfare and advancement. His services as trustee were marked by the greatest devotion to the advancement of the interests of the school.

MILLS INSTITUTE AND KAWAIAHAO SEMINARY

BISHOP WRITES IN MANY objects of his charitable interest in the Third and Fifth Sections of the Charles R. Bishop Trust deed. The first object named in the Third Section he called "Mills School." * This school for the education of boys of Chinese extraction was operated by Francis Williams Damon, son of Reverend Samuel Chenery Damon.† "Frank" Damon and his wife were masters of the Chinese language and decided to organize a school for Chinese boys in their home. The school, soon to be named Mills Institute, had its beginning in 1892. In 1896, endowment money for building needs was forthcoming from several Honolulans, including Bishop. The Third Section also directed annual contributions to the Mills Institute starting with 1895. These were continued through 1914 even though the institution had lost its identity in a 1907 merger with the Kawaiahao Seminary.

The story of Kawaiahao Seminary ** begins in 1859. Miss Ogden in that year had started a home for Hawaiian girls called "Makiki Family School." It was largely assisted by the Ladies' Benevolent Society and also by the government through the Board of Education. Studies were mainly in English, and domestic duties were stressed. The growth of the School was slow but steady: 1860, ten girls; 1862, eleven girls; 1866, twenty-one girls; 1868, twenty-five girls. The May 31, 1860, edition of the *Pacific Commercial Advertiser* carries an editorial on the need for this home as a family type of school, and also an advertisement asking for additional students, five to eight years of age, at the rate of $3.00 weekly for tuition and board. The advertisement was signed Chas. R. Bishop, Secretary. This was his first school interest.

* Mills Institute.
† See p. 14.
** Bishop used the name, Kawaiahao Female Seminary in his references to Kawaiahao Seminary in correspondence and in the Charles R. Bishop Trust deed.

Makiki had been chartered by the Privy Council in 1860 with Samuel M. Carter as President and Bishop as Secretary. During 1868 the school was suspended and then was immediately reopened and absorbed into the recently organized Kawaiahao Seminary.*

Paragraph Three in the Fifth Section of the Trust deed provides discretionary payments for the board and tuition of girls between the ages of six and sixteen, preference being given to Hawaiian girls of pure or part aboriginal blood. Kawaiahao Seminary was mentioned, but wide latitude was given to supply such payments to other schools for girls in the Hawaiian Islands. An annual gross sum of $5000 for the life of the Trust was provided on a discretionary basis. Of this amount Kawaiahao received $2400 anually from 1895 to 1954. Bishop had made a personal endowment contribution of $5000 to the Seminary before his Trust deed came into effect.

The new Mid-Pacific Institute, created through a merger of Mills Institute and Kawaiahao Seminary in 1907, experienced no lessening of interest on the part of the Charles R. Bishop Trust. The $500 payments started in 1895 to Mills Institute were continued to the new school through 1954. In addition the Trust deed provided $1200 each year from 1905 to 1924, doubled that in the years between 1924 and 1944, and authorized varying amounts on through 1954. This distinguished institution of secondary education in Hawaii has enjoyed a total contribution either by the direct personal hand of Bishop or by his Trust deed of well over a quarter million dollars.

THREE SCHOOLS FOR GIRLS

Makawao Female Seminary

Two OTHER SCHOOLS for young Hawaiian girls were mentioned to the Charles R. Bishop Trust by Rev. C. M. Hyde. These were the Makawao Female Seminary on the island of Maui, and Kohala Girls'

---

* The Kawaiahao Seminary was started as a family school for girls in the home of Dr. and Mrs. L. H. Gulick. This was in 1865. In April, 1867 the American Board of Commissioners for Foreign Missions assumed direction of the school with Miss Lydia Bingham as the first principal. Her salary was paid by the Hawaiian Mission Children's Society.

School on the island of Hawaii. Both were high in enrollment of Hawaiian girls. Both were vigorous, well managed schools. Under the Fifth Section of the Trust Deed an annual payment of $1200 was made to the Makawao Female Seminary. These payments extended from 1895 to 1908 and totalled $15,250.

In 1898 the Makawao or East Maui Female Seminary building burned, and a new Maunaolu Seminary took over the properties and the program. The Trustees continued payments to the school under the name Makawao for some time beyond 1898 and continued the $1200 annual payments to Maunaolu Seminary without a break through 1944. The Maunaolu share was $44,400 or a total of $59,650 for the overall fifty-year period. The number of girls aided by the payments ran variously from twenty to forty each year. Bishop had an early interest in this institution. It had been founded originally, in 1861, by Rev. C. B. Andrews, a missionary. At first it was called "The Home;" then it had a variety of names, including East Maui Female Seminary and Makawao Female Seminary. Bishop carried the title of assistant treasurer and banker of this school. This was in 1870 and earlier. This school for Hawaiian girls was at one time (1880) characterized as the Mount Holyoke of the Hawaiian Islands. With this background it can be well understood that Bishop would interpose no objection to Hyde's thought of directing Charles R. Bishop Trust money to aid this school, and he wrote to J. O. Carter on July 21, 1902, to that effect:

I know that the aid given to the Makawao (or E. Maui) Seminary has been well bestowed and appreciated. Many good women have done conscientious and valuable service there—such women as Miss Carpenter, Miss Malone, Miss Alexander and others are true missionaries and well deserve all the reward promised to those who are faithful.

Kohala Girls' School

Rev. C. M. Hyde was also deeply interested in the Kohala Girls' School on the island of Hawaii. It had opened December 1, 1874, with twenty-one girls, all of Hawaiian ancestry. At one time it was known by the name of *Waikupanaha*, The Wonderful Spring. It was also called Mauna Oliva Home. As with so many such schools, when the first principal, Miss Lizzie Lyons, left, the driving force was gone, and the school was closed October 20, 1882, but reopened October 2, 1889, under Miss M. F. Whittier. At this time, "Hon. C. R.

Bishop donated $100." In 1890, he gave another $100 and in 1893, $5000 to the endowment fund. The Charles R. Bishop Trust, at the urging of Hyde, paid an average annual sum of $800 beginning in 1895 and ending in 1955 until a total of $51,066.50 had been distributed against the accounts of the Hawaiian girls who were students at Kohala. On the books of the Charles R. Bishop Trust, the school is called the Kohala Female Seminary. The payments totalled over $56,500.

Waialua Female Seminary

Reverend O. H. Gulick opened a "family school" with eleven native girls on Printer's Lane in Honolulu in 1860. Three years later he moved it to Kau, Hawaii, but in 1865 he reopened it at Waialua, Oahu under the name of the Waialua Female Seminary. It was discontinued temporarily in 1869 due to the illness of the founder. Eighteen months later, in 1870, the school was opened again with Miss M. E. Green, Principal; and Bishop was a member of the Board of Trustees. Because of personnel and community difficulties the school closed in 1882.

HILO BOYS' BOARDING SCHOOL

THE BENEFACTIONS OF BISHOP, personally and through the Charles R. Bishop Trust, to the account of the historic Hilo Boys' Boarding School were extremely generous. The founding year was 1836, and in 1848 the school was chartered and granted a fee simple title to its Hilo acreage. It was intended solely for boys of Hawaiian extraction, but Japanese boys were admitted beginning in 1886. In a letter to Levi L. Lyman, December 28, 1901, Bishop wrote:

. . . The excellent work done by your grandfather [Reverend D. B. Lyman] during the many years he was the head of that school proved itself in the lives and service of many Hawaiians. . . . It was that fact, largely, that attracted my interest in the old school. . . .

Bishop was solicited many times on behalf of the Hilo Boarding School. March 11, 1882, he was asked for $10,000 for the Lyman Memorial Fund. He gave $500. On August 15, 1885, he was asked for

$15,000 for a Bishop Memorial Fund. This was undoubtedly suggested as a memorial to Mrs. Bishop, since she had passed away but nine months before. He said "he had to decline for the present." In November of that year he gave another $500 since the Hilo supporters had reported favorably that a current campaign resulted in collecting $2000.

About this time the pressures of the opening of the new Kamehameha School for Boys brought him into the market for an outstanding school man capable of planning and opening the new school. He remembered William B. Oleson, principal of the Hilo Boarding School, from an earlier contact and offered the position to him. Bishop referred to this in a letter to Oleson, February 1, 1886:

I hope that you will be able, without taxing your strength or patience or taking too much of your time, to raise the remainder so as to claim my $2,000 for the Lyman Fund; and I further hope that matters will so arrange themselves in your mind and for you that you will be ready and willing to take hold and build up the Kamehameha School for Boys. . . .

He made further subscriptions to the Hilo institution. There may have been a motive here, for but a few days earlier, on February 19, he had caused William B. Oleson to read a communication to the board meeting of the Hilo Boarding School, and the Minutes record it:

Personal communication was then made by Mr. Oleson relative to correspondence with the Trustees of The Kamehameha School for Boys at Honolulu looking towards an invitation to his becoming Principal of this new school.

On February 22, 1887, he subscribed $2000 to the Lyman Memorial Fund. Bishop's interest in the Hilo school was quickening. September 1, 1890, another $12,000 was added to the Lyman Fund. An entry in the Minute Book of the Hilo Trustees, for August 9, 1890, reveals his intention:

Hon. C. R. Bishop in response to an appeal for funds made in a circular expressed interest in the school and a desire to aid in increasing the funds of the school.

In accordance with his usual custom, his offer was predicated upon a matching arrangement. This time the Hilo officials were to raise $18,000, and they did raise that sum. In 1893 he gave another $10,000.

The parade of gifts provoked appreciative action by the Trustees of the school. The Minutes show on March 20, 1893:

Moved that Mr. Lyman write to Hon. C. R. Bishop thanking him in behalf of the Trustees and school for his gift of $10,000.

This was followed by an entry on May 13, 1893: "Dr. Wetmore nominated Hon. C. R. Bishop as Trustee to fill the vacancy caused by the death of Rev. J. D. Paris." Bishop could scarcely accept, since he had left but three days prior for California and was not to return again except for three weeks in February of the next year. Samuel M. Damon acknowledged the nomination letter for him and wrote to Mr. Terry, secretary of the Hilo Boarding School, that "Mr. Bishop would have to decline the honor. He would feel that to be a Trustee he would have to be a resident in the Country."

The obligation to Hilo was very deep. The Boarding School was a chief agency to benefit from annual subscriptions from the Charles R. Bishop Trust. In the first year of the Trust, $500 was transmitted to Hilo for operating expenses. Another $500 was sent the second year, $1500 in the third year, and in each successive year from 1898 through 1902 an even thousand dollars was paid towards the budgeted expense. The giving over the years, which had been exceedingly generous, was climaxed on March 3, 1903, when a payment of $25,000 was made toward the capital structure of the institution. This brought the grand total of $7500 for operating expense and $60,000 for capital endowment to $67,500, which was to account for the Hilo Boarding School's largest benefaction from any single source in its history.

A report on a possible plan for co-education at Hilo called forth a bit of Bishop philosophy on the subject. This was immediately after his Charles R. Bishop Trust had made the last large capital contribution. The thought was expressed in a letter to J. O. Carter, on April 1, 1903:

I'm pleased to learn that the Trustees of the Hilo Boarding School have, for the present at least, dropped the idea of attempting to build for accommodation of girls as well as for the boys and I hope that they will never attempt to provide for both sexes in the same or adjoining premises. If I had supposed that such a union would be attempted, I doubt that I would have helped toward the endowment of the old school as I have done, for I do not believe in such a school for Hawaiians, to say nothing about other nationalities. I also think that it is unwise and unnecessary to admit boys for so small a money payment as $25. Twice that sum is much too small for Kamehameha and is not too large for Hilo. But this is a matter which the Hilo trustees should be able to judge of better than I can. Of course the boys, their parents, guardians or friends will never pay *more* than they are *obliged* to.

In authorizing the last capital gift Bishop wrote the Hilo Trustees to inquire, ". . . how the funds were wanted? Oahu Railway and Land Company bonds with a 4½% yield or in cash?" It was decided to take the $25,000 in cash; and C. M. Cooke, a trustee of the Charles R. Bishop Trust, suggested that the money be placed in Kohala Plantation bonds which were available at par. Thus Bishop not only paid a long-standing debt for the direct contribution that Hilo Boarding School had made through sending William Oleson to Kamehameha as its first principal, but he also was proudly assisting a school that had supplied the inspiration to Hampton Institute and the Kamehameha Schools.

PUBLIC EDUCATION IN HAWAII

EDUCATION HAS EVER BEEN a popular public platform topic in Hawaii. It was so in the 1840's, and public pressure mounted throughout the decade to culminate in 1848 in the appointment of Richard Armstrong, one of the most effective of the missionaries, as the second Minister of Education.

Armstrong has been called the Father of American Public Education in Hawaii. He introduced a modest program of vocational education in the Kingdom long before it took hold in the United States. He also initiated the principle of tax support for public education. Under his urging the sectarian public schools were abolished in 1854. The independent Board of Education was established in the next year.

After Armstrong's passing in 1860, progress was stalled for some years. On December 21, 1869, Bishop was appointed to membership on the Board of Education. King Lunalilo reappointed him as a member in 1873 and as President in 1874. With the courageous assistance of H. Rexford Hitchcock, and later, D. Dwight Baldwin, the languishing school system was awakening. Bishop continued as President until February 17, 1883, when he and the other members of the Board, with the exception of Rhodes, were forced to resign.

Walter Murray Gibson replaced him as President. On July 7, 1887, as an appointee of King Kalakaua, Bishop in turn replaced the deposed Gibson and continued as President, this time including a re-appointment by Queen Liliuokalani, May 5, 1891, until his departure for California. He held this position under the Monarchy, the Provisional Government, and the Republic.

Benjamin O. Wist * characterizes Bishop:

. . . as a man imbued with ideals of service, possessed of faith in Hawaii and in public education as a means of promoting its social and economic welfare. He held the confidence of both the native Hawaiians and the leading industrialists. While not belonging to the missionary group, he was in no way inimical to its purpose. . . .

Bishop's practical sentiments about education were brought to bear upon public education. He wanted students educated to habits of industry. Industrial education was an imperative in his concept of the program of studies. All students were to know something of physical labor—should regard labor as dignified and not as mere drudgery. Probably, the best expressions of his educational philosophy for his nation's children are contained in his address at the fortieth anniversary of Oahu College. Said he on this June day in 1881:

No considerable proportion of the youth of a nation can be educated in boarding schools, or away from their parents or friends; and it is not reasonable to expect that they should be. The masses must work up together, gradually; and the character of the masses, (not the favored few) will be the character of the nation. In a field of cane there are large hills and towering stalks scattered here and there, but the crop depends upon the average of the field and the good cultivation of the whole.

Is it not probable that a majority of the children of foreign blood now in our schools, will spend the most of their days on these islands? If so here will be their field of duty and labor; and here their influence will be felt. Should they not be taught in common with the youth of the aboriginal stock to look upon this country as their home and their country and upon themselves as Hawaiians?

His report as President of the Board of Education for 1878 pointed up several of his concerns. He referred to the poor attitude of students towards attendance, the indifference of the parents, the general incompetency of the teachers, and the obstacles to recruitment of good teachers. He worried about the lack of good supervision and particularly the failure of the work program.

* Benjamin O. Wist, *A Century of Public Education in Hawaii* (Honolulu, Hawaii Education Review, 1940), p. 78.

The occasion of his leaving the presidency in 1883 was the signal for a second ebb-tide in public education. A statement by Mr. Henry S. Townsend, Inspector General of Education a few years later, emphasizes the change back again:

In 1887 came a revolutionary movement . . . after which a new Board of Education came into existence, being made up in large part of old material, including C. R. Bishop, as sincere and effective a friend of Hawaiian education as it ever had.

So, Bishop, an educational leader by draft originally by King Luna-lilo, gave to public education in Hawaii the leadership so essential when a new political, industrial, and social order was in the making. His influence in association with others, gave education in Hawaii its genuinely public nature. It became universal, non-sectarian, and tax supported.

William R. Castle succeeded him as President of the Board of Education and was one among several Honolulu community figures at his ninetieth birthday party. On this occasion Castle paid sincere tribute to his predecessor:

. . . He shows also his spirit. He wanted not only to have the pupils who were taught by the country, whose education was in the hands of the Country, taught to labor and to respect labor, but also to respect themselves and to be men, and I may say that the entire eighteen years that he gave to the cause of public education in this country was de-voted constantly to that spirit and that idea, of making education mean something more than a knowledge of books, by giving independence, giving dignity and the right character to individuals.

Mr. Bishop's name will be preserved as long as Hawaii lasts and will go down to the future as one of those who were the builders of Hawaii.

One note of relaxation creeps into the story. This one from the *Friend:* "On August 19, 1890, Mr. Bishop indulges the visiting and resident teachers of the Board in a railroad excursion and picnic at Remond Grove [*mauka* of Pearl Harbor]."

THE HONOLULU LIBRARY AND READING ROOM ASSOCIATION

THE HONOLULU LIBRARY and Reading Room Association, forerun-ner of the Library of Hawaii, came to be one of Bishop's most cherished objects of support. A small group of interested men of Honolulu met in the Knights of Pythias Hall, March 1, 1879. They drew up a subscription list to organize a Temperance Reading Room Association. But before that first evening came to an end, the name was changed to the Honolulu Workingman's Reading Association. Bishop was on the first subscription list for $1000. The Association received its charter on June 24, 1879. The officers and directors were great debaters: they debated the admission of females to the reading room, and they debated even about forming a debating society. They wrangled long over allowing children to read the books in the library; and after admitting public school children (in a group only with a teacher), they debated about admitting private school children.

The Association struggled along for some years and raised needed operating monies by holding benefits of one kind or another. In June, 1882, an impressive array of privately owned collections was exhibited to a delighted Honolulu public. There were bronzes, statuary, paintings, tapestries, and a large display of Hawaiian antiquities. The collection of paintings purchased by the Bishops in Europe was catalogued and made a part of the exhibit, and Mrs. Bishop's personal collection of noted Hawaiian antiquities was included. The committee responsible for this portion of the exhibit was headed by Rev. C. M. Hyde, who was largely responsible for Bishop's considerable interest in the Association. Bishop gave little attention to the library project for several years. With the passing of his wife in 1884, he became engrossed with problems of her estate and his own resultant mounting plan to retire to California. But there was a well-spring of interest which appeared in 1888. On March 1, he donated the 300-volume collection of the Fornander Library * to the Association. A motion of thanks was ordered spread in the Minutes and published in the newspapers; but Mr. Allen, member of the Board of Trustees, "was of the opinion that the publication of the letter [of thanks] would not afford Mr. Bishop any particular satisfaction." The secretary was instructed to omit the newspaper publicity.

In the Minutes of the Association meeting for October 8, 1888, Bishop's name was included in the list of nominations for Trustees.

---

* This collection is not to be confused with the Fornander manuscript collection which Bishop had also purchased and which eventually was presented to the Museum.

Nine were to be elected. Bishop came in tenth. In the October 4, 1889, meeting records, the following appears:

Judge Dole remarked that he thought he had a pleasant surprise for the members and stated that conversing with Mr. Bishop a few days ago the subject of the Library came up. When the Hon. Gentleman revealed that he should be glad to do something for the Association but objected to the debt. But if the Association would clear themselves from debt he would agree to donate $1,000 a year for five years for the purchase of books.

This was agreed to and the annual monies became the "Bishop Fund." In 1892 he approved the "temporary use of his Bishop Fund for Purchase of a vacant lot in the rear of the library."

On November 4, 1892, the secretary "cast a white ballot for thirteen names including that of C. R. Bishop." At a reconvened meeting that evening he was elected President, and he was absent. At the next quarterly meeting, April 17, 1893, the treasurer announced a gift from President C. R. Bishop for $5000, to be received on certain conditions:

Received from C. R. Bishop the sum of five thousand dollars being in full payment of a legacy given by him in his Will: to the Honolulu Library and Reading Room Association; and it is agreed that said amount shall be used in enlarging the building of said Association or in creating a fund, the income of which is to be applied to current expenses of said Association and for no other purposes.

He was also absent from this meeting. He was elected President again at the annual meeting in 1894 and this election found him settled in California. He was re-elected each succeeding year through 1906 and had not attended a meeting, either quarterly or annual, of the Association. The board members could not bring themselves to drop him after he had left Hawaii permanently. In this instance, it does not seem as if he tried very strenuously to avoid the honorary long-distance elections to the presidency. On December 1, 1894, he wrote to H. A. Parmalee, Secretary-treasurer of the Honolulu Library and Reading Room:

. . . I wish to thank the members and trustees for the compliment of reelection. Having been absent from Honolulu nearly all of the past year, and my residence there in the future being so uncertain I did not expect or merit such a compliment; and I wish the trustees to feel quite at liberty to treat this letter as my resignation if the interests of the Association or the convenience of the trustees will be promoted thereby.

They could not have foreseen his generous purposes that were detailed later in the Charles R. Bishop Trust. That agency did not come into being until the summer of 1895. In paragraph F of the Third Section, eight annual payments of $1000 are provided. In the Sixth Section he wrote in the sum of $25,000 for the Association as a capital fund contribution, thereby bringing his total benevolence to about $45,000. He can be considered a major benefactor, therefore, of the Library of Hawaii, formerly the Honolulu Library and Reading Room Association. Some of his thinking in extending this support was undoubtedly colored by the advantages thereby accruing to the Hawaiian Historical Society and the Bernice Pauahi Bishop Museum.

HAWAIIAN HISTORICAL SOCIETY AND THE POLYNESIAN SOCIETY OF NEW ZEALAND

The Minute Book of the Hawaiian Historical Society shows in the initial entry, December 29, 1891:

A few gentlemen interested in Hawaiian Antiquities and Comparative Ethnology, met at the rooms of the Hawaiian Board, 108 Beretania Street, to consider the expediency of forming an organization for cooperation in the study, preservation and utilization of material relating to the condition and progress of the Hawaiian people and cognate races.

There were present, W. D. Alexander, G. P. Andrews, C. R. Bishop, S. B. Dole, J. S. Emerson, N. B. Emerson, O. P. Emerson, C. M. Hyde, L. McCully, of Honolulu, and Chaplain Hoes of the U. S. S. *Pensacola*.

Professor W. D. Alexander read a letter which he had received from New Zealand, proposing the organization of a Polynesian Society, with branches in the different groups:

Resolved, that in view of the opportunity before us, the time has come in our opinion for the formation of a local Antiquarian and Historical Society, affiliated with the proposed Polynesian Society of New Zealand, but acting as an independent organization in its methods and administration.

As a result of that first discussion at the Hawaiian Board rooms, an organizational meeting was called two weeks later on January 11, 1892. This may be accepted as the official Founder's Day of the Historical Society. Bishop was not present at this meeting, but his name headed the nominating committee's slate of officers for the office of President. Rev. C. M. Hyde was listed as recording secretary, and both were elected. When the time came for signing the Constitution of the Hawaiian Historical Society, Bishop was accorded the honor of being signatory number one.

This was the first successful attempt to launch an historical society in Hawaii. One other, with the simple title, "The Historical Society," was formed by students of Reverend Sheldon Dibble, an able and inspiring missionary teacher of Lahainaluna Seminary, in 1841. One of the contributors at a meeting that year was a student by the name of David Malo, who read a paper on the "Reign of UMI," the first of the Lahaina manuscripts of Hawaiian history. Bishop, a half century later, was instrumental in publishing Malo's greatest manuscript under the imprint of the Bishop Museum.

Reverend Roswell Randall Hoes, USN, chaplain of the USS *Pensacola,* was among those present at the first organization meeting of the Society. The Hawaiian Historical Society undoubtedly owes its origin at this particular time to the leadership and enthusiasm of this Navy chaplain. An Easterner, he came of a literary family where bibliography, genealogy, and history, were household interests. Although Hoes was in Honolulu but a few months, he helped engineer the historical society movement into a living community agency. He had no difficulty in enlisting the interest of Hyde, who in turn suggested a small list of able community leaders as backers.

Hoes was an invaluable person. W. D. Alexander wrote to His Excellency J. L. Stevens at the U. S. Legation with a strong plea for extending Hoes' tour of duty to allow the completion of work on the bibliography of the Hawaiian Islands and early government archives. Alexander stated, "It is chiefly owing to his [Hoes] efforts that the Hawaiian Historical Society has been organized, and to his zeal and energy as its librarian, that an extensive and valuable collection of historical documents is rapidly being formed." But, an extension of the tour of duty was not approved and Hoes therefore resigned, March 7, 1893. He was accorded the signal honor of election as a Corresponding Member of the Society.

The Society met generally on a quarterly basis variously in the parlor of the Honolulu Library, Bishop's office in the upstairs room at the bank, and the YMCA Hall. Bishop was present at the meetings through the early part of 1892 and then was unable to attend another. But seemingly, the more he absented himself, the closer became his affiliation. On April 7, 1892, the "President was designated as Trustee of the Society, to hold and manage Society property."

At this same meeting the "Basis of Cooperation" with the Honolulu Library and Reading Room Association was adopted: the Association would grant permanent use and control of the front room of the Library building to the Society; all of the Association's collections of manuscripts and printed matter relating to Hawaiian history would be transferred to the ownership of the Society; association members might use the Library in the quarters now to be controlled by the Society; no financial aid would be given by the Association; and if the Society should close its doors, all property and the "front room" would revert to the Association. This, of course, was a windfall of maximum value; and the Society lost no time in moving in.

For more than a dozen years Bishop had watched the struggling Library, and had assisted it from time to time; but it was not until the five point agreement with the Hawaiian Historical Society was adopted that he swung into line behind it. He placed capital funds to its credit, provided for the purchase of additional land to enlarge the library building, and he became President. Thus, he was able to effect a practical and economical joint utilization of resources of the Society and the Association without the necessity of a merger. The two cooperative agencies were to grow and develop as strong and independent community culture centers.

Simultaneously with the organization of the Hawaiian Historical Society, and as specifically reported in the letter which W. D. Alexander read to the first meeting of the group interested in forming such a society, another group of like-minded men was meeting in New Zealand to form the Polynesian Society. This organization meeting was held in the library of the New Zealand Institute in Wellington; and the date was January 8, 1892, only seventy-two hours prior to the Honolulu meeting. Both societies elected Her Majesty, Liliuokalani, Queen of Hawaii, as Patron of their respective groups; and both societies continued her as Patron until her decease, although her title was changed to Liliuokalani, ex-Queen of Hawaii, when revolution changed the Hawaiian government. Bishop supplied another link in that he also became a charter member of the New Zealand society. This was in 1892, and his membership continued through 1903. He faithfully re-mailed all his copies of the Journals of the Polynesian Society to the Bishop Museum and in 1903 sent his membership there also. This was in keeping with his general retreat from all affiliations in Hawaii and the Pacific area after establishing residence in California.

There were several Honolulans who joined the Polynesian Society that first year; the list included many of the illustrious names of the day—W. D. Alexander, A. J. Cartwright, W. N. Castle, A. S. Cleghorn, S. B. Dole, J. S. Emerson, C. M. Hyde, A. F. Judd, and H. A. Widemann. And the Polynesian Society still continues as a distinguished center of Polynesian research and publication.

At the end of the first year of the Historical Society's existence, Bishop was re-elected President, and again was re-elected in 1893 and 1894. The Directors urged him to take another term as President in 1895, but he declined on the reasonable basis that he could not operate effectively as President that far away.

On December 14, 1895, this statement appears in the Minutes:

The Treasurer stated that he had received from the Trustees of the Charles R. Bishop Trust a check for $2000 cash, a donation from Hon. C. R. Bishop, without conditions, for the general objects of the Soc'y.

It was recommended to the Society that Hon. C. R. Bishop, Hon. G. D. Gilman, Professor A. B. Lyons be made Corresponding Members.

About a year later, on November 26, 1896, an acknowledgment was recorded:

The Corresponding Secretary was instructed to write Hon. C. R. Bishop in grateful acknowledgment of his generous gift of $2000, the only permanent fund of the Society.

Bishop was made a Corresponding Member for life, in 1897, an honor which pleased him very much.

THE HAMPTON NORMAL AND AGRICULTURAL INSTITUTE

GEORGE FOSTER PEABODY, the multimillionaire mercantilist, and Samuel Chapman Armstrong, the founder of Hampton Institute, almost cast Bishop in the role of principal benefactor of the distinguished Virginia school whose major purpose was the vocational training of the Negro and the Indian. It was Peabody's * own admission, regarding his pattern of systematic giving, that so strongly influenced Bishop even against his own inclinations. Peabody was a strong supporter of Hampton Institute, serving on the Board of Trustees for many years. The trusts which he established were designed, in part at least, to serve Hampton.

Armstrong was a *kamaaina* to Hawaii. He was born on Maui, the son of Richard Armstrong, who was a pioneer leader of the public school system of Hawaii. He attended Royal School and was graduated from Punahou School. He was a scholar in Bishop's Sunday School class at Bethel. Tall and robust, he loved humor and was a devoted student of nature. It was he who had been instrumental in shaping the vocational program at the Hilo Boys' Boarding School. He advised Bishop about the vocational program at the Kamehameha Schools and helped to select the first teachers.

Despite the bare and incomplete outline of the Peabody-Armstrong services rendered, it can be understood that Bishop might easily have become a principal donor to Hampton Institute. However, in the 1880's, things were confused and unsettled in the Bishop family. Mrs. Bishop's passing in 1884 set the wheels in motion for the organization of The Kamehameha Schools. Bishop himself was engrossed in special community efforts because of the tragic fire of 1886 which razed the bulk of Honolulu's downtown business, cultural, and religious buildings.† He was also beginning to long for the brisk climate of San Francisco and to direct a share of his planning in that direction. However, in 1886 he sent an initial gift of $500 to the endowment of Hampton. In 1889, on June 14, he wrote to Samuel M. Damon: ". . . He [General Armstrong] has been very active and painstaking in looking for teachers for us, especially for one to take the teaching of carpentry and he will write Mr. Oleson fully. . . ."

Bishop wanted to see this school so he went down to Hampton and later wrote to Damon that his visit had been very pleasant. Said he: ". . . I have ordered two harnesses, one single and one double, to be made at General Armstrong's school at Hampton." And a month later a sight draft for $1500 on the Bank of California went

* See pp. 297–299.
† See pp. 254, 270.

back to General Armstrong. Bishop had reached the coast and was on his way home to Hawaii when he wrote:

. . . [Enclosed is] part of my intended bequest to the Institute for the purposes stated in my Will and you have my permission to use it in erecting or furnishing your new Science building now partly finished. Should it suit to connect the name of my dear friend Wm. L. Lee with the new building, I shall be very glad of it.

The science building was not named for Lee presumably because he was neither a man of science nor of education and did not, except for the principalship at Norfolk, have roots or antecedents in Hampton's sphere of activity. No copies of any Will of Bishop's are known except the last one probated in 1915 after his death. There is no mention of Hampton Institute in that document. There was, however, another $1500 forthcoming in 1890; and the two sums were placed in a Charles Reed Bishop scholarship fund. The income is still available to qualified Hampton students.

Armstrong and Bishop never met again. Armstrong came to Honolulu to speak at Punahou School's fiftieth anniversary on June 25, 1891, in Kawaiahao Church; and two days earlier he gave the commencement address at Kawaiahao Church to the graduating class of The Kamehameha Schools. Bishop was on his way to Europe. Armstrong had developed a world-famous school with vocational training as its central purpose. This dedicated, tireless man died May 11, 1893, at the early age of 54. The assistance given in the early planning stages of The Kamehameha Schools constitutes the greatest monument to Samuel Chapman Armstrong in Hawaii.

8

Religion

THE CHURCH

BISHOP WROTE TO Uldrick Thompson April 19, 1899:

. . . My own creed is very short, and I have but little respect for sectarianism. What a man really is and what his life shows month after month and year after year, is more important than what he says he believes. There can be excellent and effective preaching in short sermons without offending Christians of any denomination. . . . But I will not attempt to discuss theology.

Some months earlier in a letter to Theodore Richards he commented upon the proposed employment of a pastor for The Schools, and we find a clue to his religious feeling in it:

. . . Of course we do not expect to secure a great preacher, but we do want a broad-minded, cheerful man whose *everyday* life and personal influence will be worth more than preaching.

A few weeks later, December 17, 1897, he wrote to Rev. C. M. Hyde:

. . . For myself I favor a short, broad and liberal creed probably too liberal to best switch to the position under consideration [a rather fundamentalist church philosophy had been suggested for the new church at Kamehameha], and so I am willing to trust to the reason and sincerity of the Trustees in Honolulu.

Bishop was baptized in a Methodist church in Glens Falls and attended Sunday School at a little Methodist church in Warrensburgh a few miles distant from the summit crossing between Lake George and Warrensburgh, the site of his grandfather Jesse Bishop's home. The sea voyage via the brig *Henry* provided opportunity for him to read aloud from the Bible and to pray.

References to such devotions are recorded in a journal of the trip.

In the first years of his marriage he taught a Sunday School class at Bethel Union Church, along with James Marshall.

Miss Martha A. Chamberlain * spoke at the concluding service of the Fort Street Church in November, 1892 (the congregation was about to move into the new Central Union Church), and described the church attendance practices of the Bishops:

> . . . about the center of the *mauka* middle aisle was then as now the pew of Hon. C. R. Bishop, and very regularly to the evening service came that beloved Chiefess of Hawaii—Mrs. Bernice Pauahi Bishop. She always attended in the morning, the Kawaiahao Church, of which she was a member. . . .

Most of Bishop's services to religion in Honolulu were in some aspect or other tied in with the story of Central Union Church.

The fire of April 18, 1886 burned Bethel Union Church to the ground. Scarcely had the fire been put out when an invitation was extended by the Fort Street Church to the Bethel Union congregation to use its facilities. Bethel Union Church had been organized by Samuel Chenery Damon April 3, 1850, and it met in the Seamen's Chapel. It grew so rapidly that out of it, in turn, there emerged four colony churches, the second of which was called the Second Foreign Church. Bishop's connection with this church was of long standing.

We see the name of Bishop among a committee of five including G. P. Judd, Orramel H. Gulick, John Thomas Waterhouse, and Richard Armstrong petitioning His Highness John Young for temporary use of the newly constructed Court House (1851). The petition was dated June 22, 1852:

> . . . the foreign residents of Honolulu have formed a church and separate congregation, and raised by subscription sufficient to support their Pastor the Rev. T. E. Taylor and pay the incidental expenses for the present year, but not enough to enable them to build a house of worship; and therefore, respectfully request your permission, to hold their meetings in the new Court-Room, until they shall be able to procure a more suitable place.

This request was granted and on June 3, 1853, Reverend T. E. Taylor was installed as pastor of the Second Foreign Church in the Court House. This church was called the Second Church until a permanent structure was built on the corner of Beretania and Fort

* Martha Ann Chamberlain was the fourth child of Levi Chamberlain, missionary.

Streets. For a short period in the spring of 1856, the Board of Trustees of the Second Church, among whom now was "Hon. C. R. Bishop," met every morning at 10 o'clock and spent an hour in canvassing the town for subscriptions to the building fund. The church cost $10,575 plus a steeple. The name of this church at the time of moving was changed to the Fort Street Church.

And here now was the Fort Street Church opening its doors to its disaster-stricken mother church. It was a natural outcome that two churches using the same facilities and of the same denomination would think of an organic merger. In 1887, representatives of the two churches met. Bishop was named to a new Fort Street Church merger committee. He had been a faithful visitor at the Fort Street Church for thirty-five years, but was never listed on its membership rolls. The merger committee quickly raised $10,000. The constitution, rules, articles of faith, name, and covenant of the Central Union Church of Honolulu were adopted in November, 1887. The first meeting of the new united church board was held in Bishop's home on Emma Street, and he was elected President of the Board of Trustees. Also present were Hon. J. B. Atherton, Hon. S. M. Damon, Messrs. J. O. Carter, C. M. Cooke, B. F. Dillingham, and Jonathan Shaw. Bishop was re-elected President of the Board continuously through 1895, even past the time he had moved to California. The Trustees met several times at his home and later in a room in the banking offices of Bishop and Company. Finances and a new building for the church were among his special concerns in the few years left to him in Hawaii.

Early in 1889, a Committee on Plans, consisting of Messrs. C. R. Bishop, C. M. Cooke, and Alexander Young, was asked to study all problems relating to a new church building. The committee recommended inviting Mr. Bordwell, architect of a church in East Oakland, California which seemed to most nearly fill the requirements in Honolulu, to visit; and he did so in November 1889. The committee report was adopted, and work started. At Bishop's urging the Trustees decided to construct the church of the lava rock * quarried near the Kamehameha campus. He also persuaded the Trustees to use the same construction men, Lishman and Mutch.

Bishop was a member of the boards of many associations and corporations, but his attendance record as presiding officer of the

*See p. 148.

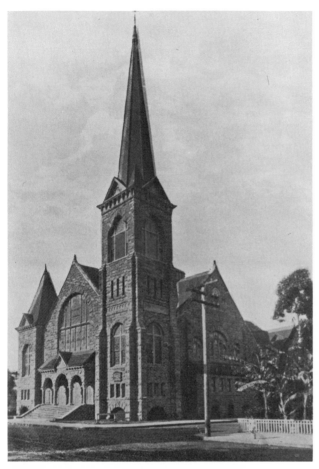

The first Central Union Church, erected under the general guidance in contracting and financing matters by Bishop, at Beretania and Miller Streets.

The Bernice Pauahi Bishop Memorial Chapel, constructed by Bishop close to the site of the present Farrington High School Auditorium.

The First Unitarian Church of Berkeley, California. Bishop attended this
church in his last years. The architect was Bernard Maybeck.

Central Union Church Board was about his best among them all. He missed but one meeting from the start through October 11, 1892. This one was to be his last meeting with the Central Union Board, for he left the next day on the *Australia* for a five-months' trip to the United States. He was back intermittently for two visits of a month each after that, but no church meetings were scheduled in those short periods.

Central Union owes more to him than has been generally recognized. He had given $5000 on the original subscription list in May of 1889. The Charles R. Bishop Trust deed authorized $100 annual payments from 1895 to 1951, and $6000 was realized through these payments. He had early been a member of the pastoral succession committee of the Fort Street Church (1858). In addition to steering the building fund campaign of the Central Union Church, he handled the necessary loans to assure good financing of both the construction of the building and of the operation of the church. He supervised the building while it was under construction and personally attended to the planning and manufacture of the stained glass windows.

Rev. Henry H. Parker, on Mr. Bishop's ninetieth birthday, had this to say:

To tell the truth, I never talked to Mr. Bishop about his church affiliations. But I know he had an interest in the Church, and we all know it, not because he said it, but from that silent, unconscious influence that went out from him into the religious institutions of these islands.

Never a member of Bethel Union, Fort Street, or Central Union, he nevertheless was a bulwark to all of them in counsel, in construction, and in business problems. He heads a long line of illustrious, faithful trustees of Central Union Church.

Other churches directly assisted by the Charles R. Bishop Trust were Kawaiahao and Kaumakapili. These institutions—the leading Hawaiian churches of the Congregational denomination—were evergreat objects of his interest. His wife was a member of Kawaiahao. The Charles R. Bishop Trust started to each church the $100 annual payments which were to continue for sixty years, and Bishop contributed about $5000 of personal funds towards the repair of the roof and belfry of Kawaiahao Church. In a letter to Reverend H. H. Parker of Kawaiahao, dated December 17, 1889, he described two memorials:

I have purchased in Boston . . . a small but neat, marble font with a silver plated bowl to be presented to Kawaiahao in the name of my late wife. . . .

I have also rec⁴ a plain tablet to Paki, Konia and Pauahi—a marble slab intended to be put into the wall of the passageway of the church . . . there is one more name to be cut in it. . . .

Kaumakapili Church was in his thoughts not only because of its Hawaiian congregation but also because of its repeated exposure to fire losses.

Other interests in Honolulu of Bishop in church-related fields included the Hawaiian Temperance Society, the Hawaiian Missionary Society, and the Hawaiian Bible Society. Not infrequently, he was asked to be treasurer of this group or auditor of that group because of his integrity and his ready access to physical banking facilities to handle bookkeeping and accounting problems. These qualities were likely factors in his relationship to the Temperance, Missionary, and Bible Societies. The Hawaiian Bible Society, oldest of the above-named groups, was organized in 1841. The Hawaiian Tract Society was organized a year later, and the two merged in 1859 under the name of the Hawaiian Tract and Bible Society. Bishop offered this new group the use of the Honolulu Sailors' Home, but even this bit of assistance did not save the work; the Hawaiian Tract and Bible Society languished and died in 1862. He was on the lists for minor annual subscriptions. Mrs. Bishop was an annual member in 1848, two years before her marriage.

The Hawaiian Temperance Society, an outgrowth of the Oahu Temperance Society organized in 1846, lists him as Vice-President along with John H. Ward, President. This was in July, 1848, only a few weeks after he decided to give up going to California to join the gold rush. Nothing of any Bishop interest appears in the record until 1852. Then, a committee consisting of Messrs. E. O. Hall, C. R. Bishop, and J. Mott-Smith was appointed by the Hawaiian Temperance Society "to report on the law regulating the sale of intoxicating liquors in the Kingdom." The members of the committee were to study the inconsistency of a professedly temperance government selling smuggled liquors which had been seized by the police. In his governmental role of Collector of Customs, Bishop was well acquainted with the problems of smuggled goods. He was a teetotaler himself. The Society went far afield in its official proceedings; its members even tried to build up an interest in establishing a savings bank in Honolulu.

"C. R. Bishop Esq." is listed as auditor in the June 5, 1851, proceedings of the Hawaiian Missionary Society. He was re-elected auditor each year through 1855 and then apparently dropped out. However, the name of the Bishops' adopted baby son, Keolaokalani Paki Bishop, was entered as a life member June 29, 1863. This Society, which was a creature of the American Board of Commissioners for Foreign Missions, was dissolved in 1863; and a special dispensation in the form of an honorary life membership in the Hawaiian Mission Children's Society was made for all its life members.

Bishop's participations in the three societies was not of great significance, except that his experiences with them occurred early in his life in Hawaii and paved the way in some degree for his later pattern of philanthropy among agencies of this type.

The story of The Kamehameha Schools' chapel properly belongs in this chapter. Practicality and religious sentiment guided his decision to build a chapel and to give it his wife's name. He waited until after his arrival in California to engage in the rather complicated chore of planning construction details of a church at Kamehameha. The idea had been discussed frequently by Bishop and Hyde prior to 1894. Hyde was the Bishop Estate Trustee closest to The Schools and his zeal finally reached Bishop's mind and heart—and pocketbook, resulting in a paragraph to J. O. Carter, July 8, 1895, from the banker: "In building, the chapel is the first thing to do, and as soon as the cholera is out of the way and there is time to attend to it I hope that men will be out at work getting out stone without waiting for the plans." The rather endless flow of Museum problems which William H. Brigham kept sending to San Francisco occasioned, on the same day, this letter: "There is not to be any chapel, (Methodist or other) built on the School premises very soon. Whenever a chapel is built it will probably be of *stone* and down toward King Street, and the trustees will say who is to be Chaplain. . . ."

One statement issuing from his pen about religion appeared in the series of letters dealing with chapel planning and was written in response to a question by Hyde. The remarks were contained, October 11, in another letter to Carter:

I cannot share Dr. Hyde's prejudice against *Methodists*. My father and mother and my grandparents on that side (Bishops) were Methodists, and I think that denomination as consistent and as nearly right as any of the orthodox denominations. New England people have a wrong idea about Methodists because in that part of the country they were largely of the ignorant classes, much more so than in New York and the Middle and Southern States.

I am a liberal Protestant, and the differences which divide Christians into denominations and sects seem to me to be non-essential, petty and weakening. I hope that the teachers in the Kamehameha Schools will be sufficiently liberal and reasonable to worship together without raising any question as to denomination or sect. . . . Kamehameha Schools are Protestant so far as the faith of the teachers is concerned, but not denominational. My wife liked the Episcopal Service and had not Kawaiahao been the church of her parents and friends she might have been an Episcopalian—though she did not favor Bishop Staley and Co. or *high* church ceremonies. She was a *liberal Protestant*.

The sentiments expressed by Bishop in the Carter letters were unmistakable evidence that he was reaching a decision to build a chapel at Kamehameha. The question of denominationalism had been raised, and he was clear on that point.

Details regarding the chapel were beginning to arrange themselves, and on October 14, he addressed himself to Richards:

About building the Chapel I know of nothing to wait for but plans. . . . It is not my wish to build a large house to be used for all sorts of meetings, but a place for worship, lectures—not on chemistry with dangerous acids etc—and Sunday School—to seat not *more* than 400. Perhaps it is well to have no evening meetings in it. Of course it cannot be used for political meetings. The door ways should be so arranged that people can enter without being blown in by the strong wind. . . .

To Hyde, on November 5, he wrote these lines:

About the Chapel . . . we will not be in a hurry. We will take time to get plans to suit before we go ahead to build. The sketch made by Mr. Ripley * does not quite suit me. The little steeple on top is really a disfigurement.

Unfortunately, he misplaced the Ripley sketch which delayed matters a bit. The planning talks were soon continued however and he wrote to Hyde, March 7, 1896:

It should be the aim to build the Chapel complete for $55,000 so that the almost unavoidable extras need not make the entire cost come to over $60,000 including suitable organ. . . . If there is any doubt that when the Chapel shall have been built that the Trustees will have control of it, I am unwilling to build at all. . . .

* Ripley and Dickey were architects of the chapel.

Again he wrote to Hyde, on April 23—the plans were being moved along rapidly:

About the internal arrangement of the Chapel as to Choir etc., the princi-pals of the Schools may have some ideas worth considering. The archi-tects may be inclined to make the building too much like a grand church, rather than as a modest Chapel, but I was not much pleased with Mr. Ripley's sketch in the elevation. There is more in the *proportions* of a building than most people imagine. Proportions count for more than ornamentation in striving for beauty in a building.

Letters followed at frequent intervals to one or another of the Trustees throughout the next twenty months. The choice of koa or something else for the organ, the type of pew, stained glass window designs, slates for the roof, the question of whether to have electricity or not—all these and many more subjects were covered. Mr. Bergstrom, long to be the chief supplier of pipe organs to Hawaii, installed the Kamehameha Chapel organ for $3100. Bishop asked Hyde to ". . . let Mr. Wray Taylor play the organ when it is dedicated. He has written me a letter praising the Hilo organ and requesting the pleasure of dedicating our new organ. . . ."

The Chapel was nearing completion in the fall of 1897, and all concerned were pointing to Mrs. Bishop's birthday, December 19, as the dedication date for the Bernice P. Bishop Chapel. On Novem-ber 8, Bishop expressed his pleasure with comments about the build-ing, already largely completed:

The Chapel seems to be generally admired. . . . If there are places in the colored glass through which the sunlight is too strong the light can be toned down by stippling the glass using umber paint mixed with Coach varnish.

He was not going to have any costly process used in "toning down" the excess sunlight.

The kind of creed which might have best represented his wife's ideas is described in a letter to Hyde on December 17:

About teaching any "special religion" in the School, I do not remember to have made any positive statement. I did not build the Chapel for my-self, and I do not expect to select or engage a pastor. Mrs. Bishop was brought up under the teachings of the Congregationalists and was a mem-ber of the Kawaiahao Church to which she was loyal and devoted to the end of her life, though she was pleased with and enjoyed the American Episcopal Service.

One week later he wrote again to Hyde:

262 *Charles Reed Bishop*

The appearance of the Chapel is much praised, and I hope that the service in it will always be attractive, elevating, and helpful toward right living, so that it may be a blessing and delight to all who are or may be connected with the Schools. It is intended for a place of worship, and I believe that the worship most acceptable to you is, such as is taught in the life and words of Jesus and as awakens and strengthens love for and helpfulness to mankind.

With this letter, he runs down the curtain on the Chapel. It cost finally about $70,000 and represented an important contribution to the spiritual training of Kamehameha students.

Shortly after Bishop moved to California he was attracted to the services of the First Unitarian Church of San Francisco. This church was a pioneer in the West, having been established about the time that Bishop was sailing around Cape Horn towards Honolulu and Oregon. He did not hold a church membership, although he is listed in the annual reports of 1895–1904 of the Unitarian Club of California as a regular member. He presented a thousand-dollar "Key Route" Bond to the church in February, 1911. C. S. S. Dutton writes of this to Philip C. Knapp, April 22, 1932:

The Charles R. Bishop gift came to the Church during the moderatorship of Mr. Arthur Smith. The bond was handed to Mr. Smith; there was no letter; Mr. Bishop merely remarked, "This is for the church." I recall that Mr. Smith mentioned that it was handed to him on California Street in front of the Bank of California.

Another $1000 bond, this of the San Francisco, Oakland and San Jose Railway #2805, was given to the church with the "Proceeds to be used for charity or other Christian work."

Here he had found a church with a philosophy he could accept. After the earthquake and fire he moved to Berkeley and transferred his interest to the First Unitarian Church of that city. He attended the Berkeley church so regularly and with such punctuality that the minister and the organist learned to time their own moves in the pulpit and at the organ by the prompt moment of his arrival. If he were ever late, and there is a record of one such occurrence, the entire service was in a bit of a dither because the man in the cutaway coat and high silk hat had not appeared at the rear of the church.

The plans for the Berkeley Church were drawn by the famous Bernard Maybeck, who was later to do the Palace of Fine Arts in San Francisco. In the University of California's plans for expansion in the 1960's, this church stood athwart the march of the new campus, and at first the authorities decided to leave it as a monument to the distinguished architect. Other views later prevailed, and it is now to be razed. Temporarily, however, this architectural gem stands in its original setting—an island in a sea of modern university construction. Bishop remembered this church in his Will with the sum of $1000. To the Starr King School of the Ministry (Unitarian) in Berkeley, he gave "seven lots in the Thousand Oaks Station Tract for Building Fund, valued at $10,000." To both the church and the school he was a generous donor in annual gifts. He was not listed as an officer; he was a member of the Board of Trustees of the school from 1904 to 1913.

THE HAWAIIAN EVANGELICAL ASSOCIATION

THE HAWAIIAN EVANGELICAL ASSOCIATION of Congregational Christian Churches is venerable, having been started virtually with the arrival of the first company of missionaries in 1820. Church historians list the year of organization as 1823. Mrs. Bishop's church, Kawaiahao, the great mother church of the native Hawaiians was a member of the Association. Bishop had been a key figure in the merger of the Bethel Union and Fort Street Foreign churches into the new Central Union Church. Churches such as these constituted the membership of the Association which initially carried the name, "Hawaiian Association."

In 1841 the name became the "Sandwich Islands Mission," and in 1854, the "Hawaiian Evangelical Association." From the beginning, it was an organization of churches. It was operated by the American Board of Commissioners for Foreign Missions (commonly referred to as the ABCFM) until 1860, when the Islands were given autonomy in church matters. The Hawaiian Board of Missions came into being at this time and continued as the directive influence in Hawaiian Evangelical Association affairs until 1952, when a complete re-organization combined the Hawaiian Board of Missions with the Evangelical Association under a new charter in which the name was spelled out as the Hawaiian Evangelical Association of Congregational Christian Churches.* Despite the fact that the ABCFM handed control of the religious work to the Hawaiian Board of Missions, the local people frequently returned to the mother board for assistance. One of these calls had to do with recommending a pastor to direct a newly opened native pastor training school, "The North Pacific Missionary Institute."

This missionary training center was started as the Theological School at Wailuku, Maui, in 1863 under the charge of Reverend W. P. Alexander. In 1870 he visited the Marquesas Islands, causing the temporary discontinuance of the school. In 1872 the buildings of the U. S. Marine Hospital, 56 Punchbowl Street, Honolulu, were purchased and refitted at the instance of Dr. G. P. Judd as the Theological Seminary. The highly respected Reverend J. D. Paris was appointed head. He resigned two years later, and the American Board in Boston was invited to suggest a younger man to lead the enterprise. After one false start the Board designated "as the head of this school of the Prophets," Reverend C. M. Hyde, D. D.† of Haverhill, Massachusetts. The institution was rechristened the "North Pacific Missionary Institute" upon the arrival of Hyde in 1877. In the *Friend* for September, 1889, is this news item:

Hon. C. R. Bishop previous to his return [he had been on a trip to San Francisco and New York and had returned August 23], remitted a donation of $1,000 to Dr. Hyde to be applied towards the proposed new building for the North Pacific Mission [ary] Institute. . . . We think that other liberal friends will be glad to imitate Mr. Bishop's example.

He also gave another $1000 to the building fund in 1890, $100 to the general fund in 1889, and $200 to that same purpose in 1891. A specific reference to a maximum of one third of the income from the $20,000 awarded to the Hawaiian Evangelical Association by the provisions of the Charles R. Bishop Trust to be allocated to the North Pacific Missionary Institute's operation was a reflection of Bishop's high regard for Hyde. The Third Section of the Trust deed defines the appropriation:

To the Board of Hawaiian Evangelical Association aforesaid, for the use of said Evangelical Association, the sum of Twenty Thousand Dollars said amount to be securely invested, and the income therefrom to be applied to Home Missionary objects, Hawaiian, Chinese and others; in which said Association may be interested, and including aid to the North Pacific Missionary Institute in said Honolulu.

* Now the Hawaii Conference of the United Church of Christ.
† See p. 54.

Not more than one-third of the net income to said Twenty Thousand Dollars shall, however, be used for the last named object.

Shortly after Hyde's death, Bishop wrote to Uldrick Thompson, principal of The Kamehameha School for Boys. The letter was dated December 12, 1900:

I hope that the idea of grafting the North Pacific Institute onto the Kamehameha Schools will not be favorably entertained by the Trustees of the Estate. This is my first thought and I believe that the first thought on such a suggestion is usually the most correct. The students in the Institute are mature *men,* and most of them, if not all, are *married.* There is no place there for the family of a student. Of what denomination would the Professor in Theology be? Although Protestant is the control Kamehameha is not denominational.

The Hawaiian Evangelical Association was, in effect, a "holding corporation" for all aspects of the work of the Congregational Church in the Kingdom. The North Pacific Missionary Institute was a constituent member. But the Association's outreach also included Mills Institute, Kawaiahao Seminary, Makawao and Maunaolu Female Seminaries, the work with the lepers at Kalaupapa, and a dozen other enterprises. Bishop was readily sympathetic and agreeable to the idea of substantial support to one organization which coordinated the work of so many of his interests. Before the systematic authorizations contained in the provisions of his Trust deed, he had given the following amounts to the Association's general fund: $500 in 1891, $300 in 1892, and $300 in 1893. In this last year he made a capital fund donation of $10,000. His benefactions ultimately totalled $35,000.

HAWAIIAN MISSION CHILDREN'S SOCIETY

IN THE MINUTE BOOK of the Hawaiian Mission Children's Society, or "Cousins" Society, there is this entry, April 9, 1910:

It was moved by R. W. Andrews, seconded by Mary Green Wilcox [Mrs. Henry] that Hon. C. R. Bishop be made an honorary member of this Society. It was thought, that inasmuch as Mr. Bishop had done so much for the Hawaiians, and so much for the Cousins through gifts to Punahou, it was an honor to the Society to make him a member. The motion was passed unanimously and F. W. Damon selected to make the announcement.

Thus belatedly—Bishop was 88 years old—the "Cousins" Society acknowledged a debt of community honor. That the gesture was acceptable we know from two letters of acknowledgment, one to Mrs. Phillip H. Weaver, May 5, 1910:

I have long been envious of those members of the Society who are not to the manner born, because from the first arrival of my dear friend Lee and myself at Honolulu the missionary families took us into their homes with confidence and treated us as friends, which we on better acquaintance became and continued to be.

You know of my dear wife's intimate and confidential relations with the missionaries, which should have perhaps won her also an honorary membership.

The other was addressed to Mrs. R. W. Andrews, Secretary of the Hawaiian Mission Children's Society, and was dated a few days later:

Your letter of April 30th informing me of my election as an Honorary Member of the Mission Children's Society came to me . . . and I am pleased by this act of courtesy and regard on the part of the members of the Society.

From the date of my first arrival in Honolulu until now the American Missionaries in Hawaii and their children have been my constant and highly appreciated friends, and my respect for those living and honor for those who have departed does not diminish by the passing of time.

Yours respectfully, "A Cousin"
[signed]   Chas. R. Bishop

[In handwriting]
Please excuse type,
used to favor weak
eyes.   C. R. B.

It was his pleasure to acknowledge receipt of the annual reports of the Society, and he did so each of the years that remained to him. He cherished his honorary membership in the "Cousins" Society as a greater tribute perhaps than any other that could have been paid to him. He was never actually eligible for regular membership, nor was Mrs. Bishop, and yet both of them were close, cordial contemporaries of the "Cousins" throughout their lives. We can share his feeling of wistfulness as he speaks of his wife's intimate acquaintance with the missionaries and that perhaps she might also have through that acquaintance won herself honorary membership. He regarded the Society with great affection. It graciously brightened his twilight days with a gentle candle of recognition. The Hawaiian Mission Children's Society was founded in 1852 with eligibility for membership limited to descendants and consorts of descendants who have been members of the American Protestant Mission of these Islands. Honorary and "adopted" memberships have been granted by the Society to a very few individuals over a period of years.

YOUNG MEN'S CHRISTIAN ASSOCIATION

THE HONOLULU YMCA is a time-honored community enterprise in the Hawaiian Islands. The date of its founding was April 30, 1869, which means it was launched in Hawaii but a very few years after the national movement reached the United States from London. The names of Sanford Ballard Dole, P. C. Jones, T. Rainwater, and a "committee of seven friends," are on the charter. Bishop's name was not included in the original list of members, but he was to be associated with the YMCA movement in a variety of relationships over the next twenty-five years.

He was an officer of the Board of Directors of the Sailors' Home of Honolulu when a committee from the newly organized YMCA called to request permission to "take charge of and have control of the Men's Reading Room for one year." This was recorded in the Minute Book of the YMCA in June 25, 1869. The Sailors' Home became the permanent headquarters of the YMCA for the next fourteen years. The minutes of the YMCA Board of Directors on September 15, 1881, show that a building fund campaign for $15,000 realized $21,068.45, and a lot at Hotel and Alakea Streets was purchased. Here or across the street the YMCA's Central Branch was located in one building or another until World War II. When the list of donors was printed Bishop's name was down for $750. At a meeting of the Board of Directors, held on March 15, 1883, he was honored with a life membership in the Honolulu YMCA.

Years later, the Honolulu YMCA undertook a program of adult education and sponsored the operation of night schools in the city of Honolulu. The operation was the forerunner of the present program of adult education carried on by the Department of Education. Bishop had left the Islands in 1894; but through the measures provided in his Charles R. Bishop Trust considerable leeway was allowed in applying monies to organized community needs, and funds were made available for night school work. Beginning in 1895, and continuing for eight years, sums ranging from $500 to $1250 were made, totalling in all $5750. This pioneer effort was not massive; but it was substantial for its day, and it started something in the field of educational endeavor which was to prove of deep and lasting significance to the culture and economy of Hawaii. This was to be especially true in the successful assimilation of the polyglot migration waves that were to wash upon Hawaii's hospitable shores.

The regular work of the YMCA also received assistance at the hands of the Trustees of the Charles R. Bishop Trust. The sum of $5000 was paid to C. H. Atherton for the capital account of the YMCA, and $150 to $450 was paid annually for the years 1895–1900 inclusive, for a total of $1650.

Meanwhile, the Chinese work which had received the sincere, devoted energy of Mr. and Mrs. Francis W. Damon also included the launching of a Chinese YMCA. This was in 1886, and Bishop made personal annual donations to the support of it. From 1886 through 1894 he contributed $50 or $100 for each year's budget, and in 1888 and 1894 he gave $500 towards the building fund. The total of this giving reached $1500.

Were all the known benefactions to be totalled, the figure would probably reach about $15,000. This is not a large sum even in terms of the value of the dollar in those days, but the security and confidence that Bishop's contributions gave to the YMCA served to strengthen the movement.

SAILORS' HOME OF HONOLULU

In the 1840's and 1850's the hunt for whales in the vast ranges of the North and South Pacific caused the whalers to headquarter in

Hawaii. The business of outfitting whaling vessels and handling financial problems of the shipowners was a community stimulant, and all agencies of commerce and communication prospered. Disgorging entire rosters of seamen "upon the town" posed grave questions for the city fathers; one primarily was that of recreation. Certain Honolulu citizens, through the medium of a series of temperance meetings, studied the sailors' troublesome situation. Early references to these preliminary talks are contained in the diary of Amos Starr Cooke:

Fri. Nov 3 1854. Last evening we had a good temperance meeting . . . talked some of a Sailors' Home. Bro. Castle proposes that we give in lumber etc towards it $1000.

Mon Nov 13: . . . Adjourned [Temperance] had a meeting about a Sailors' Home. Voted to call a meeting, Monday evening to organize some society to build a Sailors' Home.

Wed. Nov 15: Monday evening had a meeting at Chapel about Sailors' Home. Chose a com. of six to draw plans etc.

Thurs Nov 23: Past evening adopted a constitution and elected a board of 18. Monday the Privy Council granted the land *makai* of the Chapel for a Sailors' Home provided $5000 are raised in 12 months & no rum is sold in the premises, no bad women kept there & no gambling allowed. If so the land is to revert to the Govt.

November 21, 1854, a Reading Room and Boarding Home for Sailors and a Book Bible Tract Depository were open for business. Elisha H. Allen was its first president. The board consisting of S. N. Castle, H. M. Whitney, and J. T. Waterhouse obtained premises at the intersection of Bethel and Merchant Streets. Construction immediately got under way with completion marked by the opening of the Home on September 1, 1856. Bishop initially had no official role to play in the Sailors' Home. His firm, Aldrich and Bishop, contributed $500 to the first fund drive. The location was thought particularly strategic since the Home would be the first object in a sailor's range of vision upon leaving his ship. The grogshops and places of related entertainment were more "uptown." Mr. and Mrs. Thrum * presided over the 75-bed original home.

Bishop was selected treasurer of the new Board of the Sailors' Home in 1856, the year the Home was completed. Kamehameha IV was the Home President, and his close friend William L. Lee, Vice-President. In 1855, a Royal Patent No. 1893 was issued to the

---

* They were the parents of Thomas G. Thrum who published January 1, 1875, the first in his highly regarded series of *Thrum's Hawaiian Annuals.*

Sailor's Home Society for the purpose of ". . . improving social, moral and religious conditions of seamen resorting in the port." The patent was signed by Kamehameha IV and the seal bore the imprint of Kaahumanu. Bishop continued as treasurer for 35 years. In 1886 and each year thereafter through 1895 he was elected to the presidency of the Home. He was a Trustee for many three-year periods during the forty years. His donations in money and materials were not large. One year he gave five gallons of paint, and one hundred dollars another year. He joined with other officers and board members in making up annual deficits in the operating budget.

The fire of April 18, 1886 interrupted the Home's services. The fire was so dangerous that the fire fighters attempted dynamiting the already fire-gutted Sailors' Home with gunpowder to set up a fire break. That failed but the Home was destroyed. The seamen who needed a home were to be without such facilities for nine years.

An indenture dated September 30, 1886, was agreed to among Walter M. Gibson, Minister of the Interior, and Charles R. Bishop, President, and John M. Paty, Treasurer, Honolulu Sailors' Home Society:

Whereas, December 13, 1855, Kamehameha IV granted Elisha H. Allen and others by Royal Patent No. 1893 a piece of land at the northerly angle of Merchant Street and Bethel Street. . . .
They held this on a reversionary to the Kingdom basis. Now, if the Sailors' Home Society will raise $5,000 in five years and will agree to build a certain quality building the government will match this amount.

The proposal included an exchange of land. The new site was at the corner of Alakea and Halekauwila Streets. On March 27, 1890, Royal Patent No. 3474 was issued:

No intoxicating liquors shall be drunk on the premises, no woman of lewd character admitted, no gaming allowed, nor other disorder tolerated. . . . open to sailors of all governments including the Hawaiian Kingdom. The patent is allowed with a reversionary interest to the Kingdom if the property ceases to be used for a Sailors' Home. Permission to lease unneeded portions of the property and applying the avails to the operation of the home is included. . . .

[signed]   Kalakaua Rex

The second building was finished in 1896, and in that building-fund drive, with the $5000 nest egg from the government, the community raised an additional $19,000. Bishop contributed $3000.

The Sailors' Home was merged with the Seamen's Institute in 1907 and has carried the latter name ever since. In 1963, the building was razed to make way for a multi-story business structure but with certain of the lower floors reserved for the purposes of the Seamen's Institute.

AMERICAN RELIEF FUND

THE PACIFIC COMMERCIAL ADVERTISER, on February 27, 1864, reported on the newly organized American Relief Fund Association:

Organized for needy Americans who have no claim on the United States or Queens Hospital, resided here for one year and have been employed here and are not strangers. 100 names pledged to contribute one dollar per month to the American Relief Fund Association.

Bishop subscribed to the Association and became a founding member at this time. In a meeting of the members in 1865 the name was changed to the American Benevolent Fund.

The collector of dues must have attended rather tardily to his work, for there is an entry in the record dated February 28, 1868, that Bishop paid back dues for 48 months in the sum of $48. There must have been some apprehension about the condition of the books, since the membership elected him treasurer in 1871. In 1875 he was made secretary-treasurer, a post he held until 1893. He was elected President for 1894–1895, an honorary gesture since at the time of the election he was concluding his residence in Hawaii.

This benefit society ultimately adopted the name American Relief Fund. It was one of several which had been organized to supply a much needed type of welfare assistance to nationals temporarily in straitened circumstances. There was already a flourishing British Aid Society. There was another for the German citizens. It was therefore a natural sequence to organize an aid society for citizens of the United States.

The good that the American Relief Fund accomplished cannot be measured easily in dollars or otherwise, as no benefit work ever speaks fully of the energy and devotion of the leaders or the improvement in morals and welfare of those assisted. But this modest American agency expended about $6000 a year in assistance over a span of thirty-five years. One of the strongest assets it possessed in preserving its regular monthly dues-paying membership and program of giving was the presence of Bishop on the board of officers. And yet he had his qualms about its effectiveness. Rather fretfully he wrote to C. M. Hyde, January 15, 1897:

. . . I am puzzled to know for what reason the Trustees request me to increase the gift to the American Relief Fund so largely. For many years I have worked hard to get Americans to give one dollar a month to that fund.

Even at that he had been more than generous. He authorized eight annual payments of $300 each, beginning in 1895. After a total of $1450 had been paid to the Fund by 1899, the annual giving was stopped; and a final capital sum of $3000 was transmitted to the treasurer. Thus, through the Charles R. Bishop Trust a total sum of $4450 was paid in over and beyond his regular monthly dues and the rather substantial contribution in services over almost a third of a century.

Emma Kaleleonalani was the Queen Consort of Kamehameha IV and a granddaughter of John Young. She was born January 2, 1836, and died April 24, 1885. She was noted in Hawaiian history as a co-founder of the Queen's Hospital.

Bishop Home for Girls at Kalaupapa, Island of Molokai. Erected by Bishop to house young girl patients. The Order of the Sisters of St. Francis was invited by Bishop to staff the Home.

Upper: Dormitory.
Center left: Recreation hall.
Center right: Storeroom and kitchen.
Lower: Sisters' cottage.
Photographs by courtesy of Lawrence
McCully Judd.

9

Compassion

QUEEN'S HOSPITAL

OCCASIONALLY, AMONG THE community enterprises supported by Bishop there would be numbered those which were destined to undergo such complete transformation over the years as to be scarcely recognizable now. Indeed, in some instances they may have languished and passed out of existence. It was not to be so with the hospitals. The distinguishing features and purposes of each of the four major hospitals which orginally held a Bishop interest are virtually unchanged today.

The hospital story in Hawaii commences with a parade of sporadic and small scale, private citizen attempts at providing nursing care and some bed facilities, chiefly during the 1840's and 1850's. The natives were faced with decimation from the onslaught of "foreign" diseases and their culminations in major epidemics. Also, the continuous inbound migration of nationals from countries all over the globe was accompanied by strongly varied expressions of need for hospitalization in keeping with familiar and traditional practices in the countries of origin. The clamor grew in the 1850's, and after several false starts Queen Emma took up the challenge.

In the early months of 1859, the Legislature, prodded by Queen Emma, passed a hospital enabling act. The amount of $5000 was to be acquired by the corporation authorized in the act, and $5000 of government lands was to be conveyed as a matching contribution. Kamehameha IV signed the bill on April 20, 1859, and immediately set out with Queen Emma to raise the subscription needed. *The Nupepe Kuokoa* wrote sentimentally after the passing of Kamehameha IV:

. . . We remember the King, walking alone on the streets, unattended by chiefs or guards, going from house to house with book in hand. His eyes brightened to see the warm response. His heart rejoiced in knowing he could build a refuge for those of his people who were stricken with disease and poverty. He would say, "Allow me the honor of writing your name down, with any amount you wish to contribute."

The Amos Starr Cooke diary contains a reference in May 25, 1859, which resembles the modern fund raising procedure:

At 10½ o'clk the King summoned the contributors to the Hospital Fund at the Courthouse where many resolutions were passed & a committee of ten: Snow, Damon, Castle, Bishop, Austin, Hall, Waterhouse, Aldrich, Capt. Green, and Hackfeld (appointed to assist).

While Kamehameha IV was out on his "walks," his Queen Consort, Emma, was holding soirees and benefits and attracting throngs of charity minded customers. Bishop had given $100 as his personal subscription to the original "walk" drive of Kamehameha IV (Mrs. Bishop is also on that first list for $50). The two royal rulers raised $13,150.73, and the hospital opened for business with the "poor sick" Hawaiians in August, 1859.

The cornerstone for the first permanent building was laid in 1860, on July 17, by Kamehameha IV in full Masonic ceremony. The earliest entry in the Minute Book of the Trustees of the Queen's Hospital describes the Privy Council resolution declaring Kamehameha IV "elected and declared perpetual President," the constituting of the ten people representing the government, and the ten representing the subscribers—the body politic—as the Board of Trustees. Shortly after Bishop's elevation to the House of Nobles, another legislative reference concerning him is found in the Minute Book of that body, June 20, 1860. This was but a few days before the ceremony of the cornerstone laying:

A message was recieved [*sic*] from the Representatives [House of] transmitting a Bill passed by them, entitled "An Act in Aid of Queen's Hospital Corporation." The Bill was read a first and a second time and referred to a select committee consisting of Messrs. Gregg, Bishop and Armstrong.

A meeting of the ten government members was convened June 4, 1859. Bishop was selected by lot, for a two-year term, as one of the ten subscriber members of the Trustee group on June 29. The newly created full board had its first meeting the next day. Bishop was elected Treasurer, a position to which he was re-elected for successive two-year terms until his voluntary resignation upon the eve of his trip to the United States and Europe with Mrs. Bishop, 1875–1876. He was elected and re-elected Trustee without interruption through 1893. An attempt at resignation in 1891 failed when his letter of resignation written on a trip to San Francisco was not accepted. Despite the obvious fact that he would not be available much longer, the Trustees went to the other extreme and re-elected him Chairman of the Executive Committee and the Regent re-appointed him as Vice-President. He had been placed on the Executive Committee, April 4, 1863, and made Chairman, December 6, 1878. He retained the chairmanship until just prior to his move to California.

The Trusteeship was the basis of his positions as treasurer and executive committee member and chairman. It was also the basis of the call to another significant portfolio—the vice-presidency of the Hospital. His close friend Elisha H. Allen had long held that appointment. He was followed by Charles C. Harris who passed away in 1881. Whenever the Vice-President was absent, Bishop usually acted as chairman; and it was logical that he be appointed as permanent chairman upon the decease of Harris. Accordingly the Minute Book on July 15, 1881, reads:

Her Royal Highness the Princess Regent * was pleased to appoint the Honorable Chas. R. Bishop Vice President of the Queen's Hospital for the term of two years.

He was re-appointed successively for two-year terms through 1893. Thus, through the trusteeship covering thirty-four years he served variously as treasurer, member and Chairman of the Executive Committee, and Vice-president. He was valuable in both policy and finance.

Bishop participated in many committee assignments. Some of them were definitely routine, as in the case of the visiting committee. But some of the special assignments carried interesting meaning. He conferred with the consuls of the many nations represented by nationals in the kingdom, regarding the admittance of seamen to the hospital. Should people with measles be admitted? What about an insane asylum on the grounds? Were foreign women to be admitted? What about South Sea Islanders? What policy should be adopted when Hawaiians entering as patients insisted upon having their relatives and friends share the hospital room with them? He was

* Her Royal Highness the Princess Liliuokalani, proclaimed Heir Apparent to the Throne, April 11, 1877.

insistent that the specific purposes of the Hospital be carried out and the quality of care be maintained with the highest of standards. He was stirred one time by a rumor that lepers were being treated there. All his Hawaii life he had been apprehensive about lepers and had provided special means for their treatment and would not tolerate mixing the housing and treatment of such patients with the others. Years after he had left permanently for California, he wrote to A. Cleghorn:

The Queen's Hospital has strong claims upon the government and people for more generous support. It was never intended to be an Alms House nor a hospital for infectious or incurable diseases—as you know.

Bishop's contributions in dollars were significant. At the September 14, 1878, meeting he offered a motion to set $5000 as the endowment price of a hospital bed and later proceeded to endow his first bed with that sum of money. In the Trustees' Minute Book there is this entry, March 9, 1891:

The Secretary, Mr. F. A. Schaefer read a letter from the Hon. S. M. Damon, stating that he had received instructions from Hon. C. R. Bishop, to place at the disposal of the trustees the sum of $5000 for the perpetual maintenance of a bed at the hospital, under the rules, at the disposition of the President of the Stranger's Friend Society, so long as that organization is in existence and to be known as the "Bishop" bed.

The Hospital is the beneficiary of Paragraph D in the Third Section of the Charles R. Bishop Trust deed. He required the Trust to pay "To the Queen's Hospital, maintained and carried on at said Honolulu, the sum of $1000." This payment was made in each of eight years, but more beds and a nurses' cottage were provided too:

. . . to Queen's Hospital in said Honolulu, for the purchase, furnishing and perpetual support of three (3) beds, each to be known and designated as "Bishop Bed" and provided also that not more than one of these beds shall be kept in the same room, and that they shall always be a superior quality in all respects, though plain and strong, the sum of $18,000.

To the said Queen's Hospital, for Nurses' Cottage and other uses, within the discretion of the Trustees of said Hospital, the further sum of $35,000.

He made many contributions including a Bishop wing. In a Hospital Trustees' meeting, April 23, 1903, mention was made of a grant of $20,000 from the Charles R. Bishop Trust to "enable the Trustees to proceed with the building of the intended wing. . . ." Shortly thereafter the $35,000 mentioned above was paid over for another addition which on April 20, 1905, was officially named the Pauahi Annex in memory of Mrs. Bishop. This Pauahi Wing, as it came to be called, was opened June 23, 1905, and was the occasion for a bit of sentimental homage. Mrs. William F. Allen and Mr. E. Faxon Bishop commissioned an artist by the name of Duesbury to paint a portrait of Bishop for presentation to the Hospital. This gift is recorded in the Hospital Trustees' Minutes of July 27, 1905:

The Secretary read a letter from Mrs. Wm. F. Allen accompanying the presentation on behalf of herself and Mr. E. Faxon Bishop, to the Queen's Hospital of a portrait of the Hon. C. R. Bishop.

While the total of Bishop's hospital charity can probably never be accurately established, he must have given well in excess of $100,000 in various forms. He was a chief benefactor of Queen's Hospital in his financial gifts. One sidelight on his standing in the community is noted in a plea for funds for Queen's Hospital which appeared in the *Friend*, January 1, 1862, and he had scarcely started his way up the financial ladder:

. . . Should you have any scruples about passing over your contributions [for Queen's Hospital] to the pastors of churches, bear in mind that Mr. Bishop is Treasurer of the Queen's Hospital.

Kamehameha IV eloquently, and in simple sincerity, stated an eternal code of obligation for all of the citizens of Hawaii when in the dedication speech at the Masonic cornerstone laying in 1860 he said in part:

Charities like taxes for the commonwealth, have to be met from time to time. There is no commuting for a given sum, and claiming exemption for all time to come.

You give according to your means for the time being. When the next call comes, your capabilities may be greater or less, and according to your capabilities you will settle with your conscience.

There is something wholesome in being called upon from time to time to acknowledge, however strong our own health may be and however prosperous our fortunes, that—after all—the sick and the destitute are our brothers and sisters. . . . This it is that makes us human, and members of the human family.

There was an appeal in these profound words of the Hawaiian regent that burned itself unforgettably into the mind of Charles Reed Bishop.

THE OTHER HOSPITALS

Kauikeolani Children's Hospital

KAUIKEOLANI CHILDREN'S HOSPITAL was opened in 1909 after a private subscription campaign was successfully completed in 1907 and 1908. Albert S. Wilcox of Kauai was largely instrumental in the fund-raising campaign and had the assistance and support of his sister-in-law, Mrs. Elizabeth Napoleon Low, and Messrs. Sanford B. Dole and William Owen Smith. The given name of Mrs. Wilcox was Kauikeolani, and this name was subsequently selected as most appropriate for use in the official name of the new children's hospital. A small pamphlet or brochure describing the proposed hospital was printed with a date line on November 2, 1907. It was in the nature of a prospectus with letters of support from Sanford B. Dole, Albert S. Wilcox, and officials of the Hawaii Territory Medical Society.*

On April 21, 1908, Bishop having seen this, offered to give $5000 to the Children's Hospital if the committee working on the financial campaign would raise another $9000. A letter arrived shortly thereafter from Dole acknowledging the offer with an explanation of the timing of the committee's plans. This called for a reply, and he wrote Dole on June 6:

Mr. A. S. Wilcox is right in requiring a pledge of a considerable endorsement of the Hospital before any building is erected. He and his brother George are sensible men, and know that the continuous maintenance will be more difficult than the beginning of the good work.

The Hospital realized over $100,000, of which more than half was contributed by A. S. Wilcox. The descriptive qualifying masthead statement contained in the Wilcox booklet was to this effect: "to establish a children's hospital open to children of all nationalities and races, but preference shall always be given to needy children of native Hawaiian parentage." This phraseology likely attracted Bish-

* The prospectus probably refers to the Hawaii Medical Society. The Hawaiian Territorial Medical Society was organized in 1926.

op's attention. Throughout the changing years this flourishing Hospital has become an accredited open Hospital with no other restriction except that of admission being limited to children whose ages range from the newborn through sixteen years. Bishop at one point suggested that this Hospital be incorporated as a ward in the Queen's Hospital structure. A negative reply was immediately forthcoming on that idea.

Kapiolani Maternity Home

Kapiolani, wife of Kalakaua, was the real founder of the Kapiolani Home of the Hoolu Lahui Society, which was started for the purpose "of providing a maternity home where Hawaiian women can receive proper care and treatment during the period of childbirth, and for such other benevolent and charitable purposes as may be consistent with the maintenance of such Maternity Home." The founding date was June, 1890.

The original Home was located at the corner of Beretania and Makiki Streets; here was a piece of property which had belonged to Princess Kekaulike Kinoiki, sister of Kapiolani. It was familiar enough to Kapiolani since it had been her home for many years. Prince Kuhio ultimately gave the property (he was chairman of the Trustees of the Kapiolani Estate) to the Hospital for $1.00.

Bishop found an agreeable theme in the statement of purposes of the Maternity Home. His Charles R. Bishop Trust authorized annual payments, 1895 through 1900, of $150 to $450 each. The total came to $1650. He climaxed the annual giving through his Trust deed with a final contribution of $5000 which was paid over to Mrs. Flora E. Jones on January 21, 1901.

An interesting sidelight on Hawaiian life and customs turns up in a letter to C. M. Hyde, February 11, 1897:

You speak of the Maternity Home, but do not say what the Trustees have recommended regarding it. I have no doubt but that it is a good institution, and that its advantages should be availed of in many cases, but it cannot be and should not be generally. The most important thing for Hawaiians or for any other people is to teach them to rely upon themselves, to help themselves as much as possible. But few of the girls can go to boarding schools, and less of the women can go to Maternity Homes. Those old Mothers' Meetings, as they were called, that used to be held by the Missionary women years ago were helpful to the young native wives, and there needs to be something to take their place, partly perhaps by an organization of the more intelligent of the native women, assisted by their white friends. . . .

Leahi Hospital

The Honolulu celebrants of Queen Victoria's Jubilee in 1897 decided to establish a hospital "for the care and treatment of persons suffering from incurable diseases except leprosy and for the relief of those excluded from other hospitals." This was largely social talk until the devastating bubonic plague swept Honolulu in 1899. The fires which the authorities started deliberately to clean up premises got out of hand and many chronic invalids were left homeless. This emergency energized the Jubilee hospital proponents, and they organized the Victoria Hospital. The main building which became the real hospital facility, was the old kerosene warehouse at Queen and South Streets. The Hospital changed names frequently in its early days. The second name was the Honolulu Home for Incurables, the next was Leahi Home, and today it is known as Leahi Hospital.

Forty-eight subscribers were listed on the original roster of donors, and among them was Bishop. He made a personal contribution of $5000, recorded in the hospital board Minutes for August 14, 1901. This Hospital meant much to the native Hawaiians for they were susceptible to tuberculosis; and Leahi was tending to specialize in treatment of that disease. He wrote another $5000 into his Will, and this is recorded not only in the Will but also in the Hospital Minutes, November 16, 1915.

SICKNESS AND DISEASE

For one whose medical history reveals a singular immunity to sickness and disease, Bishop displayed an unusual concern for the health problems of the peoples of Hawaii. His references to his own personal illnesses are encountered regularly in his letters, but none of them could be considered serious or permanent. And his passing at the age of ninety-three was ascribed to a final natural wearing out of his physical body. As regards his personal illness, the record is replete with minor complaints. In his January 7, 1874, letter to Elisha Allen, he writes:

I have been poorly lately, and would resign immediately upon the King's return, only that I fear it might lead to several others taking the same step, and I am not willing to do an unpatriotic thing.

Lunalilo was desperately ill in Kona and returned to Honolulu to an unsettled government and his death-bed shortly after this letter was written. To R. W. Meyer, March 12, 1888, Bishop complained:

For some time back I have been poorly, having some fever and lacking appetite. Last Friday Mr. Damon and I drove to Waialua and retd. on Saturday, and I am the better for the change.

This was his first mention of his physical condition since 1874. But references continued to appear, although still scattered over the years. He was also reacting to the climate and regretted in a letter to Meyer on November 17, 1890: ". . . I am sorry to go away without seeing you, but it is late in the year for going to a cooler climate, and I should no longer delay my going." To J. O. Carter, January 9, 1895, there is a reference to his only serious infirmity: "I have had two terms of diarrhea which pulled me down some, but am pretty well now and picking up again."

There was an increasing tendency in Bishop's later years toward slight physical impairments which was undoubtedly the reason, or one of them, that he never returned to Honolulu. Excerpts from letters over the years describe a pattern of minor ailments:

February 10, 1898:
It would give me very great pleasure to spend a few weeks or days in visiting the Kam Schools, the Museum and other places in and about Honolulu, but I can hardly hope to have that satisfaction. I am an exceedingly bad sailor and have many engagements here, and (between ourselves) I have a chronic disability which makes a voyage almost an impossibility or at the least very inconvenient.

March 22, 1901:
Were it probable that good health and strength would hold out, I should like to live ten years more, or long enough to see results of the teaching at Kam Schools. . . .

February 9, 1907:
I thank you and Mrs. Griffith for your congratulations on the eighty-fifth anniversary of my birth, and am able to report myself in fairly

good health, and not strong. I think that I am having my full share of "labor" if not of "sorrow."

May 6, 1909:

My general health is fairly good, but I am sorry to say that my sight has become so defective that I have to avoid much reading or writing.

June 6, 1910:

It is an uncommon thing for me to write so much with my own hand, for trouble with my eyes has prevented.

These references indicate the general freedom Bishop enjoyed from physical and nervous disorders. But the same could not be said of the health of his beloved Hawaii. The Kingdom's susceptibility to epidemic was high, and the epidemics when they came were decimating in effect. A list of them would include these: 1848, measles; 1853, small pox; 1872, small pox; 1881, small pox; 1895, cholera; 1899, cholera.

We find no comment by Bishop regarding the 1848 measles scare. This was an eventful year. It was not only the year of the Great Mahele; but also California's gold rush was under way and had created a great demand for Hawaii's produce. It is believed that the measles were introduced possibly by passengers or crew members aboard the American frigate *Independence* out of San Francisco. One-tenth of the population succumbed to the disease. Bishop was an eye-witness to this tragedy and was never to free himself completely of an involuntary and real concern for the casualties in human life and property caused by the ravage of disease.

In 1853, small pox struck. One third of the 6500 cases were fatalities. Happily, however, Bishop could write to J. Turrill, October 7:

. . . The small pox has so far disappeared from Honolulu and vicinity that the whalers and other vessels do not hesitate to come into port at once. We have had a sad time, as you have seen by the papers, and there is still a good deal of the disease in the country districts of this island. . . .

* * * * * * *

The Hawaiians called this small pox, *"ma'i pu'upu'u li'ili'i."* There was small pox in San Francisco at this time, but how it may have been transmitted to the islands is not known.

It was this epidemic which shaped Kamehameha IV's thinking about a hospital. His first message to the Legislature in 1855 reflected his settled purpose, and the first step was taken through his joint venture with Queen Emma in raising funds personally to start

Queen's Hospital. Bishop needed no urging to become associated with support of the institution. Small pox hit again in 1872 and once more in 1881. The introduction of the 1872 epidemic was blamed on San Francisco, and the 1881 outbreak was laid at the door of passengers disembarking from some tramp steamers from China. The latter outbreak lasted seven months and took a dreadful toll.

It remained for cholera, "*ma'i 'oku'u*," in 1895 and again in 1899, to cause the greatest consternation. Nearly a century before, the Islands had almost been laid waste (1803–1804) by the historic plague, but the traces of that were largely erased from memory. This was, however, the first recorded plague in the history of Hawaii. Kamakau writes graphically of its dread effects. Kamehameha I almost succumbed to it on Oahu when he was organizing a war of subjugation of the last remaining territory of the Islands not under his control. Most of his chiefs and counselors died, and although he survived it was probably the loss of his leaders that almost turned victory into defeat and prevented the launching of a successful attack upon the island of Kauai.

The epidemic of 1895, probably introduced by a Chinese immigrant, was devastative; its effects were felt in many ways. Bishop wrote from San Francisco that a "missing" teacher probably had not embarked on a Honolulu-bound ship for fear of the cholera. Dr. David Starr Jordan told Bishop that cholera would keep him from the Islands that year. News which was received intermittently and irregularly and only by ship variously lifted the spirits of the worried people in San Francisco or left them disappointed and troubled. In a letter dated September 11, Theodore Richards received this word from Bishop:

It may not be so wicked to kill by frightening as it is by violence, but the effect upon the victim is very much the same. Ever since the *Manowai* arrived with the report of Asiatic cholera being in Honolulu, brought on Bd. the *Belgia,* and that eight, natives and Chinese, had died, and others were sick, we on this side have been suffering with anxiety, fear of the worst, and suspense, until today at noon when word arrived from Auckland N. Z. that there was no cholera in Honolulu when the *Mariposa* left there, and that the deaths referred to were caused by eating poison fish at a feast! Imagine the relief, to hundreds or thousands of people in this and other countries!

I thought of the students and pupils of the Kamehameha Schools, Oahu College and other schools, scattered and unable to come together, and some of them and many others exposed to the most fatal disease that could come into such a climate and condition! I have never been more thankful for any news than I have been for the message which came today. We have for two days been expecting news via Victoria B. C. and almost dreaded to receive it. . . .

Contrary to Bishop's assumption, cholera had actually hit and was cutting a solid and fearful swath through the ranks of the Kingdom's citizens.

The Kamehameha Schools' children, however, came through virtually unscathed due to sound preventive measures; but Bishop sounded a usual warning caution. To Richards, he wrote again, September 18, 1895:

. . . it is hardly possible that any more of your boys or of the girls will be able to return to school for some time to come, though from what I hear of the energetic action of the Board of Health and the assistance of the citizens, I am hopeful that the cholera may have a short run in Honolulu. In view of the good discipline at the schools and the precautions taken as to wholesome living, it seems to me unlikely that the sickness will reach either of the schools. . . .

And on October 14, a letter to Richards says:

The authorities and citizens deserve commendation for their energy, thoroughness and humanity. The cholera has been quickly "stamped out" and the poor have been cared for. . . . The report per *China* is that there has been no new case of cholera since that of the 28th ulto, and therefore I shall hope to learn per *Mariposa* that the schools are filling up and hard at work trying to make up for lost time. . . .

One more plague was to strike the Islands, this another attack of the dread cholera, in 1899. On January 29, 1900, Bishop got off a worried note to Ida M. Pope, who was heading the work at The Kamehameha School for Girls:

The Schools had made a good beginning for another year's work, and now the dreadful plague casts a deep shadow over everything in the Islands. . . . Of course your school will need to be kept *carefully* together until there is no danger in going to their homes or friends. . . .

And to William T. Brigham he wrote on February 3:

The visitation of plague is a great calamity, causing distress and damage in many ways. . . . I was under the impression that since visitation of cholera extraordinary care had been exercised by the Board of Health. Private individuals cannot control such conditions [overcrowding in residence districts]. . . . Several times during the last year or two I have suggested terminating leases and making changes and improvements on the Estate's property. . . . To burn more or less was no doubt necessary or the best way for getting rid of the sickness. . . . Prevention is better than cure. . . . When the time for cool reflection comes the sensible and responsible people will try to do those things that are reasonable and just. . . .

But the disease that was to disturb him more than any other was leprosy. Few subjects referred to in his letters exceed in sheer number the references to leprosy. The first known comment was in a letter dated April 28, 1873; the last was in a letter dated March 22, 1905. And in between there is an epic story of general concern, of the grasping at any rumored remedy, and the practical assistance to the welfare of the leper colony at Kalaupapa, the successor leper colony area to Kalawao, both on the lava plain at the foot of the vertical northside wall of Molokai.

Bishop's first statement on leprosy, made when he was Foreign Minister under Lunalilo, was contained in an official communication written to David I. Lee, M. D., in San Francisco:

I have just been informed by Dr. Hutchinson, that Dr. McGrew says that he delivered to you a Report by the College of Physicians of London to the British Government on the subject of Leprosy. If you have it among your books, you will please leave it with H. W. Severance His Majesty's Consul in San Francisco. The volume being unbound, you could easily overlook it. You will be sorry to hear that the Leprosy has spread a good deal since you were here. The sad work of separating them from the general community is being more energetically and strictly carried on than it has been heretofore.

Another official letter on August 4, 1873, was written to Henry W. Severance:

It is said that people are afraid to come here, because of the leprosy. There is really much less danger now than there was a year ago. Lepers are not allowed to be at large now, but are carefully looked after and sent to their place on Molokai. A stranger might walk on streets daily for months without seeing one, unless he chanced to meet some on the way to the asylum or to Molokai. For prudent and well conducted people there is no danger from leprosy.

In the effort to awaken people to the necessity for decided action of how they would rid the country of this awful disease, a great deal has been said and written, so much that a wrong impression has got abroad. The natives are still too indifferent to it.

And far to the west in Yedo, Japan, C. E. DeLong, U. S. Minister to Japan, had a letter from Hawaii's Foreign Minister dated October 15, which was all devoted to leprosy:

Your Excellency is doubtless aware that that awful disease, leprosy, has afflicted this nation for some years past. Those known to have the disease (about eight hundred in all) are strictly isolated and well cared for on the Island of Molokai, but no remedy is known to our physicians. Of course, His Majesty, His people and their friends, are anxious to know of, and to try if possible any true remedy that may be found.

I have taken the liberty to enclose . . . correspondence . . . from a Yedo doctor, who is said to have "opened a Leper Hospital in Naruko-machi," and whose specific method of treating leprosy has been introduced into Holland by Doctor Bandum.

If Your Excellency will be kind enough to furnish information as may be convenient for you to procure . . . you will confer a new favor upon His Majesty's Government.

Back across the world, in Europe, H. H. M's Consul, Victor Schar-berger, received a letter dated October 25:

The report of the Medical Congress which met at Vienna this year, proba-bly contains information which would be of value to this country, espe-cially those parts of the report relating to Leprosy. . . . If practicable, you will please procure such information in printed form . . . and forward same to this office.

To Monsieur Theo. Ballieu, Commissioner and Consul of France, he wrote November 13 in reply to a request for more liberal visiting privileges at the Leper settlement:

. . . The Board [of Health] had [has] so far modified its rules "as to ad-mit the visits of medical men and Ministers of Religion for exercise of the functions of their office, the special written permission of the Board of Health having been previously obtained."

This modification will, I am sure, be very gratifying to you, and to the Reverend Father [Damien], whose difficulties and wishes you have so kindly and earnestly presented. . . .

That there is an opportunity for the exercise of charity amongst the lepers at the Settlement on Molokai, I will not deny; and yet, I may truthfully claim that the provision made by the Government for the comfortable maintenance of that unfortunate class of the community is liberal; a large number of them being better provided with shelter, food and clothing than they were in their own homes; and others still having means of their own with which to add to the supplies furnished by the Government.

Leprosy may have been introduced into the Islands from China. It was sometime during the reign of Kamehameha III; but little atten-tion was paid to it, and in ten years it had spread throughout the Islands. Kamehameha V spoke of the need to combat it in his message to the Legislature in 1864. A receiving station was established in Kalihi in October, 1865, and a very short time later the Board of Health purchased the Kalawao-Kalaupapa peninsula and started the very unwelcome and misunderstood act of segregation. The patients were largely Hawaiian, and the Hawaiian Church organized a congregation in the new settlement in 1866. Father Damien arrived in 1873; and because his original reception was not of easy acceptance, recourse was had to the French consul. The letter quoted above relates Bishop's tactful assistance through his role of Foreign Minister in clearing Father Damien's approach to his chosen labor among the lepers.

Lunalilo's Board of Health pressed the matter of segregation with resulting wide criticism by the natives. About five hundred patients were taken to Molokai during the year of his reign, and this sudden massive increase in enrollment gave it the effect of a crash program. Popular charges that the settlement had been neglected were not borne out by the facts. It was this avalanche of new patients—an increase of two-thirds or more—all in a few months of 1873, that caused the critical situation which the churches, the patients, and the Board of Health righted in a reasonable time.

Bishop's thinking was reflected in a letter he sent to Geo. N. Oakley, H. H. M's Consul to Australia, January 26, 1874:

You are entirely right in your remarks upon the misleading and damaging effect of publishing so much in the English language upon the subject of leprosy. . . . In order to awaken the native part of our population to a proper sense of their duty in carrying out the laws enacted for their protection and the cure of the unfortunate lepers, it was necessary to publish strong appeals and warnings. . . .

The highest number on Molokai at any time past was 816. There are now 745 there. . . .

There is a greater necessity for separating the lepers from the general community in this country because of the reckless habits of our people. . . .

I have called Dr. Trousseau's attention to the report of Dr. Gavin McCray. Dr. T. is the physician of the Board of Health, and is very energetic in investigating.

We read nothing from his pen on leprosy for ten years. He had acquired the Molokai Ranch and had installed a reliable manager, Rudolph W. Meyer. The Board of Health needed a representative accessible to Kalaupapa. Bishop granted permission for the appointment of Meyer as agent. As a result he became acquainted with many of Meyer's problems in supervising the Kalaupapa operation.

The next several years of correspondence reflect his mounting solicitude for the welfare of the unfortunate community. The very first in the Meyer series, March 17, 1884, reflects this interest:

. . . Cannot the landing be improved at Kalaupapa without a great outlay? I know that a good wharf or landing cannot be made there. . . . It seems to me that a physician should be kept at the settlement all of the time. . . . He need not be a very skillful doctor or surgeon, but should be a kindly and sober man and might have authority for general purposes. . . . This leprosy affliction is to be a heavy tax upon this country for many years to come.

The Meyer correspondence continues:

July 7:
    I forgot to ask you about the effect of creosote pills upon the lepers.
August 6:
    What sum would be required to compensate fairly the owners (all) of land and houses within the boundaries of the Leper Settlement? Authority may be asked for to condemn the *kuleanas* etc. and take them for this Govt. use at an appraised valuation.
August 9:
    It is strange that so many untrue things should be said about the Leper settlement, the treatment of the Lepers, giving permits for people to go there etc. etc. I thank you for your reply to my inquiring about the value of the *kuleanas* etc. there.
March 16, 1885:
    I am sorry to hear that Father Damien is a leper. Trousseau says it is so. He could hardly hope to escape after so much exposure. What will those who do not admit its contagiousness say now?
May 11:
    I am glad that Mr. Gibson is to visit the settlement, . . . I think Mr. Gibson will see, if he is willing to see it, that the lepers can be supported better, more comfortably, and cheaply at the settlement than in the small premises here.
August 31:
    I have taken the liberty of giving Rev'd C. M. Hyde, D. D. a letter of introduction to you. He visits the settlement on some church business. You will find him a pleasant gentleman who takes an interest in everything Hawaiian.
September 7:
    Dr. Hyde spent one night and a part of two days at the Settlement and was made quite comfortable by Mr. Hutchinson and others. He was interested in the place, thinks very well of it for the purpose it is now used for, and would have liked to remain longer.

This was Reverend C. M. Hyde, * director of the North Pacific

* See p. 54.

Missionary Institute and the Social Science Association of Honolulu, who was one of the five original Trustees named by Mrs. C. R. Bishop in her Will establishing The Kamehameha Schools. This is also the Hyde who wrote a private letter highly critical of Father Damien to the Rev. H. B. Gage in San Francisco which by a roundabout series of coincidences reached the eyes of Robert Louis Stevenson in Sydney, Australia, and stimulated the 8000-word philippic * by the famous author. Bishop had an intimate and first hand acquaintance with the circumstances and details of the Hyde-Stevenson controversy but took no public part in it. He likewise never referred to it in correspondence although his sympathies lay with his close and trusted friend.

His interest in the Molokai Ranch was chiefly the production of cattle. He was in a difficult conflict-of-interest position because he was a member of the Legislative Assembly, and his ranch manager was an agent of the Board of Health for Kalaupapa. And yet it was his feeling that he ought to be permitted to supply beef on a competitive price basis with any other supplier, which some estrangement between him and the Board of Health seemingly prevented. In many of his letters to Meyer during this period he referred to his attempts to enter the market for the supplying of beef to Kalaupapa. He proposed to deliver the cattle at the Kalaupapa landing or at the head of the zigzag trail down the *pali* to the settlement. He could and would supply cattle at a more favorable price than any other ranch owner. His exasperation appeared in a letter to Meyer on May 31, 1886:

The Bd. of Health has violated the law in not asking for tenders for supplies, and had paid unnecessary prices for beef etc., and I shall in the Assembly ask for an explanation. Looking at my private interests only, such an action is not politic I know, but as a member of the Assembly and in the interest of the public and of honesty I shall do it.

August 23, he wrote of other settlement problems:

It is useless for me to try to prevent the extravagance of building more hospitals at Kalanui for Goto's experiments. If the priest wants it done W. M. G.† will say yes, without regard to cost or necessity. If I talk against it it will be taken as coming from you, and may only make a preju-

---

* Robert Louis Stevenson, *Father Damien, An Open Letter to the Reverend Doctor Hyde of Honolulu,* London (Chatto and Windus, 1890).
† William Murray Gibson.

dice against you. Goto is all the rage now because his patients are at least temporarily improved, and I fear and still believe that it is only temporary.

Then on October 18, he observes:

At last the legislature has closed, and its follies, which are many, are on record. Many of the appropriations for roads and other useful things will not be spent, but the money will be used for other purposes. If your Road Supervisor and others will, after the taxes are collected keep asking for some money for the *pali* † road, and if the lepers will ask for it as a means of giving them a chance to earn a little money, they may get it, or part of it. Throwing off the taxes from the lepers' horses and dogs was wrong, and I opposed it, but it was popular and passed.

But the ranch and the leper settlement seemed inextricably entwined, largely because Meyer was an overseer of both places. This is evident in a letter to Meyer, January 14, 1887:

Mr. Thurston is anxious to get some more houses built for the lepers as soon as possible. The large number of useless *Kokua* ** there is an annoyance to him and others of the Board, and just how to reduce the number is not so easy to decide. The question of supply of fuel has also to be considered. Somebody has told him that there is a good deal of dead wood on the lands of the ranch. . . . If the *dead* wood could be removed and utilized without destroying live wood or doing other damage, it might be a good thing. . . . Could you or your sons undertake to furnish any wood to the settlement, within reach of the people there, and if so, at how much per cord? Is there any place on the mountains from which wood can be floated down a stream to within reach of the settlement?

I suppose that many of the *kokua* went to the settlement with sick relations for the purpose, real or pretended, of taking care of them; and in many instances they may have been useful and a comfort to the sick; but in many instances the sick friends must have died long ago, and the reason for the *kokuas*' remaining there no longer exists, so that if in health, he or she might be cleansed and depart. . . . Could there be an overhauling and examination to see how many and who have no reason for being there any longer, preparatory to sending such away?

This leprosy question is the most important and difficult that the authorities have to deal with and requires much of common sense, patience, and tact. . . . The absence of fuel seems to have suggested to Mr. Thurston's mind some central cooking places. . . . The Board of Health should not make the mistake of letting you resign. . . . you are needed too.

March 28, 1887, he again wrote to Meyer:

† Precipice or cliff.
**Helper or comforter.

I hope it may be necessary for the members of the Bd. of Health and the doctors to go up and down your *pali* often, so that something may be done to that road.

Little was done about the narrow and steep zigzag trail down the face of the *pali* for these were the uneasy months of the shaky Kalakaua government. Needed public works were about at a standstill and Meyer as representative of the Kingdom's health department was powerless to press or persuade.

But Kalaupapa's affairs were soon to occupy Bishop's attention much more directly. He had grumbled about the Board of Health rigging the conditions for bidding on the supplying of beef to the Settlement, to the real disadvantage of his Molokai Ranch; and he had complained about the small amount of work done at the Settlement for the large and generous appropriations by the government. And yet he was but a bystander. The eyes with which he viewed Kalaupapa and the conditions of life there, were the eyes of R. W. Meyer who would write frequently reflecting his work as agent for the Board of Health.

Meyer also maintained a prolific correspondence with Father Damien and achieved an unusual awareness of the intimate problems and needs of the people. Among the letters in this correspondence is one that Father Damien wrote to Meyer, December 8, 1887. It is a long letter written in rather imperfect English, but it is eloquent in its direct appeal for help:

. . . I am truly sorry that the establishment of our good Sisters is again negatived between you and Father Leonor—as it was previous between him and Gibson—the Mother Superior write me repeatedly of the desire of the Sisters—to come with the lepers at Kalawao there seems to be mutual attachment between them—especially the females—who have been a certain time with them . . . but a few mothers such as the Franciscan Sisters of Kakaako who are anxious to come—why not—open the door for them. . . . *I wished you had spoken directly with Brother Herman about this matter, and not at all with Father Leonor, who always from the beginning off has been opposed—to their coming here.* Now Dear Mr. Meyer—that you have the action about this long desired question in your own hands—and that the *Sisters seem to be uneasy about their future stay at Kakaako and perhaps—at the Hawaiian Isl.*

Then Father Damien adds a kind of postscript which is a quotation from a letter of appeal to him from Sister Marianne:

(x this are her words) Our hearts are bleeding to see *them*, [lepers] shipped off—If it was the will of God, how much we would like to accompany them—*but our future look dark.*

Sist. Marianne

Meyer accepted the Damien appeal as a personal mission, and upon the occasion of his next business trip to Honolulu he did a bit of inquiring around town. He always stayed in a room which Bishop reserved for his frequent Honolulu visits. He started out by addressing himself directly to Bishop regarding the Damien plea. He likely talked with Lorrin A. Thurston, Minister of Interior. The seed was planted.

In a letter to Meyer, March 26, 1888, Bishop makes an initial inquiry regarding the need for specially trained nurses and suitable quarters for young, unmarried women patients:

There is talk of placing some sisters, either Catholic or English or both, at the Settlement, as nurses. And also about having an establishment there, partly a hospital I believe, to which to send women only, especially the younger and unmarried ones where they can be looked after and will be more independent of and less exposed to the men. Perhaps Mr. Thurston talked with you about it. Would you build a lot of *separate* houses for them or some larger houses divided into rooms? If you have in mind a plan, please let me know at your convenience, with an estimate of cost. . . .

April 3, he was getting down to cases and wrote Meyer:

There are nine Sisters at Kakaako who have their living and $20 per month each, which is more than I had supposed. They take care of the children in the Kapiolani Home as well as look after the lepers. Mr. Damon thinks that a good Superintendent and Assistant would cost nearly as much as the Sisters do and would not and could not do all they do. It seems a large number for that place beside the other help. If they (the Bd) reduce that establishment and send more to Molokai a part of the Sisters could go too, and if each would spend a part of her time at the Settlement the change would be good for their health.

Letting no time elapse on this newest venture he wrote to His Excellency, Minister of the Interior, Lorrin A. Thurston, April 13:

Having been told that there are a number of young women and girls at the Leper Settlement on Molokai who have no proper protection or guardians, and that it is the wish of the Government to provide such patients with houses separate from the general community of the Settlement, and to place them under the immediate care of Christian women, either Protestant or Catholic or both, I hereby request the privilege of paying for the cost of houses for the purpose above mentioned, up to the sum of five thousand dollars; the houses for the patients to be of such quality as have usually been provided there; and the house for the super-intendents to be plain and suitable for their use; all to be erected under direction of R. W. Meyer Esqr. and afterwards to be under the control of the Board of Health. I wish to have it understood, if your Excellency grants my request, that in the control and treatment of women and girls who may occupy the rooms to be provided, there shall be no interference, restrictions, or discrimination on account of their religious faith.

Lorrin Thurston immediately studied the matter and on May 21, wrote Sister Marianne, Mother Superior Franciscan Sisters, Hono-lulu:

The fact is no doubt well known to you, that one of the great hardships at the Molokai Leper Settlement, has been the lack of a proper residence for single women and girls. This difficulty seems now in a fair way to be remedied so far as the necessary buildings are concerned, through the generous offer of Hon. Charles R. Bishop, to provide a suitable residence for those who may have charge of the same.

If there are any of the members of your order, or of other orders . . . who would be willing to undertake the charge of the proposed Home the Hawaiian Government will thankfully accept of their assistance. . . .

On June 2, Bishop described the start of real action to Meyer:

The carpenter, Mr. Wallace . . . seemed afraid to go to the settlement. . . . I told him he need take no risk of getting leprosy; that there were clean houses for himself and his men . . . but as to poi for his native carpenters, I could not say. . . .

The next week, on June 9, he wrote: "The carpenter, Wallace, refused to go to the Settlement on any terms. I have an offer from Mr. Peter High to put up the building. . . ." On June 10, he ob-served that: ". . . The Sister Superior at Kakaako favors breaking up the establishment there and sending all lepers to Molokai, and I think such will be the decision of the legislature." To Mr. A. Hutch-inson at Kalaupapa, he wrote, June 23:

Mr. Peter High and his men (carpenters) will go to the Settlement in the "Likelike" this evening, to begin erection of the house for Sisters on the lot selected for that purpose by Mr. Meyer.

Let me ask you to bear in mind that the mechanics going to the Settle-ment to do work are some of them very much afraid of the sickness. . . . Some carpenters cannot be induced to go there at all.

The Sisters were now standing by and would sail to Molokai and set up housekeeping upon the completion of his compound of build-ings. In the meanwhile, he filled the mails to Meyer with specifica-tions, costs, and plans. The original idea of two large buildings began within a few short weeks to grow into a self-contained institution complete with dormitories, dining house, kitchen, bath house, work house, privies, and a fair amount of fencing with gates and turnstiles. All buildings were to be whitewashed with lime. He took time away from the subject of building to write to Meyer that Mr. Damon had told him:

. . . The Sisters (four in all) will be ready to go to the Settlement as soon as the house is ready. . . .
   In 1872 I procured Cashew nuts for seed, through a friend in New York. . . . I think the oil has been used on lepers here some years ago. . . .

He again wrote to Meyer on August 25, 1888:

If there is a possibility that Cashew nut oil will cure or mitigate leprosy, it should be tried: and it is very strange that, if it has such virtue it should be so little known. My faith in it is weak.

On September 17, he wrote: "I had little if any doubt that Mr. High had done his work honestly and well, and am glad to have you and Father Leonore confirm it. . . ." That same day he addressed a letter to Interior Minister Thurston:

Referring to my letter of April 13 last, I now have the pleasure of informing you that the buildings which I offered to erect at the Leper Settlement are completed at a cost of $5038.61, and are now the property of the Government.

November 19, he was able to tell Meyer that things were becoming settled: "The Sister who first went up to see the house and surroundings said she was pleased; and she talked sensibly about treatment of the women who might take advantage of the home provided for them."
November 20, a bit of typical Bishop comment was made to Meyer: ". . . If the Sisters have a sensible Chaplain it will be well for all concerned. . . ."
   There was a lull in Kalaupapa talk. Father Damien died April 15, 1889, but he had lived to realize his cherished dream of a house for young women patients at the Settlement established and staffed by the Sisters of St. Francis. Although Bishop intended to build a chapel for the Bishop Home compound, it was delayed and almost overlooked; but he revived the offer himself in a letter to Meyer,

November 17, 1890: "My authorization to enlarge or build the chapel to suit the Sisters at the House remains unrevoked."

A part of the unrest of 1893, when the Provisional Government was trying its feeble legs, was a reaction to a proposal to move the lepers of Kauai to Molokai; and in a letter to W. D. Alexander, September 27, Bishop wrote:

. . . .

. . . Mr. Gay says that since the attempt to remove the lepers from Kauai to Molokai, the people on Kauai are strongly opposed to the Provisional Govt. and to anything proposed or attempted by it. Had the Gays and others at Waimea always favored sending the lepers to Molokai, as they should have done, the late trouble and loss of life might have been avoided.

Sister Marianne wrote these very friendly little notes to Meyer in three successive weeks, January 10, 17, and 23, 1896:

. . . The Chapel building is progressing nicely and is nearly under cover. I hope the other addition to the house will go up as fast, we are so crowded.

. . . with regard to the Photograph of Mr. Bishop, I shall be thankful to you if you will kindly get them for me. Yes, I would prefer to have them from Mr. Bishop or rather I would not like to have his picture without his approval.

. . . I am sure if he knew how many poor girls he has saved from immorality he would feel more than happy for having founded this, "Home." God Bless him.

Bishop remembered the request for a photograph and wrote to Meyer, May 15, 1897:

I have not forgotten the request of the good Sister Superior for my photograph, although I have not attended to it as I should have done. Please remember me to her with great respect when you see her or write to her.

Mother Superior Marianne and Bishop never met, but the reputation of each created a mutual high regard. Mother Marianne had come to Honolulu from St. Anthony's Convent of the Sisters of the Third Order of the St. Francis at Syracuse, New York, November 9, 1883, and moved on to Kalaupapa, November 14, 1888, and remained at that post until her death August 9, 1918.

Bishop kept his eye on the Settlement's welfare and was quick to warn of danger. One time, January 23, 1899, he wrote to Hyde:

The Legislature of this State [California] now in session is making an effort in Washington to have the lepers that may be in this State and I believe other States sent to Molokai. I can hardly believe that the Government of Hawaii can be in favor of such an arrangement.

A rather matter-of-fact swan song is recorded in Bishop's letter on March 22, 1905, to L. E. Pinkham, president of the Board of Health. Bishop was eighty-three years old and still very much in tune and in touch with Hawaii's problems:

Your letter dated the 11th inst. came to me yesterday, and I am pleased to know that what I have done toward improving and repairing the Bishop Home at Kalaupapa, Molokai, is fully approved. When the further repairs, for which I have provided through Messrs. Bishop & Co., Honolulu, shall have been made (very soon now) and which will cancel an item in my will, I do not intend to expend anything more there; but I hope that the Legislature, now in session, will find it possible to add whatever may be necessary, so that the good Sisters and the unfortunate women and girls under their care may be made reasonably comfortable.

No other Country that I am acquainted with has done as much as Hawaii has for the lepers within its borders.

10

Sources

HOW THE GIVING CAME TO BE

BISHOP'S DETERMINATION AND discretion utilized in money making were valuable qualities when the time came to satisfy his purposes in money giving. The origin of his systematic pattern of giving to educational, scientific, and charitable causes may be found in a little incident heretofore unrevealed. William R. Castle was walking home from a meeting with Bishop one night, and the subject of philanthropy came up. He relates that "Bishop stated, he never liked to give, and that it was only with reluctance that he made donations. However, he had recently read something of the life of George Peabody and had come to the conclusion that it was wiser and better to dispose of wealth while alive than to leave it by Will." The following quotations from the pen of George Peabody had impressed Bishop and brought him finally to adopt a systematic order of giving of his wealth:

When aches and pains came upon me, I realized I was not immortal. I became anxious to use my millions for the greatest good of humanity. I found that there were men in life just as anxious to help the poor and destitute as I was to make money. I called in friends in whom I had confidence and asked them to be trustees for my first gift. They accepted. For the first time I felt a higher pleasure and greater happiness than making money—that of giving it away for good purposes.

I have prayed my Heavenly Father day by day that I might be enabled before I died, to show my gratitude by doing some great good to my fellowmen. [This second quotation from George Peabody is inscribed on a tablet in the floor of Westminister Abbey.]

It was not only the quotations that moved Bishop; the life of George Peabody which was very familiar to him, was a remarkable parallel to his own. Both were born poor. School was over for both of them at the end of eighth grade. Both worked as clerk-bookkeepers in the general store of a relative. Both organized companies for trade. The roster of gifts by Peabody continued the remarkable parallel. A brief list would include the following:

Scholarships for the Peabody High School.

Capital funds for the Peabody Museum and Library.

Erection of the Lexington Monument.

Reconstruction of South Church.

Financing of the Kane Arctic Expedition.

Establishment of the Peabody Education Fund.

Establishment of the Peabody Normal College in Nashville.

Founding of a library at Georgetown, D. C.

Construction of a memorial church in Georgetown, D. C.

Grants to Kenyon College, Ohio.

Grants to Phillips Academy, Andover, Massachusetts.

With the Peabody story as his inspiration, it was not difficult for Bishop to recognize in Reverend Charles McEwen Hyde,* an 1877 arrival in the Islands from Massachusetts, an individual upon whom he might rely for practical advice in his unfolding program of giving.

From public problem to public solution Bishop and Hyde walked hand in hand: Social Science Association, North Pacific Missionary Institute, the leper settlement, kindergartens, YMCA work, night schools, Chinese mission, Queen's Hospital, Central Union Church, Punahou School, The Kamehameha Schools—in all of these and more the name of Charles Reed Bishop was linked in some management or financial aspect with Charles McEwen Hyde. Bishop's dependence upon his fellow townsman was particularly important in the growth of the Bishop Museum and The Kamehameha Schools. So obligated was he to Hyde in his own estimation that he wrote a warm testimonial in a book † published two years after Hyde's death:

I trust that you will permit me, one of his friends, to offer a few lines in testimony of my respect for him and my high appreciation of his work and influence in the Hawaiian Islands. He was a whole-souled missionary, a faithful friend to the Hawaiian people, and during all the years of his residence in Honolulu, he took a deep and active interest in all that concerned their moral, social and physical welfare. Much of his time, thought

---

* See p. 54.

† Harry Knight Hyde, *Charles McEwen Hyde* (Eddy Press, Ware, Mass., 1901), pp. 117–118.

and strength were given to general education and uplifting of the various races represented in the islands, and he was especially devoted to Oahu College, The Kamehameha Schools, and the North Pacific Institute [North Pacific Missionary Institute].*

It was my good fortune to be associated with him as trustee of Oahu College; of the Estate of Mrs. Bernice Pauahi Bishop; the Bernice Pauahi Bishop Museum and other trusts, and I am indebted to him for many wise suggestions and efficient aid. In the management of the schools and the museum his experience, culture and broad intelligence were of great advantage and value. He was systematic and rapid in his work, and hence, by constant application, accomplished great results.

But few had so wide an acquaintance in the islands as he had, or will be so missed now that his work is done. His name and influence are deservedly held in honor by all who knew him well and will not soon be forgotten.

Bishop's philanthropy, the greatest that the Islands have ever seen, was thus induced from the biographical sketch of a distinguished American mercantilist and attained its maturity in action and accomplishment from the personal acquaintance of a dedicated and able minister and community leader.

THE BISHOP CORRESPONDENCE

THERE ARE IN the Charles Reed Bishop research section of my library some seventeen hundred typed copies, photocopies, and originals of letters written by Bishop. With the unfortunate loss in the San Francisco earthquake and fire of the copy press books and accumulations of papers covering the years 1894 to 1906, the true extent of Bishop's correspondence will never be known. Other tragedies through insect damage, water spoilage, fire, and simple "cleaning outs" have been encountered in the attempt to turn up Bishop letters; and such losses, added to the major catastrophe at San Francisco in 1906, limit the presentation of the Bishop story.

Bishop wrote almost all of his letters in longhand. There was a period in his eighties when he had to resort to a nurse-stenographer, but he signed his letters even to the last week of his life in a firm,

* See p. 264.

clear hand. Archives of Hawaii has in the Collector General of Customs books, the Foreign Minister books (1873), and in certain special collections about 650 letters. The Bernice Pauahi Bishop Museum has about 240. In the Charles R. Bishop Trust folders there are about 75 and the Punahou School Library has 25. The First National Bank of Hawaii files contain 130 letters, and the B. P. Bishop Estate files have 80 or so. Among collections, the Mary C. Alexander collection of letters to W. D. Alexander is outstanding with 23. The Helen Wilcox Salazar Collection has 19. Valuable letters will also be found in the Joel Turrill Collection of the Hawaiian Historical Society and the Elisha H. Allen Collection in the Library of Congress. One other important and sizeable collection contains 205 letters to R. W. Meyer. There are numerous other private and personal letters, but those listed constitute the bulk of the known Bishop correspondence.

Bishop's letters seldom failed to contain advice on thrift, economy, the value of a reserve, and adherence to a contract or agreement. Integrity was a word that Bishop never employed in a letter, and yet it was the climate of integrity that characterized his correspondence. Bishop's letters as a collection do not rank with outstanding collections of letters in American literature, but their contents throw important light on the march of history within Hawaii.

THREE ARTISTS

David Howard Hitchcock

Many artists from around the world have essayed the sharp dramatics of Hawaii's cumulus clouds and volcanic mountains or have indulged in the peaceful land and seascapes of the Islands, but it took a native son to record most effectively the glowing fire pots of Kilauea or Mokuaweoweo and the pastoral scenes of Kialoa or Kuhio Bay. In so doing he was to create a demand for his paintings, from both the sentimentalist and the connoisseur, which was never to be satisfied.

David Howard Hitchcock was born in Hilo, Hawaii, on the eve of the Battle of Bull Run. He worked hard at his easel and in the late 1880's was "discovered" by Bishop, who soon realized this polite and unostentatious painter had a potential skill worth sponsoring. A Bishop sponsored salon was held by Hitchcock in the Pacific Hardware Company showroom in October, 1891. For the young student-artist, the culmination of this assistance was the fulfillment of a dream—study at the Julienne Academy in Paris. He had preceded this by a course at Oberlin College. In 1893 he exhibited in Paris, showing one of his most widely acclaimed pictures, "The Village By-Road." He attended the National Academy of Design in New York and the San Francisco School of Art. The University of Hawaii gave him an honorary master of arts degree.

When he returned from the art training in Europe and America, he opened a studio on Beretania Street near Washington Place. He painted many pictures, selling some and paying bills with others. Punahou School had his services as an instructor in art for some time beginning in 1905, and The Kamehameha Schools enjoyed him for the school year 1918–1919. At Kamehameha, his title was instructor in mechanical drawing and his pay, $1500. He was founder and first president of Kilohana Art League.

Hitchcock was very much aware of his obligation to Bishop, and we find a satisfaction of his debt in a letter addressed to the Trustees of the Bernice P. Bishop Museum, May 21, 1897:

By means of financial assistance generously given to me by the Hon. C. R. Bishop, the Founder, and one of the Trustees, of the Bernice P. Bishop Museum, I was able to study my profession under eminent Masters in the City of Paris.

Since my return, I have expressed to Mr. Bishop, my wish to acknowledge my indebtedness to him for this assistance in some tangible form, and Mr. Bishop has been good enough to say that he should prefer that I should do something for the Museum.

As an acknowledgment therefore, of the services I have received at Mr. Bishop's hands, I beg to offer you, on behalf of the Museum four of my best efforts viz. #45 Mokuaweoweo, eruption 1896, #46 Halemaumau, in 1893, #47 Halemaumau in 1894, after breakdown, #48 General view of S. end of Kilauea, 1894, and trust that these paintings, if accepted, will be a satisfactory addition to the historical value of the Museum.

P. S. For purposes of exhibition, the above paintings were suitably framed, by the Pacific Hardware Co. May I ask that this small cost be borne by the Museum?

In the roster of outstanding artists of Hawaii, Hitchcock would rank among those at the top. Bishop's faith in his artistic promise was justified by the quality and the quantity of his protégé's works.

Frederick Yates

The Bishops were photographed, portrait painted, and sculptured at various times throughout their lives and to such an extent that quite a sizeable volume of reproductions has been made available.* The portrait-painting activity did not stop upon the decease of either Mr. or Mrs. Bishop. In one instance, an English painter named Frederick Yates, painted a portrait of Mrs. Bishop from a photograph selected by her husband and his portrait from an actual sitting.

Frederick Yates was a world-renowned artist who unfortunately was never permitted to paint until he was twenty-eight years of age. He was sent into business after completing college and therefore had to "suppress his artistic aspirations" and delay his career of painting for many impatient years. Upon making the break from uncongenial office routine, he went first to America, thence to Paris where he studied under the famous French artist Bonnat, and wound up his apprenticeships amidst the great traditions of art-minded centers in Italy. Feeling ready, Yates launched himself on a series of trips to far-off places, one of which was the "Sandwich Isles." During his stay in Honolulu, he painted highly praised portraits of Bruce Cartwright and Judge Hartwell. The latter was so pleased he arranged an exhibit of Yates' works.

Word of this new and able painter was carried all about Honolulu, and Samuel M. Damon, who had but two years before completed the purchase of Bishop and Company and who had, as the result of the gift of the lands of Moanalua, come to be doubly obligated to the Bishops, desired a portrait of each. It happened that Yates was scheduled to stop in San Francisco for a large part of 1897, and Damon was planning a trip there too (he actually made two trips there in 1897). The commissioning, therefore, of the two portraits, with Bishop selecting the likeness of his wife and approving the project in general, resulted in two excellent likenesses. They hung in the Moanalua pavilion on the Damon property until 1959

* Harold W. Kent, *Album of Likenesses; Bernice Pauahi and Charles Reed Bishop* (Honolulu, The Kamehameha Schools Press, 1962).

and were then moved by Henry Damon, Samuel M. Damon's grandson, to his home.

Yates was a superior draughtsman; and it was this fundamental skill that provided his pictures, landscapes, snow scenes, or portraits with "shrewd characterization and sterling sense of romanticism." He retired to the English lake country near Rydal, Westmoreland, gave up his portrait painting almost entirely, and devoted himself exclusively to unaffected portrayal of the countryside of his native land.

William F. Cogswell

Self-taught portrait painter, William F. Cogswell, was just about a life-span contemporary of Bishop. He was born in Sandusky, New York, July 15, 1819 (Bishop was born in Glens Falls, New York, January 25, 1822), and died in South Pasadena, California, December 24, 1903 (Bishop died in Berkeley, California, June 7, 1915). The two men never met until Cogswell arrived in Honolulu March 21, 1879, on the *Zealandia*, especially to paint a portrait of King Kalakaua. He was favored with commissions to paint portraits of many of Hawaii's leading citizens, but Bishop was not numbered among them on this visit. Others who had portraits painted at this time included John Dominis, Princess Likelike, Princess Liliuokalani, and Minister of Interior Samuel G. Wilder.

Cogswell's fame as a portrait painter preceded him to Hawaii and was the reason he was considered for the Kalakaua appointment. He had entered a portrait of Lincoln in a competition authorized by Congress in an Act, March 3, 1869. The winning portrait, for which up to $3000 was to be paid, would be selected by the incoming President and placed in the White House. Cogswell's Lincoln was one of thirteen portraits submitted and was selected by President Grant. The winning portrait is of Lincoln full standing with the Capitol in the background. It hung in the State Dining Room of the White House until 1939 when it was moved to the east wall at the east end of the foyer. Cogswell followed this with at least eighteen Lincolns and two Grants and two McKinleys. Thirteen of the Lincolns were sold to various states, one to the Pasadena Public Library, and another to the California State Capitol at Sacramento. Two are owned by individuals, and the last one was obtained for Hawaii. He had painted a Grant before journeying to Hawaii and found a ready sale in Honolulu, since the United States–Hawaii Reciprocity Act had just been signed. Both the Hawaiian Grant and Lincoln were presented by the Trustees of the Library of Hawaii to Governor Wallace Rider Farrington and now hang in the Senate Chamber of the State of Hawaii. Cogswell painted a McKinley portrait which hangs with the Lincoln in Sacramento.

Cogswell visited Hawaii again, arriving January 10, 1890, on the *Australia.* He was seventy-one years old. He opened a studio on Fort Street in the Love Building. This time he painted Sanford B. Dole, Theophilus H. Davies, Prince David Kawananakoa, Peter Cushman Jones, Judge and Mrs. Widemann, Hon. W. G. Irvine, and Hon. M. P. Robinson. He also painted at least four almost completely similar portraits of Bishop. One of these hangs in my office at The Kamehameha Schools, the second is in the main entry of the Bishop Museum, the third is in the board room of the First National Bank of Hawaii, and the fourth was donated by Mrs. W. F. Allen to Punahou in 1912. This last copy has vanished. The Board of Trustees of the Queen's Hospital authorized portraits of Queen Emma and Kamehameha IV on March 25, 1890, at $250 each. The paintings were hung on the corridor walls of the Hospital where they are today.

On June 4, 1894, but a few days after his "final" arrival in San Francisco, Bishop wrote J. O. Carter:

Mr. Cogswell, the artist, has just called. He has in Honolulu, in care of Mr. Williams, some pictures (portraits) of native girls which *he recommends* for the museum, and which he has had expensively framed. He says the eight frames—two or three of which are here—cost him about $550; and that he paid the girls not less than $30 for sitting, and he will *give* me the pictures, if I will pay the cost of the frames! Are they suitable for the museum, and desirable, at any price?

Brigham snorted at Cogswell's "Types of Hawaiians," the acquisition of which had been referred to him by J. O. Carter. He wrote Bishop that he thought the "paintings were wretched—only fit for tavern signs or coach panels." Nevertheless, Brigham's Trustees decided to purchase the pictures, an action which surprised Bishop a little. He wrote to Carter a few days later, June 30, 1894: "I did not think that the trustees would advise the purchase of Cogswell's pictures, but as I had only had a glympse [*sic*] at some of them, I consented to send his offer."

At the age of 80, Cogswell came again, this time, August 17, 1898, on the *Mariposa.* He wanted to do a portrait of Princess Kaiulani;

Two paintings of the Bishops by Frederick Yates, painted at the request of Samuel M. Damon. The portrait of Mrs. Bishop was copied in 1897 from a photograph selected by Bishop. The portrait of Mr. Bishop was painted in 1897 in San Francisco while Bishop sat for him.

but before he could make the arrangements, the young princess passed away. He returned to Pasadena and continued working in his studio until incapacitated in a street car accident in San Francisco. Upon recovering sufficiently, he returned to Pasadena and lived until December 24, 1903.

In the biographies of artists, Cogswell is widely praised for his work in New York, Philadelphia, St. Louis, Washington, D. C., San Francisco, and Los Angeles. No mention is made of his three trips to Honolulu and the magnitude of his contribution to the history-in-portrait of the leaders of the 1880's and 1890's—leaders in the Kingdom, the Provisional Government, and the Republic. Hawaii, however, is indeed the richer at the hands of Cogswell's artistry.

11

Farewell

DEPARTURE FROM HONOLULU

BISHOP LEFT HONOLULU, finally, for California on March 2 of 1894. He boarded the *Australia* and bade a sad farewell to the land he had graciously and constructively served so many years. The ship moved out of the harbor past Diamond Head and twelve days later tied up at San Francisco. Here he expected to live out his declining years. He was seventy-two and could have scarcely hoped that those years would lengthen out for another twenty-one.

Why did he leave Honolulu where he had spent the best years of his life? He had made many trips to San Francisco after Mrs. Bishop died in 1884. Even before her passing, however, he had visited the Bay area and had begun to buy land, both urban and rural. He had invested in mining stocks and public utilities, and he held a large portfolio of mortgages. Perhaps the flavor of this venture grew out of the fever he once had when he almost shipped out of Honolulu during the gold rush in 1849. Upon his first visit to San Francisco with Mrs. Bishop, in 1866, he had opportunity to examine the historic scene of the speculations of 1849. He found the tempo of buying and selling, particularly in land, was still holding; and he felt he should be numbered among the buyers and sellers. This feeling grew stronger and brought him back again and again. While he continued his massive financial operation in Hawaii and worked prodigiously at his community benefactions there, his personal San Francisco boom was inevitably nurtured.

His bereavement in 1884 foreshadowed the severance of strong sentimental, political, and financial ties with Hawaii. Mrs. Bishop was the last of the royal line of the Kamehamehas, and he was a life member of the House of Nobles. His financial house was the greatest ever erected in the Kingdom. It was a certainty that the ties would be broken; and he undertook the necessary steps to conclude his active responsibilities with his cherished financial and community interests in Hawaii, chief of which were Bishop and Company, The Kamehameha Schools, and the Bernice Pauahi Bishop Museum.

His final determination was made in the first or second year of the 1890's. His business was rounding to a satisfactory conclusion in Hawaii while his investments in San Francisco and the Bay area were beginning to demand his personal presence. Between 1890 and 1894 he spent more time in San Francisco and the Bay area than in Honolulu.

In 1894, on January 29, he wrote to W. D. Alexander in Washington, D. C. (he was leaving the next day on his last trip outward bound for Honolulu):

It is my intention to return to the city as soon as I can—within six weeks at the longest. . . . I shall go home with a heavy heart and perplexed mind [this reference was to the uncertainties facing the Provisional Government then ruling in Hawaii and the confusing actions of President Grover Cleveland relating thereto]—and so far as I am concerned it is fortunate that I have interests here which will require a speedy return, for I cannot bear the wear and tear of sleeplessness in that climate. . . .

It can be concluded also that the frequent crises arising in the Kalakaua and Liliuokalani governments were writing a portent on the Hawaiian tapestry of living that not only perplexed but grieved him. He was more than an ordinary adviser to the regents (when they would have his advice); he was financial counsellor to them. Their habits of spending, both as public servants and private citizens, disturbed his sense of propriety. He knew how social as well as political upset could result from indiscreet or inconsistent financial operations. It was partly in this feeling of utter helplessness in trying to be of service to the Hawaiian people that the ultimate move to San Francisco received some of its encouragement.

It was, therefore, a developing pattern of events, personal, political, and financial, that finally brought him to leave his Hawaii for the cooler, more exuberant climate of the San Francisco Bay area. Even in leaving he was mindful of his obligations to the many enterprises, public and private, which had enjoyed his support. No activity on his Hawaii horizon was in any way overlooked. He brought every enterprise, financial and community, to the point where self-sufficiency of purpose and backing would assure a successful continuation and growth.

SAN FRANCISCO AND BERKELEY

BISHOP USED THE OCCIDENTAL HOTEL in San Francisco when visiting California in the 1880's and the early 1890's and made the hotel his permanent residence upon moving from Honolulu in 1894. His apartment became a warm haven of hospitality for visitors travelling to and from Hawaii; royalty and commoner, businessman and planter, teacher and student, trustee, scientist, and author. It was a vantage point for maintaining contact with the news and with the trends of commerce. This location also constituted a half-way house for observation of politics as between Washington and Honolulu. He received countless invitations to return to Honolulu; and while they were strongly tempting, he did not return again. He enjoyed the cooler climate of the San Francisco Bay area. While in San Francisco for the winter months of 1890–1891, he applied for membership in the exclusive Pacific Union Club and was elected a member April 3, 1891. This club became a favorite lunch location for Bishop; and while the record does not list him as officer or director, he did request guest cards for his gentlemen friends who passed through the Bay area. He withdrew his membership October 1, 1914, just a few months before his death.

Many are the stories and impressions that emanate from his callers. H. B. Restarick wrote a touching little vignette of one call he made, among several:

. . . It was there in 1904 that his kindly nature was revealed to me. I was much disturbed and perplexed by a matter on which a life seemed to depend and I needed expert advice. I went to Mr. Bishop's room at 8 o'clock one night and told him my trouble.

Showing deep, sympathetic interest he said, "I know the person you must see." Finding by telephone that he was at home, Mr. Bishop said, "I will go with you." I protested saying it was a cold, damp night and that he was an old man—he was then 82—but he persisted in going. We walked down the stairs (this was in the Occidental Hotel) for he never entered the elevator, and taking a street car he took me to his friend's house.

I knew it was his presence that elicited the interest of the specialist whose advice was invaluable to me. In the kindest way he inquired whether I needed monetary assistance, which fortunately I did not but he had given me more than money and that was sympathetic friendship and help. That was Charles Reed Bishop, the man. He was generous from principle rather than nature or impulse.

Alexander Walker, in an interview, told me of stopping en route to college in the East, usually for breakfast, with Bishop:

Our host was always (on these stopovers) one of whom we were somewhat in awe. He would insist that we order a large complete breakfast and would say little during the meal. He was not cold but reserved. He thought a matter through carefully and thoroughly before speaking. He did not seem at all a talkative person.

Another impression comes from the pen of a reporter on the staff of the *San Francisco Examiner*. He had been asked to check a news story that Bishop "had given $800,000 to schools and societies in the Hawaiian Islands." He reported his interview in the August 22, 1895, issue of his paper:

Mr. Bishop was seen last night at the Occidental Hotel and was requested to make some mention of the matter. The gentleman who is a millionaire five or six times over, has his own ideas about things and is very dogmatic in maintaining them. He confirmed the truth about having made a very large donation of money to the island schools but refused to mention the sum. He did say it was a large sum and was particular to neither affirm nor deny that $800,000 was the amount.

"I did not wish to have my donation made public," he said last evening, with an evidently sincere show of feeling, "and I do not wish to make any comment on the subject. 'The Examiner' seems somehow to have knowledge of my action. I cannot but appreciate that its motive is to get the news, and for that reason I will say I have given the schools down there a large donation in money.". . .

The reporter's picture and the story, generally, are quite accurate except that the $800,000 referred to was the money involved in the sale of Bishop and Company to Damon.

In his eighties Bishop's eyes began to fail and many readers came to help him. One such, John H. Lathrop, his Unitarian minister in Berkeley told me:

I used to read to him for an hour every day. His interests were broad and he kept in touch with current events. He did fall asleep with my reading and I'd tiptoe out of the room. He was of good height, slender, fine features, snow white hair, courteous with courtly manners. He had a distinguished appearance. He was always treated with respect.

Another reader, Ethel Eveleth Uren, warmly described to me her experience in reading to Bishop:

Mr. Bishop was almost blind. I read to him in 1909–1910. I read newspapers and magazines to him but he'd usually fall asleep before I'd read much. He still went over to San Francisco each day and he wanted to go alone. His male companion would walk a little behind him. I heard of Mr. Bishop's need of a reader from a relative, Dr. Alderson. I was paid a bright $10 gold piece every week. He was not a tall man, very kindly. Had a large picture of his wife on the wall behind him.

Not only was he a faithful worshipper at the First Unitarian Church of Berkeley, but he was also very fond of the symphony and the opera. He attended many of the lecture series offered at the University of California. Beginning in his late eighties he was periodically forced into a wheel chair in which he was frequently seen at the world-famous Greek Theatre at Berkeley.

The most tragic single event in Bishop's San Francisco years was the 1906 earthquake and fire. Charles A. McWayne, Sr., of Honolulu, gave details to me of a visit that he and his aunt, Mrs. B. M. Allen, made to San Francisco and to Bishop; they had arrived in San Francisco the evening of April 12, 1906:

We went to the Occidental Hotel and registered and enjoyed a few meals with Charles Reed Bishop. On Tuesday night, Mrs. B. M. Allen, Charles Reed Bishop and I went to the opera—April 17. On the way home from the opera we noticed how excitable and restless the fire horses were as we walked past the fire houses. About five A.M. Wednesday, April 18, the earthquake hit. We all dressed hurriedly and made our way down to the lobby. We found Mr. Bishop already up and at work. He asked if we had any goods or clothing etc. to salvage. We piled some of our stuff, retaining only a suitcase, into a wagon alongside some things of his. He had already been out on the street and had hired a wagon and a driver. The driver then drove off and cached the load of papers and personal items somewhere beyond Van Ness. We didn't see Mr. Bishop again for two or three months and then it was he who looked us up at the Belvedere Hotel. He told us how to get in touch with the driver to regain our property.

The B. M. Allen aunt of Charles McWayne is from a different Allen family than the husband of Bishop's niece who came to get him with a newly purchased automobile and take him with some of his goods out to the house on Ashbury Street. Charles Bishop Dunham, a nephew, also hurried out to San Francisco that morning, to assist him in any possible way.

Despite the moving and burying of "goods," Bishop lost some extremely valuable papers in the San Francisco earthquake and fire. He had preserved his wife's entire correspondence, pictures, and personal papers and was intending to place them in a safe place for appropriate access for historians and writers. These materials were destroyed. He assisted Mary H. Krout in reconstructing the story of Mrs. Bishop's life, and two years later her *Memoirs of Bernice Pauahi Bishop* appeared but in nothing like the fullness or authenticity that might have been. Likewise, his own copy books of his voluminous correspondence were destroyed, and this book on his life has suffered proportionately.

A Bank of California official cabled SNOMAD in Honolulu on April 26:

> April 26th 1906.
> DAMON-S

FROM 66 OAKLAND CAL. TO SNOMAD HONOLULU
Seen Moulton thinks banks may not open two to three weeks. Sell as little exchange as possible; people should take money or drafts, if necessary, on northern branches of Calbank send eastern drawing straight to New York instructing to charge Calbank's account. New York exchange not quoted. Use Calbank's code leaving out anything written or typewritten. Mr. Bishop safe. Merrills burnt out but safe.

This cable message (SNOMAD is Damons spelled backward) served to allay rumors about Bishop's safety and health.

He did not write much about the disaster except to Samuel Damon. On May 8, Damon asked the *Honolulu Advertiser* to publish a portion of a Bishop letter. Many rumors were flying about Honolulu:

There have been many reports in circulation relative to the Hon. C. R. Bishop, and many of them were so preposterous as to be ignored by most people and believed by a few. Mr. Damon feels annoyed at the reports and requests the Advertiser to print the following, which is part of a letter he received from Mr. Bishop by the *Alameda* on Saturday. It is addressed to Mr. Damon. The writer says,

"Yesterday Mr. Moulton sent me a copy of your cablegram of the 18th in which you, Mrs. Allen and E. F. Bishop all kindly invited and advised me to go to Honolulu. I requested Mr. Moulton to cable you in reply that I was comfortable in Berkeley. It seems to me necessary, or at least best, that I should remain here to protect my own interests and do what I can for others. When the earthquake came I was sure that a fire would come and it did start under the drug store on the corner and we were ordered in an excited tone to 'dress and get out.' That fire was controlled and then came the word to leave because the building would likely be blown up to stop the fire in that direction. Everyone was excited and conveyances were almost impossible to secure. Of course many mistakes were made in saving things of small value and overlooking things of greater value.

The husband of Mrs. Allen's niece came with his auto and took me and such of my belongings as we could gather and handle, out to his house on Ashbury Street, where I remained under the good care of my hospitable friends until yesterday afternoon and then came here, where I am comfortably lodged in a house which belongs to me, and is let to a good housekeeper and I get my meals in a nice Inn near by.

It has been exceedingly difficult to get about in the city or to find anybody or be found by friends. The wrecked city is an awful and distressing sight and although the spirit of the people so far is good and they act and talk courageously, the task before them is tremendous and great mental and physical suffering must follow.

It will take several weeks yet to dig out and cool the vaults and safes so they may be opened without danger to the contents. Of course you will husband your cash as much as possible and make it serve you to the limit.

The weather is now good and there is demand for nearly all kinds of labor, but home accommodations for families is insufficient. The surrounding towns and country are receiving many of those who are burned out but many are camping with little shelter. Just where the Bank of California will open temporarily for business is not fully determined. There is some talk of putting a floor and a roof over the ruins on California Street.

With many who had good business and thought themselves well off the question now is Have I much, little or nothing left?

Our friends, the Merrills, have nothing of their dwelling left and how much of the contents I do not know. The steel framed buildings have shown their superiority in resisting earthquake shocks and fire and would have done better still if they had had some streams of water at the right point.

I received your letter of the 19th last evening. Have been unable to be useful to others but have tried to act sensibly. Am to attend a meeting of the Fireman's Fund this morning in the city. People and offices are becoming located as fast as possible. The newspapers will show you how offices are scattered in the city and in Oakland, the latter filling rapidly. To supply money will be one great difficulty.

At the meeting of the Fireman's Fund there was but one sentiment which was: to adjust and settle the losses as soon as possible, which at best will take considerable time, and go ahead. Just what is to be saved of the books and records, etc., is still uncertain and cannot be ascertained in a hurry. You will of course be advised in due time from the office, which is temporarily Mr. Levison's residence. No. 2420 Pacific Avenue. Probably the Oakland office will be headquarters for general business.

Tomorrow I am going over, hoping to see Mr. King and Mr. Anderson. The sight of so much of ruin and want is distressing. We who have comfortable lodgings and are safe have great reason to be thankful.

You are very kind to think of me but at present there is nothing you can do for me. With kind regards to all of your family, I remain

Very truly yours,
[signed] Charles R. Bishop"

In a letter a day later, Bishop wrote to Mr. Griffiths, President of Punahou:

Your kind letter of the 21st ulto. reached me on the 3rd inst. Not long after writing to me you learned no doubt, from other friends to whom cablegrams were sent, that I got away from the Occidental without personal harm and saved a part of my effects which have since been very convenient for my comfort.

Great work is being done by civil and military authorities and committees of citizens male and female as you have learned from the newspapers. I am not so located nor am I strong enough to do any considerable service. There is no lack of able, brave and good hearted people, full of courage and hope directing, planning, and working, so that every passing day shows good results. Poverty and distress of body and mind cannot be *quickly* overcome. I congratulate you upon happy conditions and pleasant surrounds.

On looking at the widespread views of the late handsome and prosperous city it is difficult to believe that such awful destruction could have come to pass in so short a time. I am comfortably located here and having a cold. Am pretty well. With kind regards to Mrs. Griffiths and yourself.

Late that fall in a note to Brigham, Bishop said: ". . . All of my books, reports etc. about the Museum were burned, and as I have not felt permanently settled I have not hastened to replace the things lost and that I miss very much. . . ." His complete sense of sadness and frustration at his loss of important historical papers was touchingly described to W. D. Alexander, June 17, 1907:

. . . The memories of Mrs. Bishop, now undertaken by Miss Krout should have been written by somebody twenty years ago. Many letters received by Mrs. Bishop from friends at home and abroad, with other memoranda and data preserved by her, and in my care at the time of the great fire in San Francisco, April 18th, 1906, were together with my letters and copies of letters etc, destroyed. My memory of names, dates, and detail, never strong, has lost a good deal by the lapse of years and by the habit of trusting to writings so that now I am greatly embarrassed when called upon to furnish material for the Memoirs. I must rely very much upon the recollection of good friends of my wife, yourself included. . . .

After the San Francisco disaster he moved to the El Granada apartments in Berkeley. From here he need walk but a few steps to the ferry for his daily journey to San Francisco to his secluded fifth floor office of the Bank of California. He was also near several nephews and nieces. He subsequently purchased the El Granada building and deeded the property to niece Emma Bernice Bishop (Dunham) one of the children of his brother Henry. This was about the time (1910) that he moved for a third time, now to the Shattuck Hotel in Berkeley. The Bay area nephews and nieces, with the addition of several cousins scattered across the United States, were about all the "family" that Bishop had.

The first correspondence originating with brother Henry Bostwick Bishop is contained in a letter to his Uncle William Brayton and Aunt Althea Anna Bishop (Brayton), June 24, 1849, while he was aboard the brig *Cecelia Louise* bound for San Francisco from Panama. Like his brother Charles, he was a soldier of fortune and had decided the Glens Falls environment was not sufficiently promising. The gold rush in California was drawing adventurers by the overland routes of the United States and territories and by Cape Horn and across the fever-ridden jungle route of Panama.

Henry Bishop joined the Sandy Hill Mining Band, took the Panama route, and after a long voyage of wild experiences arrived in San Francisco, August 13, 1849. His departure date from Panama was May 22, of that year, making the trip up the western side of the continent one of about three months' duration. Things did not work out too well in the gold fields; and at the invitation of his brother, Henry bought passage on the bark *Carolina* which set him ashore in Honolulu, July 27, 1850. He went almost immediately to Maui and remained there until 1857 when he returned to the Bay area and married Caroline Elizabeth Gilliland, March 4, 1858. This marriage produced six children.

Bishop was closely attached to this family. In making his Will he appointed George Lewis Bishop, a nephew, and Charles Bishop Dunham and Leland Stanford Dunham, both grandnephews (all direct descendants of Henry and Caroline), executors of his estate.

A fourth, Irving P. Moulton, was his lawyer. Henry was well advised in his financial operations by his brother. One typical situation is described in a letter Bishop wrote to his brother, May 20, 1870: "I hope you have made a good bargain and will not be disappointed in it—as a good many Italians have lately lost their money by the failure of a large Italian firm in San Francisco." Henry was in the act of purchasing a farm and was taking a $3000 mortgage on it. He died in Oakland in 1900, a man of considerable wealth.

The Henry Bishop family line ran into fateful difficulty among the six children: William died at age twenty, unmarried; Charles Reed (namesake) died at the age of two; George Lewis, the executor, lived to be seventy-seven, unmarried; Lee Gilliland died in infancy; and Jessie June died of tuberculosis at the age of twenty-two, also unmarried. This story, therefore, leaves only the second child, Emma Bernice Bishop, who married James Skipp Dunham. Their children were: Edna Lucile Dunham, who married Francis Logan McCaffery; Charles Bishop Dunham; and Leland Stanford Dunham. It was Emma Bernice who at the age of twelve accompanied the Bishops on the 1875–1876 trips to Europe. She had lived the three years before with them in Honolulu. He remembered her substantially in his Will, leaving some of the oil paintings purchased on the European trip, most of his personal effects, and properties of considerable value. Emma did much by way of friendly service for both her aunt and uncle. When Mrs. Bishop made the futile trip to San Francisco in search of medical relief, it was niece Emma who came from Stockton to the Palace Hotel to remain with her aunt for the full period of the examination and observation.

Nephew Leland Stanford Dunham, brother of Emma, and also highly regarded by Bishop, offered several illuminating comments to me in an interview we had in Oakland, California:

Uncle Charles gave me a lot of Hawaiian stamps and I not knowing the value of them gave them away.

My Uncle was disappointed that I had decided not to go to college. He offered to pay my tuition and expenses for four years at any college I might choose. He sent many people to college but education was not one of my chief interests then.

He had all the books on grammar, spelling, synonyms, and books on writing on his desk in Berkeley. He was self educated although he attended school through the eighth grade.

He never wanted to be helped.

To me when I was about to be married he said, "Don't forget it is easier to save money than retain it."

This nephew succeeded very well in his professional career as had his brother, Charles Bishop Dunham. Both of the nephews along with Emma received a tenth interest each in their illustrious uncle's estate.

Another line of relatives was held in close affection by Bishop. The second line (cousins) derives from but five of Bishop's nine uncles and aunts; Linus, Nelson, Sarah W., Althea Anna, and Susan Wilson. The Linus Bishops had an only son, Linus Dewey, whose family produced four cousins once removed from Charles Reed Bishop. The oldest, Frances Elizabeth did not marry. She frequently commented on her pride in her illustrious cousin. In a letter to a niece, Althea Devine, she wrote, March 23, 1891:

. . . You have no idea what a great amount of good Cousin Chas. does. Its perfectly astonishing and all in such a quiet way you never know it unless you are in the home with him and then you would not know it if it could be helped. Cordie [Mrs. W. F. Allen] used to say, now if you will never tell I will tell you something that will make you glad. Then she would tell mother & I of some nice things he had done in such a way no one knew but the receiver and Cordie as he would get her to give it so they need not thank him personally, and Cordie must not tell any-one. . . .

Later that year she wrote another letter to Althea and again commented:

. . . Cousin Charles is still at Carlsbad and some better. He is an old man [69] to improve very much with that disease, but I hope he will not suffer very severely. He has done so much good in his life that no one knew anything about until someone would die and then would come out what he had done for them. And for the natives and schools for whites and natives, its wonderful. I think I will never say again that a rich man is close or ought to do more for one does not know what they do in se-cret. . . .

Years after Bishop's death, a comment appears (1926) in another letter to Althea:

. . . Wills make a great deal of work always; seems strange they cannot be made plain enough without such a lot of "red tape." Cous. Chas. said he was going to give his away while he lived, and he did, most of it so as to prevent trouble. . . .

Next in the Linus Dewey Bishop family was Charles Hulbert,* who went to work as a boiler in the sugar mill at Lihue and later opened a money making plantation store there. There were four sons

* See p. 228.

and one daughter in this family. The oldest of the children, Linus Allen, never married and died in Miami, Florida, September 13, 1962. He willed the residue of his estate to the Bishop Museum. The second child is Frances Ethel who married Harry S. Bettis. She was graduated from Punahou in 1907 and knew Bishop well the last fifteen years of his life. She summarized her impressions of her illustrious uncle in a recent talk that I had with her in San Francisco:

He was a most immaculate man. He was about five feet, eleven inches and very slender. He usually wore a dark business suit, a black derby, and he had a full beard to the day of his death. He was a serious man but he could chuckle easily. He was dignified. He mellowed as he grew older. He aged gracefully. He had no temper, having a very mild disposition. He was not a shouting man. He was very friendly with Ogden Mills and others high in the banking and business community. He went over to the Bank of California every day and his male nurse went along too.

The second son, Raymond, married Genevieve Goodacre from Kauai. I had an interview with him in Santa Clara, California at which time he recalled many contacts and experiences with his Uncle Charles:

My brother Charles and I were sent to the Hitchcock Military Academy in San Rafael, California, at my uncle's expense. He had an office with John H. Spring in the San Francisco Savings Union Building at the corner of California and Webb before the earthquake. Afterwards he had an office by himself in the Dollar Building, where I also had an office. He endorsed my letters of credit when I entered into business. My wife and sister used to read to him frequently—he would enjoy about an hour of that in one span of time. He was always quite reserved with us and very independent. If I would try to assist him on to a street car he would elbow me away.

I was in his bedroom when he passed away. He spoke quietly, "I guess I'd better go. Goodbye." He turned over on his side and left us.

Another son of the Kauai store manager is Charles Reed Bishop (namesake). I invited him to write of his recollections of his "illustrious godfather and benefactor." The letter is dated, New Year's Day, 1963:

At my birth on the Island of Kauai, [October 24, 1889] Cousin Charles endowed me with $5000 in trust with the Hawaiian Trust Company of Honolulu. This was conserved on my behalf until the first world war, when I joined the Navy. Then my wise and dear guardian, Uncle Faxon, deemed the time had come to allow me the use of income. The original gift was the beginning of good fortune and is still the core of my estate.

After the primary teaching at home with an English governess, I was ready for boarding school. In 1904 Cousin Charles made himself responsible for the whole cost of my education. . . . I was sent to Hitchcock Military Academy at San Rafael, California, to be with my brothers, Raymond and Faxon.

On Saturdays, I left San Rafael for Berkeley, to lunch with my Godfather. Sometimes we went to a matinee. As I remember him, he was both dignified and self-effacing. He was worldshy but never nervous. He was reticent and soft-spoken, but with purpose and meaning in his quiet ways. He was the gentleman. The determination of his acts came from a fine sense of humanity.

And, once I saw him when he failed to see me. That was during the critical day of the great fire in 1905 [sic] in San Francisco. He had secured a dray and was moving his trunks. He wore a top-hat and the tails of his broadcloth coat were in the breeze.

And, yet, in a manner of speaking, his wish for me has been fulfilled. By God's grace, I have a taste for the best in everything: architecture, the dance both ballet and interpretive, painting, lectures, theatre. I still have the Complete Shakespeare given to me by Cousin Charles (*Temple Edition,* Dent, London, MCMIV, in dark red Morocco leather.). . . .

The last of the four boys, Faxon Hulbert, passed away in 1949.

Returning to the Linus Dewey Bishop family; the third child was Bradley.* Eben Faxon was the fourth and youngest. Like his brothers, Charles Hulbert and Bradley, he had been drawn to Hawaii through the urging of their astute cousin. "E. Faxon," as he came to be called, moved in with the Bishops on King Street upon arrival and lived there for the year and a half remaining before Mrs. Bishop's death. He came to know her well and delighted in her friendly company. His marriage to Annie Smith Walker was a major social event in Honolulu. Frances Elizabeth Bishop wrote about it to Althea Devine Mills (Glens Falls, N. Y.) in August, 1891:

. . . At the wedding July 21, 1891, were Mr. and Mrs. William F. Allen, Mr. and Mrs. Sam Allen, Mr. and Mrs. Bert Bishop, and five intimate friends. They were married by Reverend M. McIntosh with the American Episcopal ceremony. They stood for two solid hours afterwards receiving congratulations of the visitors. The Queen and all her suite arrived at quarter to nine and stayed till after ten. The newlyweds slipped off at half past eleven in a double team to Paul Isenbergs 12 miles away. . . .

Practical minded Cousin Charles presented the couple with $100 in cash and $10,000 in stock in C. Brewer and Company. This stock was the basis of the fortune eventually accumulated by this favored cousin.

* See p. 28.

"Aunt Annie" lived to the age of ninety-three, passing away in 1962. With real zest she recalled how seventy years earlier she nervously approached the first dinner she and her husband could have for Charles Reed Bishop. He was in Europe at the time of the wedding and did not return to Honolulu until December, 1891. She was "really worried" as she prepared for the important guest.

E. Faxon Bishop did not have the opportunity to create community agencies or pioneer in them as had his distinguished cousin, but he was instrumental in serving most of them. Of particular satisfaction to Charles Reed Bishop was the appointment of his cousin to the trusteeships of the three Bishop Trusts: Estate, Museum, and Charles R. Bishop. He served in these trusteeships for thirty-six years from the date of his appointment in December, 1904. He was the only one of the several Bishops who, having tried Hawaii at the urging of his Cousin Charles, remained to become completely identified with the Islands. In this he even out-distanced his sponsor. He was devoted to the causes which his cousin held sacred. And on the day of the great funeral procession honoring Charles Reed Bishop, from town to the Royal Mausoleum up Nuuanu Valley, it was E. Faxon Bishop who lovingly carried the ashes into the Kamehameha crypt and placed them near the casket of Bernice Pauahi (Bishop).*

From Uncle Nelson Bishop's family came Cordelia Church, Edgar, Julia Ann, and Frederick. Cordelia married William Fessenden Allen, Bishop's official host during his residence at the 21 Emma Street home. Aunt Sarah's marriage to Samuel Dunham Judd produced four children. None of these Judds had a close relationship with either Bishop or the eminent Judd family in Hawaii.

Aunt Althea Anna married William Brayton which accounts for the Brayton mentioned in Bishop's will.† A daughter in this family, Althea Augusta Brayton (Devine) received a letter from Bishop, November 28, 1895:

I am glad that you have purchased in your own name a place for a home, and with a house to spare, to let. No doubt you keep your buildings and contents covered by insurance. To put you out of debt, I now have the satisfaction of sending to you as herewith a gift, three thousand dollars

* See p. 334.
† Last Will and Testament of Charles Reed Bishop dated May 29, 1914. The Will was probated under File #20289 in the County Court House, Oakland, California, June 18, 1915.

($3000) in the sight draft No D 24696 of the Bank of California on Messers Laidlaw & Co. New York for $3000, payable to your order.

Bishop's youngest aunt, Susan Wilson, married Thurman Pattison on March 22, 1837. This union produced four children, Orville, John, Charles, and Mary Augusta. John and Charles died in youth, and Orville and Mary Augusta became great favorites of Bishop. Orville organized a bank at Elkland, Pennsylvania, a source of satisfaction to Bishop. On March 9, 1903, Bishop and Company under instructions from Bishop sent him 100 shares of stock of the Oahu Railway and Land Company. He was also remembered in Bishop's Will with a bequest of $10,000.

Bishop's mother, Maria Reed (Bishop), had a sister named Lucy Jane Reed (Blood). This aunt took over much of the responsibility and the care of young Charles when he was orphaned as a baby. A son of hers named Charles Bishop Blood was born March 22, 1852. This namesake of Mr. Bishop was ever-after an object of his favor. In an old notebook in the possession of Mattie Washburn of Fort Ann, New York, is this statement:

He [C. R. B.] married the King's daughter [Bernice] and is a very wealthy man now [1912]; has given Charlie and other relatives a good deal of money.

This namesake was the recipient of two known gifts of $3000 each. The first was contained in a letter addressed to Charles B. Blood, under date of September 6, 1894:

In my last will I have made a bequest of $3000 to you, and have decided to give it ($3000) to you now, and not leave it for my Executors to do. . . . I suppose that you will invest or deposit this money where it will be *perfectly safe* and give you interest or rent, and use the income leaving the principal untouched as long as you can.

He does the same thing in a second letter, March 3, 1900:

Dear Cousin,
Herewith I send you on account of bequest in your favor by my will, three First Mortgage Gold Bonds (6%) of the Yuba Electric Power Company of San Francisco for one thousand dollars ($1000) each, and with 59 coupons attached . . . as these bonds pay six per cent interest they will be worth more to you than $3000 in money would be. . . . Be careful and deposit these bonds in a safe place where neither thieves or fire can reach them. . . . It is my wish that you should not dispose of or part with these bonds during my life without first consulting with me. . . . With kind regard to your aunts. . . .

The Bank of California in Bishop's early San Francisco years. Construction was completed in 1867, but the building was razed in 1906, immediately prior to the time of the earthquake and fire.

The business office of the Bank of California in the 1880's and 1890's.

Another aunt of Charles Bishop Blood, Mrs. Jane Van Deusen, also of West Fort Ann, New York, had a letter from Bishop, June 20, 1904, acknowledging information regarding the passing of his namesake cousin, and we have the real reason for his generosity to his cousin:

I have seen so little of my cousin during his life that I have not felt much acquainted with him. His mother was kind to me when I was young and was very dear to me and it has been a pleasure to show kindness to her descendants.

This faithful and rather remarkable and unsolicited generosity in memory of the kind treatment of earlier years was most common with him, but little of it can be ferreted out since it was all largely personal and confidential.

As he grew older he lost some of the drive that marked his earlier years, but he never slowed down mentally. He could be expected, therefore, to continue his money-making activities; and he could be counted upon to continue his interests in philanthropy for relatives, friends, and community agencies. His public benefactions in the Bay area followed the pattern he had designed for Hawaii. Among the enterprises provided for in the Will are these:

Day Nursery for Children in Berkeley.	$200
[This nursery is still in existence and doing business under the same name.]	
Day Nursery of Canon Kipp Mission in San Francisco.	$200
[This was later absorbed in the Canon Kipp Community Home. The Home is Episcopal.]	
Girls and Boys Industrial Home and Farm.	$500
[This home is now called the Salvation Army Children's Home and is located at Lytton Springs, California.]	
Boys and Girls Aid Society of California.	$500
[This important charity is still doing business in San Francisco.]	
Associated Charities of San Francisco.	$500
[This organization has been absorbed by the United Crusade of San Francisco.]	
The First Unitarian Church of Berkeley.	$1000
Maud B. Booth Home in San Francisco.	$500
[This is now known as the Salvation Army Hospital for Unwed Mothers.]	

In addition to these Bay area charities, his Will provided $1000 for Associated Charities of Honolulu, $5000 for the Leahi Home of

Honolulu, $10,000 for Oahu College, and $2000 for the Kamehameha Alumnae Association. The First Unitarian Church of Berkeley received many annual gifts. The Golden Book of Benefactions in the Starr King School (Unitarian) Library in Berkeley lists these contributions:

1906	Charles R. Bishop for general purposes	$ 500
1907	Charles R. Bishop for general purposes	300
1908	Charles R. Bishop for general purposes	200
1908	Charles R. Bishop for furnishing Dormitory	100
1911	Charles R. Bishop for general purposes	100
1911	Charles R. Bishop for building fund	10,000
(Nov. 29)	[This contribution was in the nature of seven lots in Thousand Oaks Station Tract.]	
1912	Charles R. Bishop for general purposes	100

As with his benefactions, Bishop's complex and vast banking and investment activities in the Bay area are difficult to trace. He had begun the buying and selling of land and improved property and stocks and bonds some years before his 1894 move to California. The records of the Bank of California reveal that interest as early as 1882. On October 10 of that year he is listed as a shareholder with 100 shares.

His inclination towards the Bay area however did not develop seriously until after the passing of his beloved wife. Her death severed his chief tie to his adopted land. He waited two years before sailing for San Francisco on the *Mariposa*, October 23, 1886. Upon arrival, however, he entered upon a very active program of investments; one item he reported to Damon, December 4, 1886, was $45,000 of stock in Selby Smelting and Lead Works: "I have made some investments here besides my lot on Sutter Street and may make some money. . . ." He returned to San Francisco a year later and reported again to Damon:

My Sutter Street building looks well, but the stores are not let. The Fremont Street building is getting on well. I have bought a lot and building on Washington Street (above Mont) for $20,000 and am inclined to buy another. . . . These are not speculative purchases. . . .

He returned in 1889, and the pace of his transactions picked up. These were some of his purchases as listed in letters to Damon:

100 shares of Sather Banking Stock at $111.000 per share
Corner lot at Truman and Washington Streets $21,000
Lot and new building at 51 Stevenson Street $23,000
480 acres of land near Stockton $13,000
Stock in Farmers and Merchants Bank $10,000
492 acres of land near Lathrop $12,000
Lot on Mission between Fremont and Main $75,000
Piedmont Cable Road (Oakland) 6% bonds $50,000
Lot on corner Front and Oregon $20,500
Lot on corner of Jessie and San Francisco $22,500

In another letter to Damon, May 30, 1889, he said:

. . . You will see that I am putting out considerable money in California and when I return I may do more in the same line if B & Co's balance will admit of it. . . .

He had also continued his purchasing of Bank of California stock. In 1887 he is listed as the owner of 300 shares; in 1888 as the owner of 500; in 1890 of 677; and 1893 of 830. He attended the October 9, 1894, meeting and was elected the bank's Vice-President and a director. He served faithfully on bank committees such as the Executive Committee and the Board of Directors' meetings in the absence of the President. His principal responsibility was that of administering the internal affairs of the bank. His attendance record at directors' meetings was perfect in all his San Francisco years, and the record was not ended until the last meeting, May 25, 1915, just two weeks prior to his death.

Some notion of the scope of his securities operations may be obtained by reference to the inventory of properties in his Will when it was filed for probate, September 23, 1916. The examples listed here will serve to indicate his understanding of the principles of sound diversification and the investment interests peculiar to his day:

Bonds:
  San Francisco-Oakland Terminal Railway
  Golden Gate Land Association
  Philippine [sic] Telephone & Telegraph Company
Preferred Stocks:
  California Pacific Title Insurance Company
  Pacific Gas and Electric Company
  Classen Chemical Company
  Denis Telephone Fire Alarm Company

Common Stocks:
  Bank of California
  Hunt Brothers Company
  Fireman's Fund Insurance Company
  Mercantile National Bank
  The National Bank of D. O. Mills and Company
  The Montebello Oil Company
  Remedial Loan Association
  Union Sugar Company
  Carbo Petroleum Company
  Confidence Gold Mining and Milling Company
  Mascot Copper Company
  Mojave Water & Power Company
  National Mines Company
  North American Oil Consolidated
  Oroville Gold Dredging Company
  The Petrol Company
  The Panama Pacific International Exposition
  Poulsen Wireless Company
  Petaluma and Santa Rose Railway Company
  York Dredging Company

All was not smooth sailing in the Bay area. He complained one time to Ethel Bishop (Bettis) that "they were too sharp for him up here." He described his ventures into real estate and his heavy losses to her. In reality, he profited enormously from his real estate activities. It was his ultra conservatism that created such an outward air of pessimism. However, he did give Mrs. Bettis stock in a gold dredging company. "You'll have a nice little income from this stock." This was the Scott Mine Dredging outfit that was finally to liquidate—being unable to get the gold out because the "terrain was too rough with too many boulders encountered etc." Walter Dillingham related a visit he had as a young man with Bishop in San Francisco and of the latter's enthusiasm for making money out of dredging for gold. The enthusiasm was contagious. Dillingham, a few years later, embarked upon a highly successful dredging venture in Hawaii.

Bishop's birthday was January 25, and among the most faithful friends and relatives who remembered it was Annie Bishop. She wrote him regularly and sent some little token remembrance; chutney, handkerchiefs, pillows, and the like. He always acknowledged the thoughtfulness. On January 25, 1912, she sent him a letter and a basket of taro which brought a prompt reply that, ". . . Honolulu was the only real home that I have had since my boyhood and many of the people were truly my friends and neighbors. No other place can be quite so much to me." This particular birthday, his ninetieth, called forth a most unusual birthday party 2500 miles away from San Francisco. He was in Berkeley; the birthday party was in Honolulu. Friends gathered in the roof garden of the Alexander Young Hotel and reviewed the life and works of the Man of Hawaii and the almost forty years of his residence in the Kingdom. The speeches and resolutions were printed in a brochure and forwarded to Bishop. On the first page the following descriptive item is noted:

At the appointed time there assembled a large number of ladies and gentlemen, among whom were the Governor, Chief Justice, representatives of the Chamber of Commerce, Merchants' Association, Oahu College, Kamehameha Schools, Mid-Pacific Institute, Board of Education, Hawaiian Board of Missions, Catholic Mission, and other educational, philanthropic and religious institutions.

Professor M. M. Scott was temporary chairman and proposed that Messrs. A. S. Hartwell and Frederick March Hatch act as chairman and secretary respectively. The Honolulu papers had published an open invitation to this birthday party the day before. Resolutions which reviewed the general philanthropies of Bishop, were presented by F. A. Schaefer and P. C. Jones. W. R. Castle, who had succeeded him as President of the Board of Education, detailed the progress of the public schools when Bishop was at the helm. Following Castle, Sanford B. Dole outlined the Bishop influence in public affairs. A different slant to the story was given by Ida M. Pope, principal of the Kamehameha School for Girls. Her remarks dealt with Bishop's concern for the welfare of the young Hawaiian women and girls. Religion was considered a part of the birthday discussion, and this was well covered by Reverend Henry H. Parker of Kawaiahao Church.

The roof garden of the Young Hotel was not the only birthday observance that January day. The schools of Honolulu held exercises in his honor. At one of the public programs the retired ex-Queen Liliuokalani was an interested member of the audience. In Berkeley, California, in the El Granada, the Bay area relatives and friends gathered in reunion. Congratulatory telegrams and letters poured in from practically every country in the world. To Annie Bishop he summed up much of his sentimental love for Honolulu, February 5, 1912:

I have had a great birthday and am happy and proud by being so honored by dear old friends in Honolulu and California. It is worthwhile to live to be old if one can keep comfortably well, and retain mind and heart to enjoy life reasonably and take interest in the events of this wonderful age.

And so the story moves towards its end. Bishop never had a biographer. He shunned any attempt to have his life story described in any detail. He refused to have Mary Krout do his story, as someone had suggested. He declined to write his own memoirs. Hence, the story has had to be derived from available records, minute books, trustees' proceedings, newspaper and magazine files, history books, but primarily from the letters which he wrote. He could scarcely ever have been convinced that his story should sometime be told. It would not have occurred to him that the letters and minute books would express a special eloquence of their own when it came time to set forth the story.

12

1915

BISHOP PASSED AWAY after a week's illness in his ninety-third year on June 7, 1915, in Berkeley, California. News of his death was flashed to the Hawaiian Islands and received in a shocked sense of disbelief and loss rarely experienced among the people of a community. His impress had been that of an institution rather than that of an individual. Alive he had been a massive force for good; dead, he seemed momentarily to have removed a bulwark or wall of beneficent, helpful righteousness. The impact of his removal from the midst of his endeavors can be sensed in the memorializations of his life and works.

On June 18, 1915, the following minutes were entered in the proceedings of the Trustees of the Bernice P. Bishop Estate:

There was reported to the meeting the receipt on June 7th of cable advices announcing the death on the day at Berkeley, California, of the Honorable Charles R. Bishop; and, on Mr. Judd's motion, it was voted to appoint Messrs. Smith and Carter a special committee to prepare a set of appropriate resolutions to be spread upon the minutes of the meeting. The committee later submitted the following:

BE IT RESOLVED, that in the death of Hon. Charles R. Bishop the community of these Islands has suffered great loss.

Coming here in the early years of his life, he became identified with all that made for the advancement of high ideals, high standards in business and in social and public affairs. His interest in the education of the young, his personal services and munificent financial aid, have contributed much to the advancement of education. Through a life extending far beyond the usual span, by industry, ability and high character he attained rare eminence and rendered great public service. . . . He was a wise counselor, a loyal friend, and one whom men delighted to honor, and we mourn his loss.

In the minutes of the following meeting, June 25, 1915, this statement appears:

Mr. Smith reported to the meeting that the ashes of the Honorable Charles R. Bishop had arrived, as expected, on the S. S. *"Matsonia"* on Tuesday, 22nd inst., and that they had been immediately taken to Kawaiahao Church, where, until the hour of the funeral, representatives of Hawaiian organizations had remained in attendance, together with a guard of honor of Kamehameha cadets. The funeral services had taken place on the following day [Wednesday] from the Church, at 3 P.M., with commemorative exercises at the Kamehameha Tomb, conducted by the Rev. H. H. Parker, Pastor of Kawaiahao Church. It was mentioned that the active work of arranging and conducting the funeral exercises had been delegated to Lieutenant A. J. Booth, Acting President of the Kamehameha Schools; and Mr. Smith now expressed appreciation for the excellent manner in which this service had been rendered.

The service at Kawaiahao Church at 3:00 P.M., June 23, 1915, was simple and in keeping with the life and character of Charles Reed Bishop:

Organ Prelude
Arrival of Honorary Pall Bearers and Clergy
Music
Quartet
Reading of Scripture, Remarks and Prayer
Rev. Mr. Parker
Address in Hawaiian and Prayer
Rev. Mr. Poepoe
Music
Quartet
Benediction
Rev. Mr. Parker
Postlude

The *Friend,* of July, 1915, devoted several pages to the memorial services for Mr. Bishop:

Memorial services for the late Charles R. Bishop were held at Kawaiahao Church at 3 o'clock on the afternoon of June 23rd.*

The ashes arrived the previous day, on the steamer *Matsonia,* and were taken at once to Kawaiahao Church, where the old name chants of the Kamehamehas were sung. The *kahili* † waving ceremony was observed for the first time in the case of a white man connected with the Kamehameha dynasty since the lying in state of the body of John Young, Kamehameha the Great's trusted friend and adviser, nearly a hundred years ago.

* Wallace M. Alexander accompanied the ashes of Mr. Bishop on the *Matsonia* from San Francisco. W. O. Smith, Albert F. Judd, Alexander and a Kamehameha Schools' Guard of Honor escorted the urn to Kawaiahao Church June 22, 1915.

† Royal standard.

Hawaiian royalty, represented by Queen Liliuokalani in person; leaders in church work, representatives of the foremost business houses of the city, of educational institutions, federal officials, including army and navy, representatives of the territorial and municipal governments and hundreds of citizens, men and women, in private life filled the ancient Hawaiian church to do honor by their presence to the memory of Hawaii's great philanthropist and well-loved citizen.

The metal urn containing the ashes of the deceased, and which was in turn placed in a mahogany case, reposed on a stand in front of the pulpit. This was surrounded by a mass of beautiful calla lilies, priceless royal feather *kahilis* standing mute guard over all. To the right of the great organ, over which Miss Hattie Ayau presided, stood a number of the Daughters of Hawaiian Warriors, with rich feather capes, the insignia of the order, drooping from their shoulders, mantle-like. To the left were members of the Order of the Daughters of Hawaii. The choir was hidden in a mass of ferns, palms, beautiful magnolias and calla and other lilies.

As the Queen took her seat the honorary pallbearers entered from the vestry and sat to the left of the central aisle. The pallbearers were Hon. W. O. Smith, Judge Sanford B. Dole, A. W. T. Bottomley, P. C. Jones, Delegate J. K. Kalanianaole, Fred W. Beckley, F. W. Macfarlane, W. M. Alexander, Henry Smith and Prof. A. F. Griffiths.

A quartet, composed of Arthur Wall, first tenor; Dudley French, of the Kamehameha School for Boys, second tenor; George A. Brown, first bass, and Leslie French of Punahou Academy, second bass, sang "Still, Still With Thee," their voices blending harmoniously.

Following a Scripture reading, Rev. H. H. Parker, pastor of Kawaiahao Church, spoke feelingly of the great man, whom he had known in life as one beloved all over Hawaii. Mr. Parker said that it was twenty-one years since he had last seen Mr. Bishop. He was then leaving Hawaii to take up his residence in California.

"He spoke to me feelingly about his dead wife, the Princess Bernice Pauahi, and of the special interest she always had felt during her life for the young people of her race," said Mr. Parker, recounting this last conversation with Mr. Bishop.

"If I should say anything about Mr. Bishop, I would talk to the young people of Hawaii, especially the young Hawaiians, of Mr. Bishop and the Princess, his wife, and their great life work for the youth of this land."

Mr. Parker said that no man more upright, straightforward and honest had he ever known than Mr. Bishop.

"There was no fuss, no sham, no doubledealing about him. His word could always be depended upon," said the speaker. "Upright, square and fearless, he was a man in his every word and action. He was always loyal to right; he never believed in doing wrong that right might come of it.

"The royal Hawaiian motto, '*Ua mau ke ea o ka aina i ka pono*,' 'The life of the land is established in righteousness,' was no mere sentiment with Mr. Bishop. He believed in it and in his everyday life carried out its injunction. Mr. Bishop was human; he was humane. He was always sober and serious. His austere appearance gave one the idea that he was entirely unapproachable. This was not so; he was most approachable, in fact.

"I cannot say that he is dead. He is only away. His spirit is here. The work for good that he did in life will abide with us. As a philanthropist, I have known none greater than he."

Mr. Parker closed his address with a prayer. Rev. H. K. Poepoe, pastor of the Kaumakapili Church, who occupied the pulpit jointly with Mr. Parker, the pastor, gave an address in Hawaiian. He spoke of the life work of the deceased; of the good that he did in life and that now endures to the benefit of the human race.

The quartet next sang "Peace, Perfect Peace," after which Rev. Mr. Parker pronounced a short Benediction.

Arrived at the mausoleum grounds, the Queen's automobile was the only one allowed to enter, the funeral cortege walking afoot. The Royal Hawaiian Band, led by Prof. Henri Berger, played a number of funeral dirges while the procession filed into the grounds. This was Prof. Berger's last official act in connection with the band that he has led for upward of forty years. He retired on July 1st, having been pensioned by the last Legislature.

The ceremony at the tomb of the Kamehamehas was short and simple. The urn was carried into the tomb by the pallbearers and placed by Prince Kalanianaole * on the coffin of Mr. Bishop's wife, the Princess Bernice Pauahi, while Rev. Mr. Parker pronounced a short benediction. The pallbearers and Mr. Parker filed out of the resting place of Kings, the heavy metal doors were shut and bolted. This marked the placing of the ashes of the late Charles R. Bishop in their last earthly resting place.

Flags were at half mast throughout the city during the afternoon, over public buildings, courts, government offices, and most of the important business houses were closed.

Following adoption of the Bishop Estate resolution, the Trustees met as Museum Trustees and adopted this resolution, dated June 17, 1915:

'RESOLVED: That the Secretary record on the minutes the death on the 7th day of June, 1915, of the Honorable Charles Reed Bishop, the founder and a former Trustee of the Bernice P. Bishop Museum, and that the Trustees give expression to their feelings of admiration and regard for a life so valuable as that of Mr. Bishop, who, though born in humble circumstances and equipped with the meagre instruction of a country school, which he left at the age of fifteen years to enter upon the serious business of his life, yet had, through the force of a character deeply spiritual, fitted himself by the right use of opportunities open to all in this country, to engage with conspicuous success in various businesses requiring a high order of knowledge, perspicacity and judgment, and to recognize and perform, with the approval of his fellowmen, duties and

* See p. 334.

obligations imposed by an ideal conception of the honor and dignity and responsibility of American citizenship; and to adorn with a dignified presence, simple manners and a reverent spirit the highest offices of the land of his adoption; whose noble life had lifted him above the failings and weaknesses which are the common lot of mankind, so that it showed the possibilities of human nature and created in those who knew him a hope for the future of the human race.

Recognizing how dear to Mr. Bishop's heart was the Bernice P. Bishop Museum, the offspring of his affection for his wife and his gratitude to the amiable people among whom he had lived and flourished, and his testimony to the service science had performed in helping to free the human mind, the Trustees renew their acceptance of the trust placed by him in their hands, and pledge themselves to endeavor to execute it under the influence of that spirit of faithful and honest service which directed him in all of his works.

The Trustees donned still another hat. In the Annual Report of the Charles R. Bishop Trust the following memorial, dated August 12, 1915, is entered:

On Monday, the 7th day of June, 1915, the Honorable Charles R. Bishop, Founder of the Trust, passed away at his home in Berkeley, California, aged 93 years, 4 months and 13 days. The tidings were received locally as a public calamity, and a partial suspension of business, both on the day of the receipt of the news and on the day of the funeral, gave eloquent expression of the sentiments of the community. On Sunday, June 13th, memorial services were held at Kawaiahao Church. On Tuesday, the 22nd, the S. S. *"Matsonia"* arrived with the ashes, which were immediately taken to Kawaiahao Church, where they remained until the hour of the funeral, fixed for 3 PM. the following day, Wednesday, the 23rd. Representatives of Hawaiian organizations in the city remained constantly in attendance, and voluntarily accorded the remains of the deceased the final honors usually bestowed only upon a deceased *alii* of their own race. A Guard of Honor, formed of Kamehameha Cadets, also attended. The impressive church service was conducted by the Rev. H. H. Parker, assisted by the Rev. H. K. Poepoe, who reviewed the life and work of Mr. Bishop, speaking in the native tongue to the many Hawaiians assembled, who numbered, among them, H. M. Queen Liliuokalani and others of the *alii*. At the conclusion of the service, the casket containing the ashes, accompanied by the honorary pall-bearers (composed of representative citizens) and followed by relatives and personal friends of the deceased, by Kamehameha Cadets and members of the Hawaiian Societies, was borne by automobile to the Royal Cemetery in Nuuanu Valley, where the burial service, also conducted by the Rev. Mr. Parker, was followed by the singing of Kamehameha students, during which the casket was deposited in the Kamehameha tomb, beside the relics of the beloved wife, the Princess Bernice Pauahi Bishop. The ceremonies throughout were made as simple as possible, in compliance with an expressed wish of the deceased. Mr. Bishop's was a life of exceeding beauty, absolutely devoid of selfishness and immodesty, devoted to works of charity and usefulness. He created this Trust in 1895 to amplify and extend the great work inaugurated by his noble wife, who gave to the youth of her people the whole of her large inheritance. The Trust Deed gives general preference to Hawaiians, and the scope of its benefactions is so broad as to have reached nearly all of the private or semi-private institutions engaged in charitable, educational or religious work in the Islands. Mr. Bishop was one of the five original Trustees of this Trust, and remained such until permanent residence abroad impelled him to resign, which he did the 13th day of October, 1897, although the resignation was not actually accepted by the Trustees until January 3, 1898, when a new Trustee (Mr. S. M. Damon) was appointed to take Mr. Bishop's place. Mr. Bishop's personal interest in the affairs of the Trust did not cease, however, with his resignation, and his advice, freely sought and given when required by the Trustees will be sorely missed.

The Chamber of Commerce of Honolulu met on the second day following Bishop's death and adopted this resolution:

CHARLES REED BISHOP

The following resolution was presented by Mr. F. M. Swanzy and unanimously adopted at a meeting of the Directors of this Chamber held on June 9th, 1915:

———

"WHEREAS, it has pleased Almighty God to remove from this life the

HONORABLE CHARLES REED BISHOP

who for many years was closely identified with this Chamber of Commerce, part of the time as its President; and who during a residence of almost half a century in these Islands was ever in the front in all matters relating to their political, educational, social and commercial welfare, contributing in no small degree to their prosperity and progress; and who since taking up his residence elsewhere has manifested by many kindly acts his continued interest in and his affection for these Islands;

NOW, THEREFORE, BE IT RESOLVED:
    THAT this Chamber hereby express the profound regret of its members at the death of the said, the

HONORABLE CHARLES REED BISHOP,

whose noble character and fine public spirit have endeared him to all, and whose memory will live long in the hearts of Hawaii Nei."

———

Mr. Bishop was a member of the first Chamber of Commerce organized in these islands in 1859; was a signer of the petition which prayed for charter in 1871 and was an incorporator when new charter was granted in 1883. He was President of this Chamber from 1883 to 1885 and again from 1888 to 1894. Mr. Bishop died in San Francisco on June 7th. His ashes arrived in Honolulu by the S. S. *Matsonia* on June 22nd, and now rest in the Royal Mausoleum in Nuuanu by the side of his wife, the late Princess Pauahi Bishop.°

Back in San Francisco, the *Pacific Unitarian* in its July, 1915, issue printed the following statement:

In Memoriam
Charles Reed Bishop

On the 29th † of June at Berkeley, after an honorable and eventful life, Charles Reed Bishop died in his ninety-third year. He was a man of benignant presence, gentle and kindly in manner, retaining all his faculties and persisting in his attention to his large business affairs almost to the last. Of late years his increasing feebleness has been apparent, but he regularly crossed the Bay to attend to his duties as vice-president of the Bank of California. His mind retained its strength but eyesight was dim, and it was significant to realize how lonely he was, in the midst of his large possessions and the universal respect in which he was held. He did not like to give up, and his business life was all he had left. He had no ties of home and no family to cheer his declining days. When walking the street he appeared to be alone and without need of assistance, but a faithful attendant followed in his wake, ready if help were needed.

Much of his life had been spent in doing good and his benefactions were many and of large amount. His estate of approximately $9,000,000 was mostly left to nephews, his nearest of kin. Among many legacies the Berkeley Unitarian Church received $1,000, and the Boys and Girls Aid Society $3,000. From 1894 to 1906 he resided in San Francisco and was a constant and devoted attendant of the First Unitarian Church. After the fire he went to Berkeley, where he had considerable property, and found comfortable accommodations at an agreeable hotel.

With all his wealth, he was pathetically alone. He was respected and revered, but fortune had denied him the blessings of children, and the final waiting for the long-delayed summons was trying. He lingered in an age that had left behind a past in which he played a leading part, and ended his days among a people who knew little of what he accomplished long ago and far away.

In Hawaii, his name is among the most familiar and most deeply honored. His connection with its history was romantic and important, and his endowments princely. In early life he left New England to seek his fortune in the Far West. He was well educated and trained to business. He was first a clerk, and became a banker. He married the Princess Bernice

° The resolution was adopted June 9, but contains this last sentence which refers to later events.
† June 7th, 1915, is the correct date.

Pauahi and became an official of the government. His wife was an accomplished woman of high character, enjoying the highest respect of her people, to whom she was deeply devoted. Mr. Bishop accompanied her on a visit to England, where they were presented at court and given great honor. The Princess was in line of succession and might have ascended the throne, but she preferred domestic life and contented herself in ministering to the welfare of the people of Hawaii.

In 1884 she died, leaving a large part of her fortune to education and charity. The Kamehameha Schools, for both boys and girls, have since been strongly maintained under her endowment. In her memory Mr. Bishop established in 1889 the Bernice Pauahi Bishop Museum, popularly known as the Bishop Museum, one of the most attractive spots in Honolulu, housing a collection of great historic and ethnological value,—one of the most memorable of world exhibits.

The Bishop Estate, charged with the support and extension of the Museum, which is free to all, holds real estate in the various islands largely in excess of any other corporation or company. There is also a Bishop Trust that contributes largely to many charities, and the bank of Bishop & Co. still leads in the finances of Hawaii.

The Kamehameha Schools occupy a beautiful tract of ground within which the Museum and a handsome memorial church are also located. Last year 240 young men and 125 young women were in attendance at these excellent schools.

It is many years since Mr. Bishop last visited the Islands. He did not feel equal to the voyage and especially to the strain on his emotions involved in revisiting the scenes of his earlier life and the excitement of such a reception as he would receive.

In accordance with his expressed wishes, his ashes will be placed by the side of those of his well-beloved wife.

Eben Faxon Bishop, cousin of Mr. Bishop, wrote his sister Frances Elizabeth Bishop, June 30, 1915:

I am sending you papers giving a full account of the funeral ceremonies so I will not attempt to go over the whole matter again in this letter; the two days were strenuous ones for me and everything passed off in a solemn and dignified way.

I placed the ashes with my own hands near the casket of Cousin Bernice in the Kamehameha Tomb where rest all that is mortal of twenty-one of the Kamehameha dynasty and the tomb has now been closed up permanently.

Cousin Charles is the only one lying there who is not of the royal line which is very appropriate considering his great nobility of character. Of course the floral offerings were wonderful and in great mass; I wish you could have seen them. Mr. Parker of Kawaiahao assisted by a Hawaiian Pastor conducted the service both at church and Tomb. Mr. Parker is the only clergyman here now who was active in Cousin Charles' Day.

Somewhat similar, although distinctive, was the memorial prepared as a part of the Trustees' Annual Report of the Bernice P. Bishop Museum, October 12, 1915. It is considerably more objective than the resolution of June 17:

On Monday, the 7th day of June, 1915, the Honorable Charles R. Bishop, Founder of this Trust, passed away at his home in Berkeley, California, aged 93 years, 4 months, 13 days. On Sunday, June 13th, memorial services were held at Kawaiahao Church. On Tuesday, the 22nd, the S. S. *"Matsonia"* arrived with the ashes, which were immediately taken to Kawaiahao Church, where they remained until the hour of the funeral. On Wednesday, the 23rd, at the conclusion of the church service, the casket containing the ashes, followed by relatives and friends, was removed to the Royal Cemetery in Nuuanu Valley, where the burial service was read by the Rev. H. H. Parker, after which the casket was laid in its final resting-place near the relics of the beloved wife of the deceased, the Princess Pauahi, in the tomb of the Kamehamehas. The ceremonies throughout were made as simple as possible, in compliance with an expressed wish of the deceased.

Next to his life, the Bishop Museum is the noblest monument to the memory of Mr. Bishop. It was conceived in the desire on the part of Mr. Bishop to erect some suitable memorial which might be dedicated to his wife, one of Hawaii's greatest benefactresses. The idea bore fruit in 1889, when a small building was completed, forming what is now the Entrance Hall, Kahili Room, Hawaiian Vestibule and Picture Gallery of the present Museum main building. In these rooms were housed the Hawaiian Government, Queen Emma and Bishop House collections, which may be said to have formed the nucleus of the present Museum. Other collections came speedily, and it soon became evident that the original accommodations would not suffice; and the wing now known as Polynesian Hall was provided by Mr. Bishop, being formally opened and dedicated on December 19, 1894, the day celebrated by the Kamehameha Schools as "Founder's Day" and devoted to Mrs. Bishop's memory. The cost of these buildings, as well as all expenses of maintenance incurred to July 1, 1892, was borne by Mr. Bishop, without charge upon the liberal endowment which he settled upon the Museum. He also made the Museum the chief beneficiary of the Charles R. Bishop Trust, a source from which the Museum from time to time receives funds for special objects. Since 1892 the Museum has stood upon its own feet, but it remained under the management of the five Trustees created by the will of Mrs. Bishop [of whom Mr. Bishop was one] until it became a separate trust, October 13, 1896, with the same Trustees and two more added—making seven in all—of whom Mr. Bishop was chosen President. A year later Mr. Bishop resigned, on account of permanent residence in California, but never did he cease to take the keenest personal interest in the affairs of the Museum.

About a year later, August 12, 1916, the Charles R. Bishop Trust Minutes report the completion of a marker in Mr. Bishop's memory on the grounds of the Royal Mausoleum:

In order to provide a place on which to carve a suitable inscription to his memory, relatives of the late Honorable Charles R. Bishop, the founder of this Trust, have erected a substantial stone monument adjacent to the Kamehameha Tomb, in which repose the ashes of the deceased, and inscribed thereon a fitting testimonial to the life and work of this great philanthropist, as a "Builder of the State—Friend of Youth—Benefactor of Hawaii." As the monument is practically a part of the Tomb proper, its care and preservation naturally devolve upon this Trust, under the provision of the Deed of Trust which makes the care of the Kamehameha Tomb a mandatory and perpetual charge upon the funds of this Trust.

In the inscription of this gray granite marker in the Royal Mausoleum we find the eternal key to the beautiful life of Charles Reed Bishop, Man of Hawaii.

Builder of the State   Friend of Youth   Benefactor of Hawaii
His Ashes Rest in the Tomb of the Kamehamehas

This picture was taken of a memorial program before the Bishop marker on the Royal Mausoleum grounds, on the centennial of the arrival of Charles Reed Bishop in Hawaii, October 12, 1846.

Program participants with their titles at the time the picture was taken, are from left to right: Mr. Edwin P. Murray, Trustee of the Bishop Estate; John R. Desha, graduate of The Kamehameha Schools; Harold W. Kent, President of The Kamehameha Schools; William Bishop Taylor, custodian of the Royal Mausoleum and one of the first students of the Preparatory Department; Rev. Henry P. Judd, a distinguished citizen of Hawaii; Rev. Stephen Langhern Desha, Jr., graduate of the Preparatory Department and Chaplain of The Kamehameha Schools.

Appendix

SCHEDULE OF TRAVELS
MR. AND MRS. CHARLES REED BISHOP
TO THE MAINLAND AND EUROPE

Destination	*Means of Travel*	*Date*
	1846	
1. To Honolulu	Brig *Henry*	Arrived
	Charles Reed Bishop	Oc-
	1866	tober 12
2. To San Francisco	*Ajax*	April 4
	Mr. and Mrs. Bishop	
To Honolulu	*Swallow*	June 18
	Mr. and Mrs. Bishop	
	1871	
3. To San Francisco	*Moses Taylor*	June 8
	Mr. and Mrs. Bishop	
Montreal		
Quebec		
Washington,		
D. C.		
New York		
Boston		
Glens Falls		
To Honolulu	*Moses Taylor*	November 20
	Mr. and Mrs. Bishop	
	1875	
4. To San Francisco	*City of Melbourne*	May 29
	Mr. and Mrs. Bishop	
To Europe	*Bothnie*	July 7
Cork		July 17
Edinburgh		August 20
To New York		September 15
San Francisco		October 1
New York		October 20
To Europe	*Main*	October 23
Bremen		November 7

Cologne		November 8
Coblenz		November 9
Frankfort		November 11
Heidelberg		November 13
Vienna		December 2
Trieste		December 5
Naples		December 17
Rome		December 24

1876

Mentone		
Monte Carlo		
London		May 24
To New York	*Britannia*	May 30
Troy, N. Y.		July 4
Glens Falls		July
Fort Edward		July
Boston		July
Isle of Shoals		July
Philadelphia		July
To Honolulu	*City of New York*	September 21
	Mr. and Mrs. Bishop	

1879

5. To San Francisco	*City of Sydney*	March 19
	Mr. Bishop	
To Honolulu	*City of Sydney*	April 22
	Mr. Bishop	
6. To San Francisco	*City of New York*	May 13
	Mr. Bishop	
To Honolulu	*Zealandia*	July 14
	Mr. Bishop	

1880

7. To San Francisco	*Australia*	July 6
	Mr. Bishop	
To Honolulu	*Zealandia*	October 2
	Mr. Bishop	

1882

8. To San Francisco	*Zealandia*	March 13
	Mr. Bishop	

To Honolulu	*Zealandia*	April 13
	Mr. Bishop	
	1883	
9. To San Francisco	*Alameda*	November 1
	Mr. Bishop	
To Honolulu	*Mariposa*	December 9
	Mr. Bishop	
	1884	
10. To San Francisco	*Alameda*	April 1
	Mrs. Bishop	
To San Francisco	*Mariposa*	May 15
	Mr. Bishop	
To Honolulu	*Mariposa*	June 9
	Mr. and Mrs. Bishop	
	1886	
11. To San Francisco	*Mariposa*	October 23
	Mr. Bishop	
To Honolulu	*Zealandia*	December 25
	Mr. Bishop	
	1887	
12. To San Francisco	*Australia*	September 27
	Mr. Bishop	
To Honolulu	*Zealandia*	November 26
	Mr. Bishop	
	1889	
13. To San Francisco	*Umatilla*	April 12
	Mr. Bishop	
New Orleans		April 19
Mobile		
Atlanta		to
Chattanooga		
Cincinnati		May 19
New York		May 27
Boston		June 22
Glens Falls		July 9
St. Paul		July 13
Tacoma		July 25
To Honolulu	*Australia*	August 23
	Mr. Bishop	

1890

14. To San Francisco	*Australia*	November 21
	Mr. Bishop	

1891

New York		April 23
New York		June 11
Carlsbad,		July 23
Bohemia		
To New York from	*Umbria*	October 3
Europe		
New York		
Washington,		
D. C.		
Chicago		
San Francisco		
To Honolulu	*Mariposa*	December 10
	Mr. Bishop	

1892

15. To San Francisco	*Australia*	May 24
	Mr. Bishop	
To Honolulu	*Australia*	August 10
	Mr. Bishop	
16. To San Francisco	*Australia*	October 12
Hampton	Mr. Bishop	
Institute		
Hampton,		
Virginia		

1893

Washington,		February 23
D. C.		
New York City		February 27
To Honolulu	*Australia*	April 18
	Mr. Bishop	
17. To San Francisco	*Oceanic*	May 10
	Mr. Bishop	

1894

To Honolulu	*China*	February 5
	Mr. Bishop	
18. To San Francisco	*Australia*	March 2
	Mr. Bishop	

Occidental Hotel
San Francisco, California
March 5, 1891

To Her Majesty Queen Liliuokalani,

Your Majesty's kind letter of the 24th ulto. reached me yesterday and I give you many thanks for it. On opening it and my other letters I was surprised and grieved to learn that the question as to whether or not it was the duty of the Ministers appointed by the late King to resign because of his decease had not been settled authoritatively for I had received the impression that it was referred to the Justices of the Supreme Court some weeks ago, and no doubt settled satisfactorily as to the law. When the King died questions as to the effect it would have in the government and in business, and as to the disposition of his successor toward Americans and the American interests were freely and frequently asked. The impression was strong here that Kalakaua had been particularly friendly to this Country; and in some minds there was a suspicion that your Majesty had stronger sympathies in other directions.

I said without hesitation that the affairs of the Government would move on smoothly, without a jar, and with no important changes; that I had the honor of knowing you well, and that there was no reason for doubting your friendly disposition toward Americans or American interests; that there would be no change of Ministry, unless the incumbents chose to resign, which was not likely as they had been sustained by the Legislature only recently prorogued and had just gotten fairly to work; and that I was hopeful that your reign would be honorable to yourself and satisfactory to the people generally, etc., etc.

When abroad and among strangers it has been my habit to speak quite as favorably of Hawaiian affairs as truth and conscience would permit; always presenting the best side and not always saying all that was in my mind; but in my expression of confidence in your Majesty there was no reservation.

From my knowledge and impression of the terms, spirit and intention of the Constitution I was of the opinion that the Ministers were under no obligation, loyal or other, to resign—that their Commissions were good until the legislature should have passed a vote of want of Confidence in them; and I expressed that opinion without hesitation—just as frankly and sincerely as I would express it to your Majesty now. Should a majority of the Justices give a different opinion from mine, upon a proper submission of the question, I should accept and adopt it.

Under the former Constitution the Minister held office during the pleasure of the King, and as he could displace them at any moment—(besides its being the rule for them to resign on a vote against them by the Legislature) it was a matter of course for them to tender their resignations to the new Sovereign immediately— Messrs Hall, Sterling, Judd and I did so on the accession of Kalakaua. We were told to retain our portfolios for a time, and we did so. Our acts under the *new* King and our *old* Commissions were perfectly legal. The theory is that "The King does not die" and the fact is that the Government does not die.

From the taking of the oath by your Majesty you were the lawful Sovereign according to the Constitution, and though you did not give new Commissions to the Ministers, there is no doubt about the legality of their subsequent acts.

The Constitution is the Organic and the Supreme law of the Hawaiian Kingdom and it does not matter that it is not altogether like that of any other country. It is supposed to be adapted to the condition and wants of the nation to which it belongs, and is subject to changes as provided in itself. No two countries have the same constitution. The Constitution of Great Britain and those of every Country of Europe have been changed from time to time and always in the same general direction that Hawaii's has. The present Constitution was intended to restrict the former power of the Sovereign in some things—notably, to make the tenure of office of the Ministers more secure, and to make them really responsible and answerable to the Legislature only.

Having in the foregoing hastily written lines stated some of my ideas about the Constitution, which have led me to express an opinion which may not accord with that of your Majesty or of that of wiser men than I am (but I still hold my opinion), I will not tire your Majesty by adding more on that point.

You have advised with some excellent men, and I shall not question the honesty of their advice. Were you to ask for my opinion or advice you would expect me to be honest, frank and truthful with you, though my opinion and advice might be ever so disappointing to your wishes.

I am satisfied that Your Majesty has been ere this become convinced that you have made one error unintentionally and, intending to do what is right, you will not adhere to it.

What you have written about the Commissioner surprises me—for I had supposed that he was not only quite acceptable to the late King, but that he would also be the same to your Majesty; that he would exert himself to be obliging and kind so far as he could be so without detriment to his position as Minister or exposing himself to censure by the legislature.

It cannot be expected that people with minds of their own shall always think alike—but they can differ and be friendly; and between Sovereign and Ministers there should be confidence, frankness and respectful politeness, with a strong disposition to agree—bearing in mind that no one can relieve the Ministers of their responsibility or excuse any neglect or violation of law on their part. It is not an easy thing to make up a really good Cabinet, for many of the men best fitted to be Ministers, cannot afford to take office. I am in favor of appointing natives to such offices as they can fill fairly well and with safety to the public interests—but the simple fact of a man's being a native does not fit or entitle him to hold a responsible and difficult position.

It is now only a little over a year to the meeting of the next Legislature, and there is much work to be done in the meantime. Frequent changes of Ministry are wasteful in the carrying on of the business of the Govt. and shaky confidence in the stability of the Country both at home and abroad.

If the Ministers feel that they cannot do their duty, or that the best interests of the public would be served by their giving way to others then they would be excusable for resigning. The King and the Legislature put upon them the duty and responsibility of carrying on the affairs of the Govt. and they accepted them. Would it be right for them to let others whom they believe could not or would not do the business properly, take their places, and hold them in spite of anybody until removed by the legislature? I am not saying that the present Ministers are altogether satisfactory or are better than any other available—but I am now trying to explain the principle against changes under such circumstances.

Your Majesty has in all the years past treated me with so much kindness and respect, and our relations have been as agreeable, that it has encouraged and helped me in the work for the Hawaiians, in which you have also taken a deep interest—and this friendly feeling makes me exceedingly anxious that you should make no mistakes.

Your love for our dear Bernice would of itself win my regard. Were she living now her large heart would be full of sympathy for you in every trial and of joy for every honor that you may gain.

There are not many left who have in years past associated with and enjoyed the friendship of the noble Chiefs old and young of whom you are the last of the higher class. Yourself, your husband and I have many pleasant and many sad recollections of those who have gone before. Permit me now, dear friend, to congratulate you upon your grand opportunity for usefulness and honor—and to give some advice which you have not asked for, but which I trust will not seem to be bad. I regard the moral influence which you can execute upon the community, and especially upon your own race as of much more importance than anything you can do in the politics or business of the country. Your position as Queen gives redoubled force to your example and influence, and I have no doubt that you intend to take advantage of it. In the politics and routine of the Government the Ministers have the responsibility, annoyances and blame—and usually very little credits. Let them have them, and do not worry yourself about them. You will live longer and happier and be more popular by not trying to do too much.

The decrease of the Hawaiians which the recent census shows is still going on, in the adults, at least—is caused mainly by two things: intemperance, and the influence of Kahunas. Is there no hope of winning the people to wiser and better habits? The children are better cared for and are doing better than in times past, but the adults and old people are behaving badly.

Pardon me for inflicting upon your Majesty such a long letter.

Mrs. Allen is much better, but the doctor has not set a time when it will be safe for her to start from New York for home, but I think in two or three weeks she will be coming this way.

P.S.

The names mentioned in your letter would certainly make a better cabinet than those first reported here as being your choice.

It seems to me likely that the Ministers will resign after the justices hand in their opinions, which I cannot help thinking will sustain their views of their rights. If the opinion should be against their view, they will of course resign.

> Your Majesty's old friend
> and obedient servant
> Chas. R. Bishop
> [signed]

Index

A

Academy of Sciences, 207, 211
Adviser to royalty, 100
Agassiz, Louis, 199
"Aikupika," Bishop home, 33
Ajax (ship), 47
Alakea Street Cottage, 32
Alameda (ship), 311
Aldrich and Bishop, 43, 109, 269
Aldrich, William A., 43, 45, 47, 109, 127
Alexander and Baldwin, 53 n
Alexander, Arthur C., 232
Alexander, Brevet Brig. Gen. B. S., 60–61
Alexander Liholiho Iolani, *see* Kamehameha IV
Alexander, S. T., 131
Alexander, Wallace M., 328n
Alexander, William DeWitt, letters to, 58, 84, 87, 219–221, 248, 295, 307, 313
Alexander, Rev. W. P., 264
Allen, Cordelia Church Bishop (Mrs. W. F.), cares for Pauahi in final illness, 29–30; daughter of Nelson Bishop, 319; donates Bishop portraits to Punahou, 304, Queen's Hospital, 277; hostess at "Keoua," 36; marries W. F. Allen, 36
Allen, Elisha H., biography, 49 n; boarded at Ladds, 32; President Sailors' Home, 269; immigration, 126; Kalakaua, 70; Lunalilo, 66; reciprocity, 63–64, 111; Vice-President Queen's Hospital, 275
Allen, Mrs. W. F., *see* Allen, Cordelia Church Bishop

Allen, William Fessenden, attends Annie S. Walker's wedding, 318; gifts of, 235; Bishop's hosts at "Keoua" Hale, 36, 141, 185; marriage, 319
Alumni Association, 176, 228
Alvord, William, 131
American Benevolent Fund, 271, *see also* American Relief Fund
American Board of Commissioners for Foreign Missions, 215–219; approves election Castle, Bishop to Punahou board, 233; artifact collection, 215, 218, 229; Hawaiian Missionary Society, 259; operates Hawaiian Evangelical Association, 263; organized, 215; sends mission groups to Hawaii, 7
American Museum (New York), 207
American Relief Fund, 271–272; Association, 47; gift to, 49; offices held by Bishop, 271; Chas. R. Bishop Trust, 229
Andrews, Rev. C. B., 239
Andrews Cottage (Nuuanu Valley), 32
Andrews, Judge Lorrin, 26, 40
Andrews, R. W., 265
Annexation, 91, 174
Annuity (Bishop), 230
Anthony, J. Garner, 149
Aquarium, *see* Marine Aquarium
Armstrong, Rev. Richard, Bethel Union Church, 255; father of American public education, 243; marries Pauahi and Charles, 24–27; pioneer in Hawaiian public education, 252; reconciles Paki and Bishop, 27